FORCE OF WORDS

Columbia Studies in Terrorism and Irregular Warfare

COLUMBIA STUDIES IN TERRORISM AND IRREGULAR WARFARE
Bruce Hoffman, Series Editor

This series seeks to fill a conspicuous gap in the burgeoning literature on terrorism, guerrilla warfare, and insurgency. The series adheres to the highest standards of scholarship and discourse and publishes books that elucidate the strategy, operations, means, motivations, and effects posed by terrorist, guerrilla, and insurgent organizations and movements. It thereby provides a solid and increasingly expanding foundation of knowledge on these subjects for students, established scholars, and informed reading audiences alike.

Ami Pedahzur, *The Israeli Secret Services and the Struggle Against Terrorism*
Ami Pedahzur and Arie Perliger, *Jewish Terrorism in Israel*
Lorenzo Vidino, *The New Muslim Brotherhood in the West*
Erica Chenoweth and Maria J. Stephan, *Why Civil Resistance Works: The Strategic Logic of Nonviolent Conflict*
William C. Banks, editor, *New Battlefields/Old Laws: Critical Debates on Asymmetric Warfare*
Blake W. Mobley, *Terrorism and Counterintelligence: How Terrorist Groups Elude Detection*
Jennifer Morrison Taw, *Mission Revolution: The U.S. Military and Stability Operations*
Guido W. Steinberg, *German Jihad: On the Internationalization of Islamist Terrorism*
Michael W. S. Ryan, *Decoding Al-Qaeda's Strategy: The Deep Battle Against America*
David H. Ucko and Robert Egnell, *Counterinsurgency in Crisis: Britain and the Challenges of Modern Warfare*
Bruce Hoffman and Fernando Reinares, editors, *The Evolution of the Global Terrorist Threat: From 9/11 to Osama bin Laden's Death*
Boaz Ganor, *Global Alert: The Rationality of Modern Islamist Terrorism and the Challenge to the Liberal Democratic World*
M. L. R. Smith and David Martin Jones, *The Political Impossibility of Modern Counterinsurgency: Strategic Problems, Puzzles, and Paradoxes*
Elizabeth Grimm Arsenault, *How the Gloves Came Off: Lawyers, Policy Makers, and Norms in the Debate on Torture*
Assaf Moghadam, *Nexus of Global Jihad: Understanding Cooperation Among Terrorist Actors*
Bruce Hoffman, *Inside Terrorism*, 3rd edition
Stephen Tankel, *With Us and Against Us: How America's Partners Help and Hinder the War on Terror*
Wendy Pearlman and Boaz Atzili, *Triadic Coercion: Israel's Targeting of States That Host Nonstate Actors*
Bryan C. Price, *Targeting Top Terrorists: Understanding Leadership Removal in Counterterrorism Strategy*
Mariya Y. Omelicheva and Lawrence P. Markowitz, *Webs of Corruption: Trafficking and Terrorism in Central Asia*
Aaron Y. Zelin, *Your Sons Are at Your Service: Tunisia's Missionaries of Jihad*
Lorenzo Vidino, *The Closed Circle: Joining and Leaving the Muslim Brotherhood in the West*

Force of Words

THE LOGIC OF TERRORIST THREATS

Joseph M. Brown

Columbia University Press
New York

Columbia University Press
Publishers Since 1893
New York   Chichester, West Sussex
cup.columbia.edu
Copyright © 2020 Columbia University Press
All rights reserved

Library of Congress Cataloging-in-Publication Data

Names: Brown, Joseph M., author.
Title: Force of words : the logic of terrorist threats / Joseph M. Brown.
Description: New York : Columbia University Press, 2020. | Series: Columbia studies in terrorism and irregular warfare | Includes bibliographical references and index.
Identifiers: LCCN 2019056686 (print) | LCCN 2019056687 (ebook) | ISBN 9780231193689 (cloth) | ISBN 9780231193696 (paperback) | ISBN 9780231550451 (ebook)
Subjects: LCSH: Terrorism. | Propaganda. | Threat (Psychology)
Classification: LCC HV6431 .B776 2020 (print) | LCC HV6431 (ebook) | DDC 363.325—dc23
LC record available at https://lccn.loc.gov/2019056686
LC ebook record available at https://lccn.loc.gov/2019056687

Cover design: Chang Jae Lee

For my family.

Contents

Acknowledgments ix

Introduction 1

1 Threats: A Theoretical Framework 18

2 The Provisional IRA: A Full Spectrum of Threats 29

3 ETA and the Tamil Tigers: Comparable Threats for Social Control and Negotiation; Contrasting Threats for Legitimacy, Disruption, and Advantage 62

4 The MRTA and the Shining Path: Common Enemy; Virtually No Threat in Common 94

5 The Taliban, ISIL, and Boko Haram: Comparable Threats for Social Control; Contrasting Threats for Legitimacy, Negotiation, Aggrandizement, and Advantage 115

6 Quantitative Analysis: When to Expect Truthful Warnings 145

Conclusion 166

Appendix 181
Notes 217
Bibliography 265
Index 281

Acknowledgments

I owe thanks to many people who supported me through the long process of writing this book. First, I thank my family. I could do nothing without their love and support. I also thank Robert Jervis and Page Fortna, the academic advisors who oversaw the earliest stages of this project. For their reading of my work, I thank Erica Chenoweth, Peter Krause, Severine Autesserre, Stuart Gottlieb, Austin Long, Robert Shapiro, Shuai Jin, Tanisha Fazal, Victor Asal, Luis Jimenez, Leila Farsakh, Paul Kowert, Michelle Jurkovich, Samuel Barkin, Jeffrey Pugh, Stacy VanDeveer, John Horgan, Max Abrahms, Friederike Kelle, and Costantino Pischedda.

I thank the political science departments at Columbia University and the University of Massachusetts Boston for providing institutional support. For their generous financial support, I thank the Horowitz Foundation for Social Policy and the Advanced Consortium on Cooperation, Conflict, and Complexity (AC4) at the Earth Institute at Columbia University. I also thank Professor Christopher Coker and the Department of International Relations at the London School of Economics and Political Science for hosting me as a guest researcher during my fieldwork in Ireland and Great Britain. I thank the MIT Security Studies seminar for their useful comments on my work.

I thank my research assistants for their help in producing the quantitative database for my research: Nidale Zouhir, Nathan Akin, Uluç Karakaş, Vaibhav Sabharwal, Osama Mohamed, Mallory Rosso, Vivian Grossman,

Gi Jae Han, Addy Sonaike, Antoine Sander, Katie Garcia, David Ray Anderson, Fatima Dar, and Kangdi Li. I thank Matthew Eaton for his advice about statistical modeling, and Jon Lizarraga Díaz for his assistance in translating Basque interviews. I thank the many academics who assisted me in obtaining IRB approval for my research: Rebekka Friedman, Diego Navarro Bonilla, Zachariah Mampilly, Xabier Irujo, Roger Mac Ginty, Richard English, Neil DeVotta, Mark Whitaker, Roland Vazquez, and Zoe Bray.

I thank the Coiste na nIarchimí Republican ex-prisoners support group for making former IRA prisoners available for interviews. I also thank the Falls Road office of Sinn Féin, Northern Ireland Retired Police Officers Association (NIRPOA), Police Service of Northern Ireland, Northern Ireland Policing Board, Samaritans organization, Department of Justice of Northern Ireland, Irish Republican History Museum, Royal United Services Institute, and CAIN project at the University of Ulster. For their special assistance in Northern Ireland, I thank Seánna Walsh, Danny Morrison, Robert McClanahan, John O'Hagan, Eamon Mallie, William Mawhinney, Jonathan Blake, Joanne Murphy, Brendan Birt, Geraldine McAllister, Peter Gilleece, Kevin O'Brien, Jo Black, Leanne Donly, Tim Farrell, Patrick Thomson-McQuiston, Maura Scully, and Louise Quinn. For their assistance in Britain, I thank Jonathan Powell, Gordon Barrass, John Bew, Richard English, and Peter Neumann.

For their assistance with my research in Spain, I thank Antxon Etxebeste, the Guardia Civil, Urko Aiartza, the New York Euzko-Etxea, Brian Currin, Gorka Espiau, Paul Rios, Joseba Zulaika, and the Lokarri organization. For their assistance with my research in Sri Lanka, I thank M. A. Sumanthiran, Jayantha Dhanapala, Jayadeva Uyangoda, the British Tamils Forum, the Federation of Tamil Sangams of North America, Tamils Against Genocide, John Rogers and Ira Unamboowe of the American Institute for Sri Lankan Studies, Jehan Perera, and the National Peace Council of Sri Lanka. For their assistance with my research in Peru, I thank Maria Cruz-Saco, Salomón Lerner Febres, Ricardo Caro, Gustavo Gorriti, Paula Muñoz, Jean Franco Olivera, Maria Rae, Eduardo Toche, Talia Castro-Pozo, Cynthia Sanborn, Orieta Pérez, the Instituto de Democracia y Derechos Humanos, and the Centro de Información para la Memoria Colectiva y los Derechos Humanos.

Finally, I thank Caelyn Cobb and Bruce Hoffman at Columbia University Press for supporting this project and helping me bring my research to the public.

FORCE OF WORDS

FORGET THE ALAMO

Introduction

Saturdays are quiet in Bishopsgate, an orderly commercial neighborhood in the heart of London. On the morning of April 24, 1993, the international banks were closed, leaving the streets and skyscrapers populated by weekend security and maintenance staff.[1] Few took note of the Iveco tipper truck that rolled up in front of the Hongkong and Shanghai Bank at 9:00 a.m. Two occupants hastily exited the vehicle and shuffled a short distance before boarding a car driven by a third person, who pulled away from the scene.[2] The unaccompanied truck drew the attention of two London Metropolitan police, who began to make inquiries about its missing drivers.[3] What the officers could not immediately perceive was the peculiar nature of the lorry's cargo: 2,200 pounds of ammonium nitrate and fuel oil (ANFO) explosives, manufactured in a makeshift facility in County Armagh, Ireland, and just as powerful, pound-for-pound, as TNT.[4] The otherwise normal-looking truck was an enormous ticking time bomb.

The danger did not become apparent to police until 9:30 a.m., when a series of nine telephone calls, originating at a phone box in Ireland, arrived at the switchboards of media organizations and emergency services in Britain.[5] These calls conveyed an urgent warning: the Provisional Irish Republican Army (IRA), a secessionist group demanding independence for Northern Ireland, had parked "a massive bomb" in Bishopsgate; authorities should "clear a wide area" to prevent bloodshed.[6] The switchboards relayed this message to London police, who rushed to Bishopsgate, sirens wailing, to evacuate buildings and cordon off the neighborhood. Thanks to their efficient work, only one person, photojournalist Ed Henty, remained in the vicinity. Instead of heeding instructions to evacuate, Henty moved in to take pictures of the suspicious truck. It was a fatal mistake.[7]

The bomb's explosion, at 10:30 a.m., was monstrous. It sent a pulverizing shockwave in all directions, blowing a five-meter crater into the pavement and shattering five hundred tons of skyscraper glass over a half-kilometer area.[8] The NatWest building, a nearby landmark, was unrecognizable, "black gaps punching its 52 floors like a mouth full of bad teeth."[9] Repairs and insurance payouts would amount to an estimated £1 billion, yet the only fatality was the dead journalist, Henty.[10] The human toll would surely have been far greater, had it not been for the IRA's telephone calls in advance of the explosion. These bomb threats were frightening, but they were also helpful, even merciful, to London's civilian population. With warning of the attack, civilians could evacuate to avoid being caught in the blast.

After the Bishopsgate bombing, the IRA issued new threats, generally less helpful and more coercive in character. Dozens of foreign-owned banks and other businesses in the London area received the following message: "We do not seek to target those with whom we have no quarrel but the reality is that simply by virtue of their location many businesses will suffer the effects of our operations. In the context of present political realities, further attacks on the city of London are inevitable. This we feel we are bound to convey to you directly to allow you to make fully informed decisions."[11]

The language was subtle, but the meaning was clear: the IRA was threatening businesses to drive them out of the city. The threat to financial institutions also had frightening implications for the British government. If international banks left London, they would take billions of pounds worth of business with them. This was a dagger aimed at Britain's economic heart. To underline the threat, but also to offer a way out, the IRA issued a public ultimatum giving the British government a choice between "ending its futile and costly war in Ireland" and a dark future in which further attacks would hollow out the U.K. economy.[12] The British could negotiate or suffer the consequences. The decision was theirs to make.

These are just a few examples of the threats the IRA made during its roughly thirty-year conflict with the United Kingdom. They are illustrative of the types of threats the IRA issued—in fact, the types of threats we see in many terrorist campaigns. Threats are diverse. Each IRA message was directed at a different target—the civilians on London's streets, the owners of international banks, and the U.K. government. Each message had a different purpose. The communiqués to the government and banks embodied the conventional notion of "threat" as a hostile statement foreshadowing violence. These threats were coercive, demanding that the government negotiate, urging businesses to relocate, and promising consequences if they did not. But the threats immediately prior to the Bishopsgate bombing had a different quality. Directed toward civilians, the phone warnings signaled restraint: the IRA was eager to destroy property and damage the economy, but it was unwilling to kill indiscriminately. The IRA was, nevertheless, willing to lie and induce panic on occasion. Consider a series of bomb threats issued by the group on April 3, 1997. The messages, again transmitted from telephones in Ireland, promised attacks on major English highways. Fearing mayhem on the motorways, British authorities shut down much of the country's road transit infrastructure. Yet the IRA never attempted to fulfill these threats. With just a few words, the group caused transit disruptions and an estimated £80 million in economic losses to the British economy—an impressive return on a ten-pence phone call.[13] The IRA used this tactic sparingly, however, hoaxing some of the time and otherwise leaving the transit system alone.[14]

Whether directed at civilians or the state, coercing or sparing, informing or deceiving, threats are powerful instruments of terror. In fact, their importance goes beyond their utility as means to an end: threats are integral to terrorism itself. In the general use of the term, *terrorism* is a violent form of political communication, intended to convey some message or produce a psychological impact on a wider audience.[15] "Terrorism is theater," RAND Corporation analyst Brian Jenkins observes.[16] Violence is one part of the production, generating terrorism's "sound and fury," but threats play an equally important role.[17] They make the violence meaningful, telling us what terrorists will do next and what concessions they demand in exchange for stopping the performance.

There is considerable variation in terrorist threats, even those emanating from the same group. What explains the specific patterns we see? Why should the IRA, which killed civilians much of the time, call in bomb warnings to spare civilians at other times? Why call in a rash of hoax threats on one day and not call in more every day after? The terrorism literature has only just started to tackle these questions. Scholars note, as an aside, the use of threats by the IRA and the Basque separatist group ETA to disrupt their adversary states' economies.[18] This research is accompanied by more focused studies of particular tactics such as hoaxing.[19] To my knowledge, I am the only author to have attempted, albeit in a shorter article format, a unified theoretical account of terrorist threats—their varieties, their functions, and the political circumstances that incentivize them.[20]

This is the first full-length scholarly study of terrorist threats. A book like this is long overdue because threats have always played a central role in the coercive practices of the IRA and other terrorist groups. The scholarly inattention to threats is even more striking, given the clear implication, in major theoretical accounts, that threats are essential to terrorism. Consider the role of threats in the "costly signaling" paradigm.[21] This literature observes that militants use terrorism because they begin from a position of weakness and their talk is perceived as "cheap." Unable to make credible coercive threats, militants take symbolic actions to demonstrate their destructive capabilities and their resolve to fight until their political demands are met.[22] Terrorist violence is a deadly strategy to earn credibility so that one's talk is no longer cheap. But then what? What do terrorists do with the credibility their violence has bought them? How do they hope to obtain political results?

Clearly, the answer implied by the literature is that terrorists issue *threats* to obtain concessions. But this part of the story is not investigated systematically in its own right. We have an extensive literature on the most spectacular aspects of terrorist violence—suicide bombings, the pursuit of weapons of mass destruction, and the importance of claiming credit for attacks so that the destructive capability can be attributed to the perpetrator.[23] To comprehend terrorism fully, we must also examine the other half of the story, the half in which terrorists use threats to translate violence into political outcomes—concessions, social control, and perhaps a more humane image if we factor in the role of warnings. Naturally, this returns us to a discussion of terrorism as communication with an audience. Terrorism operates through a symbolic, psychological logic that shapes perceptions and structures political incentives. Only by examining threats in detail can we understand how terrorists communicate specific messages to their various political audiences.

The Argument

Throughout this book I argue that threats are the crucial link between terrorist violence and its political outcomes. As nonstate actors, terrorists cannot achieve their coercive goals by force of arms alone; they must also employ the force of words, using threats to manipulate others' behavior and beliefs. Table 0.1 lists the types of threats we observe in terrorist campaigns, the objectives they serve, and the target audiences they influence.

We can identify four broad classes of threats: warnings, pledges, hoaxes, and bluffs. These categories are distinguished by their temporal relation to violence (prospective or immediate) and the intended truthfulness of the message. Pledges and bluffs (respectively, true and false) threaten violence in the indeterminate future. These threats are useful for strategic purposes: obtaining political concessions in negotiations with the state, altering civilians' behavior, aggrandizing the terrorist group's reputation, and distorting the state's allocation of counterterrorism resources in ways that strategically advantage the militant group. For instance, by pledging attacks on

TABLE 0.1
Typology of Threats (Audiences in Parentheses)

	Immediate	Prospective
True	**Warning** Objectives: legitimacy (civilians) disruption (state, civilians) tactical advantage (state)	**Pledge** Objectives: social control (civilians) negotiation (state) aggrandizement (state, civilians) strategic advantage (state)
False	**Hoax** Objectives: disruption (state, civilians) tactical advantage (state)	**Bluff** Objectives: social control (civilians) negotiation (state) aggrandizement (state, civilians) strategic advantage (state)

airports, terrorists can force the state to spread its counterterrorism resources thinly across all airports—or spend tremendous new sums to protect airports adequately. Borrowing a term from chess masters, I describe this function of threats as *strategic prophylaxis*—forcing the opponent to make moves that benefit oneself.[24] Terrorist groups can also use bluffs to negotiate, control civilians, aggrandize themselves, and distort the state's counterterrorism strategy. However, if the state or the population calls a bluff by disregarding it, the exposure of the terrorists' lie will deplete the group's reputation and its ability to make credible threats in the future.

Warnings and hoaxes (respectively, true and false) threaten immediate violence. These threats relate to specific terrorist operations, shaping their physical outcomes and fine-tuning their political effects. Immediate threats can spare civilian life to enhance terrorists' legitimacy, disrupt the economy in a strategy of attrition, and secure tactical advantages over security forces. For instance, truthful warnings or hoaxes can draw police into ambushes. Terrorists may use hoaxes for disruption and tactical advantage as well. At times they may link hoaxes with real attacks—for instance, a rash of false bomb threats that spread police out and distract them while physical attacks commence elsewhere. I term this use of hoaxes *tactical prophylaxis*.

In addition to identifying the types and functions of threats, I develop a speech/kinetic action model of terrorism.[25] This model, depicted in figure 0.1, differs from other conceptions of terrorism, which distinguish attacks from speech acts (threats, credit claims, and so on).[26] Examples such as the Bishopsgate attack show that terrorists integrate threats with kinetic violence as part of the same tactical plan. These threats alter the physical outcomes of an attack, making it more effective politically. This is particularly important as terrorist groups face what I call the *multiple audiences conundrum*—when the violence used to coerce an opponent risks alienating casualty-averse supporters on whom the terrorist group depends. Warnings mitigate the multiple audiences conundrum by adding an element of discrimination to terrorist tactics. By focusing harm on property, they signal strength to the state while communicating restraint to terrorists' civilian supporters. The ability to send different signals to different audiences with the same attack (what I term *signal splitting*) is one of the key functions of immediate threats. Hoaxes advance this strategy as well, causing economic disruption with no physical harm. If violence alone would send suboptimal

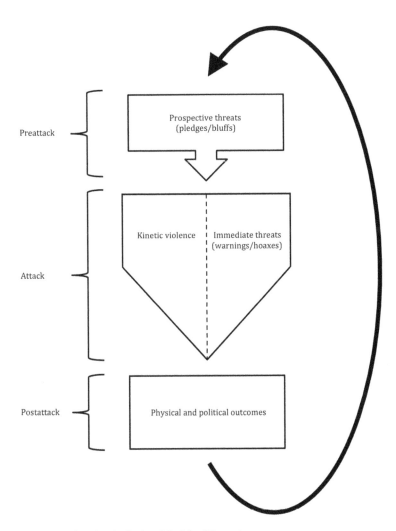

Figure 0.1 Speech/Kinetic Action Model of Terrorism

signals to one or more audiences, terrorists can use threats to alter the pattern of damage and send more effective political signals to each audience.

Because terrorist violence cannot be understood in isolation from the speech acts that determine its physical and political effects, immediate threats should be considered part of the attack. We can think of hoaxes as attacks consisting of speech alone.[27] Figure 0.1's arrow represents the link between threats and kinetic violence in the current episode of terrorism and the ex ante conditions for the next episode. For example, fulfilling a threat builds the terrorist group's reputation for potency and truthfulness. These postattack outcomes lend credibility to future threats, making it easier to extract political concessions and control civilian behavior.

We can derive a number of propositions from the framework I have laid out. For instance, referring back to table 0.1, we can infer that terrorist groups with greater needs for popular legitimacy (including those with intense multiple audiences conundrums) are more likely to issue warnings to reduce civilian casualties. Groups pursuing political negotiations with the state are more likely to issue pledges and bluffs against government targets. Groups seeking to build their reputations, or to restore them in periods of decline, will issue pledges or bluffs to aggrandize themselves. Groups facing particularly strong counterterrorism pressures are likely to avail themselves of prophylactic threats to spread out, confuse, or victimize the state's security forces. All told, my theoretical framework gives rise to six propositions about when terrorists will issue particular types of threats:

1. Terrorists will issue warnings when they seek political legitimacy.
2. Terrorists will issue warnings and/or hoaxes when they seek to disrupt the state's economy.
3. Terrorists will issue pledges and/or bluffs (against civilians) when they seek social control.
4. Terrorists will issue pledges and/or bluffs (against the state) when they seek negotiations.
5. Terrorists will issue pledges and/or bluffs when they seek to aggrandize their reputations.
6. Terrorists will issue warnings, hoaxes, pledges, and/or bluffs to seek advantage against strong counterterrorist opponents.

The Evidence

I provide support for these propositions using a mixed methods research design, including a quantitative analysis of terrorist attacks and case studies of specific terrorist groups: Euskadi Ta Askatasuna (ETA), the Liberation Tigers of Tamil Eelam (Tamil Tigers), Peru's Sendero Luminoso (Shining Path) and Túpac Amaru Revolutionary Movement (MRTA), Boko Haram, the Afghan Taliban, and the Islamic State of Iraq and the Levant (ISIL). First, however, I present a detailed case study of the IRA, based on thirty-three interviews of IRA members, former Northern Irish police and military officers, government officials, and a group of charity workers, journalists, and civil society members who served as conduits for communicating the IRA's threats to British authorities. This case study illustrates the speech/kinetic action nature of terrorism with rich qualitative data from a historically significant terrorist group. It gives examples of the four varieties of threats I identify in my theory. It also explicates my theory's causal processes, tracing the paths from specific political variables to the types of threats issued by the IRA. In this way, the IRA case study enables me to make clearer, more testable predictions about what behavior to expect from the other terrorist groups I analyze.[28]

I choose the IRA for this initial case study because the Northern Ireland conflict is exceptionally data rich. The IRA signed a peace agreement with the British government in 1998. Hundreds of formerly incarcerated IRA members can discuss their activities during the conflict without legal repercussions because they have been pardoned and released from prison as part of the peace process.[29] The postconflict environment also facilitates interviews of police, whose safety concerns, as frequent assassination targets during the conflict, are now dramatically reduced. It would not be feasible to conduct a detailed primary-source case study of an active group like the Afghan Taliban or Boko Haram without running prohibitive legal and safety risks.

The interviews I obtained in Northern Ireland show how the IRA perceived its political environment and how it used threats to achieve strategic and tactical goals. The group used pledges and bluffs to coerce its adversary state, to control the civilian population, and to aggrandize itself relative to rival terrorist organizations. The IRA used warnings and hoaxes to finetune the physical damage from each attack, sending more effective political signals to its audiences. These audiences included the British government, local civilians, and Irish Americans who provided money and political assistance from abroad. Certain revelations from this chapter stand out as particularly significant. First, the IRA case study shows which political factors intensify the multiple audiences conundrum. This group sheltered in local civilians' homes while fighting a liberal democracy that set a relatively high standard of legitimate political behavior. To remain in the good graces of its civilian hosts, the IRA had to ensure that its violence did not appear indiscriminate. The group gave warnings when attacking commercial targets so that it could destroy property without causing mass casualties. The IRA used hoaxes to cause bloodless economic disruption, although it limited its use of this tactic to avoid wearing out the willingness of police to respond to warnings. The IRA also instituted an elaborate system of code words and standard procedures to enhance the credibility of its threats—both in relation to physical attacks and in the context of bargaining with the state. Finally, the IRA used prophylactic threats to incapacitate a highly proficient British counterterrorism apparatus that would otherwise have made short work of the group.

Having demonstrated the logic of my theoretical framework in the IRA context, I show how the framework explains the behavior of other terrorist groups. I present a series of case studies, comparing groups that were ideologically similar but quite different in their political circumstances and their resulting uses of threats. The patterns of threats in these cases conform closely to the expectations laid out in my six theoretical propositions. First, I compare ETA and the Tamil Tigers, two ethnic separatist groups from Spain and Sri Lanka, respectively. This case pair shows the divergent patterns of threats from groups with different legitimacy concerns, emphases on economic disruption, and levels of counterterrorism pressure to overcome. For instance, ETA did not control territory and had to shelter among civilians. The Tamil Tigers possessed secure territorial bases and could arrange their own shelter. ETA's greater dependence on local civilians created an intense multiple audiences conundrum and a correspondingly greater need to adhere to civilians' norms of legitimate revolutionary behavior. Consistent with my theoretical argument, ETA issued warnings, particularly when the group attacked commercial businesses and infrastructure. At other times, it used warnings to obtain tactical advantage over a vastly superior counterterrorism opponent. The Tamil Tigers issued warnings and prophylactic, advantage-seeking threats far less often than ETA did. At the end of the Sri Lankan civil war, however, as the Tigers' military position deteriorated, the group issued prophylactic bluffs to draw the government's attention away from the battlefront toward civilian targets elsewhere. Certain consistencies between ETA's and the Tamil Tigers' behavior also support my argument. Both groups sought negotiations with their state opponents and social control over the civilian population. They were similarly liberal in their use of pledges for these purposes.

Next, I contrast the Shining Path and the MRTA, two Marxist rebel groups that fought simultaneous wars against the government of Peru. This is an exceptionally well-controlled pair of cases. Because the groups are local contemporaries, their relationships with civilians, attitudes toward political compromise, and changing power relationships with the state are easy to compare without being confounded by the peculiarities of time and place. The Peruvian cases are best suited for observing the different patterns of threats that arise when groups have differing incentives to seek legitimacy, economic disruption, negotiation, social control, and self-aggrandizement. For example, the MRTA depended on urban civilians for shelter, while the Shining Path controlled rural territory of its own. The MRTA also targeted *yanqui* (U.S.-owned) businesses, while the Shining Path preferred to target civilians and state forces directly. Consistent with my theoretical argument, we see more warnings and hoaxes from the MRTA, as it sought to earn civilians' support through reduced-casualty armed propaganda. The Shining Path rarely gave warnings, but it did pledge spectacular retribution against civilians who defied its iron regime of social control. Other differences relate to the issue of negotiation: the MRTA sought peace talks with the state, but the Shining Path vowed never to compromise. Also consistent with my argument, the MRTA directed more pledges and bluffs at the state, pairing its peace overtures with threats. At other times, the MRTA issued pledges and bluffs with a boastful and self-aggrandizing character. This is what we expect from a small, militarily weak group like the MRTA, competing for headlines with a more formidable peer rival like the Shining Path, which rarely issued self-aggrandizing threats.

I compare the uses of threats by jihadist groups as well. To give broader coverage of a global religious and political movement, I profile three groups: the Taliban of Afghanistan, ISIL, and Nigeria's Boko Haram. These cases show consistency in the use of threats for social control. All three groups seek to govern territory under conservative Islamic religious law. Like the governments of Westphalian states, they proclaim authority over civilians' political and social lives and pledge violent retaliation against those who violate their rules. The three groups differ, however, in their other political incentives and uses of threats. Boko Haram has difficulty controlling territory and fights a relatively functional democracy. We expect (and in fact we observe) a pattern of casualty-reducing warnings from this group.

The Taliban and ISIL, which have controlled more territory and fought less democratic states, are less prone to issue warnings. Nonetheless, in the warnings these groups do issue, we see a common theme: ex post moral justification for killing civilians. Jihadists warn civilians not to engage in sinful behavior—for instance, attending secular schools. When these groups fulfill their threats, they rationalize any civilian deaths by noting that they warned their coreligionists in advance about their transgressions; those injured in the attack chose to ignore the warnings, so they were not truly innocent. Regarding negotiation, Boko Haram and the Taliban have expressed a desire for political dialogue and compromise with their adversary states; ISIL has not. Consistent with my theoretical argument, Boko Haram and the Taliban issue more threats against their government opponents. There is an exception, however, in ISIL's more recent history. As ISIL has lost territory, it has issued an increasingly fanciful array of bluff threats to "conquer" the European countries whose air strikes have now destroyed its caliphate. This bravado is also consistent with my argument: a group that is suffering physical losses will seek to bolster its reputation by threatening revenge. Finally, we see more advantage-seeking threats from Boko Haram and the Taliban, which have fought intense insurgencies against capable counterterrorism opponents. ISIL, which has fought more conventional military battles with defined front lines, has not issued as many prophylactic threats.

I support my argument with additional quantitative evidence, using a large-N statistical research design to generalize my more practical insights about warnings to a wider variety of militant groups. My comparative case studies treated ideology as a constant, but the quantitative research design allows me to test hypotheses when ideology varies across groups. I conduct the analysis using my own 12,235-observation database of bombings and bomb threats by 131 terrorist groups in the years 1970–2016.[30] I use multilevel logit analyses to test two theoretical predictions: warnings are more likely when terrorists face legitimacy concerns (operationalized as when they lack territorial strongholds and fight democracies) and when terrorists pursue strategies of economic disruption. My results uphold both hypotheses. They also provide practical insight for people and institutions who receive threats. Purported warnings from groups without territory, groups fighting democracies, and groups attacking economic targets should be taken more seriously. These threats may indicate actual danger, and responding to them may save lives. Supposed warnings from groups with territory, groups fighting nondemocracies, and groups attacking noneconomic targets are more likely to be hoaxes. We should view such threats with greater skepticism.

Scholarly Implications

This book reorients terrorism studies by placing threats at the center of the field. Academic researchers regard threats and violence as "equally important" in the abstract, but they have tended to fixate on the violent half of terrorists' coercive tool kit, scrutinizing the physical actions that terrorists carry out but largely neglecting the question of how those actions produce political results.[31] For weak nonstate actors, it is not violence that enables coercion but the threat of more violence to come.[32] By explaining the role of pledges and bluffs in coercion, I show how terrorists hope to achieve their political goals.

I also show how terrorists use warnings and hoaxes to advance their coercive campaigns without alienating their civilian supporters. I develop this portion of my argument by introducing two key concepts: the multiple audiences conundrum and signal splitting. The first concept summarizes a pervasive problem faced by terrorists: the same attack that signals strength to the enemy may inadvertently signal brutality to civilian audiences. Terrorist groups can mitigate this conundrum by issuing warnings and hoaxes along with their violence. By altering the pattern of damage, warnings and hoaxes split terrorism's signal, communicating strength to enemies and restraint toward friends. My analysis shows how threats render terrorism politically sustainable. It also demonstrates that the physical and political outcomes of terrorism can be understood only by accounting for the role of threats. Warnings and hoaxes should therefore be understood as part of the attack, not as mere adjuncts to it.

My theoretical innovations and empirical findings enhance several key areas of the terrorism literature. First, they expand our existing account of terrorism as signaling. The costly signaling framework is based on the assumption that terrorist threats are "cheap talk" in the absence of violence.[33] Terrorists use violence to communicate their capability and their resolve.[34] But once they have carried out a certain amount of symbolic destruction, terrorists' talk is no longer cheap. This possibility receives scant attention in the terrorism literature (although scholars of interstate conflict address the issue in depth).³⁵ By turning the focus to threats, I show what terrorists do with the credibility their violence "buys": they issue pledges and bluffs to obtain concessions from the state and an impressive degree of social control over civilians. My account elaborates the "theory of victory" in terrorism studies by showing that violence is not enough to achieve success; threats are essential as well.³⁶ I also show how threats enable terrorists to signal different things to different audiences simultaneously. Excessive violence may signal inhumanity, a counterproductive message that may alienate terrorists' civilian supporters and ultimately jeopardize a group's prospects for victory.³⁷ By mixing violence with warnings and hoaxes, terrorists are able to signal capability and restraint at the same time. My explication of signal splitting is novel. It shows how threats enable terrorists to speak out of both sides of their mouths.

Second, my study advances the literature on terrorist propaganda. Scholars have analyzed the communiqués, websites, propaganda videos, and claims of credit produced by terrorist organizations.³⁸ This body of literature explores the various forms of terrorist propaganda, but it does not explore the logic of the threats that are conveyed in it. By laying bare the logic of threats, I provide insight into the significance of terrorist propaganda. My research unifies the study of propaganda with the above-mentioned studies of costly signaling and coercion. It also expands the notion of propaganda by noting the role of threats as image management. For terrorists facing an acute multiple audiences conundrum, ex post justification may not undo the political harm wrought by civilian casualties. By altering the pattern of damage to focus on property, threats bring terrorists' "propaganda by the deed" in line with the explicit propaganda narrative they create in text.³⁹

Third, this book speaks to an evolving literature on credibility and reputation in terrorism. Existing studies consider what happens when terrorists sit opposite the state at a negotiating table.⁴⁰ Should the state believe terrorists' promises and threats? This literature is empirical, lacking a general theory of credibility as exists in the state-centric coercive diplomacy literature.⁴¹ I show that terrorists' credibility is built through violence and truthful threats. Credibility may be spent down with a moderate amount of bluffing or hoaxing. By exploring the use of false threats, my theory contributes to a small but growing literature on lying by terrorist groups.⁴² My IRA and ETA interviews, however, also show that terrorists are careful not to issue too many false threats. Terrorist organizations protect their credibility through truth telling, standard procedures, and institutions that distinguish their messages from those of impostors.

Fourth, my findings advance the literature on civilian targeting in terrorism. Killing civilians is certainly the most spectacular way for terrorists to signal their capabilities. The terrorism literature explores the logic of casualty maximization via tactics such as suicide bombing and the pursuit of weapons of mass destruction.[43] But maximizing casualties is not always advantageous politically. This possibility receives limited consideration in the terrorism literature—although civil war scholars address it in more detail.[44] Given their role in reducing casualties, warnings give us an indicator of what makes terrorists choose a strategy of restraint. Terrorists give warnings when they face acute legitimacy concerns—for example, when they depend on civilians for shelter and when they fight democracies. My analysis suggests that terrorists' propensity to spare or target civilians does not follow from the other factors emphasized in existing literature: religion, ethnic grievances, separatism, and state sponsorship.[45] My findings are a challenge to conventional wisdom. They also show that the civil war literature's theories regarding civilian targeting cannot be directly imported to the analysis of terrorism.

Practical Implications

This book addresses practical questions as well. When should polities, social organizations, and individuals believe the threats they receive? My findings offer useful guidance. First, my quantitative analysis of warnings shows that these truthful threats are most likely when a militant group lacks territory, when it fights a democracy, and when the target is economic in nature. A threat meeting all three conditions has greater prima facie credibility. My concluding chapter broadens this analysis by identifying three essential elements of credibility in any terrorist threat. First, can the terrorist group possibly carry out the threatened attack? Second, if the terrorist group were carrying out such an attack, would it have political incentives to issue truthful threats in advance? Third, is it likely that the threat emanated from the terrorist group, as opposed to some unscrupulous individual hoaxer? If the answer to all three questions is "yes," we should take the threat seriously. If the answer to some or all of the questions is "no," it may be best to deprioritize the threat. In all likelihood, the greatest danger is overreaction. My broader hope for this book is that by considering terrorist threats rigorously, we can gain some mastery over an otherwise confusing and psychologically disorganizing phenomenon. A fuller understanding empowers us to respond in a fashion that is less fearful, less reflexive, and more appropriate to the finite danger that terrorism poses.[46]

Plan of the Book

The rest of this book proceeds as follows. Chapter 1 lays out my theoretical framework for understanding threats. I discuss the existing literature on threats in terrorism, showing how this body of research lags behind the more extensive scholarly investigation of threats in international diplomacy. I import several concepts from the coercive diplomacy literature to develop my own ideas about the functions of threats in terrorism. I explain my theoretical argument and the empirical implications that follow.

Chapter 2 presents my case study of the IRA, showing the four varieties of threats in context. My interviews of IRA members and police reveal how the IRA perceived its political environment: the audiences that supported it, the adversaries it sought to coerce, the tactics that would assure the former while intimidating the latter. The IRA interviews show how each variety of threat advanced the organization's coercive goals. Chapters 3–5 present further case studies to demonstrate the predictive power of my theoretical argument. Chapter 3 contrasts ETA and the Tamil Tigers. Chapter 4 compares the Shining Path and the MRTA. Chapter 5 contrasts the Afghan Taliban, ISIL, and Boko Haram. Chapter 6 presents the large-N quantitative analysis of warnings.

The concluding chapter summarizes the evidence supporting my argument. It brings these insights together with a practical discussion of what constitutes a reasonable response to any given threat. I present some anecdotes of civilian institutions overreacting to purported jihadist threats and stories of Nigerian schoolmasters calibrating responses more effectively over time. These examples suggest some best practices for assessing the credibility of a given threat in light of its content and the known political incentives of the terrorist group that allegedly issued the message. This system of best practices, combined with insights from my own analysis, offers a template for locally appropriate responses to threats. I also offer some predictions about the types of threats we are likely to see in the future. Although technological developments will increase the volume of threats that institutions and individuals receive, most of these threats are likely to be hoaxes or bluffs emanating from pranksters rather than terrorist groups. I argue that the social media–driven trend toward "crowdsourced" terrorism is blurring the line between threats and incitement. Organized terrorist groups and lone terrorist actors will circulate threatening memes and viral videos that may be understood both as direct threats against particular targets and as invitations for like-minded individuals to attack those targets on their own initiative. A forward-looking analysis of these trends will enable the recipients of threats to react effectively to those that require a response, while deprioritizing those that are quite unlikely to be true.

CHAPTER I

Threats

A Theoretical Framework

In this chapter I lay out the theoretical framework that structures the rest of the book. The framework includes a speech/kinetic action model of terrorism, in which threats and violence jointly determine the physical consequences of the attack and the resulting political messages conveyed to different audiences.[1] My framework also includes a four-category typology of threats, mapping the different types onto their tactical and strategic functions. Threats include warnings, hoaxes, pledges, and bluffs. We can distinguish these categories based on the timing of the threatened violence (immediate or prospective) and the intended truthfulness of the message. Immediate threats (warnings and hoaxes) may increase or decrease bloodshed, disrupt the economy, and secure tactical advantage over security forces. Prospective threats (pledges and bluffs) control social behavior, facilitate negotiation, aggrandize the perpetrator, and secure strategic advantage over the state. A single threat may serve several functions. It may also enable terrorists to communicate different messages to friends and foes with the same attack. I describe this phenomenon as signal splitting. When violence alone would produce suboptimal messaging outcomes, threats alter the pattern of damage, sending more effective signals to each audience.

Before explaining my theoretical framework in full, I lay some conceptual groundwork. As a scope condition, I define terrorism as *the use of violence and threats to influence the beliefs or behavior of a broader political audience.*

As terrorism scholars are quick to admit, there is no consensus definition of terrorism.[2] In general, scholars agree that terrorism is a symbolic activity. The purpose is not merely to cause destruction but to communicate something. As Brian Jenkins puts it: "Terrorism is aimed at the people watching, not at the actual victims. Terrorism is theater."[3] This conception of terrorism echoes the thinking of nineteenth-century anarchists, who described their insurrectionary activity as "propaganda by the deed."[4]

Beyond this point of broad consensus are several areas of controversy. One concerns the identity of the actors in terrorism: are "terrorist groups" different from rebel groups, insurgents, and guerrillas? Some scholars define terrorism as encompassing only the activity of small clandestine groups, too weak to control territory or engage the state's military formations.[5] I do not make an inherent distinction between terrorists and rebels because my concern is with terrorism as a type of behavior, which may be carried out by diverse perpetrators. Rebel groups employ communicative violence that is virtually indistinguishable from the violence of clandestine actors.[6] Moreover, my study shows that militant groups of various sizes use threats in quite similar ways. I do, however, restrict my study to terrorism by nonstate actors. I am mindful of the fact that common state practices—area bombing, forced disappearances, public execution, torture, and punitive incarceration—have broader communicative functions and could conceivably fit the definition of terrorism.[7] I do not discount the significance of these issues. Nor do I adopt any normative assumptions about the inherent legitimacy of state violence or the illegitimacy of nonstate violence. I do seek to limit my own investigation to a manageable scope. State terrorism and nonstate terrorism transpire under vastly different conditions—power dynamics, legal frameworks, and political relationships with civilians. I cannot address both phenomena in the same book, so I focus on nonstate terrorism.

Readers may also note that I include some attacks on security forces within my definition of terrorism. Other authors exclude such attacks, but there are many examples of nonstate actors targeting police and military forces outside of battlefield environments to send broader political messages.[8] The May 22, 2013, killing of British Army fusilier Lee Rigby provides a vivid example. Two professed jihadists ran Rigby down with a car on a London street and then hacked him to death with meat cleavers while encouraging bystanders to film the act with their camera phones. One of the men gave a statement, asserting that "Muslims are dying daily by

British soldiers" and British troops should "leave our lands" if citizens wish to "live in peace."[9] Such attacks target military forces, but they are clearly intended as terrorist theater. Moreover, my empirical analysis shows that militants use threats to victimize security forces, drawing them into traps and exploiting their reactions in furtherance of terrorist operations against civilians. One cannot comprehend the role of threats in terrorism without including certain attacks on security forces within the scope of the analysis.

Perhaps my most significant scope condition is to include threats within the definition of terrorism. I part ways with those who define terrorism as violence alone, instead adopting the approach of those who view violence and threats as "equally important."[10] In fact, this book represents the most extensive effort to date to demonstrate that threats and violence are coequal in terrorists' coercive tool kit. Terrorists cannot achieve their political ends without combining their violence with threats.

The importance of threats is already anticipated, if not directly explored, in the terrorism literature's costly signaling paradigm.[11] As nonstate actors, terrorists typically lack the military capabilities of governments. They may possess some ability to inflict harm, but because they have no tanks, armies, or police in uniform, it is difficult to assess their strength. From a position of weakness and obscurity, terrorists cannot make credible threats to attain their political goals. They can change this situation, however, by carrying out acts of violence for demonstration (i.e., signaling) purposes. Physical attacks signal terrorists' capabilities and political resolve.[12] Terrorist violence is thus a deadly strategy to gain credibility and increase one's leverage over state and society.

Scholars have devoted most of their attention to terrorism's credibility-generating process: the varieties of violence, the importance of claiming credit for attacks, and so on.[13] These are important contributions. But to understand terrorism fully, we require an equally detailed investigation of what terrorists do with the credibility their violence has bought them. How do terrorists translate credibility into political results? The literature on coercive diplomacy by states explores these issues in considerable depth.[14] Governments extract concessions from one another by making threats. Typically, we think of threats as a prelude to violence, but the logic of coercion is the reverse: violence is an instrument to make one's future threats credible. Thomas Schelling writes: "To inflict suffering gains nothing and saves nothing directly. . . . The only purpose, unless sport or revenge, must be to influence somebody's behavior, to coerce his decision or choice. To be coercive, violence has to be anticipated. . . . It is the *threat* of damage, or of more damage to come, that can make someone yield or comply."[15] This may be an overstatement in an interstate context because many nations have militaries capable of overpowering their enemies outright. But for nonstate actors seeking to coerce states or impose their rule over much larger civilian populations, the logic applies quite well: brute force is inadequate to achieve results, except when paired with threats.

Terrorism scholars do not discuss threats as systematically as Schelling does, but they do explore certain aspects of his logic. Authors note the importance of articulating clear demands in order to obtain political results.[16] Other scholars explore the dynamics of peace talks between terrorists and states.[17] Their focus, however, is on the state's perspective, not the threats that brought the government to the bargaining table or the threats a terrorist group makes if its initial demands are not met. When terrorism scholars do discuss threats, it is in a vague sense: a "threat of terrorism" that exists because some person or group has carried out an attack.[18] This use of the term *threat*, although grammatical, obscures the strategic utility of threats. It connotes a state of affairs—what could more precisely be termed a *risk* of terrorism, regardless of any explicit threats the militant group has or has not made. But risks are not especially useful for inducing specific policy concessions. The most efficient way to obtain concessions is to confront the target of coercion with a clear cost/benefit calculation. The victim must be made aware of what harm to expect and what to give up in order to avoid that harm. As Schelling observes, "the object of a threat is to give somebody a choice," and, by making the alternatives clear, to push the victim toward the desired outcome.[19]

We require a direct investigation of threats in order to grasp the coercive logic of terrorism. How do terrorists use threats? What sort of threats do they issue—and to whom? An analysis of threats should help us to discern the specific functions of each type of threat in shaping the beliefs or behavior of the audience. An analysis of threats should also address the interrelation of speech acts and violence in the complex arena of terrorist signaling. Because the signal of terrorist violence is often issued in public, multiple audiences may observe it. The message may be intended for one set of viewers—the state, the general public, supporters of the militant group—but all these audiences are likely to observe the signal and draw their own conclusions about the sender. It is possible that in communicating one message to the intended audience, the terrorist group may communicate a second, undesirable message to other audiences. I describe this situation as terrorism's *multiple audiences conundrum*.

The multiple audiences conundrum arises because of the violent and often repulsive nature of terrorist signaling. Several authors have noted the high likelihood that in carrying out attacks to signal strength to the state adversary, terrorists will also appear inhumane to civilian observers.[20] Extreme bloodshed may be effective for signaling to the enemy, but it risks alienating friendly civilians on whom the terrorist group depends for shelter, finance, and other resources. Terrorism may thus be self-defeating. How do militants solve this problem? One possible means is through target selection—attacking infrastructure instead of public spaces where many civilians are likely to be present.[21] But these ostensibly low-casualty targets may be inaccessible or situated in densely populated areas. There are many examples of militants attacking physical infrastructure like transit lines and pipelines with horrific results.[22] Is there another way to mitigate terrorism's multiple audiences conundrum?

Threats offer the militant group a potential solution. They shape the violence, reducing damage to certain types of targets while heaping extra damage onto others. This use of threats is distinct from the logic of coercion, which involves longer time scales and actions that can be called off if the target grants concessions. Violence-shaping threats immediately precede a specific physical action, giving detailed information about what is about to occur. The attack may be set in motion already, but the reaction to the threat by government and civilian actors can influence the physical consequences in ways that advantage the terrorist group. For example, the IRA and ETA issued warnings prior to their bombings, allowing civilians to escape harm.[23] Additional "hoax calls following a real bomb" shut down economic infrastructure and caused bloodless disruption beyond what the bombs themselves achieved.[24] In each case, the combination of bombs and threats created a distinctive pattern of reduced-casualty property destruction. The IRA and ETA could thus send two different signals at once. To civilian audiences, they communicated restraint; to state audiences, they signaled their ability to cause economic ruin.

How widespread are these practices? Do threats serve any other functions? To answer these questions, I present a new theoretical framework based on two innovations. First, I reconceive terrorism as consisting of speech and physical actions.[25] This insight applies not only at the strategic level (i.e., the use of threats in coercion) but also at the level of the attack, when a group mixes violence with warnings or issues disruptive hoax threats that can be thought of as attacks in their own right.[26] To grasp the logic of terrorism, one must account for terrorists' kinetic actions and their threats, which jointly produce the attack's physical and political outcomes.

My second theoretical innovation is a four-part typology (table 0.1) that classifies threats and facilitates an empirical investigation of their functions. We can categorize threats based on their temporal proximity to violence and their intended truthfulness. Immediate threats (warnings and hoaxes) foreshadow violence in the very near future. These threats help to constitute the attack. They shape the attack's physical outcomes—or they can substitute for physical violence. Prospective threats (pledges and bluffs) promise violence at some indeterminate time in the future. These threats may not shape the attack's physical outcomes, but they do shape the political consequences. The long-term strategic dynamics within a conflict, and the ultimate success of terrorism in obtaining policy concessions, depend on the terrorist group's issuance of coercive pledges and bluffs.

The speech/kinetic action model and the typology of threats work synergistically. Recall figure 0.1. The figure divides terrorism into three temporal moments: preattack, attack, and postattack. Pledges and bluffs occur in the preattack moment. The attack moment contains some mix of kinetic violence and immediate threats. The mix may be dominated by one component or the other, or it may consist of one element alone. A hoax attack, for instance, contains threats alone in the attack moment. Certain moments can also be "empty." For instance, a strategic bluff during political negotiations would include prospective threats in the preattack moment but no violence or threats in the attack moment. An "out-of-the-blue" attack contains no threats in the preattack moment but kinetic violence in the attack moment.

The postattack moment contains the physical and political outcomes of threats and violence. These outcomes will include particular messages sent to one or more political audiences, such as the militant group's state adversary and its political supporters. Some outcomes in the postattack moment will shape the strategic conditions for future terrorist incidents. For instance, a successful kinetic attack that elevates opponents' perceptions of the terrorist group's capability will increase the perceived credibility of the group's future coercive threats. This is the core logic of costly signaling.[27] Figure 0.1's arrow represents the link between threats and kinetic violence in the current episode of terrorism and the ex ante conditions for the next episode. Terrorists choose their actions today mindful of their conditioning effect on the strategic environment for threats and violence tomorrow.

By unpacking terrorism to appreciate its speech and kinetic action components, my framework allows us to identify the specific functions of terrorist threats. It shows what pledges, bluffs, warnings, and hoaxes (separately or in combination) *do* for terrorist groups. My framework exposes the role of threats in achieving particular objectives. It also enhances our understanding of terrorism as political communication with an audience. By examining threats systematically, we gain insight into how terrorists shape perceptions and structure their audiences' political incentives.

My theoretical framework allows us to make predictions about when terrorists will issue particular types of threats. Recall table 0.1, showing the four varieties of threats along with their functions. By alerting civilians to an impending attack, a warning offers them the chance to escape harm.[28] Warnings may therefore be useful to militant groups seeking to cultivate an image of restraint and political legitimacy among civilian populations. A group with a particularly intense multiple audiences conundrum may find this variety of threat useful. Immediate threats are also disruptive. The state reacts to warnings and hoaxes by mobilizing police, shutting down transit and commercial hubs, and dispatching bomb squads. The state undertakes these emergency responses to reduce casualties and damage, but the interventions also carry costs. A bomb with a warning imposes extra economic disruption on the state, beyond the physical effects of the device. Warnings allow terrorists to signal strength to the state (via property destruction and economic attrition) while attenuating casualties and signaling restraint to civilians. This is one example of signal splitting. Terrorists can augment a reduced-casualty property destruction campaign with hoaxes that impose economic disruption with no bloodshed and no operational cost to the militant group.

Terrorists can also use immediate threats to seek tactical advantage over the state's security forces. For example, they can use warnings or hoaxes to draw police into areas where they are vulnerable to ambush.[29] Another use of immediate threats is *tactical prophylaxis*: issuing warnings or hoaxes to deter security personnel from entering particular areas or to pin them down in areas they cannot escape.[30] Prophylactic threats restrict security forces' movements so that militants' own operations are more likely to succeed. This increases the militant group's ability to signal strength—to adversaries or to civilian populations who may choose to support a group based on whether it appears capable of winning its struggle. Terrorists can use hoaxes for intelligence-gathering or rehearsal purposes as well. The militant group issues a false threat and observes the reaction of security forces. These reactions can be exploited in the next real attack. (Recall figure 0.1's arrow, representing the role each attack plays in establishing conditions for the next.) Having observed security forces' reaction to a hoax threat, militants will know approximately how long they have to carry out operations before security forces arrive at the scene of a terror alert. They may also know the route security forces will take to arrive at the scene of an alert. This information is useful for staging ambushes of security personnel. By making future attacks more lethal and more likely to succeed, intelligence-gathering/rehearsal hoaxes increase terrorists' ability to signal strength to the state. The practices described—using threats to draw police in, to disrupt counterterrorism operations, or to obtain intelligence—are useful for militant groups facing highly capable counterterrorism opponents. The more capable the opponent, the greater the terrorist group's incentive to seek tactical advantage using hoaxes and warnings.

Prospective pledges and bluffs shape the political dynamics of a conflict. Their relationship with specific acts of violence is more distant temporally. Terrorists can therefore make their threats contingent on some desired behavioral change by the recipient. This is the sort of threat discussed in the coercive diplomacy literature.[31] Terrorists may announce, for instance, that they will commence attacks on politicians who allow foreign military occupiers to remain in the country. If the terrorists are sincere and politicians do not concede, the militants will fulfill their pledge. If the terrorists are not sincere and politicians refuse to concede, the bluff will ultimately amount to nothing—except perhaps a blow to the terrorist group's reputation for truthfulness. Note, however, that if politicians grant the concession, the ultimate truth or falsehood of the threat will be known only to the militants. Because bluffs are "cheap," requiring no physical preparation to fulfill, it makes sense for terrorists to bluff if they believe the state will accede to their demands. In general, we should expect pledges and bluffs against the state when terrorist groups are seeking to negotiate concrete issues with the government.

Pledges and bluffs are also effective tools for controlling the civilian population. A group whose core mission includes social control is likely to issue more pledges and bluffs against civilians. For example, a religious terrorist group may threaten to attack civilians who engage in proscribed behavior—consuming drugs and alcohol or associating with the military forces of apostate foreign occupiers.[32] The truthfulness of these threats will not be known to outsiders if civilians comply with the militants' demands. If civilians violate the rules, the truthfulness of the initial threat will become clear to all. A terrorist group that fulfills a pledge increases the credibility of its future threats, even if the present threat was ineffective at shaping behavior. Having observed the consequences just visited on those who failed to heed the first threat, civilians are more likely to obey the militants next time. But a terrorist group that bluffs to achieve social control may see the strategy backfire if civilians disobey. To claw back their credibility, terrorists may need to issue more threats and fulfill them before civilians will believe the group's words.

Pledges and bluffs can aggrandize the terrorist group's reputation relative to the state and other militant groups. Pledging an attack before carrying it out renders the success of the attack more impressive. Even with advance notice, the state was incapable of stopping the terrorists from carrying out their plans. By showing that the state is incapable of self-defense, the terrorist group may convince politicians that concessions are the only way to obtain relief from further attacks. By demonstrating their capability to overwhelm the state's defenses, terrorists may also achieve greater popular support. This postattack outcome is particularly useful to marginal terrorist groups seeking to outbid more powerful peer rivals and attract more recruits.[33] Bluffs serve the same purpose as long as they are never revealed. For example, a terrorist group that pledges to attack military patrols may never need to do so if the state ceases those patrols. The militants appear to be strong, even if they never had the capability or intent to carry out their threat. Thus bluffs aggrandize a terrorist group for as long as they are effective at shaping behavior. But if the state calls the bluff by ignoring it, the reputational effect is precisely the opposite. In general, we should expect terrorist groups to issue self-aggrandizing pledges and bluffs when their status is most in question: when they are competing against larger or more capable militant organizations, when they suffer strategic reverses, and when they enter periods of decline. In the latter case, we might expect to see more bluff threats, as the terrorist group tries to reclaim the limelight or perhaps provoke a government reaction that makes the group look relevant again.

Finally, terrorists can use pledges and bluffs for *strategic* advantage or prophylaxis. The purpose of these threats is not to interfere with the tactics of security forces but to force an alteration to the state's counterterrorism strategy—taking certain options off the table or requiring the state to undertake policies it would otherwise have forgone as suboptimal. For example, terrorists may threaten government officials working on education and economic development projects. This may foreclose counterterrorism strategies built on positive community interaction, as opposed to militarized search and seizure operations.[34] We should expect terrorist groups to issue pledges and bluffs for strategic prophylaxis when their counterterrorism opponents are especially strong, forcing the militants to seek advantages wherever they can.

This survey of threats and their functions gives rise to several propositions about when we can expect particular varieties of threats. Table 1.1 summarizes the relevant incentives and predicted behaviors. I give supporting evidence for these propositions in the chapters that follow, in my contrasting case studies of ETA and the Tamil Tigers, the MRTA and the Shining Path, and the jihadists of the Afghan Taliban, ISIL, and Boko Haram. Each of these comparisons is suited to testing particular propositions, based on which political factors vary across the militant groups in each ideological grouping. My quantitative analysis focuses on testing

TABLE 1.1
Theoretical Propositions

	Objective	Expected Behavior
1	Legitimacy	Warning
2	Disruption	Warnings/hoaxes (vs. economic targets)
3	Social control	Pledges/bluffs (vs. civilians)
4	Negotiation	Pledges/bluffs (vs. the state)
5	Aggrandizement	Pledges/bluffs
6	Tactical/strategic advantage	Warnings/hoaxes/pledges/bluffs

propositions 1 and 2, concerning warnings. This sets the stage for a discussion, in the concluding chapter, about credibility and emergency responses to purported warnings. I lay out a set of recommendations for those who receive threats to assess the credibility of a given message and calibrate emergency responses to the degree of danger. To set the stage for all this, I first present my primary source case study of the IRA, illustrating the logic of all six propositions in the words of militants themselves.

CHAPTER II

The Provisional IRA

A Full Spectrum of Threats

This chapter illustrates the various functions of threats through a primary source case study of the Provisional Irish Republican Army (IRA). I have chosen the IRA as my first case study because of the rich data available on this group and the relative ease of obtaining interviews with former conflict participants. A study of an active militant group would be hampered by serious legal and safety concerns for the interviewees and myself. These issues do not arise with the IRA owing to the more or less settled nature of the Northern Ireland conflict. Formerly incarcerated IRA members are free to discuss their activities during the conflict without fear of legal consequences, having been pardoned by the British government as part of the 1998 peace deal that ended the so-called Troubles.[1] The safety concerns of police and other conflict participants on the opposing side are likewise reduced now that the IRA has disarmed. The political environment in Northern Ireland presents an ideal opportunity for a detailed case study characterizing the varieties of threats and explaining, in conflict participants' own words, the strategic and tactical logic behind each. My interviews show how each variety of threat advances a particular function: seeking political legitimacy, economic disruption, social control, negotiation with the state, tactical and strategic advantage, and self-aggrandizement. These functions relate back to my four-category typology of threats and my speech/action model of terrorism.[2]

An IRA case study is also well suited to elucidating the multiple audiences conundrum and signal splitting. Violence may produce suboptimal messaging outcomes if militants are signaling to two or more political audiences, at least one of which is casualty averse. In the IRA's case, the most relevant audiences were the British state adversary and the IRA's nationalist supporters in Ireland and the United States. A persistent tension for the IRA was the need to signal strength to the British state without alienating sympathetic nationalist civilians. My interviews show how the IRA used threats to mitigate this problem. Warnings created a pattern of damage that spared civilians while heaping physical and financial ruin on the state. The signal of IRA violence was split: the IRA's supporters perceived the group's restraint toward noncombatants, while the British state perceived the IRA's strength as a fighting force. The IRA used hoaxes to compound the economically disruptive effects of bombings and warnings. It also used hoaxes to distract police and draw them into traps. To shape the broader political dynamics of the conflict, the IRA used pledges and bluffs. These prospective threats aggrandized the IRA relative to the state and rival militant groups. They facilitated social control of the Irish population and political bargaining with the government. Pledges secured strategic advantages as well, preventing local civilians from collaborating with British security forces.

These insights and their implications emerge through the words of interviewees. First, I contextualize the data with an overview of the conflict and my procedures for recruiting and interviewing subjects. I then explore the political dynamics of the IRA's support base. This context is essential to understanding the IRA's political strategy and how the group used specific types of threats to advance it.

The Troubles, 1969–1998

The Northern Ireland conflict, colloquially known as the Troubles, lasted roughly from 1969 to 1998. The Troubles were a struggle for political control of Northern Ireland, the six northernmost counties of historic Ireland, which remained part of the United Kingdom following the Irish Revolution of 1919 and the creation of an independent state in the southernmost twenty-six counties.[3] The partition of Ireland was a compromise solution to a simmering conflict between Catholics (a majority in the South) and

Protestants (a majority in the North). Predominantly Catholic nationalists were dissatisfied with an agreement that left part of Ireland under British control. Catholics also suffered job and housing discrimination and barriers to political participation in Protestant-dominated institutions.[4] Unionists in the North defended Northern Ireland's inclusion in the United Kingdom.

In the late 1960s Catholic civil rights demonstrations sparked violent police responses and a cycle of tit-for-tat sectarian attacks in cities such as Belfast and Derry (known by unionists as Londonderry). Northern Ireland's parliament requested British military intervention in 1969 to keep the rioting factions apart.[5] Remnants of the Irish Republican Army, the revolutionary force that overthrew British rule in the South, initiated their own effort to secure northern nationalist communities against sectarian attacks. A more radical faction calling itself the Provisional IRA began an armed campaign against the government and security forces, with the intention of seceding from the United Kingdom and establishing a single all-Ireland republic.[6]

There were three discernible phases in the violence.[7] From 1969 to 1974 the Provisional IRA sought independence from British rule through a campaign of violent destabilization. IRA forces attacked British troops, local police and military reservists, pro-British loyalist paramilitary groups, and commercial and political targets in Northern Ireland and England. The IRA gained international notoriety for this last mode of violence, carrying out hundreds of bombings.[8]

From 1975 to 1993 the IRA pursued a "long war" of attrition. It sought to impose costs on the British state while insisting that the U.K. government negotiate a peace settlement with the IRA's political wing, Sinn Féin. As part of this strategy, the IRA fought a public relations battle for legitimacy in the eyes of Irish, British, and international publics. IRA members in military prisons launched a series of protests and hunger strikes, demanding "political" rather than "criminal" status. Ten hunger strikers died.[9] The spectacle of the strikes brought international media attention to the IRA's political demands. It solidified the IRA's new strategy to take power "with a ballot paper in this hand and an Armalite in this hand."[10]

From 1994 to 1998 the IRA and Sinn Féin pursued a political settlement with the British government while strategically manipulating the level of violence in the armed campaign.[11] The Army Council, the IRA's leadership body, declared a ceasefire in August 1994 to make way for Sinn

Féin talks with the Conservative John Major government. When talks broke down in 1996, the IRA carried out spectacular bombings in English cities such as London and Manchester, seeking to force the British government back to the bargaining table.[12] With the election of Tony Blair's Labour government and a fresh start to negotiations, the IRA declared a new ceasefire in July 1997. With American diplomats and Irish politicians acting as brokers, Blair, Sinn Féin negotiator Gerry Adams, and Army Council representative Martin McGuinness reached the so-called Belfast or Good Friday agreement in April 1998.[13] Although the peace settlement left Northern Ireland under British control, it did make several concessions in exchange for the IRA's disarmament. These include a statutory ban on ethnic discrimination, a devolved Northern Irish government with power sharing between nationalists and unionists, a demilitarized border between Northern Ireland and the Republic of Ireland, dual British/Irish citizenship for Northern Ireland residents, and formal political and economic links between the North and South.[14]

Research Methods

To understand the IRA's use of threats, I conducted thirty-three interviews of former IRA members, police, British Army personnel, government officials, and journalists and civil society members who served as intermediaries for communication between the IRA and British authorities. I recruited as diverse a set of interviewees as possible within my core subject population. My IRA interviewees had been active at various command levels in the organization, in the capital city, Belfast, and in County Armagh, a rural area of heavy IRA guerrilla activity. I recruited these individuals through social organizations providing services to formerly imprisoned militants, through direct personal approaches, and through referrals by other interviewees (the "snowball technique").[15] All IRA interviewees had been imprisoned for political crimes before being pardoned and released on license as part of the 1998 peace agreement. This legal status allowed them to discuss their former IRA activities without criminal liability, as long as they confined their autobiographical discussion to the specific offenses for which they had been pardoned. (Otherwise, the interviewees discussed their general understanding of what the IRA as an organization did and what the organization's strategic thinking was at the time.) The interviewees' past IRA activity was quite diverse, from weapons possession and bomb making to causing explosions and assassinating police and army personnel.

To understand security forces' reactions to threats, I interviewed veterans of the Royal Ulster Constabulary (RUC), the police force that operated in Northern Ireland during the Troubles.[16] I recruited RUC veterans who served at a variety of command levels, including the highest levels of the organization. The interviewees had diverse specializations within the RUC, from operations (those who responded to street-level concerns, including bomb alerts and shootings) to investigations and the counterterrorism "Special Branch." I recruited RUC subjects through universities and think tanks, security-oriented businesses employing former RUC officers, and direct personal approaches.[17]

I recruited Irish charity workers (specifically, crisis hotline operators) and journalists who had reported for a variety of print and broadcast media in Belfast during the Troubles. Some subjects had served as points of contact for IRA threats and credit claims. Others had worked at news offices and switchboards that received telephone threats from the IRA. These individuals served as middle links between IRA members making threats and the British authorities who responded to them.[18]

Many individuals I consulted preferred not to sit for formal interviews. Eleven preferred to be left on background and not quoted directly. Of those who agreed to be interviewed and quoted, the sources included eight former IRA members, four former police, and seven journalists. Several interviewees requested anonymity, for legal, safety, or professional reasons. I refer to these interviewees with generic identifiers (e.g., Republican #1) or in the case of RUC veterans, by rank and specialization. I conducted my interviews in a semistructured format, with basic questions to frame the important subjects of discussion (types of threats, political functions of threats, etc.) but no formal questionnaire.[19] I ceased recruiting interviewees upon reaching the point of "theoretical saturation," where the accounts of new interviewees (on and off the record) yielded no new information, only confirmation of previous interviewees' statements.[20] The appendix contains an overview of the interviews I conducted, a description of my recruitment and interview procedures, sample interview questions, and the human subjects protections I employed in this portion of my research.

The IRA's Strategy and Audiences

The IRA pursued a two-track strategy in its guerrilla campaign against the British state. On the first track, the IRA sought to undermine the British government's grip on Northern Ireland by carrying out attacks on security forces and installations. The group hoped that these attacks would make Northern Ireland ungovernable except by extreme militarization, a move that would cost Britain too much money and too many lives to be sustainable.[21] Republican #1 describes the types of targets attacked in the military portion of the IRA campaign:

> Any deployment by the British government in terms of propping up the state . . .
> British army, RUC, locally recruited regiments the likes of the UDR [Ulster Defence Regiment], RIR [Royal Irish Regiment], that sort of thing. . . . They're all armed. They're all put here for a specific reason. It was about defeating republicanism. . . . It was about upholding the state as it was. So they were the enemy and were considered as such. . . . They were considered military targets.[22]

On the second track, the IRA pursued a bombing campaign directed at commercial facilities and public infrastructure. The logic of the second track was to stretch out military and police resources, force the further militarization of the conflict, and inflict economic losses, which the British government would have to reimburse out of its own pockets.[23] Republican #2, an operative from one of Northern Ireland's border counties, recalls the strategy underlying the IRA's "commercial bombing" campaign:

> It meant the retail centers of towns, or administrative centers in towns, government offices or offices of government departments, and public transport infrastructure. . . . Those targets were attacked for the purpose of disrupting the economic life in Northern Ireland under the rule of the British government . . . to demonstrate to the British government that Northern Ireland wasn't a workable entity and that the IRA would prevent it from being a viable economic entity.[24]

As the IRA pursued this two-part strategy, it drew support from republican sympathizers in Northern Ireland and the Irish American diaspora. In Northern Ireland, the IRA's local base provided material support, including "call houses" where IRA members could meet to plan operations, store weapons, and sleep. Community members who did not offer up their homes as call houses would still allow IRA members to use their homes as getaway routes and hiding places. Brendan Hughes, operations chief for the IRA's Belfast Brigade, later explained: "Most people cooperated with the IRA; they left their back doors open, or if they saw you jumping over the yard wall, they'd open the back door if it was closed."[25]

Rank-and file IRA members developed a politically sophisticated understanding of their relationship with the local population. Of particular importance were the theories of Mao Zedong, as articulated in his text *On Guerrilla Warfare* (1937). Regarding the relationship between the local community and a guerrilla force, Mao writes: "The former may be likened to water and the latter to the fish who inhabit it. . . . It is only undisciplined troops who make the people their enemies and who, like the fish out of its native element, cannot live."[26]

Seven out of the eight on-the-record IRA interviewees made specific reference to Mao's analogy. Séanna Walsh, the final public spokesman for the IRA, gives a typical account: "The IRA operated here in the North with the support of the community that they came from. It's like Mao Zedong talked about, the fish in the sea. Our community were our sea, and we swam amongst them."[27]

Robert "Dinker" McClanahan, an IRA member who served eighteen years in prison for causing explosions in Belfast, offers a similar analysis: "You were the fish swimming in the sea. And you depended on the community to give you food, to give you shelter, to give you transport . . . to give you help and assistance, to look after your guns, to look after your explosives. And they could have went to jail equally as ourselves, so they were putting themselves at a certain amount of risk."[28]

In addition to local republicans, the IRA relied on the Irish American diaspora as a second base of support. Rather than supplying daily needs such as shelter, Americans' role was to provide money, weapons, and political leverage from afar. When the Provisional IRA first formed in 1969, it possessed only a few outdated firearms to defend Catholic communities against Protestant vigilante violence. Commencing an armed campaign against British forces would have been impossible without substantial acquisitions of new weapons. During this early phase and well into the 1970s, sympathetic Americans were the IRA's main source of weapons. Lax gun laws allowed American IRA sympathizers to purchase military-style weapons, including the Armalite AR-15, which later came to symbolize the IRA's armed campaign. Individual Americans shipped guns by mail or inside the coffins of deceased relatives who wished to be buried in Ireland.[29] Dedicated gunrunning operations brought more weapons, first in small shipments and later in large ones. Robert McClanahan recalls: "In the early years, I'm talking say 1970 until probably '76, '77, your main source of weapons was coming from the U.S. Whether it was old Second World War issue Garand rifles and M1 carbines and Thompson machine guns or Colt 45 revolvers, and then the Armalite, the AR-15 or AR-18 and the Vietnam stuff coming home, the M-16."[30]

Many of the sophisticated "AR" weapons were acquired and shipped by Irish Northern Aid (Noraid), a self-described humanitarian relief organization established in coordination with IRA Belfast brigade commander Joe Cahill, who traveled to the United States repeatedly to raise funds and procure arms.[31] Noraid raised money in pubs, churches and social clubs, via direct mail, and through fundraising events featuring speeches by Cahill and other IRA members.[32]

Aside from the issues of fundraising and gunrunning, the IRA saw the United States as a powerful source of political leverage to influence the British government. After the January 30, 1972, "Bloody Sunday" incident, in which British paratroopers shot and killed fourteen Catholic civil rights demonstrators, Irish-American politicians such as Senator Ted Kennedy (D-Mass.) put pressure on the British government to suspend Northern Ireland's parliament.[33] Their near-term motivation was to halt sectarian abuses of Catholics by a Protestant-dominated northern regime. However, the long-term effect of shutting down the local government was to make Britain's involvement in Northern Ireland more direct, reinforcing the IRA's self-portrayal as a grassroots resistance to a foreign military occupation.[34]

Even more significant than Ted Kennedy's role was the role of U.S. President Bill Clinton. Clinton made a crucial decision in 1994 to grant Sinn Féin president Gerry Adams a visa, against the wishes of the British government. The visa allowed Adams to address the Irish American public through high-profile media appearances.[35] Americans' acceptance of Adams helped to legitimize Sinn Féin's role as a political party and a central player in the Northern Ireland peace process. The appointment of a special Northern Ireland negotiator, Senator George Mitchell (D-Maine), helped to secure the IRA-U.K. peace settlement, which President Clinton endorsed with a visit to Belfast and a high-profile handshake with Adams. Séanna Walsh expresses the IRA's understanding of America's role in the peace process:

> One of the lessons that we had from the previous ceasefires of the mid-70s was that to get any movement from the British we had to internationalize it. If it was internationalized, well then in that context, you could be a wee bit more relaxed. If the British said something and you had international guarantors to ensure that, "Actually this is what you said," once you do that, once you bring people like that into the equation, well then that changes the whole context. So it was crucial that people like Bill Clinton and the whole Irish American diaspora really bought into what was going on here.[36]

The Multiple Audiences Conundrum

Although the IRA was fortunate to have strong support bases locally and internationally, it faced a dilemma: carrying out its two-part war, attacking military targets and commercial targets, was likely to alienate at least some of its supporters. By IRA members' recollections, the Irish republican community was averse to civilian casualties. Although they perceived themselves to be living under a colonial occupation, the level of repression was lower than in other colonial contexts. Catholics had representation in government, ethnic gerrymandering and housing and job discrimination notwithstanding. The British government also provided public works and social services to members of all religious groups. "We weren't the Palestinians," Republican #3 recalls.[37] Danny Morrison, a former IRA member and public spokesman for Sinn Féin, concurs. Although the IRA was capable of carrying out mass casualty attacks on a regular basis, nationalists "weren't that oppressed" and there could be no justification for "indiscriminate actions."[38]

However, an urban guerrilla campaign always puts civilians at risk. The problem was most acute in commercial bombings. Although the IRA claimed to be carrying out these attacks to fight off British oppression, the attacks themselves were directed at civilian structures and were very likely to kill bystanders. IRA members perceived the moral contradiction. Republican #1 recalls: "You can't on the one hand be saying you'll be fighting on behalf of a people and about removing some sort of tyranny and then at the same time being so very blasé about human life. . . . [I]f you're engaging in a war you have a responsibility that those who aren't involved in the war don't become the casualties of it."[39]

The IRA's local base perceived the tension as well. Their support depended on the IRA carrying out a relatively "clean" war. Séanna Walsh explains: "Activities that killed civilians, or even hurt civilians, could have a detrimental effect on IRA operations. People would tell you, if you went to their house after something happened. They'd say, 'That's disgraceful. Why did you do that?' . . . And people would tell you, 'I don't want you coming back by the house,' or 'I'm not prepared to mind those weapons in my house if this is what you're involved in.'"[40] Danny Morrison's recollections are similar: "Who's going to support an organization that is seen to be killing civilians, without thought, or without any ethics at all? Why, I know people who were thrown out of houses after certain attacks!"[41]

Several IRA atrocities in 1972 make the interviewees' points concrete. A March 4 bombing at Belfast's Abercorn restaurant killed two civilians and injured dozens more. On March 20 another car bombing in Belfast's Lower Donegall Street killed four civilians. These incidents alienated local Catholics, particularly women, who began local peace movements in opposition to the IRA's armed campaign.[42] Another incident, the "Bloody Friday" bomb blitz of July 21, caused an even wider rift. In this attack, the IRA detonated at least twenty bombs throughout Belfast in the space of eighty minutes, killing 5 civilians and wounding 130 more.[43] Grisly television footage of the aftermath disillusioned even staunch republicans and drove moderate nationalists away entirely. Those who favored constitutional solutions to Northern Ireland's problems would remain hostile to "armed force" republicanism for the duration of the Troubles.[44] British authorities capitalized on the new political situation, accelerating the planning and execution of "Operation Motorman," a massive military operation to dislodge the IRA from "no-go" zones it had declared in Catholic areas of Derry and Belfast. Sensing itself at a political nadir, the IRA leadership instructed cadres not to resist these incursions but to abandon their safe houses and retreat. The IRA lacked the political standing even to protest what should have been a highly controversial action: a massive military operation by a Protestant-dominated government against Catholic civilians in their own homes.[45]

Civilian casualties were politically toxic in Irish America as well. Relatively radical republican sympathizers were willing to support the IRA, but their support depended on the maintenance of a freedom fighter image. To that end, IRA speakers at Noraid "humanitarian relief" fundraisers emphasized their links to the original Irish revolution and the progress of Irish self-determination. They eschewed direct references to bombs. In public appeals to more moderate Irish Americans, Noraid claimed that the group's charity supported the families of imprisoned Republicans—not the purchase of weapons. This distinction was important not only for legal reasons but also to reassure moderate Americans who would not have donated money specifically to buy guns.[46] Yet Noraid's implicit association with IRA violence remained. A very high-ranking RUC Special Branch veteran recalls the political conundrum for Noraid and the IRA in the early 1970s: "Could you continue to kill people in the numbers that you were and still maintain [support in] your American diaspora? Because you're not a couple of freedom fighters coming down from the hill fighting an armored car. You're actually blowing up innocent people shopping. . . . You can't do that."[47]

The effect on Noraid's work is measurable in dollars, looking at the monthly fundraising totals reported in the group's tax filings. Fundraising increased after the government's August 1971 introduction of indefinite internment for suspected IRA members and revelations about abusive interrogation practices; it peaked after the January 1972 "Bloody Sunday" incident. Monthly fundraising dropped by $200,000 after the IRA's Bloody Friday atrocities that July.[48] Noraid leaders were so distressed that they contacted high-level IRA members to complain about the bombings' negative effect on their work.[49] As Robert McClanahan recalls, atrocity "plays bad in the bars and in the clubs of New York and wherever, when you're asking for money to send back to the IRA."[50] Atrocity also "plays bad" on the world stage. Because Catholics were an economically disadvantaged minority and commercial bombings took place in affluent areas, civilians killed in commercial attacks were likely to be Protestant. These deaths reinforced a British government narrative about the purpose of its military involvement. Séanna Walsh explains: "The way the British portrayed what was happening here was, there were two warring communities, Catholics and Protestants, and [the British] were in the middle trying . . . to keep these warring factions apart. Which is absolute bollocks as far as we're concerned."[51]

The IRA thus faced a potentially fatal multiple audiences conundrum: in carrying out its campaign of coercion against the state, it risked alienating local republicans, Irish Americans, and U.S. politicians whose support the IRA desperately needed. To maintain its local safe houses, its American gun supply, and the legitimacy of Sinn Féin in American political circles, the IRA needed to ensure that its violence did not kill too many civilians.

Threats and Their Functions

Threats mitigated the IRA's multiple audiences conundrum. They optimized the group's signals so that friends and enemies would perceive messages that advanced the IRA's strategy. In the following sections I describe the varieties of threats used by the IRA and the political purposes served by each type. I begin by addressing the uses of immediate threats (warnings and hoaxes), which exert their greatest effects on the near-term physical consequences of an attack. Interviews of IRA members show how the group used warnings and hoaxes to prevent harm to civilians while simultaneously increasing damage to the British security apparatus and economy. Warnings enabled the IRA to split its signals, projecting strength toward its state adversary while at the same time signaling restraint to civilians. I then turn to the uses of prospective pledges and bluffs, which exert their greatest effects on the long-term strategic and political dynamics of a conflict. The IRA used pledges and bluffs to exert social control over the Irish population, to burnish the group's reputation, and to increase its leverage in bargaining over Northern Ireland's future.

Warnings: Seeking Legitimacy by Splitting Signals

With its commercial bombing campaign, the IRA sought to turn Northern Ireland into an enormous money sink for the British government. At the same time, IRA leaders sought to minimize civilian casualties that would delegitimize the group in the eyes of its own supporters. The challenge was to identify tactics that achieved two apparently contradictory goals simultaneously. IRA leaders resolved the quandary by issuing warnings, offering civilians a chance to flee commercial areas before bombs went off. A former RUC Special Branch intelligence expert explains that the IRA "didn't send volunteers out to kill and maim indiscriminately. . . . [I]f you were told to do a thing called a 'commercial bombing,' which they did in the center of town, which was against commercial targets, you didn't want any collateral [damage]. Invariably somebody is going to get hurt somewhere along the line, but you try to minimize that by giving some sort of a warning." The intelligence expert likens the IRA Army Council to "early risk management strategists" attempting to keep civilian casualties to "an acceptable level of violence" that IRA supporters would tolerate.[52] The IRA could sometimes minimize the risk to civilians by using specialized weapons—small incendiaries instead of bombs, for instance.[53] But when an operation required the destruction of buildings, protecting civilians meant ensuring their physical exit from the target area. Bomb warnings accomplished this, if everything went as planned.

Consider the IRA's June 15, 1996, attack on the city of Manchester, England. At roughly 9:20 on a Saturday morning, IRA operatives parked a truck containing a 3,000-pound ammonium nitrate and diesel fuel bomb outside the Marks and Spencer department store in the city center. Eighty thousand people occupied the commercial center of the city at the time. Although the IRA had created the conditions for mass casualties, it averted them by making warning phone calls to media and emergency services, giving the location of the bomb and the approximate time when it would explode.[54] The emergency hotlines and media organizations relayed the warnings to police, who had roughly ninety minutes to find the truck containing the device, clear the surrounding area, and cordon it off so that no one would be caught in the blast.[55] When the bomb went off, it laid waste to empty real estate. The largest peacetime explosion in the history of the United Kingdom caused £700 million in damage but killed no one.[56]

The IRA's April 1993 bombing at Bishopsgate in London used a similarly large bomb—2,200 pounds of explosives packed into the back of a dump truck. The IRA's telephone warnings allowed police to evacuate the area. Despite causing an estimated £1 billion in damage, the bomb killed only Ed Henty, the photojournalist who defied police instructions to leave.[57] There are dozens of similar cases from England and Northern Ireland, bombings that could have caused mass fatalities but did not because of the IRA's advance warnings.[58]

To appreciate the life-sparing effect of these warnings, it is worth considering what a no-warning bombing by the IRA could look like. The IRA did carry out such attacks, sometimes intentionally and sometimes because of operational failures to communicate warnings in a timely fashion.[59] On February 17, 1978, the IRA planted a blast-incendiary bomb at the La Mon House hotel near Belfast. IRA bombers hung the device in the window of a crowded dining room, left the scene, and attempted to give a warning, but the pay telephone nearest to the hotel had been vandalized and the bombers could not immediately find another phone. Their eventual warning gave police virtually no time for an evacuation. Twelve people died and thirty were injured in one of the worst atrocities of the conflict.[60] The casualty tolls from the IRA's massive truck bombs would have been far worse than those at La Mon had the IRA not given warnings beforehand.

In general, the IRA kept fatalities in its commercial attacks low. In 582 bombings of civilian targets, the IRA killed 245 people, an average of 0.42 per incident.[61] In comparison, the IRA's 538 bombings of military and police targets (attacks generally carried out without warning) killed 441 people, an average of 0.82 per incident.[62] Warnings, when the IRA chose to give them, shifted the pattern of damage, focusing harm on property rather than people. The group was able to continue its two-track military and commercial bombing campaign while keeping civilian casualties at a level that its local and diaspora supporters would tolerate.

Warnings and Hoaxes to Disrupt the Economy

The IRA also used threats to enhance the disruptive effect of its commercial bombing campaign. Each time police responded to a bomb warning, their reaction—evacuations, traffic stoppages, public transit shutdowns, etc.—caused additional harm to the British economy. The disruption from these threats enhanced the IRA's ability to signal strength while avoiding politically unhelpful bloodshed.

The economic effect of bomb threats was particularly pronounced when the IRA attacked public transit. A bomb alert at any point in a public transit system tends to cause cascading delays across the entire system.[63] The IRA could also issue general warnings that did not specify a particular location, forcing authorities to shut down large sections of a public transit system. For example, on December 17, 1991, the IRA issued a vague bomb threat against London commuter rail stations, prompting a full shutdown of commuter rail travel. A small bomb went off harmlessly at one of the empty train stations. However, the shutdown itself stranded a thousand trains and 450,000 commuters, costing roughly £50 million in lost economic productivity.[64]

A threat does not have to be true to cause disruption on this scale. The IRA sometimes mixed hoax threats with truthful warnings to induce evacuations across much wider areas. Another tactic was to issue hoax threats following a real attack, forcing police to extend the evacuation and the associated disruption of commercial life and travel. Republican #2 recalls: "If on the same day you planted one bomb but you gave three other bomb warnings, you could cause major disruption: traffic disruption, business disruption, you would treble the effect of just planting one bomb by issuing other hoaxes at the same time."[65]

On other occasions, the IRA issued hoaxes that were entirely unrelated to real violence. These hoaxes can be understood as attacks consisting of threats alone. Because the IRA was known to give truthful warnings at least some of the time, police were forced to respond to all IRA threats as if they were real. Danny Morrison recalls: "You could use the authority which had been built up as a result of your military capability to tie [security forces] down with little or no expense. . . . [A]ll commercial life is going to be dead for the next four hours. The cops and the Brits are going to be sitting there looking at a car or looking at a package which contains nothing but a pair of socks."[66]

Hoaxes of this kind were incredibly disruptive while physically endangering no one and costing the IRA virtually nothing to carry out. For example, the IRA issued bomb threats against English highways on March 26 and April 3, 1997, at a stage in the conflict when physical violence might have set back peace negotiations.[67] The hoaxes caused £80 million in economic losses, but they injured no one. Another series of bloodless hoaxes from April 18 to 21, 1997, shut down most of England's major transport infrastructure, including London Heathrow, Gatwick, Luton, and Stansted airports, the M6 highway, major rail lines around Leeds, London Tube stations, and Trafalgar Square.[68] John O'Hagan, an alleged "senior member of an intelligence-gathering unit" of the IRA, recalls the group's enthusiasm for hoaxing as a cost-effective tactic of disruption: IRA members nicknamed hoaxes "the 10p," after the ten-pence cost of making the telephone call.[69] Sinn Féin's official newspaper, *An*

Phoblacht, applauded hoaxes' "low risk" and "maximum effect" on the British economy.[70]

Warnings and Hoaxes for Tactical Advantage: Come-Ons

Not all threats are bloodless. The IRA used immediate threats to increase the lethality of certain attacks, particularly those on police and military personnel.[71] These threats enhanced the IRA's ability to signal strength to the British state by heaping additional destruction on those perceived by the group's supporters as legitimate targets. One common tactic was the "come-on": using warnings or hoaxes to lure security forces into ambushes. Come-ons were frequently used in combination with commercial bombings. A bomb warning drew police to the scene to investigate. According to the very high-ranking RUC Special Branch veteran, the police response was "a triage-type approach": RUC units moved in "to evacuate, to clear and cordon, and to make an assessment" of whether a suspicious device was present at the scene.[72] If they found a suspicious device, police notified the British Army's 321st Explosive Ordnance Disposal (EOD) squadron, an elite unit tasked with defusing or destroying IRA bombs.[73] The IRA planned each commercial attack well in advance, so it could station snipers or additional explosive devices in the vicinity of the main bomb, springing a trap on police and army units that responded to the warning.[74] John O'Hagan, the alleged IRA intelligence agent, describes these come-ons as common adjuncts to commercial attacks: "It would have been a very rare occasion that [the IRA] didn't look for the second opportunity."[75]

The IRA also used hoaxes to stage come-ons. These attacks incorporated false bomb threats, vague threats, and threats leading to fake bombs when real explosive devices lay ticking away nearby. Hoax come-ons posed a lurking danger to police and army personnel. The RUC Special Branch intelligence expert recalls that "uppermost in your mind" when investigating bomb threats "was that every single one of them was a come-on."[76] Army bomb disposal teams' job was especially dangerous since the IRA regarded them as high-value targets. (From 1969 through 1998 the 321st EOD defused roughly 6,300 bombs, containing fifty tons of explosives.[77]) The IRA attacked bomb technicians as they approached suspicious devices and rigged commercial bombs with hidden components that detonated when disturbed by the technicians' hands. The British Army lost twenty bomb-disposal technicians during the conflict, several of them to commercial bombs booby-trapped in this way.[78]

I asked my IRA interviewees whether they perceived any moral contradiction in attacking security forces as they responded to bomb warnings. Police, in particular, were helping to evacuate civilians—a rare area of shared interest between the IRA and the authorities. IRA members objected strongly to the question. Republican #4 gave a typical account, claiming that all security forces were, by definition, legitimate targets regardless of the circumstances: "They were always open season if somebody could have a shot at them."[79]

The IRA used come-on tactics against police and army targets, but it is also possible for a militant group to use similar tactics against civilians. We can see this potential in certain IRA attacks that went disastrously wrong, with bomb warnings inadvertently drawing civilians into harm's way. The most infamous example is the August 15, 1998, bombing at Omagh, carried out by a breakaway IRA faction that rejected the Northern Ireland peace agreement. The Omagh attack involved a commercial bomb and a garbled telephone warning that caused police conducting the evacuation to move bystanders closer to the device. Twenty-nine civilians perished.[80] A terrorist group with political incentives to maximize civilian bloodshed might use warnings or hoaxes deliberately to move civilians toward a bomb or an ambush.

More generally, this analysis of come-ons shows how speech acts are integral to certain terrorist attacks. Come-ons cannot be said to consist of violence alone. The violence is only enabled by the use of threats to draw targets into danger. As part of the terrorist group's tactical plan, the come-on threat should be understood as part of the attack itself.

Warnings and Hoaxes for Tactical Advantage: Prophylaxis

If come-ons were a bonus or "second opportunity" arising from the IRA's practice of warning before commercial attacks, come-ons themselves raised tertiary opportunities. The specter of come-ons increased the caution of police and bomb squads when approaching the scene of a bomb threat. The bomb disposal experts of the British Army's 321st EOD unit began to describe their approach toward a suspicious device as "the long walk."[81] The reluctance to rush toward a bomb decreased the chance of bomb technicians defusing the device before it went off. The need to surround a site and advance with caution also tied security forces down for hours at a time. While police and army units were preoccupied, IRA units could commence operations elsewhere without interference. For instance, a relatively insignificant commercial bombing or hoax threat could provide cover for a more significant IRA operation such as a prison break.[82]

I describe these uses of threats as tactical prophylaxis—predetermining the movements of one's opponent in a way that makes one's own moves more likely to succeed.[83] Warnings and hoaxes could draw security forces away from an operation, or they could be integrated with the main operation to deter security forces from intervening. Danny Morrison recalls how the IRA might issue one or more hoaxes in conjunction with a real operation involving bomb warnings. The mixing of warnings and hoaxes "meant that [police] had to clear a wider area . . . and it meant that they were afraid to go near the bomb . . . a real IRA car bomb with two or three false warnings around the outside would mean that they couldn't go in and defuse that car bomb."[84] The IRA also used hoaxes to misdirect police and army units after an attack took place. "It may be useful," an IRA tactical manual explains, "to employ a delaying tactic (such as a hoax bomb or booby trap) which apart from having obvious military advantages, also allows for time to lapse during which forensic evidence may be dispersed or destroyed."[85]

Hoaxes for Intelligence Gathering and "Rehearsals"

The IRA also employed hoaxes to gather intelligence and conduct dry runs of attacks. The very high-ranking RUC Special Branch officer recalls: "When's a hoax not a hoax? When it's a rehearsal."[86] Hoaxes can thus increase the probability of later kinetic attacks succeeding. A hoax threat might be used to gauge the response time of police arriving at the scene of a bomb alert, or to observe the physical movements of police and army units as they approached the scene and conducted their investigation. A retired RUC chief superintendent recalls: "We had five days in a row at the same time of day, a phone call that said, 'There is a bomb in the railway station.' It came at the same time every day. . . . There was nothing there that we could find." After five days of receiving very similar hoax threats, the chief superintendent realized, "There's somebody watching our response."[87] By gauging the response time of police, IRA planners could set their bomb timers with just enough time for police to evacuate bystanders but not quite enough for bomb disposal teams to arrive on the scene. The intelligence gained from a hoax could also be used for deadly purposes, such as planning a come-on. The retired chief superintendent recalls how the IRA would station "a couple of people" at the scene of a hoax threat, "watching what the police do and where they go.... They pull up there, they always park beside the lamppost. The lamppost has a bin attached to it. So [the IRA] fill the bin with explosives."[88] The IRA would phone in another hoax threat and catch police in the explosion of the hidden bomb.

Pledges and Bluffs for Social Control and Strategic Advantage

My theoretical framework includes prospective pledges and bluffs as well. These threats are useful for shaping the long-term strategic and political dynamics within a conflict. By threatening violence at some point in the future, and possibly making this threat contingent on a desired behavioral change by the recipient, a terrorist group can extract political concessions, change social behavior, and outcompete rival terrorist groups for public support. Pledges and bluffs can also force the state to alter its counterterrorism strategy in a way that plays into militants' hands. For example, pledges and bluffs may drive a wedge between the civilian population and the state. A revolutionary group obtains strategic advantage by undermining the state's access to civilians and the intelligence they provide about the militant group and its activities.[89] The IRA also sought to prevent civilians from providing labor to the state's security forces. Republican #2 describes the IRA's threats against civilians who performed cleaning, maintenance, and other services at British military and police barracks:

> People working in a civilian capacity in military bases, the IRA would issue a warning that anybody cooperating with British crown forces would be considered a target and that they should desist from carrying out any work.... And as the IRA would have termed it... "anyone who's contributing to the British war machine" in such a fashion would be considered a target, and... they wouldn't guarantee their safety.[90]

Another use of prospective threats is deterring undesirable social behavior. The IRA claimed to be the legitimate government of the original Irish Republic.[91] To give credibility to this assertion, the group sought to show that it could govern, stamping out behavior that might erode society's foundations. One problematic behavior was the sale of illicit drugs. An article in Sinn Féin's newspaper, *An Phoblacht*, in 1974 lists drugs among the greatest threats to republicans' revolutionary consciousness: "The politicians won't put it in these words but instinctively they know the conscience of the nation can only be deadened in our present circumstances if it is perverted and degraded by a diet of bread and circuses, by the excesses of drugs, drink and sexuality."[92]

To preserve republicans' moral focus and stamp out an illicit economy of addiction, the IRA threatened punishment shootings, colloquially known as "kneecappings," of those caught selling drugs. It warned civilians in Catholic neighborhoods of the prohibition on drugs and the crippling punishment that would befall offenders. A drug dealer might be offered leniency and one or more warnings after the first offense. If caught again, however, the dealer would suffer the IRA's justice. Civilians were so familiar with the system that drug dealers would submit to the punishment rather than face execution if they attempted to hide or flee. Republican #3 recalls:

> There came a point where people are selling drugs, you tell them, "I want you to report at seven o'clock." And they would go, "Can I go home and change my trousers?" And they would voluntarily go up and get shot for criminal activity. . . . You usually get three warnings and after the third warning you'd be shot. They [the IRA] would tell you to report 'round the back of the flats, you know, the apartment building somewhere. They [the drug dealers] would all sit there waiting. There'd be four of them waiting to get shot in the leg.[93]

Bluffs may serve the same social control function as pledges. But they are effective only as long as the public does not cross the behavioral line and expose the militants' threat as a lie. Because social control is an ongoing process, bluffing is unlikely to work for very long. In the IRA's case, public adherence to the prohibition on drug dealing was sustained by the group's follow-through on previous threats to kneecap drug dealers—or to kill those who refused to submit to kneecapping.

Pledges and Bluffs for Aggrandizement

Pledges and bluffs can also aggrandize the terrorist group relative to the state and peer competitors. By announcing an attack in advance, the militant group renders its success more impressive. It shows the state to be incapable of self-defense. The IRA's attacks on barracks facilities exemplify this logic. IRA propagandists trumpeted the successful mortar attack on a police barracks in the city of Newry on February 28, 1985, as "indicating our ability to strike where and when we decide."[94] A state that knows it cannot protect itself may be more willing to engage in negotiations or offer political concessions. Sympathetic civilians who observe the militant group's ability to attack may be more willing to support the group over its rivals. A strategy of pledging attacks before carrying them out may be particularly useful for militant groups seeking to outbid rivals for the support of the population.[95] The strategy may also help militants to turn the civilian population against the state because civilians may be seeking protection by whichever side is able to keep them safer.[96] The IRA adopted this strategy in the early days of the conflict as it sought to outcompete rivals like the Marxist "Official IRA" and undermine Catholics' faith in the government to protect them from Protestant mobs. Following a successful engagement with Protestant paramilitaries who attacked a Catholic church, the IRA touted itself as the only armed force that "could and would defend the oppressed nationalist people."[97] The IRA's later engagements with Protestant paramilitaries would serve as proof of the group's potency.

Bluffs aggrandize a terrorist group as long no one calls them out. Some of the Provisional IRA's early boasting was empty bravado, intended to attract civilian support and undermine the Official IRA, the larger and better-known IRA faction at that time. The Provisional IRA promised not only to defend Catholics from Protestant mobs but also to defend Catholic neighborhoods against government incursions. The IRA's "no-go zones," barricaded areas in Derry and Belfast, looked impressive, but the fledgling Provisionals lacked the capability to defend them if the state decided to enter a neighborhood in force. The government was reluctant to try such a gambit, however, for fear of inflaming tensions with Catholic communities and driving more Catholics to militancy.[98] The government allowed the IRA's barricades to stand until July 31, 1972, when thirty thousand British troops moved in to reassert control, encountering no resistance.[99] This rout by a vastly superior force did not enhance the IRA's reputation. However, for as long as the barricades stood unchallenged, the Provisional IRA could claim bragging rights for defending (or appearing to defend) Catholic neighborhoods.[100] The Official IRA and the Social Democratic Labour Party (SDLP), a nonviolent party promising moderate political solutions, could not make the same claims.[101] Bluffing may thus be an effective public relations strategy for a small, marginal group seeking to increase its reputation and entice recruits away from its larger rivals.

Pledges and Bluffs for Negotiation

Pledges and bluffs also facilitate negotiation with the state. The goal of the IRA's armed campaign was to coerce the British government to relinquish control of Northern Ireland. The logic of coercion in terrorism is the same as that in international crisis bargaining. The coercer threatens violence unless the target of the threat gives up a particular policy concession. The logic cannot operate, however, if the threat is incredible—for instance, if the would-be coercer does not possess the capability to execute the threat. In cases where the coercer's initial capabilities are unclear, the threat must sometimes be "made lively" by a demonstration of violence.[102] Once terrorists have demonstrated their violent capability, they can issue credible coercive threats.

The IRA issued one of its more famous threats following its failed attempt to kill British prime minister Margaret Thatcher. In this particular attack, an elite IRA member built a time bomb into the wall of the hotel in which Thatcher would stay during a Conservative Party conference. The October 12, 1984, explosion collapsed a central portion of the hotel, nearly killing Thatcher and causing five incidental deaths.[103] The attack failed in its immediate purpose, but it did demonstrate the reach of the IRA. The group was capable of killing British politicians at the highest level, even if it hadn't succeeded on this occasion. The IRA's message to Thatcher, typed and presented to Belfast journalist #1 on "mauve-colored paper," read: "Today we were unlucky, but remember, we only have to be lucky once. You will have to be lucky always. Give Ireland peace and there will be no war."[104]

The IRA would certainly have followed through on its threat if offered another chance to do so. However, a threat does not have to be sincere to be effective. Terrorists can also obtain policy concessions by bluffing. In fact, they may prefer to attain their goals by bluffing because bluffs bear no operational cost. (One must at least prepare to carry out a pledge, even if the threatened attack is later called off in response to concessions.) The IRA has, at times, attempted to obtain concessions by bluffing. In 2005, during the weapons decommissioning stage of the Northern Ireland peace process, the IRA allegedly carried out (or authorized others to carry out) an armed bank robbery in the city of Belfast. Analysts interpreted the Northern Bank Robbery as a final attempt to raise funds for the Sinn Féin party or as a signal of the IRA's dissatisfaction with certain aspects of the weapons decommissioning process.[105] Responding to allegations of its responsibility, the IRA leadership issued a blistering denial, promising to withdraw from the decommissioning process and possibly from the peace process itself: "We are taking all our proposals off the table. It is our intention to closely monitor ongoing developments and to protect to the best of our ability the rights of republicans and our support base."[106]

Many interpreted the promise to "protect . . . the rights of republicans" as a veiled threat of violence, and ultimately a bluff. The IRA simply lacked the weapons to follow through on such a threat. At the time, however, a bluff was probably the best the IRA could do to express its frustration, given its "new, weakened position" and the likelihood that British and Irish government negotiators would force it "to crawl back to the negotiating table" anyway.[107] In general, we may expect to see bluffing early in a conflict (when a group lacks capability but seeks to aggrandize itself among civilians) or late in a conflict, as a formerly potent group spends down its credibility, the only resource it has left to make itself relevant. Terrorists in the midst of a coercive campaign will bluff sparingly. They will issue bluffs that the government is unlikely to call, so that their lies are not exposed and their reputations are not negatively affected.

Credibility and the State's Response

The IRA used threats to achieve a variety of tactical and strategic ends. These threats were effective only as long as audiences believed them. Bomb warnings, for example, can spare civilian life only if the recipients heed them and flee the scene. Yet the IRA's practices of issuing hoax threats and come-ons created uncertainty about whether any individual threat was sincere. Police responding to an IRA bomb threat did not know whether they would be saving lives or potentially losing their own if they were caught in a come-on attack. In other cases, police conducted evacuations in response to hoax threats, causing business and transit disruption that advanced the IRA's strategic goals. Some of these hoax incidents weren't even the IRA's doing but rather the work of teenage pranksters. Given the potential for hoaxes and come-ons, cynical observers might wonder why police bothered to respond to purported warnings at all.

One could raise similar questions about the credibility of the IRA's prospective threats. In the mid-1970s, during its earliest years, the IRA was small enough, and the political situation fluid enough, that high-level members of the group could meet British authorities in person to discuss the possibility of peace.[108] But as the IRA grew and the conflict became entrenched, the group's leaders began to communicate by sending emissaries.[109] How could British authorities know that a person approaching with threats or peace offers truly represented the IRA Army Council? And could the Army Council be trusted to honor its peace commitments if the government granted concessions? Republican #4 summarizes the persistent challenge facing the IRA and the British: "You have to trust your enemy as well as your friends, don't you?"[110]

The IRA resolved its credibility problem via a combination of truth-telling and clever institutional design. The group's leaders devised a system that would restrain operatives from issuing false threats while assuring the receiver of a threat that the sender truly represented the IRA Army Council. We can best understand this system by examining the use of immediate threats first. The IRA's credibility problem was especially urgent with regard to immediate threats because of the group's political interest in sparing civilians via warnings. Former Sinn Féin spokesman Danny Morrison recalls the IRA leadership's understanding that too many hoaxes might spoil police willingness to respond to truthful warnings: "The danger with that was that they [police] might become lethargic and say, 'Well, that's just another hoax,' and then you can have people killed. There was always a danger, a line there that you were walking."[111]

John O'Hagan, the IRA intelligence officer, has similar recollections. Although hoaxes were "very effective," O'Hagan explains, they "weren't used on a regular basis" to avoid spoiling the credibility of truthful warnings.[112] Several interviewees, IRA and RUC alike, suggested that operatives could be disciplined for violating the Army Council's policies on unauthorized hoaxes. The penalties might include expulsion, kneecapping, or worse.

Despite the IRA leadership's internal effort to limit hoaxes, it was still possible for outside parties to impersonate the group and issue hoax threats of their own. Spurious threats could overwhelm the ability of police to respond to the IRA's real warnings. Republican #2 recalls:

> Some person, with a few beers in them or not, might decide for any one of one hundred thousand reasons, to issue a few bomb warnings. Now it could be an A-level student under pressure in school. It could be somebody at work who didn't want to be there. . . . You just have to extend your imagination to try and cover all the possibilities. . . . [I]f the IRA had an actual device in an area, but by an unfortunate coincidence some other people were ringing in bomb warnings at the same time causing confusion, then it could result in mayhem.[113]

The inability of police to respond to bomb warnings on "Bloody Friday" in 1972 was partly due to confusion over hoax threats received at the same time.[114] Indeed, the problem was pervasive throughout the conflict. The Royal Ulster Constabulary reported 658 hoax incidents in 1971–1972, including "some twenty each day in the city of Belfast."[115] The British Army's 321st EOD unit investigated 572 bomb hoaxes from July 1976 to July 1977, a figure that excludes incidents that the RUC investigated without calling for army assistance. The situation on the other side of the Irish Sea was even worse, with London police receiving hundreds of hoax calls daily.[116] Unless something could be done to mitigate the problem of non-IRA hoaxes, there was a good chance of police ignoring truthful warnings.

The IRA adopted several remedies to distinguish its own warnings from those of pranksters. The first was simple: if the nature of the operation permitted the IRA to do so, its volunteers would warn civilians verbally as they delivered the bomb. "If a device was carried into the shop by masked men," Republican #2 explains, "the shopkeeper would be directly informed: 'This is a bomb! Get everyone out!'"[117] This tactic worked with short-fused bombs—a type used to attack pubs and other crowded locations where hiding a time bomb was infeasible, or where bombs planted in advance were likely to be picked up and moved by unsuspecting civilians.[118] When verbal warnings were not feasible, the IRA employed an elaborate phone chain procedure, typically involving a third-party intermediary and secret code words. The resulting system enhanced the credibility of threats and locked British authorities into a policy of responding to all bomb threats they received.

To understand the system devised by IRA leaders, we must first consider the phone procedures used for conveying bomb warnings to police. Convicted IRA bomber Robert McClanahan recalls that IRA units often employed a spotter who, after following the bomb team "to make sure everybody's getting away . . . just drove over to the nearest telephone" to make the warning call.[119] The RUC Special Branch intelligence expert describes this method as vulnerable to breakdown because of the inexperience of IRA volunteers (many of whom were teenagers) and the unreliability of pay phones.[120] IRA volunteers also tended to garble warnings, occasionally causing police to move civilians *toward* bombs. According to the intelligence expert, several of the IRA's most notorious atrocities "looked very different in the planning stage" and were not "planned to be bloodbaths."[121] To avoid miscommunication, the IRA adopted a new procedure in which a commander at the battalion level or higher made the warning call from a remote site. The commander would know the target of the attack and the time the bomb was set to go off and would also be able to choose a functioning pay telephone well in advance. When everything went as planned, the warnings from battalion commanders were both timely and accurate.[122]

To distinguish its truthful warnings from pranks, the IRA developed an ingenious phone chain procedure. The phone chain always included a neutral third party who could be trusted to relay the message to police—and who could not trace the phone call back to its source. The IRA communicated warnings via the Samaritans organization's 24-hour suicide hotline; the switchboards of the BBC, Irish News, and RTÉ (Irish state broadcasting); the switchboards of local hospitals; members of the clergy; even taxi dispatchers and insurance companies.[123] According to Robert McClanahan, the intermediary could be "anybody who you thought was going to lift the phone immediately," but the IRA generally chose intermediaries "with credibility or with stature within the local community" so that police would believe the warnings.[124] Journalist #2 gives a detailed description of how their organization handled warning calls from the IRA:

> The call would come through to the switchboard and staff were trained to handle such calls because they were reasonably frequent. . . .

Usually [the IRA] would say the message they wanted to say, that there's a bomb at such-and-such a place and it's timed to go off at such-and-such a time. . . . Sometimes you don't get that much detail. They would just say there's a bomb in the street, or a certain area. . . . You knew that it was serious when they said, "Have you got a pen and paper?" because they want the information to be recorded accurately and they would speak more slowly and more deliberately to make sure that you get the information, so that it's passed on properly to the authorities.[125]

To make its messages stand out from the background noise of pranks, the IRA placed multiple warning phone calls for the same bombing. An angry drunk or a student trying to get the day off from school might not have the initiative, pocket change, or phone numbers to call several different intermediaries. So, according to Republican #3, the IRA might make "two or three phone calls [and] once the emergency services see that there's a number of phone calls we made, they know that it's probably for real."[126]

The IRA also included secret words in its messages to police. The Army Council would select code words that were incongruous in conversation ("just something outside your normal speech," Robert McClanahan explains).[127] The obscurity of code words drew attention to them and made it difficult for anyone outside the IRA to guess what they were.[128] Examples included "Excalibur," "Wonder," "Kerrygold," and "Martha Pope" (a peace negotiator working under U.S. senator George Mitchell).[129] At the BBC and other news organizations, staff who received warning calls might be responsible for recording the information, but the news editor assumed responsibility for checking the code words and passing the messages on to police. Journalist #2 recalls a high degree of compartmentalization in this process to protect the code words: "Our process at the moment is that if a member of staff receives a bomb warning . . . that a more senior person contacts the police. And we are limited in what we can say, but there are times that the more senior person may not even know what the code word is, because we try and keep it quite tight."[130]

If a code word leaked out, or if the IRA had used the same word long enough so that its compromise could be reasonably expected, the IRA changed the word.[131] IRA intelligence specialist John O'Hagan explains: "It would be an approach made to all outlets saying that the IRA's code word is—whatever. And every time the code word was changed they would use the old code word to make the new word active.... Usually the leadership of the army would do that.... There was one code word for the entire IRA structure. And the one code word would be decided, signed off on, by the leadership of the army."[132]

As elaborate as these procedures were, they did not give police 100 percent certainty about the authenticity of a bomb threat. There was no particular place in the phone chain where the warnings and code words converged to allow the authentication of a message. Intermediaries often preferred not to tell police which code word was used. "We feel that the fewer people who know it, the better," journalist #2 explains.[133] Nor did the intermediaries filter messages, passing on only those with recognized code words. As a result, police received the full set of purported warnings, including messages with no code words, messages with authenticated code words, and messages purportedly authenticated but not containing the code words themselves. Retired RUC officers recall that code words made little difference in how they responded to a bomb threat. In fact, some were confused as to the purpose of the system. The RUC chief superintendent recalls: "I served for thirty-one years and retired fairly senior in my division. No one was ever able to explain to me this issue of the code words. No one.... There was never a list in the police stations of these code words.... At least never one that I was ever aware of."[134]

The predicament of security forces in Great Britain was similar. Peter Gurney, a British Army ammunition technical officer (ATO) tasked with dismantling IRA bombs in London during the 1970s, writes that "from 1973 onwards it was not unusual for the Metropolitan Police to receive up to 200 hoax calls a *day* [emphasis original], at least fifty of them with alleged code words. The hoaxers read that this was IRA practice and so invented their own; we had no way of finding out what was real and what was not."[135]

So what did code words actually accomplish? There are several answers to this question. First, although police could not ignore warnings without code words, the words did let the RUC know that certain calls came from the IRA. According to another retired RUC superintendent, police would be informed by their radio dispatcher if "a recognized code word" had been used in the warning call.[136] (Ostensibly, the dispatcher obtained this information via the intermediary passing on the warning.) If the message contained a code word, police would "treat it as the IRA," assuming a higher likelihood of a bomb or a come-on attack waiting for them. This assumption could affect the amount of time RUC officers spent investigating an incident before definitively declaring it a hoax. The very high-ranking RUC Special Branch veteran explains that police would take "graduated steps" before declaring a warning a hoax: "If you got a call, you did a cursory check, there was no code word, it wasn't credible, there was no intelligence to support it, [then] that cursory search and check may have been sufficient."[137] All things being equal, a code word and no apparent come-on would have increased RUC suspicions of a real device and encouraged police to stay on the scene and continue their search. The retired RUC superintendent recalls that the IRA would also use the code word to reiterate the warning and direct police back to the scene of a bomb if the device failed to go off as planned.[138] In these cases, the IRA actually wanted army ATOs to find the device and dispose of it because of the risk it posed to civilians. A code word offered a way of linking the follow-up phone call to the initial warning, giving police reason to recanvass the scene.

Code words also reassured the British government, at a high level, of the IRA's overall degree of truthfulness. Because high-level police intelligence specialists did have a list of known code words, those investigating any given bombing after the fact could determine whether the IRA itself had issued a warning beforehand. Those investigating come-ons and economically disruptive hoaxes could also determine whether the IRA directly authorized these incidents. It thus became possible for British authorities to assess in general the IRA's frequency of warning when attacking and its frequency of threatening falsely. A news story from 1997 explains: "More than 80 per cent of coded warnings in recent years have been made without devices being found. A national system for assessing the likelihood that a warning could be genuine was introduced almost a decade ago linked to the handful of code words which are now used."[139] By including code words in its messages, the IRA reassured British officials that, although it lied on occasion, the frequency of truthful warnings was knowable and sufficiently high to justify a policy of responding to every threat.

The elaborate communication chain and the institution of code words reassured the IRA as well. Mistrust ran in both directions of the IRA-government relationship. Several IRA interviewees alleged that police, working in collaboration with British military and intelligence personnel, deliberately ignored bomb warnings at times. None of the Republican interviewees could cite a specific occasion when police or the army ignored a bomb warning, but the belief that the authorities ignored warnings goes back at least to the Bloody Friday attack, when the IRA's warnings failed to prevent five civilian deaths. In an interview years after the event, IRA chief of staff Seán Mac Stíofáin explained: "It required only one man with a loud hailer to clear each target area in no time. . . . Republicans were convinced that the British had deliberately disregarded these . . . warnings for strategic policy reasons."[140]

The RUC Special Branch intelligence veteran offers a different interpretation of events. What the IRA could not see was that the RUC had its own internal phone chain, stretching from a headquarters switchboard and Force Control office to Belfast Regional Control or the divisional or subdivisional headquarters corresponding to the target location, to a dispatcher who would notify RUC patrols of the alleged bomb in their area. IRA spotters might be watching the time bomb tick away, and police might be in the vicinity doing absolutely nothing to evacuate civilians. "The brutal fact," according to the RUC intelligence veteran, was that the warning "may not have gotten around to them because of the chain that it had to go through."[141] IRA members like Seán Mac Stíofáin would interpret any casualties in these attacks as the results of intentional malfeasance, but the situation was more complex than they appreciated.

Nonetheless, the IRA sought a means of forcing police to respond to every warning. Communicating warnings through intermediaries imposed a degree of political accountability on police. Republican #3 describes the phone chain as a way "to get a witness" and have it "on the record" that a warning was given.[142] Particularly if journalists were serving the intermediary role, the details of the warning and its time of arrival would become public information. A slow response or nonresponse left police open to criticism and political blame for any civilian deaths.[143] The IRA leveraged police accountability further by making redundant warning calls, using "a number of organizations to spread the warning and to get the information out" (journalist #2's words).[144] Redundancy put the information into the hands of several organizations, who could offer mutually reinforcing accounts of the IRA's warning later on if the police failed to respond and civilians were killed by the bomb.

All the RUC officers I interviewed maintained that public accountability was unnecessary to ensure a response to IRA warnings. However, the specter of accountability may have influenced police and other government officials at the policy level, where people made decisions about standard operating procedures and how risk averse to be in investigating threats at each graduated level of response. For instance, after a particularly costly hoax shut down English transit infrastructure in 1991, the British transport secretary stated that his preference was to investigate every threat rather than "risking death and injury to the public."[145]

All the institution building around immediate threats helped to enhance the credibility of the IRA's prospective threats as well. Unable to meet with British government representatives directly, the IRA leadership would send an envoy to communicate its messages—both threats of violence and promises of peace if the government granted concessions. Although initial contacts between the envoy and British representatives might be made face-to-face through a mutually trusted broker, that broker and envoy might not be available later. The code word provided a way of verifying the permission of a new envoy to represent the Army Council in discussions with the government. According to the high-ranking RUC Special Branch veteran, "if you have your initial point of contact . . . but that person is no longer going to be able to do it, [the Army Council] would give you the password that legitimizes engagement with the next [envoy]. That password then becomes the legitimate vehicle for the next [envoy]."[146]

The IRA used a similar system for communicating statements to journalists. The group's representatives would approach journalists face-to-face or through personal connections. Subsequent statements could be given by phone or in person, by the original IRA emissary or by some other emissary, as long as the approach was made with the same code word. According to veteran Belfast journalist Eamonn Mallie: "Somewhere along the way you will meet somebody or somebody will call you and they will literally say, "From now on, the IRA will use the following code word," so you know, and they know that you know. Then you will be the contact point."[147]

Many of these statements would be claims of responsibility for attacks that the IRA had already carried out. Code words prevented rival militant groups like the Official IRA from claiming the IRA's attacks and stealing the reputational benefit.[148] Code words also enhanced the credibility of prospective threats by demonstrating that they came directly from the IRA Army Council.[149] Finally, code words demonstrated the Army Council's degree of control. They reassured British authorities that the IRA could command its cells to stop the violence if the government granted political concessions. Without code words, it was theoretically possible for renegade IRA cells to sabotage a peace deal by carrying out attacks and claiming them in the group's name.[150] But it was much harder to do this, given the Army Council's practice of embedding secret code words in each warning call made in advance of an attack. The code words showed which attacks were centrally authorized and, by implication, which attacks the Army Council was able to call off if the British government responded positively to the IRA's peace overtures. The RUC Special Branch intelligence expert explains:

> [The code word] was a sign to them [the British government] of how much in control the Provisional leadership were of their organization. So I'm sitting talking to you and you say . . . , "You've got all these guys out there. All these guns, all these bombs, all these renegades . . . wanting to kill people—How can you control those?" I'll tell you how I control them. "Every time there's an act, I'll attach the word to it, and then you'll know. . . . And they do as I say. And I'll tell you better than that, it's a tap. I can turn it on and I can turn it off." It proved control over a very large terrorist organization.[151]

Having established a secure channel of communication, with institutions to demonstrate the IRA's truthfulness and control of its cells, the Army Council could be confident in the credibility of its threats and promises in bargaining settings.

Insights from the IRA Case

This analysis of the IRA shows the sophistication with which terrorists use threats. They issue immediate threats to shape the pattern of damage from attacks. The IRA's warnings spared civilians and made the group's violence appear more legitimate. The IRA also used warnings and hoaxes to draw security forces into attacks—and to misdirect security forces away from operations so that they were more likely to succeed. The IRA's hoaxes complemented physical violence by disrupting the British economy. In general, this case study shows how threats can mediate or augment the effects of kinetic violence so that a group can send optimal political messages to different audiences.

The IRA case also shows how threats influence the long-term political dynamics of a conflict. The IRA used pledges and bluffs to aggrandize itself relative to rival republican paramilitaries and the state. It used pledges to intimidate civilians, dissuading them from collaborating with the government and deterring them from antisocial behavior such as drug dealing. Threats were also critical to the IRA's political negotiations with the state. Having built its reputation by carrying out violent attacks, the IRA could issue credible threats of future violence and credible offers to stop the violence if the government granted policy concessions on Irish self-determination. An analysis of the IRA shows how threats give terrorism its political force.

This IRA study also shows how particular political incentives predict the use of threats. For example, this group's sophisticated use of prophylactic threats was driven by intense counterterrorism pressure. The IRA confronted perhaps the most intimidating military, police, and intelligence apparatus in the world at the time. It used threats to deceive, misdirect, and gather tactical intelligence so that its attacks could succeed against long odds. The IRA's self-aggrandizing pledges and bluffs addressed other insecurities—in the 1970s, competition from the larger and better-established Official IRA; in the 2000s, the loss of capability in the disarmament process. The IRA's bomb warnings helped to mitigate a pervasive multiple audiences conundrum. Republicans depended on local civilians for shelter while fighting a democracy that set a relatively high standard of legitimate political behavior toward those civilians. The IRA had to give warnings so that civilians would tolerate its presence in their communities. We should expect other organizations under similar political pressures to use threats as the IRA did.

I devote the next three chapters to testing my theoretical propositions, laid out in the introduction and reiterated in chapter 1. Rather than undertaking one detailed case study, as I did in this chapter, I compare different militant organizations. I match organizations to control for broad ideological factors. I then characterize the variation in the terrorist groups' political incentives to issue threats: their drives for legitimacy, economic disruption, social control, negotiation, self-aggrandizement, and advantage versus the state's counterterrorism forces. I show that within each ideologically controlled group of cases, the variation in terrorists' threatening behavior follows from the variation in these six political incentives, as predicted by my theoretical argument.

CHAPTER III

ETA and the Tamil Tigers

*Comparable Threats for Social Control and Negotiation;
Contrasting Threats for Legitimacy, Disruption, and Advantage*

This chapter is the first of three testing my argument's predictions with comparative case studies. I contrast the use of threats by Euskadi Ta Askatasuna (ETA) and the Liberation Tigers of Tamil Eelam (LTTE—colloquially, the Tamil Tigers). I pair these groups because of the similarity in their grievances and their political goals. Both groups were motivated by ethnic nationalism, representing the grievances of a minority group—in ETA's case, the Basque population of Spain; in the LTTE's case, the Tamil population of Sri Lanka. Both groups were secessionist in their goals, demanding that the ethnic majority government cede territory to the minority group. Pairing organizations with similar ideologies and political goals allows me to control for fundamental group characteristics while showing how subtler political incentives influenced each group's use of threats. For example, ETA and the LTTE were quite different in their relationships to local civilian populations. The LTTE governed territory it had conquered from the Sri Lankan state. It could arrange its own shelter and extract resources from the civilian population under its control. ETA did not govern territory and instead depended on state-controlled civilian populations for shelter and other support. This pair of cases is well suited to show the role of threats in legitimacy seeking, disruption, and advantage seeking. ETA's greater need for civilian charity, its greater emphasis on economic disruption as a means of coercion, and its need to seek advantage over a superior counterterrorism opponent led the group to issue more warnings, hoaxes, and some prophylactic pledges. (The LTTE resorted to prophylactic bluffs in its last years.) There is less variation in the groups' social control-seeking and negotiation-seeking tendencies. Both groups made extensive use of pledges for these purposes.

I develop these insights through a focused comparison of the two groups' political circumstances and observed behaviors. I enumerate the strategic incentives for each type of threat and discuss how these incentives varied between the two cases. I then show how the cross-case variation in threats follows from the variation in the groups' political incentives, in keeping with the logic of my theoretical argument. To set the stage for this comparative analysis, I first summarize each group's history individually.

Euskadi Ta Askatasuna, 1975–2018

Euskadi Ta Askatasuna (Basque Fatherland and Freedom) was an ethnic nationalist group, seeking to establish a homeland, Euskal Herria, for Basque people. The Basques are concentrated in a coastal region along the Bay of Biscay in the Northeast of Spain and Southwest of France. Their cultural lineage is unique among European peoples. The Basque language, for instance, is the only Western European tongue not derived from the Indo-European linguistic group.[1] In fact, it bears no familial relation to any other language currently spoken. The Basques have lived as a minority ethnic group under the political rule of Spanish and French governments for hundreds of years.[2]

I focus my analysis on ETA's activity during Spain's democratic period, following the death in 1975 of fascist dictator Francisco Franco. ETA's story begins, however, in the 1930s, with the Spanish Civil War that brought the fascists to power. Basques fought on the losing side of the civil war, suffering various atrocities at the hands of Franco and his German and Italian allies.[3] From the conquest of the Basque country through the end of fascist rule, the Spanish government banned public expressions of Basque culture. Linguistic anthropologist Jacqueline Urla describes the "attempted annihilation of all official traces of Basque" as extending "from birth certificates to tombstones."[4] Some Basques responded by starting underground language schools or staging general strikes. A youth coordinating committee, Ekin ("to do"), sought to unify these campaigns with the outside agitation of exiled Basque politicians. Frustrated with the failure of these efforts, Ekin broke off in the 1950s and reconstituted itself under the moniker of ETA.

Although today ETA is known for its violent actions, the group's early activism was equally about building nationalist and class consciousness. ETA was fundamentally an ethnic self-determination movement, but it also espoused the revolutionary socialism common to many twentieth-century anticolonial movements.[5] To build nationalist consciousness, ETA sought to rehabilitate the Basque language via a network of *ikastolas*, semiunderground Basque schools.[69] These cultural revitalization efforts were complicated by Franco's industrial initiatives of the 1950s through the 1970s and a wave of immigrants arriving from Spanish-speaking areas to seek industrial jobs in the Basque country.[7] ETA's socialism, however, offered a means of integrating Spanish-speaking industrial laborers with the Basque nationalist struggle—if the struggle could be framed as a fight against "the capitalist Spanish state" rather than Spaniards themselves.[8] In the 1960s and early 1970s ETA managed to cement a coalition of ethnic nationalists and class-conscious socialist immigrants, who would turn out together in the streets for workers' strikes and nationalist demonstrations alike.[9]

ETA's political situation changed with Spain's transition away from fascist government in the mid-1970s. In fact, ETA helped to bring about the transition: the group's December 20, 1973, assassination of Admiral Luis Carrero Blanco, Franco's likely successor, ensured that fascism would die with Franco himself.[10] With Franco's death in 1975, ETA lost the common enemy that had cemented the coalition of Basques and Spanish-speaking socialist workers.[11] The introduction of democracy also offered Basques and socialists new, nonviolent political vehicles to pursue their respective interests. The formerly banned Basque Nationalist Party (PNV) replaced ETA as the most powerful force in Basque politics, empowered to govern by a new Spanish constitution granting limited autonomy to the Basque country.[12] ETA, however, rejected limited autonomy. Instead, it demanded that the new Spanish government recognize the sovereignty of an independent Basque state.[13] The group would spend the next four decades carrying out a guerrilla campaign to compel the government to grant its demands.

ETA's campaign resembled the IRA's "long war" of attrition against commerce and security forces.[14] Roughly a third of ETA's attacks targeted businesses, with another 35 percent focusing on police and military targets. In total, the group's 2,031 attacks produced 829 fatalities.[15] Concurrently with the assassinations and bombings, ETA pushed for peace negotiations with the Spanish government. The group declared seven ceasefires over the course of the conflict.[16] Two of these were reciprocated by the government—one in the 1980s and another in the 2000s.[17] Yet neither round of negotiations produced a peace settlement acceptable to both sides. The Spanish government was unwilling to concede Basque statehood, and ETA's campaign could not inflict sufficient pain to change the government's mind. In 2018, after more than forty years of violence, ETA disarmed unilaterally and left the issue of Basque self-determination in the hands of politicians.[18]

Liberation Tigers of Tamil Eelam, 1983–2009

As bitter as ETA's conflict was, the Sri Lankan civil war was far bloodier. The underlying dispute concerned the nationalist aspirations of Sri Lanka's ethnic Tamil minority, which sought an independent Eelam state in majority Tamil areas of the country. Since gaining independence from British rule in 1948, Sri Lanka's largest ethnic groups, the Tamils and Sinhalese, have struggled to stake out their respective roles in Sri Lankan politics. With 75 percent of the country's population, the Sinhalese have used the nation's democratic institutions to enact their policy preferences over those of the 11 percent Tamil minority. The Tamils' grievances include the designation of Sinhala as the country's official language, the designation of Buddhism as the country's national religion (most Tamils are Hindu), and discriminatory university admissions policies that made it difficult for Tamils to hold administrative positions in Sri Lanka's government.[19] Tamils have also faced outbreaks of ethnically motivated violence, including riots in 1956, 1958, 1977, 1981, and 1983.[20] The "Black July" riots in 1983 killed as many as 3,000 Tamils, spurred half a million to flee to other countries, and set off the civil wars that killed up to 100,000 people over the next twenty-six years.[21]

The LTTE was both an instigator of the Sri Lankan conflict and the primary belligerent on the Tamil side. Active on a small scale since the 1970s, the Tigers vaulted to prominence on July 23, 1983, ambushing a Sri Lankan Army patrol in Jaffna province and killing thirteen army soldiers. This event helped to provoke the Black July pogroms.[22] It also prompted interventions by the Sri Lankan Army to root the Tamil rebels out of northern areas such as the Jaffna peninsula.[23] These military interventions soon devolved into indiscriminate retaliation against Tamil civilians.[24] Sri Lanka's neighbor, India, then faced a political crisis. As refugees and news of atrocities arrived from Sri Lanka, sympathetic Tamil politicians in the southern Indian state of Tamil Nadu staged strikes and demanded that the Indian government assist their besieged coethnics. The Indian intelligence services covertly assisted the LTTE and other guerrilla groups, arming them and training them to push Sri Lankan forces out of Tamil areas.[25] The tit-for-tat cycle of atrocities by the LTTE and Sri Lankan military forces only escalated, however. India attempted to resolve the conflict by brokering a diplomatic accord in 1987, with Sri Lankan forces returning to their barracks, Tamil rebels disarming, and an Indian Peacekeeping Force (IPKF) arriving to supervise a transition to limited self-government for Tamils in Sri Lanka's North and East.[26] Although the LTTE expressed support for the arrangement initially, it balked at disarmament and instead turned its fire on the IPKF, forcing them out of the country by 1990, after three years of bloody fighting.[27] (As a final act of revenge, an LTTE suicide bomber assassinated Indian prime minister Rajiv Gandhi in 1991.[28]) The LTTE then turned its sights on the Sri Lankan government. Over the next decade, the LTTE managed to conquer substantial portions of northern and eastern Sri Lanka: the districts of Mullaituvu and Killinochchi, portions of Vavuniya and Mannar, and portions of Trincomalee, Batticaloa, and Ampara.[29] When the LTTE enacted a ceasefire with the Sri Lankan government in 2002, it had much of its intended Tamil homeland under control.[30] The LTTE administered a de facto state, with banking, postal, educational, and immigration systems.[31] But when peace talks broke down and the conflict resumed in 2006, a reinvigorated Sri Lankan Army swept all this away. In 2008 and 2009 the army corralled the LTTE into a small area of the northern coast, shelling the Tigers and up to forty thousand civilians out of existence.[32]

Comparing Incentives and Patterns of Threats

Tables 3.1 and 3.2 summarize how ETA and the LTTE differed in their political incentives and uses of threats. The main differences in the groups' incentives concern legitimacy seeking, the use of economic disruption, and the incentive to seek advantage over counterterrorism forces. Because ETA lacked a territorial stronghold and fought a democratic government, it needed to employ reduced-casualty tactics that Basque civilians would accept as legitimate. ETA also employed a strategy of economic disruption, incentivizing warnings and hoaxes as useful adjuncts. It eventually curtailed its use of hoaxes, however, to ensure the credibility of its casualty-reducing warnings. ETA's heavy emphasis on credibility is idiosyncratic. I spend a portion of this chapter discussing why this group was so preoccupied with credibility and describing the institutions the group devised to demonstrate the credibility of its threats. Another difference between ETA's and the LTTE's behavior concerns tactical prophylactic threats: ETA issued more of these, as it sought advantage over the formidable Spanish counterterrorism apparatus.

With respect to prospective pledges and bluffs, my theoretical framework leads us to expect broadly similar behavior from ETA and the LTTE. The groups had similar emphases on negotiation and controlling civilian populations. They both dominated their political environments, mitigating the need for aggrandizement versus peers (although the LTTE may have sought aggrandizement versus the state in its waning years). The pattern of pledges and bluffs from these groups generally comports with my expectations: both issued pledges of violence along with their negotiating demands, and both pledged violence against civilians who defied their rule. One area of divergence between the two groups concerns the use of threats for strategic advantage seeking. At first, ETA issued more prophylactic threats (pledges) as it confronted a strong counterterrorism apparatus on state territory. During the later years of the Sri Lankan civil war, however, as the Tamil Tigers' military position deteriorated, the LTTE issued a number of

TABLE 3.1
Group Characteristics: ETA and LTTE

Incentive	Relative Values
Legitimacy seeking	ETA > LTTE
Disruption	ETA > LTTE
Social control	ETA ≈ LTTE
Negotiation	ETA ≈ LTTE
Aggrandizement	ETA ≈ LTTE
	(after 2006: LTTE > ETA)
Advantage seeking	ETA > LTTE
	(after 2006: LTTE > ETA)

TABLE 3.2
Predictions: ETA and LTTE

	Prediction	Observed
Warnings	ETA > LTTE For legitimacy, disruption, tactical advantage	ETA > LTTE
Hoaxes	ETA > LTTE For disruption, tactical advantage	ETA > LTTE (After 1987: ETA ≈ LTTE ≈ 0)
Pledges	ETA ≈ LTTE For negotiation, social control, strategic advantage	ETA ≈ LTTE
Bluffs	ETA ≈ LTTE (After 2006: LTTE > ETA) For aggrandizement, strategic advantage	ETA ≈ LTTE (After 2006: LTTE > ETA)

high-profile bluff threats against civilian targets behind government lines. The LTTE's reliance on prophylactic threats exceeded that of ETA, as the Tigers sought to misdirect government attention away from military fronts where the state was winning.

Warnings and Hoaxes

The characteristics of ETA and the LTTE give us reason to expect more warnings and hoaxes from the first group. ETA had greater legitimacy concerns, a greater strategic emphasis on economic disruption, and a stronger counterterrorism opponent over which to seek tactical advantage. The first factor increasing ETA's legitimacy concerns was its lack of territorial control. The Basque militants operated clandestinely on territory ruled by the state, sheltering among local civilians who also provided intelligence, material support, and aboveground political support for ETA's violent campaign.[33] The multiple audiences conundrum is particularly intense for such a group, which seeks to project strength through violence while avoiding excessive civilian deaths that could alienate supporters among the state's population.

ETA's legitimacy concerns were further sharpened by the Spanish government's democratic regime and the general expectation of a good life under Spanish rule. As the brother of one ETA leader remarked, "The young worker receives his pay, in the evening he feeds his cows, works in the garden. He is one of the first to have a Vespa. If Franco had not been there, the situation would have been idyllic."[34] After Franco's death, the worst restrictions on Basque self-expression were removed. Political parties such as the PNV could contest elections in a semiautonomous Basque homeland established under Spain's new constitution.[35] To justify the use of violence, ETA had to make a moral and political case that oppression still existed.[36] It had actually complicated its own task by deemphasizing ethnic grievances early in its history in order to bring Spanish-speakers into the socialist dimension of the Basque struggle. ETA had to reassert its position as the legitimate leader of Basque nationalism in an already-improving political environment, with partial self-determination, democratic rights, and relatively good relations between ethnic groups. One writer observes that it was necessary for ETA "only to use arms or explosives in extremely limited and always symbolic cases . . . in direct harmony with the expectations of the population to which it related."[37]

Basque citizens were somewhat tolerant of selective violence targeting people and institutions formerly associated with fascism. The more militant nationalists adopted an attitude of *algo habrá hecho*—"he must have done something" to rationalize such attacks.[38] Basques were less accepting when ETA extended its target list to local politicians, intellectuals, and civil society members.[39] And Basques were positively intolerant of mass-casualty violence. On December 11, 1987, an ETA *kommando* (the group's basic military unit) detonated a car bomb outside a police barracks in the southern Spanish city of Zaragoza. The bomb killed eleven people, including five children who were living at the facility with their fathers.[40] The Basque public's reaction was to denounce ETA, even though the attack was intended to target police. Mainstream Basque nationalist parties responded by signing a pact with Spanish parties, denying ETA any future role in negotiations on the status of Basque region.[41]

Given the Basque public's aversion to civilian casualties, ETA needed to take a softer approach. To gain insight into the group's strategic thought,

I consulted a former top leader of the group, Eugenio "Antxon" Etxebeste. Etxebeste served as ETA's lead representative in secret diplomatic talks with the Spanish government, held in Algiers under French auspices during the 1980s.[42] He describes ETA's coercive strategy as having two tracks, much like the IRA's: "The two pillars . . . of the armed actions to destabilize the state are the . . . occupying forces, then infrastructure."[43]

Of ETA's 2,031 attacks, a plurality targeted economic infrastructure, broadly defined, with 665 attacks on businesses, 92 on transportation, 73 on utilities, and 23 each on telecommunications and tourism targets. Most of ETA's other attacks targeted Spanish police (562 incidents) and military personnel and installations (147 incidents).[44] Although many of the attacks on police and military personnel used "direct fire" weapons such as guns, the economic campaign made extensive use of bombs and incendiaries to destroy property. ETA's "summer campaigns" were a prime example of this strategy, using time-delay bombs to demolish vacation resorts and beaches vital to Spain's tourist economy.[45] At other times, ETA employed car bombs, a "logistically simpler," if potentially indiscriminate, way of delivering explosives to their targets.[46] For example, ETA's van bombing of a parking garage at Madrid's Barajas airport on December 30, 2006, used more than a thousand pounds of explosives, destroying the five-story parking garage and damaging 1,300 parked cars.[47] ETA's hope was that the economic attrition from such attacks would coerce the Spanish government to enter negotiations and concede Basque independence. A strategy of disruption generally incentivizes warnings and hoaxes.

Consistent with my argument, ETA used warning tactics regularly. Looking at the group's bomb attacks on civilian targets (a type of attack that is quite likely to injure civilians if no warnings are given), ETA gave warnings for roughly 45 percent.[48] Antxon Etxebeste describes the issuing of warnings as a matter of "revolutionary ethics." ETA understood itself as being "in an armed clash between military forces," which nonetheless transpired "in places where . . . there would be possible risks to civilians." "The aim was to meet the military objective, economic destabilization of the state, and always avoid any possible side effect of civilian casualties. Etxebeste explains the process of warning in detail:

> In cases in which you needed to give an alert for having placed an explosive, it was the *kommando* itself which advised various organizations, not so much the police, but various agencies of a public,

institutional character—it could be the Red Cross, radio stations themselves, or other organizations of an institutional character. [The phone call] was normally made with a sufficient time interval—if the explosive was to explode at midnight, then three quarters of an hour or half an hour in advance, precisely to give a chance to evacuate so that there was no liability to civilians in the action itself.[49]

ETA's summer campaigns show how the group's warning procedures reduced casualties. At the start of tourist season, ETA *kommandos* buried bombs in Spanish beaches, with long fuses set to detonate weeks later. Shortly before the bombs were to explode, ETA representatives would call Spanish emergency services to inform them of the impending detonations. Press reports describe a typical operation that took place on July 20, 2008: "Four low-power devices" exploded "in Laredo and Noja after a telephone call on behalf of the terrorist group warned of their placement in the sands . . . The announcement took place at half past ten, through a recording in which a distorted woman's voice was heard saying that the bombs would explode between noon and three P.M." Spanish police evacuated the beaches, warning residents of nearby homes to stay inside and sealing off roads and waterways until the bombs exploded. These emergency interventions prevented all but one minor injury.[50] By scaring off tourists, ETA's summer campaigns caused millions of dollars in financial losses to the Spanish economy. One study estimates that each bomb dissuaded roughly 140,000 tourists from visiting Spain.[51] However, the physical attacks harmed mostly the sand, so Basque nationalists would continue to tolerate ETA's activity.

ETA also gave warnings before larger bombings. The group's 2006 van bombing of Madrid's airport parking garage is one example. The ETA *kommando* made warning calls to four different media organizations and emergency hotlines, giving more than an hour's notice of the attack. Despite the warnings and authorities' effort to evacuate the garage, the thousand-pound bomb killed two Ecuadoran citizens who were sleeping in their car.[52] The deaths of the Ecuadorans were unintended and politically unhelpful to ETA. There are many such cases, but it is worth considering how much greater the death toll could have been if ETA had not given warnings. To make the point concrete, consider the disastrous bombing of a Hipercor supermarket in Barcelona on June 19, 1987: although ETA attempted to warn police forty-five minutes in advance of the attack, police failed to arrive promptly at the scene and failed to conduct a thorough search before deeming the warning a hoax and leaving. The building was full of shoppers when the bomb went off; twenty-one were killed.[53] The atrocity accounted for roughly a quarter of all deaths caused by ETA's commercial bombings during the conflict.[54] ETA could have caused hundreds of such atrocities had it chosen, as a matter of policy, not to give warnings. With the counterfactual in mind, the civilian toll of ETA's campaign, 83 fatalities in 634 bombings, is strikingly low.[55]

Antxon Etxebeste also describes the use of warnings to limit civilian casualties when attacks on security forces went wrong. If ETA laid a remote-controlled bomb near a police facility or along a road traveled by police patrols, there was always a risk that civilians would enter the area before the device could be detonated. The leader of the *kommando* made the decision, in Etxebeste's words, "to squeeze or not to squeeze" the button; the choice was "always not to do so" if civilians were at risk.[56] Nonetheless, an extremely dangerous situation remained, with a hidden bomb lying undetonated in an area full of civilians. To avoid disaster, ETA would make a warning call informing the government of the aborted attack so that the unexploded bomb could be defused by military ordnance disposal experts.

A final factor incentivizing warnings and hoaxes was the high competence of the Spanish police apparatus. Although Franco was gone, the newly democratic Spanish state retained the efficient law enforcement structure that had suppressed Basque militants for decades. To thwart ETA, the Spanish government relied on the Guardia Civil, a paramilitary police force founded in 1844 to suppress the government's internal enemies. The Guardia Civil were well trained and equipped, with intelligence specialists, police barracks throughout the country, and an extralegal death squad to feed them information and hunt down ETA operatives.[57] The pressure on ETA increased in the 1980s, when France joined Spain's counterterrorism effort, rounding up ETA members on the French side of the border.[58] To carry out its violent campaign, ETA would need to use every trick available, including prophylactic threats.

Etxebeste describes several ways in which ETA's warnings obstructed, misdirected, and victimized police and army personnel called to the scene of bomb alerts. Extra warnings distracted police and complicated their approach toward bombs. ETA *kommandos* ambushed police as they approached bombs. They also booby-trapped bombs to explode as explosives technicians attempted to defuse them. Another ETA tactic was the *cazabobo*, literally "fool-catcher": the attachment of bombs to Basque flags or contraband items that police would notice and attempt to remove, with deadly consequences. Although it may seem cynical to target security forces as they responded to bomb warnings, Etxebeste disagrees: "The distinction is clear. . . . We never considered the occupying forces victims."[59] The results of ETA's attacks on security forces were grim. The group's 299 bombings of police and military targets (counting both no-warning attacks on security forces and ambushes piggybacked onto commercial attacks) killed 157 and wounded 1,015.[60]

The LTTE had a very different political situation, with less need to seek legitimacy from the state's civilians, a lower emphasis on economic disruption, and a less challenging counterterrorism environment (at least off the battlefield). For most of its history, the LTTE controlled swathes of majority Tamil territory in Sri Lanka. In its secure bases, it could arrange its own shelter and "tax" local civilians to obtain resources and recruits.[61] The LTTE did not depend on the state-controlled civilian population to a high degree, so it had low incentives to integrate casualty-reducing, legitimacy-seeking warnings in its terrorist operations.

Sri Lanka's government did nothing to increase the LTTE's legitimacy concerns. Although Sri Lanka's postcolonial governing institutions were democratic in form, Tamils never enjoyed the full rights and representation their Sinhalese neighbors received. Sri Lanka's disconnect between democratic institutions and civil rights is apparent when comparing the country's yearly scores on common indices of regime type and human rights practices. During its civil war, Sri Lanka scored moderately well on the Polity IV Project's widely used Polity2 scale of democratic political institutions.[62] From 1983 through 2009 the country earned scores of 5 or 6 on a scale that ranges from -10 (totally undemocratic) to 10 (fully democratic).[63] However, Sri Lanka also scored highly on the 5-point Political Terror Scale (PTS), which indicates the frequency of state-sanctioned torture, political imprisonment, forced disappearance, and extrajudicial killing. The government generally scored a 4 or 5, with 5 indicating the most intense and widespread abuse.[64] (Spain scored between 1 and 3 on the PTS and 10 on the Polity2 scale during the same years.[65]) The Black July riots of 1983 are perhaps the best illustration of Tamil grievances: Sinhalese mobs murdered thousands of Tamils while government security forces did virtually nothing to intervene.[66] The Sri Lankan government's policies of discrimination, neglect, and abuse convinced Tamils that the state was not only unresponsive but actively hostile toward their ethnic group.

Rather than appealing for within-system reform, Tamils looked to the LTTE to represent their interests. M. A. Sumanthiran, a Sri Lankan Member of Parliament and human rights lawyer of the Tamil National Alliance (TNA), recalls: "[Tamils] found the LTTE to have been the only force that was able to stand up to the government in an effective way. Political parties couldn't. We talk, we shout, we scream, but we couldn't deliver anything. It was only the LTTE that could actually physically hold the government forces at bay."[67]

Tamils were also willing to tolerate a certain amount of inhumanity by the LTTE if it brought security and the prospect of an independent Tamil homeland. Sumanthiran denies that Tamils ever "approved of attacks on civilians." But at the time the LTTE convinced many Tamils that atrocities were "a necessary evil to put up with . . . for the moment until we attain our objective and once we have obtained it, then things will be different." "Nobody will say that was right," Sumanthiran adds, "but even today there are people who say, 'But at that time, it was necessary to have done that.'"[68] The Sri Lankan government's dearth of legitimacy among Tamils gave the LTTE little reason to restrict its own targeting of civilians.

Nor was the LTTE's prevailing coercive strategy conducive to warnings. The group's preference was to target security forces and civilians first, with economic coercion playing only an auxiliary role. Of the LTTE's 1,614 attacks, 573 targeted the Sri Lankan or Indian militaries, with 412 attacks targeting private citizens, 272 targeting police, and 146 targeting government personnel and facilities. Just 53 attacks targeted commercial property or businesspeople. An additional 122 targeted transportation, an economically significant class of target.[69] Yet as the examples below will show, the LTTE's intent in many of these transportation attacks was not to target the economy per se but to kill as many civilians as possible in crowded bus and train stations.

Indeed, the LTTE is best known for its deliberate attacks on civilian soft targets. The group's most notorious acts include the massacre of 146 civilians at a bus station and a Buddhist shrine in the city of Anuradhapura on May 14, 1985; the massacre of 110 civilians at two mosques in the Batticaloa district on August 3, 1990; the massacre of 109 Muslims in Palliyagodella, Polonnaruwa district, on October 15, 1992; and the massacre of more than 50 Sinhalese villagers in Gonagala, Ampara, on September 18, 1999.[70] These direct attacks on civilians signaled the LTTE's strength and the Sri Lankan government's inability to defeat the Tigers militarily. The strategy was reinforced by the Indian intelligence agents who armed and trained Tamil rebel groups during the early and mid-1980s. In 1987 Indian agents reportedly told one rebel leader: "As long as the south remains quiet, no pressure can be brought" on the government to settle the conflict.[71] That same year, the LTTE bombed Colombo's central bus station, killing 113 people.[72] Velupillai Prabhakaran, leader of the LTTE, personally endorsed the idea of civilian targeting in a BBC interview in 1991. Given the escalating civilian death toll, Prabhakaran argued, "The Sri Lankan government now knows it can't impose a military solution on the ethnic problem."[73]

Certain LTTE atrocities can be understood as symbolic responses to operational setbacks on the battlefield. For example, the January 31, 1996, suicide truck bombing of the Central Bank of Sri Lanka in Colombo (91 killed) and the July 24, 1996, bombing of a commuter train in a Colombo suburb (64 killed) followed the government's conquest of the LTTE's stronghold in the Jaffna peninsula in December 1995.[74] Stung by the loss of their de facto capital, the Tigers caused mayhem in Sri Lanka's capital. In February 2009, as the Sri Lankan Army approached the point of final victory over the LTTE, the Tigers again turned their sights on Colombo. The LTTE's "Air Tigers" packed two small aircraft with an enormous quantity of explosives and attempted to crash them into buildings, only to be shot down by the Sri Lankan Air Force.[75] Warning would have squandered the signaling value of these attacks, which were deliberately planned to maximize surprise and casualties. A statistical analysis of the LTTE's bombings shows how few warnings this group gave. Compared to ETA's roughly 45 percent frequency of warning when bombing civilian targets, the LTTE gave warnings just 1.4 percent of the time.[76]

We also see little evidence of tactical prophylactic threats from the LTTE. This is what my theoretical argument would predict, given the low degree of police pressure faced by the LTTE on government-held territory. The weakness of Sri Lankan policing was a long-term problem, predating the LTTE by more than a decade. The police had failed to suppress past uprisings by the Janatha Vimukthi Peramuna (JVP), a Marxist student party that rebelled against the government in 1971 and again in 1987–1990. Twice the JVP nearly toppled the Sri Lankan state. Twice the government resorted to brutal and indiscriminate repression by the Sri Lankan Army, which killed or "disappeared" approximately fifty thousand Sinhalese youth in the two episodes.[77] But the army was hardly an efficient substitute for civilian policing. It was "poorly equipped, paid, and led" until 2005, when incoming army chief Gotabaya Rajapaksa instituted reforms, training programs, new weapons acquisitions, and the recruitment of fifteen thousand new troops.[78] Yet the primary role of these troops was to fight the LTTE on the battlefield. The police defending against terrorist operations were woefully inadequate, and the LTTE's use of suicide tactics could bypass such defenses as existed. Despite extensive searches in secondary historical accounts and news reportage, I am unable to find any evidence of prophylactic warnings or hoaxes, as envisioned by my theoretical argument.[79] The closest approximation I find is a threat directed in 2000 at Sri Lankan civilians (not at security forces) to cover the retreat of an LTTE commando squad.[80] The assailants' threats cleared civilians from their escape route and prevented bystanders from providing information to the pursuing police. The logic is similar to tactical prophylaxis, although my argument more narrowly concerns prophylactic threats against security forces to affect their tactical movements. The fact that I cannot find clear instances of tactical prophylaxis lends support to my argument: the LTTE, facing a weaker counterterrorism opponent, issued fewer prophylactic threats than ETA did.

Hoaxes, Truth-Telling, and the Institutionalization of Communication

Comparing ETA and the LTTE, the Tamil group's tendency to eschew commercial targets gives us less reason to expect hoaxes. We expect more hoaxes from ETA, given its greater strategic emphasis on targeting commerce and disrupting the Spanish economy. These predictions bear out empirically. The International Terrorism: Attributes of Terrorist Events (ITERATE) dataset, which includes hoax incidents, shows only two hoaxes by the LTTE, both on March 26, 1993.[81] These incidents targeted businesspeople, although they occurred at the individuals' homes, suggesting that their purpose may have been extortion rather than economic disruption.[82] The ITERATE dataset shows four hoaxes by ETA—one each in 1984 and 1985 and two in 1986. The first incident targeted an airline flight bound from Spain to Mexico; the others targeted businesses, commercial property, and public spaces.[83] These hoaxes are consistent with the logic of economic attrition and with my theoretical expectations.

In absolute terms, however, four hoaxes in a protracted guerrilla campaign spanning several decades is not very many. Why didn't ETA use hoaxes more liberally, paralyzing transit systems and commercial districts, as the IRA did during its own campaign of bombing and disruption? One possible answer is that ETA's hoaxes are underreported. The ITERATE dataset only includes incidents of a transnational character. As such, it does not record hoaxes exclusively affecting domestic nationals and domestic businesses.[84] ETA's domestic-oriented hoaxes may also be underreported by the news media because they did not cause injuries. Yet the generally noninjurious nature of IRA hoaxes did not prevent the British press from reporting these incidents, particularly when they caused disruption to transit infrastructure and the economy. Had ETA perpetrated such hoaxes regularly, more of them would have shown up in the news.

If underreporting is not the reason, what else might explain the lower than expected frequency of ETA hoaxes—in fact, the absence of any reported hoaxes after 1986? To answer this question, I again queried Antxon Etxebeste. By his account, ETA deliberately restrained its use of hoaxes to ensure the credibility of the group's truthful bomb warnings.[85] ETA's leaders feared that by issuing hoaxes, they might give the Spanish government reason to ignore bomb warnings later on, with deadly consequences for civilians. Such fears peaked after the disastrous Barcelona Hipercor supermarket bombing killed twenty-one civilians in 1987. These deaths resulted from police officers' premature dismissal of a bomb warning and their decision to allow shoppers back into the store.[86] The officers' decision was understandable: ETA had carried out at least four hoax attacks on commercial targets from 1984 through 1986. After a few minutes of searching the Hipercor facility for a bomb and failing to find one, police assumed, reasonably enough, that the telephone warning was another ETA hoax, or perhaps a hoax perpetrated by unscrupulous individuals impersonating ETA on the phone. The decision to dismiss the warning was disastrous for shoppers, and also for ETA, as the civilian deaths sparked outrage and mass protests in the streets of Barcelona.[87]

Chastened by the disaster, Etxebeste and his fellow *etarras* resolved to shore up the credibility of their warnings. ETA never again used hoax tactics against economic targets. "Never," Etxebeste recalls, "precisely so that the credibility of the organization was complete." The way to avoid further atrocities was to convey the message that "ETA never lies."[88] Two high-level Guardia Civil counterterrorism specialists, speaking on condition of anonymity, confirmed Etxebeste's account. This is remarkable, because the Guardia Civil have every reason to report negative information about ETA—including any allegations of hoaxing. Yet these interviewees could not recall a case in which ETA gave deliberately false warnings. Unlike the IRA, which issued false threats a certain proportion of the time, ETA seems to have abandoned the use of hoaxes as of the mid-1980s.[89]

Of course, the fact that ETA abstained from hoaxes did not prevent pranksters from issuing false bomb threats in ETA's name. To prevent these false threats from spoiling the credibility of ETA's truthful warnings, the group took several steps. Like the IRA, ETA established a system of intermediaries to communicate warnings to police. According to Etxebeste, the intermediaries included "various agencies of a public, institutional character . . . the Red Cross, radio stations . . . or other organizations."[90] ETA made redundant warning calls through multiple intermediaries, assuming that mutually reinforcing messages would help convince police that the warnings were not pranks. The practice of using intermediaries also put witnesses in the middle of ETA's phone chain. Like the IRA, ETA held a cynical view of police, assuming that if they could, Spanish authorities would ignore ETA's warnings and allow civilians to die. *Etarras'* distrust of the police grew with the Hipercor disaster. Although ETA accepted responsibility for the attack and expressed regret at the deaths, the group harbored a lingering anger. Police "set a trap for us," Etxebeste claims. After Hipercor, he and other ETA leaders assumed that "the police themselves might not acknowledge the warning."[91] The intermediary system ensured that witnesses could confirm, after the fact, that warnings were given, establishing (by ETA's reckoning) that any casualties were the fault of police.

ETA's intermediaries were also crucial to interpreting threats, rendering otherwise unintelligible information actionable to emergency responders. The group's practice of attacking tourist beaches and railway tracks meant that in many cases, there was no street address or landmark to identify the location of the bomb. To increase the precision of its threats, ETA established a unique system of dead-drops and maps that could identify the specific area to be evacuated. Etxebeste explains that bombs might be buried under a particular section of beach or railroad, with long electronic fuses set to go off weeks later at a specific time. ETA would know the time and precise location of the attack, down to the sand dune or rail trestle. Days or weeks in advance of a bombing, a map "was deposited . . . in an impersonal mailbox" for "the media or an organization like DYA [a Spanish emergency service] to pick up." ETA would call the intermediary organization, inform them that "there is a map," and tell them where to find it.

The map would show the section of coastline or railway in which the bombs were hidden, but it would not show the precise locations of the devices. Intermediaries and police would not have enough information to locate the bombs in advance using the map alone. But on the day of the attack, minutes or hours before the explosion, ETA would telephone the intermediary again, informing them that bombs were "more or less in this area of the beach" (Etxebeste's words) or "from this kilometer to that kilometer" of the railway shown on the map.[92] The phone call would give police just enough time and information to evacuate civilians from the targeted area. However, because the map showed a sufficiently large area to be useless without the phone call, ETA could use the same map for different bomb attacks throughout a campaign. The idiosyncrasy of the system also set ETA's messages apart from pranks, making it harder for pranksters to call in credible-sounding threats against beaches and railways.

Another factor setting ETA's messages apart was the peculiar sound of the group's telephone calls. Etxebeste recalls how ETA used "instruments" to distort callers' voices.[93] The distortion made it difficult for anyone to identify the voice of an ETA caller and incriminate them after the fact. But it also gave ETA's messages a distinctive timbre that was difficult for pranksters to mimic. One media report describes the sound as "a recording in which a distorted woman's voice was heard."[94] ETA's responsibility claims after a bombing used the same sound, which was readily identifiable by media organizations that received such calls. Etxebeste describes this as ETA's "authorized voice" (*voz autorizada*). The voice served as "a code of authentication. . . . When that voice is put on the telephone, when that voice calls, that is the voice of ETA."[95] Coupled with ETA's strict practice of only making truthful threats, the authorized voice lent any given threat an air of credibility and urgency.

Pledges for Social Control

Turning now to prospective threats, my argument predicts that terrorist groups attempting social control will pledge attacks on proscribed places, institutions, and social behaviors. One manifestation of social control is the use of threats to extort taxes and recruits from civilian populations. The target of these pledges is not the state but the civilians that terrorists hope to control by inducing fear. The threats are issued in the preattack moment, and they have a contingent character: the terrorist group pledges to follow through on the threat if civilians cross a specified behavioral line or fail to pay the requested tribute. If civilians disobey and terrorists fulfill their threat, the group's future pledges become more credible and may induce the behavioral compliance the group seeks. Given the ethnic secessionist aspirations of ETA and the Tamil Tigers, we should expect both groups to issue social control-oriented threats against their "citizens." The scope of their demands may vary, given the LTTE's success in conquering territory and its ability to meddle in many aspects of residents' lives. But both groups portrayed themselves as governments in the making, and we should expect them, like governments, to use threats in enforcing their rule.

ETA claimed to be the legitimate focal point of Basque nationalism. As such, it claimed the moral right to govern Basques' social and economic lives. One example of ETA's drive for control was the group's vehement opposition to infrastructure projects that threatened the natural beauty and health of ecosystems in Euskadi. Such projects included a nuclear power plant, new highways, and a new high-speed rail system (the "Basque Y").[96] In opposing these projects, ETA stood on the side of a growing Basque environmental movement, against the national government and legal Basque parties that supported the projects as useful for economic development.

Although mainstream Basque activists pursued nonviolent protest strategies, ETA employed a mix of violence and threats to advance its vision for Euskadi. In late 1990 the group sent a threatening letter to the Basque business consortium set up to manage the Leizarán highway construction project. The letter informed the businesses that ETA would treat them as a "priority target" unless they abandoned the project. ETA's political arm, Herri Batasuna, made a follow up visit to the corporations and "recommended" against beginning construction.[97] The business consortium agreed to change the highway route, conceding the issue. ETA's threats and violence against nuclear energy development prompted the cancelation of a major nuclear reactor project as well.[98] Although ETA helped to deliver these policy victories for the Basque left, the group found itself at odds with pacifists, who demonstrated publicly against the *etarrras*' violent tactics. ETA deployed a mix of street violence and intimidation against peace activists, seeking to regain its monopoly over Basque protest culture.[99]

ETA also used threats to collect revolutionary taxes from Basque businesspeople.[100] Basque businesses were regularly "invited" to contribute a portion of their profits to the group's cause.[101] Those who refused received menacing notes on ETA letterhead, informing them that "you and all of your assets are operational targets." These letters might be followed by in-person harassment, threats against the businessperson's family, kidnapping (to collect the extortion money as ransom), or in some cases, assassination. A study of the long-term effects of ETA's extortion campaign counts "more than 10,000 victims," including businesspeople and their families, with intergenerational consequences including "chronic psychological disorders and, often, social withdrawal" resulting from their repeated traumatic exposure to threats.[102]

Turning now to examine the LTTE, this group used threats to implement social control on the territory it conquered from the Sri Lankan government. The precise borders of the LTTE's territorial strongholds varied with the group's military fortunes. During the 2002–2006 ceasefire, however, the Tamil Tigers governed thousands of square miles, with an administrative bureaucracy that rivaled that of a state. The LTTE established courts, a health care system, and an education system. It maintained order with a national police system and official media that broadcast the Tamil Tigers' message on radio and television.[103] The LTTE also exercised influence on the diaspora Tamil community, including Hindu temples, businesses, and a network of activist groups that provided funding, materiel, and political leverage.[104]

The LTTE used threats to extract resources from civilians. Of particular importance were the financial resources and military recruits that local populations could provide. A news account from 1991 describes life in LTTE-held territory from the perspective of a local Catholic priest:

> The Tigers tax the local population in gold, as they do elsewhere in the territory they control, and while the practice of requiring families to give up one of their sons to the movement has not become widespread here, there is a mixture of resentment and ambivalence toward the guerrillas among the people of this shrinking town. "They presume to talk for us," Father Miller said, "but nobody asked us. We didn't choose them. But they have the guns."[105]

As the 1990s wore on and the LTTE experienced some battlefield losses, the group began to recruit children to replenish its ranks. A pamphlet urging "young men and maidens [to] rise and come to us" also pledged that LTTE recruiters would "call on you and speak to you directly in your home." By the decade of the 2000s, the LTTE's child recruitment had evolved into "a noxious combination of lethal force, strong-arming, threat, trickery and blackmail." To deter Tamil civilians from fleeing, the LTTE imposed a rule that anyone leaving rebel-controlled areas had to leave behind "a guarantor, usually a relative, to ensure their return."[106] It is easy to imagine what might befall a "guarantor" whose relative fled Tamil Eelam, leaving the family member behind. Extortion extended to diaspora communities in Europe and North America as well: a significant number of the Tigers' explosives acquisitions were financed by money collected under threat of force by LTTE front organizations in Canada and the United States.[107]

An extreme manifestation of LTTE social control was the ethnic cleansing of non-Tamils (and non-Hindu Tamils) from Tiger-held areas. In Jaffna, a far northern region viewed by the LTTE as its future capital, the Tigers sought to expel Sinhalese and Tamil-speaking Muslims, who made up at least 10 percent of the population. One journalistic account recalls: "In October 1990, the Tamil Tigers issued a warning in which all Muslims were given a few hours to leave Tiger-controlled territory: 75,000 people fled south into towns controlled by the government."[108]

In general, the LTTE's and ETA's social control–oriented threats are concordant with my argument. Both groups pledged violence to influence the behavior of their respective ethnic groups. Their use of threats varied in extent: ETA could extract taxes, intimidate rival activists, and prevent local businesses from collaborating with government infrastructure projects, but it could not impose the state-like regime that the LTTE instituted in its zone of territorial control. With an iron grip on the land, the LTTE could use threats for the most extreme purposes, including the ethnic cleansing of outgroups. What emerges from these case studies is that terrorist groups with secessionist aims will use pledges to govern populations and extract resources, much like the states they emulate.

Pledges for Negotiation

My argument also holds that militant groups seeking to negotiate concrete political issues will make pledges of violence against the government. These pledges are issued in the preattack moment and may have an explicitly contingent character: the terrorist group threatens attacks if the state does not meet its demands—or if the state refuses to participate in negotiations. In some cases, the contingent character may be unstated: the terrorist group threatens violence while hinting that it is open to negotiations. If the state refuses to concede and the terrorist group fulfills its threat, subsequent pledges will carry greater credibility. In the future, they may be sufficient to obtain the concessions the terrorist group seeks.

ETA and the LTTE both sought to negotiate with their state adversaries regarding specific political demands. ETA described its approach to diplomacy as a "spirit of armed dialogue."[109] The group would carry out attacks and make peace overtures at the same time, seeking negotiations over the Basque people's future. My interviewee, Antxon Etxebeste, was the central player in one round of negotiations, the so-called *Mesa de Argel* (Algiers table) of the late 1980s. Spanish representatives met Etxebeste in Algiers under French government auspices. ETA enacted several ceasefires during these years, as Etxebeste demanded changes to the Spanish constitution to allow full sovereignty for the Basque country. ETA coupled its diplomatic outreach with threats, pressuring the government to negotiate, to concede ETA's demands at the bargaining table, and to return to the bargaining table after diplomatic breakdowns. The *Mesa de Argel* ceasefires were temporary, with an expiration date declared in advance. As the scheduled end of the ceasefire approached, Etxebeste and ETA would offer to extend the peace, promising a return to violence if the government rejected the invitation. In 1989 it became clear that the government was only willing to offer limited concessions on Basque autonomy—not a constitutional amendment for Basque independence. Etxebeste issued three final demands to sustain the *Mesa de Argel*: the continuation of political dialogue, the release of several imprisoned ETA members so that they could participate in negotiations, and the opening of formal talks between the Spanish government and ETA's political wing, Herri Batasuna. The failure to meet these demands would result in a return to hostilities. When the Spanish government refused to concede, ETA recommenced its bombing campaign with a communiqué declaring "all fronts open."[110]

The failure of the *Mesa de Argel* doomed Spain to another seventeen years of terrorist violence. But in 2006 Basque politicians were able to broker a new round of diplomatic talks between ETA's top leaders and the socialist government of José Luis Rodríguez Zapatero. Although Zapatero accepted ETA's offer of a ceasefire, the two sides found it difficult to bridge their differences on the fundamental issue of Basque statehood. As negotiations appeared to be breaking down, ETA issued an ominous communiqué stressing "the gravity of the political situation." Three masked ETA members appeared in public, firing symbolic gunshots into the air in front of a gathering of Basque nationalists. The *etarras* read from a document reiterating their "firm commitment to retaining our weapons until we reach independence and socialism."[111] ETA broke its ceasefire later that year with the car bombing at Madrid's Barajas airport.[112]

At other times ETA's threat-laden diplomacy has been more mundane. The group has attempted to force government concessions on the treatment of political prisoners by kidnapping politicians and security personnel. One such gambit, the kidnapping of Partido Popular councilor Miguel Ángel Blanco in July 1997, failed spectacularly. ETA representatives gave the Spanish government forty-eight hours to move imprisoned ETA members from facilities in the south of Spain to prisons in the Basque country. When the government failed to respond, ETA killed their hostage and dumped his body in a forest outside the city of Donostia/San Sebastián. Basque civilians condemned the killing, with thousands turning out in the streets to protest ETA's behavior.[113] An even more ignominious episode occurred in 1983, when an ETA *kommando* kidnapped a Spanish Army captain in Bilbao. The *etarras* threatened to kill their hostage unless Spanish state TV broadcast a communiqué by the group. The TV network aired the statement, but ETA killed the hostage anyway.[114]

The LTTE engaged in armed dialogue as well. The group summarized its political demands in a document known as the Thimpu Declaration or the Thimpu Principles. The LTTE reiterated these demands in public and in private negotiations with the Sri Lankan government, listing the conditions that any political solution would have to meet:

1. Recognition of the Tamils of Sri Lanka as a nation.
2. Recognition of the existence of an identified homeland for the Tamils in Sri Lanka.
3. Recognition of the right of self-determination of the Tamil nation.
4. Recognition of the right to citizenship and the fundamental rights of all Tamils who look upon the island as their country.[115]

LTTE and Sri Lankan diplomats engaged in peace negotiations from 2002 to 2003, supervised by peace negotiators and military observers from Norway. The LTTE withdrew from direct talks in 2003 because the Sri

Lankan government was unwilling to concede a fully sovereign homeland to Tamil people.[116] Even after withdrawing from bilateral talks, however, the Tigers' leader, Prabhakaran, continued to make public demands on the Sri Lankan government.

Prabhakaran's yearly "Great Heroes Day" speeches, given every November 27 from 1991 through 2008, contain a mix of diplomatic demands and threats against the Sri Lankan state. The stated purpose of the speech was to honor the sacrifice of LTTE members who lost their lives in the war, but the speeches also conveyed messages to the Sri Lankan government. As one LTTE-run press outlet explained, the Great Heroes Day speech was "awaited and listened to eagerly by devotees and enemies alike." Prabhakaran's speeches stopped short of issuing explicit threats, but analysts noted the "sinister sub-textual interpretation of the martyr celebration," which venerated the same suicide bombers who carried out the LTTE's deadliest attacks. "Thus the Tiger leader is acutely aware of the psychological impact the heroes day has on the Sinhala masses and their political leaders. . . . [Tamils'] willingness to die for freedom is extended to bombs in the South and the loss of Sinhala life, a price the Sinhala nation is reluctant to pay."[117] Prabhakaran brought the menacing subtext to the fore in his speeches from 2002 through 2005. In 2002 he asserted: "If our people's right to self-determination is denied and our demand for regional self-rule is rejected we have no alternative other than to secede and form an independent state." Prabhakaran delivered similar messages in 2003 and 2004, intensifying his rhetoric in 2005 as the ceasefire began to break down. In the 2005 speech he made an "urgent and final appeal. If the new government rejects our urgent appeal, we will, next year, in solidarity with our people, intensify our struggle for self-determination, our struggle for national liberation to establish self-government in our homeland."[118] This implicit threat was underlined by a more explicit one from an LTTE front group, the High Security Zone Residents' Liberation Force (HSZRLF). The HSZRLF would later become famous for claiming suicide bombings the LTTE did not wish to claim outright, but the December 8 communiqué was the HSZRLF's first. The ominous message asserted that a new war had already begun, but physical violence could be avoided if the government pulled its troops out of the contested Jaffna district and returned to negotiations: "High Security Zone Residents' Liberation Force will continue its armed campaign until all military personal [sic] vacate the High Security Zone.

We the internally displaced people of Jaffna district have reached the limit of our patience. As a result we have decided to wage an armed campaign against the occupying Sinhala Army to liberate our homes."[119]

A week later, anonymous posters appeared near Sri Lankan Army positions, threatening to kill troops who failed to vacate the region: "If you don't want war, go from here. If you want to die, stay back."[120] The threatening messages continued in 2006. On April 25 a suicide bomber blew herself up at Sri Lankan Army headquarters, nearly killing Chief Lieutenant General Sarath Fonseka.[121] The LTTE officially denied responsibility, and the supposedly independent HSZRLF claimed credit. An LTTE spokesman warned that the climate in the north of Sri Lanka was "like a war situation," and the LTTE would "be forced to take military defensive action" if the government continued its operations in LTTE-held areas. Full hostilities erupted. In August, as Tamil civilian casualties mounted, the HSZRLF threatened "to carry out attacks against civilian targets in southern Sri Lanka if Sri Lankan armed forces continue to massacre innocent unarmed civilians in the Northeast."[122] A more specific threat against dams and hospitals followed in November: "We are sure that the people of the south are fully aware of the sort of humanitarian catastrophe they would have to face if one of the dams in the south is to burst. . . . There are several hospitals in southern Sri Lanka. Not all are guarded by barbed wire and special forces."[123]

Pledges like this, coupled with demands on the government, are precisely what we expect from groups seeking to negotiate specific political issues with the state.

Lower Incentives for Self-Aggrandizing Threats

My argument also predicts that groups facing reputational concerns—those competing against more capable peer rivals and those suffering strategic reverses or declines—will issue pledges and bluffs to aggrandize themselves. Neither ETA nor the LTTE faced a peer competitor with greater fighting power. This removed one key incentive for self-aggrandizement. Although ETA and the LTTE both experienced strategic reverses that might predict self-aggrandizing threats, the groups' very strong incentives to seek negotiations could just as easily explain the pledges and bluffs we see. The presence of other incentives for pledging and bluffing and the lack of between-case variation in the two groups' incentives for aggrandizement make it difficult to test this portion of my argument on ETA and the LTTE. (I do test it in subsequent chapters.) What I can say with confidence is that the historical evidence does not contradict my argument: neither ETA nor the LTTE regularly issued pledges or bluffs of an obviously self-aggrandizing character.[124] When we do see threats of a potentially self-aggrandizing nature, they tend to follow strategic setbacks, more or less as my theoretical framework predicts.

As noted previously, ETA lacked true peer competitors, having dominated Basque nationalist politics since the 1950s.[125] It had large numbers of supporters, including non-Basques, and as much political clout as an underground group could have under an oppressive fascist regime.[126] When ETA turned to terrorism, it retained its position as the vanguard of armed force Basque nationalism. ETA did experience a temporary split in the 1970s and early 1980s, with a hard-line *militar* and a moderate *politico-militar* faction competing to represent Basques' struggle.[127] (As the name implies, the *politico-militar* faction favored a two-track approach combining military struggle with a political party structure.) Yet the ETA-m/ETA-pm split did not introduce incentives for self-aggrandizement as envisioned in my argument. If the split had been lopsided, with one group exceeding the other in the capability for physical violence, we might have expected the weaker faction to make up the difference with self-aggrandizing bluster. The split was not lopsided, however. Analysts describe ETA-m and ETA-pm as "two substantial forms," both showing "themselves able to conduct, for the first time, a sustained campaign of bombing, kidnapping and murder."[128] As a result, the split "produced a marked increase in violence. Targets for assassination included members of the Civil Guard and National Police, people accused of being security service informants, and council leaders in Basque towns and villages."[129] From 1977 through 1982 the two branches of ETA carried out no fewer than 50 attacks per year, with attacks peaking at 171 in 1979, the highest number of any year in ETA's campaign.[130] Internecine killings are absent from these totals, aside from a pair of police informants murdered in the late 1970s by their former associates.[131] Compared to other militant rivalries, the ETA-m/ETA-pm split seems almost collegial, the two factions attempting to outdo each other in their attacks on the government. The split ended amicably as well: ETA-pm disbanded in 1982, its more militant members folding themselves seamlessly into ETA-m, which continued its work under the simple moniker, "ETA."[132] This unified formation lacked credible rivals for the remainder of its history.

Given the lack of peer competition, it comes as no surprise that we see few, if any, self-aggrandizing threats by ETA. Despite extensive searches in the LexisNexis news database and other historical sources, I am unable to find any prospective threats of an obviously self-aggrandizing character.[133] There is one ambiguous case in 1992, a year in which ETA experienced several humiliating defeats: the arrest of its entire three-person leadership council, two of the operatives meant to replace the leadership council, and the group's alleged "financial mastermind."[134] These strategic reverses introduced an incentive for self-aggrandizement to prop up ETA's reputation. Then, in July 1992, just prior to the start of the Barcelona Olympics, ETA made a seemingly incongruous offer of a two-month ceasefire, in exchange for the Spanish government entering peace talks with the group. The same statement threatened that if the government refused ETA's offer, the group would "maintain open all fronts in the struggle." This promise of violence, coupled with a peace overture, could be interpreted as a pledge of violence by a group seeking negotiations. Yet in the absence of a "proper infrastructure in Barcelona" following the leadership council's arrest, ETA's threat seems more like a bluff.[135] (The fact that ETA adhered to its ceasefire through mid-August, despite the government's refusal of the ceasefire offer, reinforces this view.[136]) The question is whether the bluff was intended as a bargaining ploy or as a self-aggrandizing distraction from ETA's strategic setbacks. Without knowing the group's intentions, it is not possible to say whether this piece of evidence supports my argument, but it certainly does not cut against it.

Just as ETA dominated militant Basque nationalism, the LTTE dominated Tamil nationalism in Sri Lanka. As my interviewee M. A. Sumanthiran recalls, Tamils "found the LTTE to have been the only force that was able to stand up to the government in an effective way."[137] The LTTE faced some early competition from other militant groups, but it killed them off or absorbed them in the opening years of Sri Lanka's civil war.[138] Even while these competitor groups survived, the Tamil Tigers vastly overshadowed them in revolutionary productivity. The Eelam People's Revolutionary Liberation Front and the Tamil Eelam Liberation Organization, the LTTE's main rivals, carried out a combined total of 15 attacks from 1984 through 1989, the years of their activity. During the same years, the Tamil Tigers carried out 274 attacks.[139] The Tigers' deeds spoke for themselves, giving the group generally low incentives for self-aggrandizing pledges and bluffs.

In keeping with my theoretical expectations, I find few clear examples of competitive self-aggrandizement in the LTTE's threats.[140] Having searched the available news record, the closest approximation I can find is a threat directed at leaders of rival Tamil groups. In 1990 the LTTE kidnapped the leader of the Eelam Revolutionary Organization of Students (EROS). The Tamil Tigers' spokespeople "asked EROS to disband and . . . threatened to annihilate the leadership and its members."[141] The threat apparently worked, as the captive EROS leader dutifully folded his organization into the LTTE.[142] Although the Tamil Tigers issued this particular threat in the context of intergroup competition, its immediate purpose appears to have been related to negotiation (albeit negotiation with a rival militant group). The threat does not obviously fit the notion of competitive self-aggrandizement I have set forth, as outcompeting rival militant groups for the support of the civilian population.

However, there are examples of threats seeming to aggrandize the Tamil Tigers versus the state at times of great difficulty for the LTTE. One example comes from February 1993, after the Indian Navy intercepted and destroyed a smuggling ship captained by a top Tamil Tiger cadre, "Kittu." After announcing Kittu's death, the LTTE "threatened to explode bombs in busy areas" and "vowed that it would strike on an Indian leader to avenge the loss."[143] Another example comes from 2007, after the Sri Lankan Army reconquered the country's eastern region and the Tigers entered an inexorable decline. As the government announced a "national day of celebration" to commemorate its victory, a top LTTE political official, S. P. Thamilselvan, threatened "crippling" counterattacks. A news report at the time noted that Thamilselvan's "comments will raise fears in the capital Colombo that the separatist movement will return to the suicide bombings of its bloody past."[144] Both of these threats, coming immediately after strategic setbacks, show elements of self-aggrandizement. They seek to distract from LTTE losses and project images of potency. However, they could also be interpreted in other ways. The 1993 threat might represent an effort to deter further Indian intervention in the Sri Lankan conflict. The 2007 threat, coming from the LTTE's top political leader, might have had some role in negotiation seeking or in strategic misdirection, slowing the Sri Lankan Army's advance and forcing the government to move security resources southward to reinforce Colombo.

In sum, the evidence from the ETA and LTTE cases is consistent with my argument regarding threats as self-aggrandizement, but there are other possible interpretations of the data. These cases cannot provide a strong test of my claims about self-aggrandizement. Fortunately, the Peruvian groups and jihadist groups I analyze in subsequent chapters do permit such tests, and my argument stacks up well against the evidence from those cases.

Pledges and Bluffs for Strategic Advantage

In addition to their uses in bargaining and social control, pledges and bluffs can interfere with counterterrorism efforts. Threats can force police to concentrate their energies on self-protection, sabotage their attempts to build community relationships, and force them to protect targets they otherwise might not have felt it necessary to defend. We should expect militants to adopt this sort of strategic prophylaxis when facing particularly strong counterterrorism opponents.

As I have noted, ETA confronted a counterterrorism apparatus that was more efficient and more capable than that faced by the LTTE—at least until the final years of the Sri Lankan civil war, as the balance of power came increasingly to favor the Sri Lankan state. Consistent with the goal of achieving strategic advantage, ETA at times used pledges to interfere with Spanish police deployments. One of ETA's key demands on the Spanish government was to replace all Guardia Civil in the Basque country with Basque police officers.[145] A necessary first step was the removal of police barracks (*casa cuarteles*) where the Guardia Civil and their families lived. The presence of the families was problematic for ETA because it meant that the group could not attack the *casa cuarteles* without harming civilians. ETA attempted to solve this problem by issuing public threats and demands. Antxon Etxebeste paraphrases: "First remove the *casa cuarteles*. And if the *cuarteles* are not removed, at least civilians should leave the barracks." If the families remained, ETA would assume that the Guardia Civil was using spouses and children as "*escudos humanos*"—human shields—and it would attack anyway.[146] The Spanish government did not acquiesce, perhaps because it believed ETA would not follow through on the threat. This was an unfortunate miscalculation. A car bomb attack on a *casa cuartel* in Zaragoza on December 11, 1987, killed eleven people, including five children.[147] An attack in the city of Vic on May 29, 1991, killed nine people, also including five children.[148] ETA's prophylactic threat, intended to dislodge the *casa cuarteles*, induce desertions, or at least separate civilians from the police, had failed. ETA's follow-through on the threat brought political disaster: mainstream Basque parties responded to the Zaragoza atrocity by signing a pact to deny ETA any future role in negotiating the status of Basque regions.[149]

Although we see few threats of a prophylactic nature from the LTTE in the early and middle parts of its conflict, we do see some threats of this type in the conflict's later years, as the Tigers' military position worsened. The LTTE's downward slide began during the 2002–2006 ceasefire. A high-ranking Tamil Tiger officer in the eastern theater, Colonel Karuna, defected to the Sri Lankan government side.[150] With the return of hostilities, the LTTE's eastern front rapidly collapsed and the government was able to concentrate its attention exclusively on the northern front, including the LTTE's de facto capital, Kilinochchi. The Tigers' defense was far less effective than in past episodes of the civil war. This was attributable in part to the Sri Lankan regime's ability to concentrate forces, and in part to Colonel Karuna's contributions of intelligence and 600 ex-LTTE troops who understood the Tigers' defensive tactics. By 2008–2009 the Tamil Tigers were in serious decline, lacking the metaphorical teeth that had mauled Sri Lankan forces and civilians so many times before.[151] In the final phase of the civil war, as the LTTE sought reprieve from the government's military advances, prophylactic pledges and bluffs became more useful.

We can interpret the LTTE's bluff threats against dams and hospitals in 2006 as attempts to draw the government's attention and resources away from the northern front—and away from hard targets the group was planning to attack in the South.[152] (Recall that in April 2006, Tamil Tiger suicide bombers attacked Sri Lankan army headquarters, nearly killing the chief of staff.[153]) The LTTE issued bluff threats again in May 2009, during the final days of the war. Shortly after the government announced the battlefield death of Velupillai Prabhakaran, LTTE spokespeople conceded that their armed struggle was at an end. Simultaneously, a communiqué from the Tamil Tigers' HSZRLF front group threatened a new wave of attacks against government-held cities in the South. The threat was both implausible and incongruous, given the Tigers' simultaneous announcement, via official propaganda channels, that the group had "decided to silence our guns." However, the text of the LTTE communiqué suggests a strategy of "good cop/bad cop." The Tamil Tigers' surrender message linked the cessation of hostilities to the welfare of "our people ... dying now from bombs, shells, illness and hunger.... We remain with one last choice to remove the last weak excuse of the enemy for killing our people."[154] The contemporaneous HSZRLF statement, threatening suicide attacks against Sinhalese civilians, may be interpreted as an unsuccessful ploy to halt government shelling of the remaining Tamil areas in the North. This is speculation because those who made the LTTE's strategic decisions are not available to tell their stories, having been killed in the final days of the war. The general trend in the Tamil Tigers' behavior, however, with bluffs increasing as the group's military position declined, is consistent with my argument about the use of prophylactic pledges and bluffs.

This chapter affirms several aspects of my argument about threats. The pairing of ETA and the LTTE shows how different degrees of legitimacy seeking, disruption seeking, and advantage seeking incentivize different uses of threats. We see a greater frequency of warnings from ETA, the group with greater needs for legitimacy among the state's population, a greater emphasis on economic disruption, and a greater need for tactical advantage versus the state's counterterrorism apparatus. We see generally similar patterns of prospective pledges and bluffs by ETA and the LTTE. This is consistent with my argument, given the groups' similar emphases on social control and negotiation with their state adversaries. The LTTE's use of bluffs, however, increased as its position in the Sri Lankan civil war worsened. The group's empty threats, from 2006 on, bolster my claims about bluffs as strategic advantage–seeking tools for terrorist organizations on the decline.

One question unanswered by this chapter concerns the use of pledges for aggrandizement. Because ETA and the LTTE dominated their respective political environments, neither group had strong incentives to pledge attacks for the sake of reputation building. The lack of incentives for aggrandizement is overshadowed by the positive incentives to pledge attacks for social control and negotiation. Thus these cases are not well suited for testing my argument's predictions about self-aggrandizing threats. However, I am able to apply this portion of my argument to the Peruvian and jihadist cases I discuss in the next two chapters.

Another question raised in this chapter concerns the tradeoff between credibility and the instrumental utility of false threats. ETA's strategy of disruption offered incentives for hoax threats that could add noninjurious economic destabilization to the physical destruction of the group's bombing campaign. Yet ETA's sensitivity to civilian casualties gave the group reason to restrain its hoaxing. Excessive false threats may spoil the credibility of truthful threats—including the helpful warnings a terrorist group gives to spare civilian lives. The IRA navigated this tradeoff without giving up hoaxes, yet ETA found it necessary to abandon hoaxes altogether. What explains this difference?

Part of the answer seems to be local culture. ETA paid an especially high price when its attacks went wrong and killed civilians. The Hipercor disaster killed twenty-one shoppers because police dismissed ETA's bomb warning as a hoax.[155] The IRA caused similar atrocities—twelve civilians killed in the La Mon hotel attack, five on Bloody Friday, nine in an attack on a Belfast fish shop, twenty-nine in the "Real IRA" splinter group's 1998 bombing in Omagh.[156] None of these incidents provoked the mass street protests that followed the Hipercor incident, when 750,000 Barcelonans took to the street.[157] There is clearly some idiosyncratic variation in the political consequences for harming civilians, which cannot be fully explained by factors such as territorial control and regime type. The existence of unexplained variation calls for some caution when making firm predictions about a group's likely hoaxing or bluffing behavior—unless one can point to informative accidents, where a group's attacks have caused unintended civilian deaths and the latent costs of harming civilians can be directly observed. The unusually high costs in ETA's case appear to explain this group's scrupulous and risk-averse avoidance of hoaxes.

CHAPTER IV

The MRTA and the Shining Path

Common Enemy; Virtually No Threat in Common

In this chapter I present case studies of the Túpac Amaru Revolutionary Movement (MRTA) and the Shining Path (Sendero Luminoso). This is a very well controlled pair of cases, the two Marxist groups having fought simultaneous revolutionary wars against the government of Peru. The groups' collocation, contemporaneity, and ideological similarity hold otherwise perturbing variables constant, permitting a more focused comparison of their relationships with local civilians, the locations of their support bases, their attitudes toward political compromise, and their changing power relationships with the state. This chapter offers an excellent opportunity to observe how militants' threats are influenced by their incentives for legitimacy seeking, economic disruption, social control, negotiation with the state, and self-aggrandizement. There is no variation in the groups' adversary regime, so the incentives for advantage seeking via prophylactic threats are harder to compare. (The generally weak character of Peruvian policing did not offer strong incentives for prophylactic threats, and we do not observe many empirically.) However, there is intriguing within-case variation to note: in the late 1980s, new counterterrorism initiatives began to take a toll on the Shining Path's rural strongholds. These peasant-led counterterrorism programs affected only the countryside, so they exerted no appreciable effect on the MRTA. As the Shining Path began to feel heavier counterterrorism pressure, its leaders issued bluff threats, hoping to divert government resources into an urban crackdown that would take the heat off of the group's rural strongholds and radicalize Peruvians to support its cause. These empirical findings are consistent with my argument's predictions about bluff threats for strategic advantage. To set the stage for this chapter's analysis, I first present an overview of the Peruvian civil war in which the MRTA and the Shining Path participated.

The Peruvian Civil War, 1980–2000

The political conflict in Peru began in 1980, lasting roughly twenty years and claiming the lives of at least sixty-nine thousand Peruvians.[1] The Shining Path and the MRTA were the two main rebel actors. Although they shared a Marxist ideology, their origins were different. The MRTA's roots lay in mainstream, urban Peruvian socialism, including labor movements and the "legal left" electoral politics of the Alianza Popular Revolucionaria Americana (APRA). The MRTA espoused a Leninist brand of communism and a concept of guerrilla warfare borrowed from Cuba's Fidel Castro and Che Guevara.[2] At the same time, the MRTA was open to working with APRA, other left parties, and reformist elements of the Catholic Church to achieve its goals of "a socialist economy," "land reform," "popular democracy," and "a new Peruvian identity."[3] In contrast, the Shining Path originated in the interior region of Ayacucho. The group espoused a radical interpretation of Maoism developed by Abimael Guzmán, a philosophy professor at the National University of San Cristóbal of Huamanga. Guzmán (alias "Presidente Gonzalo") advocated the destruction of existing economic and social institutions. These would be replaced by the Shining Path's own structures: neighborhood committees, labor committees, peasant committees, and so on. Guzmán's cadres would "militarize" Peruvian society, destroying state forces and bringing "the masses" in line with the Shining Path's program, using extreme force against anyone who did not submit to the party's "democratic centralism."[4] Not surprisingly, the Shining Path perpetrated most of the violence during the conflict: 31,331 deaths—54 percent of the total people killed, compared to 37 percent killed by state agents and 1.8 percent killed by the MRTA.[5]

The Comisión de la Verdad y Reconciliación (Truth and Reconciliation Commission, CVR), convened by the Peruvian government and civil society to investigate the former political conflict, divides the war into five periods. The first, from May 1980 through December 1982, began when the Shining Path burned ballot boxes in Cangallo province to protest Peru's transition from a center-left military dictatorship to democracy. The period ended when Peru's new democratic government placed Ayacucho under military control, effectively acknowledging that police could not contain the growing Maoist insurgency. The second period, from January 1983 through June 1986, began with the militarization of Ayacucho and ended with simultaneous riots in three prison facilities in the Lima region. Shining Path and government forces escalated their violence (the government killed 238 people in the prison riots alone), and in 1984 the MRTA began its own armed campaign. The year 1984 was the bloodiest of the conflict, with more than four thousand deaths and disappearances. During the third period, from June 1986 through March 1989, violence spread to all parts of Peru. This period culminated with a brazen attack by Shining Path guerrillas and drug traffickers on a police station in the department of San Martín. The attack convinced the government to adopt a new strategy of aligning itself with local *campesino* (peasant) militias, relying on them to dislodge unwelcome Shining Path elements from rural towns. The fourth period lasted from March 1989 through September 1992. During this time the MRTA tried and failed to take control of the city of Tarma, losing many of its best officers.[6]

As the government's new antisubversive strategy loosened the Shining Path's hold on the countryside, the group expanded its operations in Lima to include "armed strikes" and car bombings.[7] The escalation of urban violence coincided with a severe economic crisis, helping to precipitate a self-coup (*autogolpe*) by President Alberto Fujimori, who assumed quasi-dictatorial powers in April 1992. Despite the chaos, police in Lima apprehended Abimael Guzmán and MRTA leader Víctor Polay. The civil war's fifth period lasted from Guzmán's September 1992 capture through November 2000. Reeling from Guzmán's loss, the Shining Path slowly succumbed to the government-backed *campesino* militias. Government forces finally defeated the MRTA in a gunfight on April 22, 1997, at the Japanese ambassador's residence, which the MRTA had occupied in a futile attempt to exchange hostages for imprisoned leaders of the group. Although he had vanquished both the Shining Path and the MRTA, President Fujimori fled the country in November 2000, attempting (unsuccessfully) to avoid prosecution for corruption offenses committed during his autocratic rule.[8] Fujimori's flight effectively ended the conflict, although some Shining Path elements have remained at large in remote regions, skimming money from the cocaine trade and occasionally carrying out acts of violence.[9]

Comparing Incentives and Patterns of Threats

Tables 4.1 and 4.2 summarize how the MRTA and the Shining Path differed in their political incentives and uses of threats. Although the Shining Path possessed rural strongholds, the MRTA was forced to shelter among civilians in Peru's urban centers. The Shining Path could afford to carry out no-warning attacks, but the MRTA had to employ casualty-reducing warnings to keep its violence within the bounds that its civilian hosts would tolerate. The MRTA also employed a strategy of disrupting the capitalist economy, making warnings and hoaxes useful auxiliary tactics. Although the MRTA pursued a degree of social control, seeking to deter Peruvians from collaborating with the capitalist state and U.S. businesses, the Shining Path sought to control Peruvians' lives entirely. The groups' uses of pledges were proportional to their social aims: the MRTA threatened targeted violence against *yanqui* abettors, while the Shining Path pledged spectacular retribution against entire villages who defied their reorganization of Peruvian life. With regard to threats against the government, the Shining Path and MRTA approaches were initially reversed. The MRTA issued pledges and bluffs, boasting of its potency and seeking negotiating

TABLE 4.1
Group Characteristics: MRTA and Shining Path

Incentive	Relative Values
Legitimacy seeking	MRTA > Shining Path
Disruption	MRTA > Shining Path
Social control	Shining Path > MRTA
Negotiation	MRTA > Shining Path
Aggrandizement	MRTA > Shining Path (as of late 1980s, MRTA ≈ Shining Path)
Advantage seeking	MRTA ≈ Shining Path (as of late 1980s, Shining Path > MRTA)

TABLE 4.2
Predictions: MRTA and Shining Path

	Prediction	Observed
Warnings	MRTA > Shining Path For legitimacy, disruption	MRTA > Shining Path
Hoaxes	MRTA > Shining Path For disruption	MRTA > Shining Path (Few hoaxes recorded)
Pledges	MRTA > Shining Path For negotiation Shining Path > MRTA For social control	MRTA > Shining Path For negotiation Shining Path > MRTA For social control
Bluffs	MRTA > Shining Path (mid-1980s) MRTA ≈ Shining Path (late 1980s–1990s) For aggrandizement, strategic advantage	MRTA > Shining Path (mid-1980s) MRTA ≈ Shining Path (late 1980s–1990s) For aggrandizement, strategic advantage

leverage over the state. The Shining Path issued few pledges, preferring to let its many actions speak. The group had no need to boast and no interest in negotiating with the government. As its military fortunes waned, however, the Shining Path issued a series of increasingly strident bluffs. These empty threats had a dual function: self-aggrandizement, as the group's leaders sought to distract from physical setbacks; and strategic advantage seeking—attempting to provoke a government crackdown that would radicalize Peruvian society and restore the Shining Path's political fortunes.

Warnings and Hoaxes

The MRTA had greater incentives to issue warnings and hoaxes, owing to the group's more intense multiple audiences conundrum and its emphasis on attacking economic targets. The MRTA's legitimacy concerns arose from its lack of territorial control. Without a rural stronghold, it needed to maintain a positive rapport with civilians in Peru's cities.[10] A minimum condition for the MRTA's survival was for local civilians not to denounce the group to state authorities.[11] To achieve victory, the MRTA would need to earn even more substantial support. Interviewed by the CVR, MRTA second-in-command Miguel Rincón explained that the MRTA's "conception . . . of revolution" was "as the work of the masses themselves." The MRTA's role was to act as instigator of an "organic" process, to carry out exemplary acts that would awaken "the enormous brain of a people, the imagination of millions" of Peruvians, who would take up the struggle as their own. Rincón recalls: "All of our guerrilla actions sought to convey a message of justice and revolution to our people."[12] MRTA violence was political theater, intended to cultivate the broad popular support that would sustain the group and swell its ranks in preparation for the overthrow of the capitalist state and its neocolonial U.S. allies. (The naming of the MRTA after indigenous rebel hero Túpac Amaru II symbolically aligned the group with the anticolonial dimension of Peruvian nationalism.)

The MRTA selected its targets to appeal to urban leftists and their anti-imperialist class solidarity. For example, on January 26, 1991, as the United States embarked on its Persian Gulf war against Iraq, the MRTA rocketed the facade of the U.S. Embassy in Lima, leaving behind leaflets that proclaimed, "Gringos out of the Middle East and Peru!!!" The leaflets previewed the MRTA's campaign against American business targets and symbols of U.S. oppression, in solidarity with "the Iraqi people" and all "peoples of the third world."[13] The MRTA carried out other symbolic attacks during this period, dynamiting a public statue of former U.S. president John F. Kennedy (described by the MRTA's newspaper, *Cambio*, as "the smiling face of imperialism for Latin America") and destroying several U.S.-operated Binational Centers (BNCs) for education.[14] Statistics from the Global Terrorism Database show that among the MRTA's 563 recorded attacks, attacks on businesses are the modal category, accounting for 223 (40 percent). Attacks on government facilities are the next most common category (17 percent), followed by attacks on military and police forces (12 percent) and on private citizens (9 percent).[15] The MRTA frequently attacked businesses representing *yanqui* capitalism. Citibank was a favorite target, as were American chain restaurants. The MRTA carried out at least six attacks on Kentucky Fried Chicken restaurants—on March 20, 1985 (when three restaurants were attacked simultaneously); June 5, 1990; February 2, 1991; and February 16, 1991.[16] An urban armed propaganda campaign against economic targets, by a group with no territorial stronghold, tends to incentivize warnings and additional hoaxes for disruptive purposes.

In its relationship with local civilians and its overall political strategy, the Shining Path was essentially the reverse of the MRTA. First, the group was based in Peru's rural hinterlands, where it could control territory and dominate civilians rather than relying on their voluntary provision of support. Abimael Guzmán's followers sought to reorganize the peasant masses "from the bottom up," creating "a secure foundation among elements of Peru's rural population."[17] Their approach was not to ask or encourage communities to offer support but to rely on *caudillismo*, "the tradition of political bosses."[18] When rural civilians resisted the social transformation, the Maoists disciplined them with extreme violence. For example, in April 1983, when peasants refused the Shining Path's attempts to reorganize the town of Lucanamarca, its cadres massacred sixty-nine of them.[19] In other cases, the group used the state to do its dirty work. In areas they did not yet control, the guerrillas would strike government targets and melt back into the villages and towns, where state forces could not distinguish civilians from combatants.[20] The Shining Path would thus "induce genocide" against *campesinos*, who would have little choice but to support its revolution.[21]

The Shining Path's targeting strategy was different from the MRTA's, emphasizing bloody destabilization of the state rather than armed propaganda and economic attrition. Of 4,597 Shining Path attacks listed in the Global Terrorism Database, just 752 (16 percent) targeted businesses. The modal category was attacks on police and military forces (23 percent), followed by attacks on private citizens (19 percent) and on government targets (18 percent).[22] As noted previously, Abimael Guzmán's goal in the countryside was to reorganize society based on a new Maoist model. The security forces and governing institutions of the state would be swept away, and civilians would be forced to conform to Guzmán's vision for society. When the Shining Path brought its campaign from Ayacucho to Lima, it implemented the same strategy, using extreme violence to shock, intimidate, and provoke. Maoist cadres commenced a new effort to "lead the masses to resistance" with the "armed strike"—essentially a work stoppage enforced by threats of retaliation against any who dared to show up for work. At roughly the same time, the Shining Path began a wave of car bombings in Lima.[23] Guzmán regarded Lima as "a drum" to be beaten, an instrument that could amplify the Shining Path's message, making the group seem stronger and more threatening.[24] By striking Lima hard enough, "Presidente Gonzalo" hoped to collapse the national government and step into the power vacuum as the new leader of Peru. This sort of strategy, destabilizing the state through extreme violence, does not incentivize warnings or hoaxes.

Because its approach was to cultivate Lima, not to beat it, the MRTA gave warnings of certain attacks, particularly those targeting commercial facilities. Any casualties in these incidents would have run counter to the MRTA's message, alienating the very people the group sought to recruit. According to Miguel Rincón, the MRTA planned each of its attacks "to ensure that the blow only affected those it ought to affect."[25] In his own interview with the CVR, MRTA leader Víctor Polay recalls how his group chose discriminate tactics to differentiate itself from the extreme violence of the Shining Path and the "corporate and fascist" conduct of the government.[26] The MRTA made sure to emphasize the discrimination of its attacks when claiming responsibility for them. For example, a story in *Cambio*, the MRTA newspaper, reports an attack on a Lima Kentucky Fried Chicken franchise on February 2, 1991 (an attack that left "Kentucky in Ruins"):

> Four people arrived at the premises, three men and a woman, posing as customers. One of them placed a travel bag under a dining table, while the woman warned the dozen attendees to leave the premises, which "would be blown up in a few moments." With that said, the visitors and staff moved to safety, away from the premises, as the rebels took the moment to escape. . . . Four minutes later a tremendous explosion brought down the premises' cement structures, destroying tables, cabinets, and all furniture in the restaurant, without causing deaths.[27]

The U.S. State Department reported a similar attack on February 16, 1991, destroying a Kentucky Fried Chicken restaurant and a Pizza Hut franchise housed in the same building:

> Up to 13 well-dressed MRTA members simultaneously entered both restaurants and immediately disarmed the restaurant guards. Some of the terrorists then guarded the exits while others robbed the patrons

and cash registers. Still others placed explosive devices on the floors of both restaurants. After the explosives were in place, the terrorists ordered everyone to leave the premises.[28]

The MRTA's bombs destroyed both restaurants without causing injuries. Other attacks on *yanqui* restaurants, banks, and Binational Centers followed a similar pattern.[29] Considering all the MRTA's bomb attacks on civilian targets during the conflict, the group gave warnings for approximately 6 percent; the Shining Path gave warnings for just 0.5 percent of such attacks.[30]

In fact, the Shining Path attacked without warning even when civilians were quite likely to be harmed. The group's surprise car bombings of civilian targets in Lima offer a bloody contrast to the MRTA's commercial bombings in the same city. On June 5, 1992, Shining Path cells exploded five bombs simultaneously, including a 1,200-pound truck bomb outside the Canal 2 television station, killing 5 people, wounding 20, and knocking the station offline in midbroadcast. On July 16 of the same year, cadres detonated a 1,000-pound car bomb on Tarata Street in the affluent Miraflores neighborhood, killing 25 people and wounding 155. On September 6 Maoists detonated a 700-pound car bomb at a gas station, killing 7 and wounding 10.[31] These car bombs are just a small sample of the Shining Path's atrocities. They are, however, some of the most spectacular incidents of bloodshed. They fit Abimael Guzmán's strategy of using Lima as "a drum" and a "sound box" to amplify his message and undermine popular support for the Peruvian regime.[32] They also fit the Shining Path's pattern of victimizing civilians to advance their own supposed liberation. In the words of one patriotic song taught to Maoist recruits, "Blood does not drown the revolution, but irrigates it."[33]

My argument also leads us to expect more hoaxes from the MRTA than from the Shining Path. The data on hoaxes are generally sparser than data on physical attacks, which produce damage and casualties and thereby make their way into news reporting and terrorism event databases. The available data, however, show at least one high-profile hoax by the MRTA and none by the group's peer competitor.[34] The best-documented MRTA hoax occurred on February 2, 1991—the same day as the MRTA bomb attack on a Kentucky Fried Chicken restaurant described earlier, and an attack on the U.S. ambassador's residence in Lima.[35] These incidents were part of an MRTA offensive against American businesses and diplomatic targets in retaliation for the U.S. invasion of Iraq the previous month.[36] Contemporaneously with the MRTA's physical attacks, a "false bomb threat by subversives . . . forced an American Airlines flight from Asunción to make an emergency landing at an air force base at Pisco, 240 km south of Lima"; Peru's public radio service attributed the threat to the MRTA.[37] News reports describe at least three other hoax threats against Peruvian civil aviation during the country's civil war: a general threat on the weekend of July 27–28, 1985; a threat against an outbound KLM flight on December 30, 1988; and a threat against Lima's Jorge Chávez airport on May 29, 1991.[38] None of the three incidents was claimed, either by the MRTA or by the Shining Path. It is possible that all three were the work of pranksters. However, the sparse evidence available in this case supports the prediction of more hoaxes from the MRTA than from its Maoist rival.

Pledges for Social Control

My argument predicts that groups attempting social control will pledge attacks on civilians who frequent proscribed places, associate with forbidden institutions, or engage in antisocial behaviors. These threats are useful in shaping the long-term political dynamics of conflicts. They occur before the moment of the attack and can be made contingent on the behavior of the recipient. If civilians do not comply with the terrorist group's demands, the fulfillment of the threat adds to the militant group's reputation for capability and resolve. Future threats will carry more coercive weight and may be successful in producing the behavioral compliance the terrorist group seeks.

The MRTA and the Shining Path both sought social control, albeit of very different scope. The MRTA sought to purge foreign influences from Peru's culture and economy. Its grievances were with U.S. diplomatic, business, and cultural projects in Peru, so we should expect threats only against civilians supporting those projects. The Shining Path sought a complete reorganization of Peruvian society. All existing institutions would be effaced and replaced with Maoist party structures.[39] Given the scope of the Shining Path's ambitions, my argument leads us to expect threats against many civilians—potentially anyone clinging to the existing social order.

Consistent with its limited social control aims, the MRTA issued threats against civilians who collaborated with American government agents, U.S.-owned businesses, and U.S.-based social organizations. The January 26,

1991, rocket attack on the U.S. Embassy in Lima was accompanied by leaflets demanding a U.S. exit from Peru.[40] Attacks against U.S. restaurants, banks, and other businesses were claimed triumphantly in *Cambio*, which promised still more attacks on American-owned targets.[41] Even U.S.-based religious organizations came under threat. An attack on a Latter Day Saints (LDS) church in Tarapoto on December 29, 1989, was followed by a pledge of violence giving "Mormons and DEA agents" thirty days to leave San Martín department "or face the consequences."[42] The MRTA claimed subsequent attacks on LDS churches with graffiti reading "Yankees go home" and "Yankees out." One of the threatening messages gave North American missionaries fifteen days to leave the country.[43] In keeping with the MRTA's ethos, the fulfillment of these threats was generally nonlethal: MRTA guerrillas tended to return to the LDS churches and bomb them at night—or give warnings if attacking the churches during the day. Between Christmas Day 1989 and May 2, 1991, the MRTA carried out at least twenty-six attacks of this kind.[44]

The Shining Path's regime of terror was more extensive, particularly in rural villages the group sought to collectivize. Initially, villagers welcomed some of these interventions. A resident of a small town in the Upper Huallaga Valley recalls the Maoists' first actions: "They helped us get rid of the homosexuals, prostitutes, and criminals that used to gather around here. They told them to leave; those that didn't showed up dead in the road. No town official was about to intervene."[45]

Once Shining Path cadres gained control of an area, they collected taxes from cocaine cartels and tolls from road travelers. Guerrillas established checkpoints, verified travelers' identification documents, and issued permissions to remain within rebel-held areas for specific lengths of time, under close surveillance.[46] Shining Path recruiters also demanded a "quota" of child soldiers from each village, "threatening or assassinating those who opposed them."[47] Adults who spoke out against the party were threatened, mutilated, or killed. A traumatized villager recalls: "They threatened to kill me. They hit me and kicked me like an animal. Afterwards they told me never to speak out against the party again. . . . They shot my friend. They doused him with gasoline and set him on fire. Another person turned up with no eyes, no tongue, no fingernails."[48]

The Shining Path used selective terror and indoctrination to produce popular compliance.[49] If a village resisted, the group's retaliation was absolute. In an interview with the CVR, Abimael Guzmán explained the logic of the 1983 Lucanamarca massacre: "to strike a massive blow and reprimand [the peasants], making them understand that they were dealing with another kind of people's combatants, that they were not dealing with the kind of combatants that operated earlier . . . we were willing to do anything to gain everything."[50] The CVR report describes the cumulative result of the "psycho-social tactics" of the Shining Path (Partido Comunista del Perú-Sendero Luminoso, PSP-SL) in the Huánuco region by the end of the conflict: "The local people had been reduced to servitude by members of the PCP-SL, who kept them isolated, threatened them and held them under ideological control. Anyone who tried to flee was shot by armed PCP-SL militants stationed at piers and near the mouths of rivers, the only routes out of the areas."[51]

The Shining Path announced its arrival in Peruvian cities by hanging dead dogs from light posts overnight.[52] Some of the animals bore signs reading "Deng Xiaoping, Son of a Bitch"—a reminder that Abimael Guzmán's followers were a breed apart from China's self-moderating Maoists and Peru's center-seeking urban leftists.[53] They would not shy away from using violence to advance Guzmán's agenda of social control. The Shining Path soon embarked on a campaign of threats and assassination to gain control of labor groups and other community institutions.[54] The group's cadres escalated their campaign with armed strikes (*paros armados*) to demonstrate that the rebels, not the government, controlled the population.[55] Guerrillas "laid the groundwork by sabotaging buses to intimidate public transportation workers."[56] They threatened the workers with violence if they returned to their usual jobs and murdered any violators in exemplary fashion—strapping drivers into their vehicles and setting them alight.[57] The widespread use of coercive pledges by the Shining Path and their comparatively limited use by the MRTA confirm my theoretical predictions.

Pledges for Negotiation

My theoretical framework also predicts that groups seeking to negotiate concrete political issues will pledge violence against the government. These pledges will be associated with specific demands or with a general demand that the government negotiate with the terrorist group.[58] Pledges in the preattack moment foreshadow what the terrorist group will do if the government rejects its demands. If the terrorist group fulfills its threats, its future pledges will carry greater coercive weight. Enough repetitions of the pledge/attack cycle may bring the government to the bargaining table and force it to give up concessions.

Of the two Peruvian groups, only the MRTA was interested in negotiations. The MRTA expressed openness to working with APRA, other leftist parties, and even reformist elements of the Catholic Church. The apparent contradiction of a Leninist group advocating such compromises was conveniently papered over by leaving the MRTA's publicly stated ideology "deliberately ill-defined," beyond broad pronouncements in favor of social justice, socialism, and opposition to U.S. influence.[59] As a concrete gesture of its willingness to negotiate, the MRTA declared a unilateral ceasefire following the ascension in 1985 of an APRA president, Alan García.[60] In announcing the ceasefire, MRTA leader Víctor Polay acknowledged that Peruvians "had overwhelmingly placed their hopes in the APRA Party," and the MRTA, as a popular organization, would offer to engage in political dialogue toward the "release of all political prisoners," the "formation of a Peace Commission and establishment of [a] minimum level of justice."[61]

In keeping with my argument's theoretical predictions, we see a pattern of threats accompanying the MRTA's peace overtures. The group's declaration of a ceasefire made several specific demands on the new García government, including the prosecution and punishment of Peru's former military government for its role in political violence and corruption. Asked by reporters what the MRTA would do if the García government did not administer justice against the former regime, MRTA representatives replied: "If the government does not comply with us we will apply popular justice and in due course it will be carried out." They also noted that their organization had set off a car bomb outside of the Ministry of the Interior immediately prior to the ceasefire to underline the threat accompanying their demands: "This attack is made in moments prior to the transmission of the [ceasefire] command: We say clearly, this is a warning. We have put a car bomb to show that we are capable of hitting the heart of the enemy and demand that the APRA government punish those guilty of violations; punish those guilty of disappearances, of torture; and, of course, of immorality."[62]

The MRTA reiterated these threats in subsequent public statements. A month into the ceasefire, a new communiqué reminded President García:

"Violence is the inalienable right of the victim; it is the penalty to the unpunished aggressor; it is the guarantee of victory over the decrepit and murderous system. WITHOUT JUSTICE THERE WILL BE NO PEACE!"[63] A statement several months later added: "If the Aprista government of Alan García does not take the necessary steps that lead to change . . . the people will rebel and take away their support, the MRTA will be at the head of this our people, defending our rights and conquering our aspirations with weapons in hand."[64]

The MRTA continued to berate the García administration with communiqués, but the president ignored them. Sensing the futility of their diplomacy, the MRTA's leaders reopened the armed campaign in June 1986.[65] Yet the group's leaders kept some options open: in later years they reached out to the International Committee of the Red Cross (ICRC) in an effort to broker prisoner exchanges with the Peruvian state.[66]

While the MRTA pursued its strategy of armed diplomacy, the Shining Path dedicated its full energies to making war. Guzmán's Manichean ideology ("Gonzalo Thought") called for the destruction of the Peruvian state—not negotiation with it. Guzmán explained his views in an interview in 1988: "In diplomatic meetings the only things signed at the table are those gained in battle, because no one hands over what has not already been lost, which is obviously understood. . . . Dialogue is only aimed at stopping, undermining the people's war, nothing more."[67]

It followed that the only acceptable solution was the "complete, total and absolute surrender" of the government. All elements of Peruvian society would be subjugated. A party document distributed to Shining Path cadres in 1980 recommended death for "class enemies" who stood in the way of the Maoists' campaign of purification. The document spoke of "putting a noose around the neck of imperialism and reactionary forces; they will be grabbed by the throat, choked and, when necessary, strangled. The flesh of the reactionaries will wither and be shredded, and the black scraps will be submerged in the mud, what remains will be burned."[68]

Guzmán changed his tune dramatically after his capture in 1992. From a maximum security prison cell, the Shining Path leader proposed a ceasefire to spare Peruvians the horrors of continued war. Guzmán's about-face, possibly under coercion by his government captors, handed the state a propaganda victory.[69] Most of the Shining Path's forces were demoralized by Guzmán's words, assuming that the war was over and abandoning their struggle. A smaller group of committed radicals acted as if Guzmán had never changed his line at all. The hard core redoubled its emphasis on "Gonzalo Thought" and the need to overthrow Peru's government, rather than rewarding the government with negotiations: "The people have assumed more highly the task of Conquering Power throughout the country and the people's war developed at a higher level defending the life of Chairman Gonzalo and preparing the strategic counteroffensive to which we will necessarily come with the implementation of the [plenary session] VI military plan."[70]

As for Guzmán's own peace overtures from behind bars, they were entirely toothless, full of requests to the Peruvian government but devoid of threats that would typically back up a militant group's demands.[71] This is not surprising, as Guzmán, incarcerated and cut off from his own organization, was in no position to threaten the government. An interesting finding emerges: for their own reasons, the two factions of the Shining Path, Guzmán's defeatists and the hard-core fighters, adhered to a consistent strategy of not threatening the government. This strategy was quite different from that of the MRTA, which always took a more moderate public stance, making specific demands on the state and issuing threats to back them up. The behavior of both groups is consistent with my argument about negotiation as an incentive to issue coercive pledges.

Self-Aggrandizing Threats

My argument predicts that terrorist groups with reputational concerns—weaker groups competing with more capable ones, and organizations facing strategic reverses or declines—will issue pledges and bluffs to aggrandize themselves. Recalling my theory of threats, pledges and bluffs occur in the preattack moment. By threatening an attack in advance, a terrorist group calls attention to the action and makes its success more impressive. This is a useful strategy for militarily weaker groups looking to amplify the political effects of their actions so that they can keep up with stronger rivals, whose actions may be more numerous and more impressive individually. Bluffs may also add to the terrorist group's reputation, as long as the government does not expose their insincerity. For example, an empty threat against universities will increase the terrorist group's reputation if the schools acquiesce by closing. Observers will not know that the threat was empty, but they will see that it was effective. A bluffing strategy may be useful for an up-and-coming organization or a declining group that cannot carry out as many attacks as it used to. Occasional bluffing can keep the group's name in the headlines and maintain the appearance of potency for some time.

The Shining Path rarely needed to aggrandize itself. The group's steady accretion of physical attacks—more than 4,500 by the end of the conflict—overwhelmed the Peruvian government and the rival MRTA, which committed a comparatively modest 563 attacks during the war.[72] By 1990 Guzmán's Maoists could "control or contest for control over a significant slice of rural Peru."[73] They accomplished all this with little bravado. The Shining Path's strategy documents describe a "clear and defined orientation: that the actions speak."[74] Indeed, the group's pace of action was so furious, and its reputation so fearsome, that it rarely felt the need to claim its own attacks.[75] When the Shining Path did release communiqués, they consisted of ideological propaganda: invitations to rebellion,[76] Marxist analyses of Peruvian society and politics,[77] statements commemorating Mao Zedong and fallen guerrillas,[78] speeches by Guzmán,[79] and party-line documents conveying the Central Committee's instructions to cadres.[80] Self-aggrandizing boasts are absent because the Shining Path's physical potency made them unnecessary.

The MRTA's weaker position gave it greater incentives to pledge attacks or bluff to increase its stature. In general, the MRTA implemented a publicity-driven revolutionary model, in which high-profile armed propaganda would draw sympathetic Peruvians to the group's cause. This approach allowed the MRTA to grab headlines, but it fell short of building actual military strength or deeper links to communities that might otherwise have supported the group. As a result, the MRTA lacked the Shining Path's characteristics of growth and resilience. It also lacked political influence. Even as it experienced some publicity successes associated with individual operations, the MRTA developed a pathology noted by the Peruvian Truth and Reconciliation Commission: "a fluctuation between successes and failures, the inability to achieve sustained growth in any area of the country or sector, an image of an armed group supported mainly by volunteers and the risks and confidences placed in media coverage of its actions as a way of accumulating political strength."[81]

Consistent with my theoretical expectations, the MRTA issued quite a few self-aggrandizing threats. The group's early communiqués foreshadow its intentions in general: "We are expanding the guerrilla [war] and armed propaganda! . . . With the masses and weapons, we will triumph!"[82] Later communiqués are more specific, trumpeting the MRTA's alleged development of rural guerrilla elements that would soon commence their revolutionary action. (At the time, the MRTA had barely any military capability in the countryside.) A May Day 1985 communiqué boasted that the MRTA's urban and rural guerrillas "will act in a combined and simultaneous way, under the same political and military direction. Guerrilla warfare will generate in its own movement the creation of a powerful popular army capable of disputing the power of the enemy at the political, military, territorial or geographical level."[83] The purported rural insurgency was slow to develop, although the MRTA did discover that by moving forces to distant rural areas, it could take and briefly hold undefended or lightly defended towns. These victories gave the group credibility to issue more threats and, by projecting potency, to enlarge its support base. A good example is the triumphant New Year's communiqué that followed the MRTA's brief takeover of several towns in the department of San Martín in late 1987. After trumpeting the MRTA's successes in "the Northeastern Front," the press release boasted that the government "will not be able to prevent us from concentrating our forces for larger blows."[84] Other self-aggrandizing MRTA threats appeared in February 1991 in the pages of *Cambio*, the MRTA's newspaper. Stories boasted of MRTA successes in carrying out attacks and its plans to carry out more attacks, despite Peruvian security forces' flailing efforts to beef up security.[85]

The MRTA's bluster and the Shining Path's "actions speak" strategy are what my theory would predict, respectively, from a group with military deficits and a group with no need to worry about its formidable fighting reputation. My argument, however, also leads us to expect bluffs from groups that suffer strategic reverses and declines. We do observe some bluffs from the Shining Path, precisely as the group began to suffer defeats in the rural strongholds that had constituted its power base in the countryside. Peasants alienated by the Shining Path's brutality expelled the group's cadres from many areas. The Peruvian government accelerated the process by arming peasant militias, the *rondas campesinas*, which protected villages from reinfiltration by Maoists. Sensing the shift of momentum away from the Shining Path in the countryside, Guzmán made a strategic gamble. He turned his forces' attention to the cities, where economic and political decay had left the state vulnerable to destabilization. Guzmán's hope was to create a crisis, provoke a U.S. military intervention, and make the Shining Path's war a "war of national salvation."[86]

This campaign would be based on a deliberate misrepresentation of the Shining Path's capabilities, which no longer posed a genuine threat to the state. Nonetheless, Guzmán announced that his insurgents had achieved "strategic equilibrium" with the state and could now lay the groundwork for a conventional "war of movements" against Peruvian army formations. Victory, Guzmán claimed, was "just around the corner." Captured Shining Path cadres later described their leader as "fighting a Nintendo war." His public statements referenced "battalions," but each consisted of a handful of cadres and forty *campesinos* recruited, willingly or not, to swell the ranks.[87] What the rebels lacked in actual capability, Guzmán sought to make up by bluster. Perhaps the tough talk could induce a new wave of state repression, catapulting the Shining Path back to political relevance. For a declining organization, it was not a bad gamble to take. It simply failed.

Low Incentives for Advantage-Seeking Threats

My argument predicts that militant groups fighting highly competent security forces will seek to gain the tactical and strategic initiative using prophylactic threats. This part of my argument is difficult to test on these cases because the MRTA and the Shining Path fought the same government at the same time. It is not possible to draw contrasts between these groups in a way that would predict different behavior, at least on a tactical level. It is clear that neither group had strong incentives for tactical advantage seeking, though. Peruvian security forces were not competent to the same degree as the British and Spanish security forces discussed in the earlier case studies of the IRA and ETA. The Peruvian Truth and Reconciliation Commission describes the government of Peru as "not prepared to deal with . . . armed subversion."[88] The poor preparation of security forces was particularly apparent at the tactical level. In one notorious example, police and intelligence agents failed to detect a brazen MRTA operation to free captured leaders Víctor Polay, Alberto Gálvez, and Miguel Rincón:

> Police efforts under the Aprista government . . . were overshadowed by the jailbreak on July 9, 1990, by 47 MRTA inmates—including Polay, Gálvez and Rincón—through a tunnel built into the Miguel

Castro prison. The MRTA escape exposed the precariousness of the country's maximum security prison and the limitations of the intelligence services, which had not detected a 300-meter tunnel that had been dug over several months.[89]

With police and intelligence services unable to deal with the worsening security environment, the government delegated substantial authority to the Peruvian Army. A dynamic of competition and dysfunction emerged between police and army formations that did not communicate with one another, or worse, undermined one another's countersubversive efforts.[90] The decision to lean on the army also encouraged heavy-handed tactics and indiscriminate violence against civilians. The CVR report explains:

> The police forces' initial efforts did not have time to mature or produce results before authorities decided to put the armed forces in charge of the anti-subversive fight. The immediate result of this decision, which was adopted without a comprehensive strategy for dealing with subversion on different fronts—ideologically, politically, economically and militarily—was the abdication of civilian authority in a broad swath of territory that was placed under a state of emergency, creating a drastic worsening of the violence that increased the number of casualties to levels unparalleled during the remainder of the internal armed conflict.[91]

These atrocities played directly into the rebels' hands, reinforcing their propaganda narratives about state oppression. In such a disorganized security environment, we do not expect a high frequency of tactical prophylactic threats from the militants. Nor do we observe a high frequency. In my review of secondary and primary sources, I am unable to find a single example of the MRTA or the Shining Path using threats to achieve tactical advantage. I find one confirmed hoax (by the MRTA, disrupting air travel) and a number of casualty-reducing warnings by the MRTA, but nothing resembling the come-ons, misdirection, or intelligence-gathering hoaxes observed from the IRA and ETA. The paucity of tactical prophylactic threats, in an environment of generally poor state capabilities, is consistent with my argument.

There is, however, some evidence of strategic advantage seeking by the Shining Path as the group entered its death spiral in the late 1980s.

Abimael Guzmán's "Nintendo war" can be interpreted both as aggrandizement and as an advantage-seeking strategic bluff. By announcing the Shining Path's supposed final push on Lima, Guzmán sought to induce a Peruvian government overreaction and a U.S. military invasion that would make the Maoist insurgency a "war of national salvation." The U.S. invasion never came, but the provocative bluffing continued more insistently after Guzmán's capture in 1992 (by a unit of Peruvian police detectives who refused to let the military handle counterterrorism). A 1993 communiqué by hard-core Shining Path loyalists proclaimed: "We are building the conquest of power. Why has this become more urgent? We have passed the four key moments in the leap from guerrilla warfare to the war of movements and this demonstrates how the process is unfolding."[92]

These words seem absurd, particularly after Guzmán's capture, but they make sense in light of the Shining Path's weakened position. The group's remaining cadres likely realized that their only chance of victory was to provoke the government with threats. This use of threats, by a besieged organization seeking to derail the government's counterterrorism policy, is consistent with my theoretical expectations.

The MRTA and the Shining Path present a unique opportunity to test my argument about terrorist threats. These groups were Marxist peer competitors, fighting to overthrow the same government at the same time. With few confounding variables, it is possible to focus on the subtler political factors that incentivize different uses of threats. Because the MRTA lacked a territorial stronghold and fought in Peru's cities, it had a greater need to seek legitimacy among urban civilians. The group also placed a heavy emphasis on economic disruption. My argument correctly predicts a higher incidence of warnings and hoaxes by the MRTA compared to the Shining Path.

This chapter's analysis of pledges and bluffs highlights two important possibilities: a group can have incentives to threaten civilians without threatening the state or incentives to threaten the state without threatening civilians. The Shining Path demonstrates the first possibility. This group sought to reorganize every aspect of Peruvians' lives, imposing a rigid political, social, and economic structure based on a neighborhood committee model. The MRTA sought a narrower goal of purging *yanqui* and capitalist influences from Peruvian society. My argument correctly predicts a more extensive use of pledges by the Shining Path to control civilians' behavior.

The incentives were reversed, however, when it came to threats against the Peruvian state. The MRTA sought to force the government into negotiations. It also sought to raise its own public profile among Peruvians more accustomed to hearing of the Shining Path's violent exploits. The Maoist rebels' incentives to threaten the state were low: Abimael Guzmán publicly rejected negotiation and announced his preference for action over words. As expected, we see more extensive pledges and bluffs from the MRTA against the state, particularly in its early years as it sought to negotiate with the APRA government.

One mark of a good theory is the ability to predict change within a case when the relevant independent variables change. The Peruvian cases show my theoretical framework's potential to predict change. In the late 1980s, as the Shining Path suffered losses in its rural insurgency, the group's incentive structure shifted. Now the group had reasons to bluff: both to draw attention away from its losses and to provoke the government into excessive counterterrorism interventions that would drive the population to the rebels' side. The Shining Path's announcement of an impending "conquest of power" seems bizarre and irrational to us now, but it can be explained by a theory that appreciates the strategic use of bluffing when terrorists are off balance, struggling to appear resilient, and aware that their best hope is to induce blunders by their state opponents.

CHAPTER V

The Taliban, ISIL, and Boko Haram

Comparable Threats for Social Control; Contrasting Threats for Legitimacy, Negotiation, Aggrandizement, and Advantage

In this chapter I examine the use of threats by a trio of jihadist groups: the Afghan Taliban, the Islamic State of Iraq and the Levant (ISIL), and Boko Haram. By analyzing jihadists, I am able to test my argument's application to terrorist organizations with very different ideological foundations from those I discussed earlier. This is an important consideration in assessing the generalizability of my theoretical framework. My argument would not generalize if the political variables that induce particular patterns of behavior in secular groups do not exert the same effects in religious groups—or if their effects are overridden by countervailing factors specific to a religious context.

Previous terrorism scholarship gives us reason to expect different behavior from religious and secular groups, particularly regarding the issue of civilian victimization. Religion may narrow militants' political constituencies to coreligionists alone.[1] This may mitigate the multiple audiences conundrum by shrinking the size of the civilian audience the militant group has to appease. Alternatively, religion may shrink the audience to include only the Supreme Being, sanctifying any behavior God supposedly condones.[2] The strong sacred/profane dichotomy may discourage negotiation with the secular state, attenuate the political relevance of democracy, or intensify the militant group's drive to control the minute details of private life. In fact, religion may enable the most brutal varieties of social control.[3] A framework for understanding terrorist threats must pass the test of application to religious groups, or we must qualify it as applying differently to secular and religious terrorist organizations.

My analysis of Boko Haram, the Afghan Taliban, and ISIL shows that my argument travels well to religious cases. There are certain distinctive aspects of religious groups' threats, however. One fact that emerges from my analysis is that social control and casualty reduction often overlap. A threat to kill Sunni Muslims who vote in an upcoming election functions as a deterrent to voting. It also functions as a helpful alert to those who might otherwise be harmed in the attack. Such a threat falls on the temporal line between prospective pledges and immediate warnings. The terrorist group issues the threat sometime before the attack, but it gives a specific date on which the attack will occur, enabling civilians to avoid harm by staying away from the polls.

One can see how a religious context incentivizes such threats. A doctrinal preoccupation with guilt and innocence may collide with the political incentive to threaten or kill civilians who side with apostates against the religious movement. A group that claims moral justification from religion faces a fundamental contradiction if it kills coreligionists—or if it kills noncombatants, children, or women defined by sacred doctrine as inherently innocent. Any of these contradictions intensifies the multiple audiences conundrum for a religious terrorist group. It becomes especially important to minimize civilian casualties—or at the very least shift the blame for civilian deaths onto the victims themselves. A group that issues threats in advance, stating which behaviors are forbidden by religion and punishable by death, gives itself room to "spin" civilian casualties after the fact: the victims were warned, but they chose to undertake the proscribed behavior anyway. They were not truly innocent, so the act of killing or injuring them is not technically a violation of normal religious prohibitions on targeting civilians. In fact, it may represent divine vengeance. This type of rhetoric is on full display among the jihadist groups I analyze. To develop these insights, I first provide a brief summary of each jihadist group, before moving to the cross-case comparisons that constitute the rest of the chapter.

The Taliban, 2002–2019

My first case study in this chapter is the Afghan Taliban. I focus on this group's insurgent period, from 2002 through the end of 2019, as this book goes to press. In fact, the Taliban have a much longer history, having fought in Afghanistan's civil wars of the 1990s and having served as Afghanistan's national government from 1996 to 2001.[4] My comparison of the Taliban to the other jihadist groups in this chapter is based on the group's current insurgency, so these earlier periods are outside of my scope. However, I provide some background on them here as useful historical context.

The Taliban are a religious movement based in the Pashtun ethnic communities of Afghanistan. They espouse a deeply conservative Deobandi worldview, mixing fundamentalist Islam with Persian cultural elements.[5] The word *taliban* means "students," but the organization is best known for the fighting skills it honed in Afghanistan's long-running internal conflicts. The Taliban's future leaders began as *mujahideen* in the 1980s, fighting to overthrow the pro-Soviet government of the Democratic Republic of Afghanistan.[6] The Soviet defeat and the collapse of the Afghan Republic in 1992 left a power vacuum in Afghan politics.[7] Pashtuns were frustrated by the country's descent into banditry and instability, and many were willing to support a group that promised a return to order under Islamic *sharia* law. Founded in 1994 by a one-eyed ex-*mujahid*, Mullah Mohammed Omar, the Taliban grew from a small group of a few dozen fighters to a formidable militia that managed to overrun the Afghan capital, Kabul, by 1996.[8] By 1998 they had conquered the rest of the country, except for a northern sliver that remained in the hands of opposition rebels belonging to the Tajik, Uzbek, and Hazara ethnic minorities.[9]

The Taliban governed Afghanistan from 1996 to 2001. They banned women and girls from education and work, suppressed most forms of art and entertainment, persecuted minority Shia Muslims, and enacted harsh corporal punishments such as mutilation and public execution for offenses such as theft and adultery.[10] The Taliban also gave safe harbor to Osama Bin Laden's al-Qa'ida organization, which used its Afghan base to launch attacks on U.S. embassies in Kenya and Tanzania in 1998 and on the U.S. mainland on September 11, 2001. The Taliban's leader, Mullah Omar, rejected U.S. demands to deliver Bin Laden to U.S. custody.[11] U.S. and NATO troops, working with the Taliban's remaining enemies in northern Afghanistan, drove the Taliban from power in late 2001.[12]

Although the Taliban lost tens of thousands of troops in the NATO offensive, the organization's leaders found shelter across the border in Pakistan.[13] There they regrouped to mount an insurgency against the Western-backed Afghan government—a corrupt regime with questionable human rights practices and a divisive policy of suppressing the opium trade, one of the few sources of wealth for poor Afghan farmers. As the Taliban have chipped away at the government's control of rural areas, they have revived the local drug economy as a source of revenue.[14] They promote themselves as an indigenous Islamic resistance, in the tradition of past Afghan insurgencies against the Soviets and the British Empire.[15] They have also cultivated a softer image, seeking to distance themselves from past practices such as summary executions and massacres of civilians.[16] Through a combination of local politicking and asymmetric warfare, the Taliban have reconquered roughly 15 percent of Afghan political districts; they contest control of another 30 percent.[17] Forces loyal to ISIL have made small territorial gains as well (see the next section), and the two insurgent groups sometimes clash.[18] This development may be partly responsible for a thaw in relations between the Afghan government, the Taliban, and the U.S. government. The year 2018 brought hope of a negotiated settlement. The Taliban enacted an Eid-al-fitr ceasefire with Afghan forces and all parties endorsed the idea of peace talks, pending some agreement on the format.[19] The Taliban engaged in nearly a year of secret negotiations with the administration of U.S. president Donald Trump, but the September 2019 press revelation of these talks led President Trump to declare the peace process "dead."[20] The Taliban have made further public overtures for negotiations, however, and more peace talks are possible in the future.[21]

The Islamic State of Iraq and the Levant, 2013–2019

As this chapter's second case study, I consider the Islamic State of Iraq and the Levant. I focus specifically on the period from April 2013 through December 2019, but I provide a broader historical overview of ISIL and its precursor organizations for context. ISIL's origins lie in the invasion of Iraq by the United States and a handful of other Western nations in 2003. By removing Saddam Hussein's Baathist regime, the U.S.-led coalition provoked resentment among former members of the Iraqi government and army. They also unleashed Shia-Sunni sectarian grievances that culminated in widespread interethnic killing. Abu Musab al-Zarqawi, an al-Qa'ida militant who fled the 2001 invasion of Afghanistan, formed a small Sunni militant group, Jama'at al-Tawhid w'al-Jihad, and developed it into a fearsome fighting force.[22] Zarqawi's organization made a name for itself with attacks on coalition forces and the Iraqi government, as well as bloody suicide attacks on Shia civilians.[23] Zarqawi offered his allegiance to Osama Bin Laden in 2004, changing the name of his organization to al-Qa'ida in Iraq (AQI).[24]

AQI underwent several stages of evolution on its way to becoming ISIL. Under Zarqawi's personal command, the group mounted attacks on Shia, hoping to provoke retaliation against Sunnis and embroil the U.S.-backed government in a sectarian civil war.[25] However, the attacks on Shia displeased Bin Laden and his top lieutenant, Ayman al-Zawahiri, who preferred to focus on attacking U.S. interests to force an American exit and establish a new base for jihadist operations.[26] Zarqawi ignored this advice, stoking long-term tensions between AQI and the top leaders of "al-Qa'ida Central."[27] After Zarqawi's death in a U.S. airstrike in 2006, his successors rebranded their organization as the Islamic State of Iraq (ISI), hoping to blunt criticism of AQI as a foreign jihadist outfit imposing its political agenda on Iraqis. Sunni tribes frustrated with ISI's gory tactics nonetheless switched their allegiance to support the Iraqi government.[28] The Sunnis' shift coincided with the U.S. military's "surge" of troops in 2007–2008 to fight the jihadists and stabilize Iraq's regime.[29] Only the withdrawal of U.S. forces, in December 2011, rescued ISI from the brink of defeat.[30] The Iraqi government, easily criticized for its corruption, pro-Shia sectarianism, and failure to award promised military positions to Sunni tribesmen, struggled to maintain order. ISI recruited disgruntled Sunnis and former Baathist military officers, using its new strength to launch offensives and take portions of Iraqi territory in 2012 and 2013. ISI's leader, Abu Bakr al-Baghdadi, capitalized on the chaos of the Syrian Civil War by expanding his group's operations to that country.[31]

In April 2013, having conquered areas on both sides of the Iraqi-Syrian border, Baghdadi renamed his organization ad-Dawlah al-Islāmiyah fī 'l-'Irāq wa-sh-Shām, the Islamic State of Iraq and the Levant. Baghdadi declared a merger between his organization and Syrian jihadist groups, a move that led al-Qa'ida's leaders to disown ISIL in February 2014.[32] Nonetheless, ISIL forces overran more territory, conquering Iraqi cities such as Mosul and Fallujah and Syrian cities such as Raqa.[33] ISIL administered these cities as a de facto government.[34] In June 2014 Baghdadi declared the organization to be a global caliphate, shortening its name to the Islamic State and claiming jurisdiction over all Muslims worldwide.[35] (I continue to describe the group as "the Islamic State of Iraq and the Levant" to differentiate the core Islamic State organization from affiliate groups in other regions.)

ISIL globalized after achieving quasi-statehood. Jihadists in countries such as Libya, Nigeria, Yemen, Afghanistan, and Egypt pledged their allegiance to the group's caliphate. ISIL's new "provinces" expanded the organization's reach by carrying out attacks in its name.[36] ISIL dispatched clandestine cells and used mobile phone apps to direct "remotely controlled" attacks, primarily against civilian targets, in countries such as France, Germany, Belgium, Britain, and the United States.[37] Autonomous "lone jihadists" carried out attacks as well, claiming their actions in ISIL's name and citing the group's propaganda as inspiration for their actions.[38] Yet even as ISIL exported its name and its violence, the group suffered setbacks to its original state-building project in Iraq and Syria. The United States, Western European powers, and Russia began a campaign of airstrikes against ISIL ground positions in 2014. This coalition of countries provided assistance to militia groups and the local governments fighting the Islamic State in Iraq and Syria. Although the geopolitical interests of the anti-ISIL countries do not always align, their combined efforts helped the Syrian and Iraqi militaries roll back the caliphate's territorial holdings.[39] U.S.-backed militias announced the liberation of ISIL's last remaining stronghold in March 2019.[40] In October 2019 the United States announced the death of Abu Bakr al-Baghdadi and his most likely successor in a pair of U.S. raids in northern Syria.[41]

As this book goes to press in December 2019, ISIL's future is uncertain. The loss of Baghdadi and the destruction of the territorial caliphate are major setbacks, but the Islamic State has reemerged from apparent oblivion before. There was also good news for ISIL in October: a Turkish invasion of Kurdish-held areas in northern Syria allowed the group some respite from local militia pressure, and hundreds of suspected ISIL fighters broke out of formerly Kurdish-controlled prison facilities.[42] ISIL retains a portion of its former fighting strength, with the capability to carry out ambushes, kidnappings, roadside bombings, and other asymmetric attacks.[43] It seems likely that the group will revert to a posture of insurgency in Syria and Iraq, at least for the time being. If ISIL is able to persist there, it will promote "inspired" and "remote-controlled" attacks and claim credit for the activities of ISIL-affiliated jihadists in other conflict zones.[44]

Boko Haram, 2009–2019

Boko Haram is a Salafi jihadist militant group operating primarily in Nigeria. Like the Taliban and ISIL, Boko Haram seeks to implement a conservative interpretation of Islamic religious law, or *sharia*. The group originated in Borno State in the northeastern part of Nigeria in the mid-2000s. The organization's official name at its founding was Jama'atu Ahlis Sunna Lidda'awati w'al Jihad (People dedicated to the propagation of the Prophet's teaching and jihad). Westerners, however, typically know the group by the unofficial moniker Boko Haram, translated roughly as "Western education is forbidden" or "Deceitful education is forbidden."[45]

Boko Haram's founder, Muhammad Yusuf, combined charisma, political savvy, and a willingness to use violence to advance Salafi ideals. Yusuf also possessed multilingual speaking abilities that would benefit him and his nascent political movement as they navigated northeastern Nigeria's tribal landscape of Hausa- and Kanuri-speaking Muslims.[46] Salafism is relatively common in Nigeria, but many Salafis were content to advance their ideals via nonviolent means, working within with Nigerian federal institutions that granted official status to Islamic law in majority Muslim states.[47] To the chagrin of the moderate Salafis, Muhammad Yusuf adopted a more extreme position: democratic politics were by definition un-Islamic, and no Muslim could submit to majoritarian rule without placing human laws and judgment above God's. For Yusuf and Boko Haram, the Nigerian government's democratic system constituted an oppressive force that all faithful Muslims must resist.[48]

Boko Haram escalated from preaching to open violence in 2009. Government forces put down the group's poorly organized uprising, capturing and executing Muhammad Yusuf without trial.[49] The surviving elements of Boko Haram vowed revenge, promising to "make the country ungovernable, kill and eliminate irresponsible political leaders of all leanings, hunt and gun down those who oppose the rule of Sharia in Nigeria and ensure that the infidel does not go unpunished."[50] Boko Haram reemerged in 2010 with a series of prison breaks and drive-by assassinations of police and government officials in Borno.[51] The group expanded its operations with a wave of bombings targeting Christian churches in both the north and center of the country.[52] Boko Haram also extended its terror campaign to the capital city, Abuja, with suicide bombings of the National Police Force headquarters and the headquarters of the United Nations in Nigeria.[53] These incidents, more sophisticated than previous attacks, appear to have involved some collaboration, in the form of training, with al-Qa'ida in the Islamic Maghbreb (AQIM), the North African affiliate of the infamous transnational terrorist group. Indeed, the new leader of Boko Haram, Abubakar Shekau, made public statements linking Boko Haram's struggle with that of AQIM. Although Shekau made private inquiries about the possibility of a formal affiliation, al-Qa'ida's leaders turned him down.[54]

Boko Haram's treatment of civilians worsened as its insurgency progressed. In 2012 the group publicly demanded that Christians vacate northern Nigeria.[55] At the same time, Boko Haram asserted a scriptural right of *takfir*, the power to declare progovernment (or simply nonjihadist) Muslims as unbelievers and therefore as legitimate targets of violence.[56] Boko Haram also became increasingly tolerant of "collateral damage" as Muslims were caught up in the group's attacks on Christians and the state.[57] Yet the Nigerian government's inept and abusive treatment of civilians provided political cover for Boko Haram's atrocities, lending credence to the group's allegations of anti-Muslim bias by the government.[58] With a limited degree of popular support, Boko Haram was able to assert de facto territorial control over a protostate in Nigeria's Northeast, from 2014 to 2015.[59]

Nigerian forces and allied troops from neighboring Chad, Niger, and Cameroon recaptured Boko Haram's territory in 2015.[60] Abubakar Shekau attempted to change the public narrative from one of Boko Haram losses to one of international jihadist solidarity by proclaiming his allegiance to ISIL in March 2015. Although the union with ISIL made short-term political sense for Shekau, it brought few operational benefits.[61] In mid-2016 ISIL decided to recognize another commander, Abu Mus'ab al-Barnawi, as the official "governor" of the Islamic State's West African province.[62] Even by ISIL standards, Shekau was a divisive figure, showing a willingness to victimize Muslim civilians who had committed no particular crime.[63] By elevating Barnawi as the head of the Islamic State in West Africa (ISWA), ISIL distanced itself from Boko Haram's former excesses, but it also opened a rift among Nigerian jihadists.[64] Between three thousand and five thousand of Shekau's former troops acknowledged ISWA's authority, but Shekau himself refused, and a core group of fifteen hundred fighters remained loyal to him.[65] Shekau's Boko Haram faction retains the ability to attack civilian and military targets. The group carried out a spate of attacks in 2018 and 2019, including mass-casualty suicide bombings, village raids, and raids on Nigerian military outposts.[66] Meanwhile, Barnawi's ISWA faction focuses more on attacking military and police targets.[67] It also shows greater interest in state building, controlling small pockets of territory near Lake Chad, collecting taxes, offering rudimentary services, and showing marginally greater respect for civilians than Shekau's faction typically does.[68] This is the state of Boko Haram's two main factions as this book goes to press.

Comparing Incentives and Patterns of Threats

Tables 5.1 and 5.2 summarize the political incentives and patterns of threats exhibited by the three jihadist groups. These organizations show variation in legitimacy concerns and the incentive to warn, given Boko Haram's lesser degree of territorial control and the more liberal political system of its adversary state, Nigeria. The incentives for economically disruptive hoaxes are generally low for all three groups, given their focus on attacking security forces, civil society, and civilian targets. The incentives for tactical and strategic advantage–seeking threats are generally higher for Boko Haram and the Taliban, given their greater contact with police forces and ISIL's greater contact with military formations. (Battlefield encounters are outside the scope of my study.) The incentives for self-aggrandizing threats are more acute for Boko Haram and ISIL, which have sought to regain

TABLE 5.1
Group Characteristics: Taliban, ISIL, and Boko Haram

Incentive	Relative Values
Legitimacy seeking	Boko Haram > Taliban ≈ ISIL
Disruption	Boko Haram ≈ Taliban ≈ ISIL
Social control	Boko Haram ≈ Taliban ≈ ISIL
Negotiation	Boko Haram ≈ Taliban > ISIL
Aggrandizement	ISIL ≈ Boko Haram > Taliban
Advantage seeking	Boko Haram ≈ Taliban > ISIL

TABLE 5.2
Predictions: Taliban, ISIL, and Boko Haram

	Prediction	Observed
Warnings	Boko Haram > Taliban ≈ ISIL For legitimacy	Boko Haram > Taliban ≈ ISIL
Hoaxes	Boko Haram ≈ Taliban > ISIL For tactical advantage	Boko Haram ≈ Taliban > ISIL
Pledges	Boko Haram ≈ Taliban > ISIL For negotiation, strategic advantage Boko Haram ≈ Taliban ≈ ISIL For social control	Boko Haram ≈ Taliban > ISIL For negotiation, strategic advantage Boko Haram ≈ Taliban ≈ ISIL For social control
Bluffs	ISIL ≈ Boko Haram > Taliban For aggrandizement, strategic advantage	ISIL ≈ Boko Haram > Taliban

prominence after nearly being destroyed by state forces. In ISIL's current state of degradation, the group has issued increasingly baroque bluff threats against public events in European countries. ISIL's incentive to threaten governments is low, however, since the group has forsworn high-level negotiations with Western states. Boko Haram and the Taliban have at times called for negotiations, a posture that helps to explain their frequent public pledges of violence against their state opponents.

Finally, all three groups seek to control civilians by means of violence and threats. Their rhetoric often blurs the line between pledges and warnings. Somewhat general threats deter civilians from engaging in sinful activities, but they also warn civilians away from elections, schools, and other institutions that are likely to be attacked. Perhaps more important, jihadists' threats establish boundaries of guilt and innocence. Civilians killed in attacks on sinful institutions are to some extent to blame for their own deaths. The jihadists warned them of their crimes, yet they chose to transgress anyway. This reordering of the moral circumstances, placing the guilt on the victims, is vital to groups that would otherwise run afoul of normal Islamic prohibitions on killing noncombatants, women, and children.

Warnings and Hoaxes

My argument leads us to expect more warnings and hoaxes from Boko Haram than from the Taliban and ISIL. The first reason to expect more warnings from the Nigerian jihadists is the heightened legitimacy concern that arises for militants without territorial strongholds. Although Boko Haram briefly controlled an area the size of Belgium in 2014–2015, its dominion was fleeting.[69] For most of its history, the group has sheltered among state-governed civilian populations. In contrast, the Taliban and ISIL have exercised de facto sovereignty over large portions of Afghanistan, Iraq, and Syria, governing those areas as quasi-states for years at a time.[70] Without strongholds, Boko Haram is more accountable to civilians, while the Taliban and ISIL have had greater latitude to carry out no-warning attacks. (This may be changing for ISIL, now that the group has lost its territory.)

The second reason to expect more warnings from Boko Haram is the greater degree of democracy in Nigeria. We saw in the earlier IRA and ETA case studies how the state's example sets civilians' expectations for legitimate political behavior. Even an avowedly antidemocratic group may be forced to adopt warning tactics if its civilian constituents are accustomed to democracy and liberal notions of individual rights. Since Boko Haram's founding, the Nigerian government has earned positive scores on the Polity2 scale of democratic regime characteristics, which ranges from -10 to +10.[71] From 2009 through 2014, the Nigerian regime's Polity2 score was a 4 (open anocracy); since 2015, Nigeria's Polity2 score has been a 7 (democracy). In contrast, Afghanistan has alternated between nonfunctioning government and a mixed system with mostly authoritarian characteristics. The Polity2 data series gives no score at all to the Afghan government from 2002 to 2013 (indicating a lack of functioning state institutions to code). The data series assigns a Polity2 score of -1 (closed anocracy) from 2014 through 2018, the most recent year for which Polity2 data are available. ISIL's adversary regimes set questionable examples as well. Iraq had a Polity2 score of 3 (open anocracy) in 2013 and a score of 6 (democracy) from 2014 through 2018. But ISIL's caliphate spanned the Iraqi-Syrian border, bringing it in contact with the vastly more repressive Syrian regime of Bashar al-Assad. The Syrian government is among the world's most abusive, with a Polity2 score of -9 from 2013 through 2018.[72] ISIL's multiple audiences conundrum is less severe than Boko Haram's, and possibly less severe than the Taliban's, depending on which state adversary (Iraq or Syria) one uses as the basis for comparison.

My argument also predicts warnings and hoaxes from groups employing economic coercion strategies. Statistics generated from the Global Terrorism Database show that none of the three jihadist groups employed economic coercion as its primary strategy.[73] Of Boko Haram's 2,683 attacks through the end of 2018, the most recent year for which GTD data are available, just 132 (4.9 percent) targeted businesses.[74] The modal category of target was private citizens (1,451 attacks) followed by military targets (435 attacks). Only 308 (4.8 percent) of ISIL's 6,451 attacks targeted businesses.[75] The modal category of target was private citizens (2,975 attacks), followed by military targets (1,820 attacks).[76] Of the Taliban's 8,789 attacks, 292 (3.3 percent) targeted businesses.[77] The modal category of target was police (3,271 attacks), followed by private citizens (2,314 attacks). Although these jihadist groups' low emphasis on economic coercion gives no additional incentive for disruptive warnings and hoaxes, Boko Haram's incentive to warn for casualty reduction remains. We should expect a greater frequency of warnings from this group compared to the other two. As for whether to expect more warnings from the Taliban or ISIL, my theoretical framework does not produce a clear prediction. We should expect a low frequency of warnings from both.

These predictions bear out well. Policy analysts and local citizens alike have noted Boko Haram's tendency to foreshadow its attacks. A report from 2017 by the Institute for Security Studies notes that Boko Haram will often "give notice to opponents prior to the initiation of violent operations. This process was described by [Boko Haram spokesman Abu] Qaqa as an opportunity for innocent civilians to protect themselves, by avoiding association or proximity with the aforementioned groups" named in the threat.[78] Boko Haram often delivers warnings directly to civilians, verbally or in notes written in the local language and deposited at the scene of the foreshadowed attack.[79] A witness to a September 8, 2011, attack on a Maiduguri beer hall describes the warnings that preceded the incident: "Around 6pm we saw some leaflets warning residents about impending attack in the area and people quickly closed their shops.... So around 8pm the attackers came and opened fire on the beer parlour." Those who heeded Boko Haram's warning escaped unscathed, but the attack killed the bar owner and three others who stayed behind.[80] Another news report describes warnings that preceded a Boko Haram attack on a prison in Ganye, Adamawa State, in 2013: "Boko Haram sent message that they will raid the prison and free their members." Residents were warned to "steer clear of the area," but Boko Haram had never carried out an attack in Ganye before, and "no one took the matter seriously" until they heard the first gunshots.[81]

However, in Borno State, the center of Boko Haram's activity, civilians do not question the group's credibility. In June 2014, two months after Boko Haram kidnapped 276 girls from a school in Chibok, town officials received a letter threatening additional attacks. Officials took the threat seriously, noting that Boko Haram had fulfilled its previous warnings: "Whenever Boko Haram tells you that they are coming, they never fail to come. Our fear now is that we don't know when and how they are going to come, but our people are living in terror. We are calling for prayers as well as the government to provide adequate security in Chibok."[82]

My own analysis of Boko Haram's bombings of civilian targets shows that in 459 attacks through 2016, Boko Haram gave warnings roughly 4.6 percent of the time. (These statistics are drawn from my 1970–2016 warnings dataset, described in the following chapter.[83]) The importance of territory in shaping Boko Haram's behavior is highlighted by within-case variation in the group's frequency of bomb warnings. In years when Boko Haram held territory, its frequency of warning was substantially lower—roughly 2.1 percent. In years when the group did not hold territory, its frequency of warning was 7.4 percent.

Boko Haram's warnings often blur the temporal line between immediate and prospective threats—i.e., warnings and pledges. The logic of these threats derives from Boko Haram's religious nature, and the fact that attacking civilians, Muslims, women, and children runs afoul of mainstream Islamic principles. As Nigerian Muslims have criticized Boko Haram for violating religious norms, the group has adopted at least two defenses: First, in its public statements, Boko Haram restricts the category of civilians to include only Muslims—or only Muslims who practice Boko Haram's version of *sharia*. Second, Boko Haram warns civilians to dissociate from the institutions and facilities the group is likely to attack in the future.[84] For instance, after an attack on the UN's facilities in Abuja killed a Nigerian civilian in August 2011, Boko Haram stressed that "the U.N. is the bastion of the global oppression of Muslims all over the world. . . . As such, we have warned everyone to steer clear of such places."[85] Boko Haram issued a similar statement after a February 2012 attack on street vendors. To justify its targeting of these individuals, the group alleged that the vendors had been "conspiring with security agents" and that it had "warned the public to desist" from collaborating with the state.[86]

Threatening an entire category of targets is not the most efficient way to spare civilian lives. Yet it does offer Boko Haram a way of spinning the casualties that result when its threat is fulfilled. Another example, from May 2012, exemplifies this public relations strategy. Boko Haram's warning seems half directed at deterring civilians from entering government facilities and half directed at blaming rule-breakers for their own wretched ends:

> We have decided that in the coming days, every Nigerian, especially in the North, including Abuja, should vacate any government quarters or buildings—residential, official, classroom or anything owned by the government. Every government building, whether occupied or empty will be blown up. Whoever is caught up in the attacks has his or herself to blame. We have done our best by issuing this warning.[87]

Compared to Boko Haram, the Taliban are less disposed to issue warnings before they attack. Of 1,159 bombings of civilian targets through the year 2016, just 31 (2.7 percent) were preceded by warnings.[88] When the Taliban do give warnings, they often have a general character. For example, the Taliban issued a warning to civilians in June 2008, telling them to vacate contested areas in which the group was about to commence operations against NATO forces.[89] The Taliban have also issued warnings prior to attacks on polling places.[90] These warnings are not specific as to the precise locations of the attacks, but they do offer civilians a preview of the violence the Taliban are likely to unleash at some polling places on election day. The Taliban make other threats in so-called night letters. Pasted onto the outsides of mosques and government buildings overnight, the letters warn Afghan civilians not to associate with NATO forces, the Afghan government, and social institutions that the Taliban plan to attack.[91] These letters' general character and their tendency to quote scripture suggest the same versatility of function seen in Boko Haram's warnings: reducing casualties somewhat, while also deterring sinful behavior and blaming any casualties on the victims themselves.[92] A news report from 2006 describes one night-lettering campaign against Afghan schools: "In the past two months, insurgents have burned down 11 schools in the [Kandahar] region. Some of the attacks were presaged by night letters warning parents to keep their children home."[93] Other night letters are less specific, showcasing the social control aspect of these threats. To guarantee their safety, Afghans are instructed to avoid government facilities, hotels frequented by Westerners, and roads traveled by government and Western vehicles (likely targets of Taliban ambushes and booby traps).[94]

ISIL gives warnings even less frequently than the Taliban do. Of 1,962 ISIL bombings of civilian targets through 2016, the group gave warnings for just nine—0.5 percent.[95] The few warnings ISIL has given seem to follow the logic of sparing civilians, although the group's definition of "civilian" is quite narrow, applying to women, children, and Muslims in the act of prayer. Two examples come from July 2014. Prior to destroying Mosul's mosque of the Prophet Yunus, ISIL cadres warned worshippers to vacate the facility.[96] ISIL also warned the nurses of a Tikrit hospital to seek shelter in the basement while the rest of the hospital was destroyed.[97] Like the Taliban, ISIL has issued general warnings of attacks on Western-style elections. In April 2014 the group announced that any Sunnis who voted were placing their lives at risk.[98] The threat may have reduced civilian casualties by deterring some Sunnis from the polls. The warning also reframed the civilian casualties resulting from the attacks as the fault of the victims.[99] These few examples aside, ISIL's general pattern is to attack without anything resembling a warning. The group often uses suicide tactics to get as close as possible to civilians before slaughtering them en masse. The most atrocious examples include the July 17, 2015, attack on a public market frequented by Shia Muslims in Bani Saad, Diyala province (120 killed); the October 10, 2015, double suicide bombing of a pro-Kurdish peace rally in Ankara, Turkey (103 killed); and the July 3, 2016 suicide bombing of a shopping center in Baghdad's Karada area (382 killed).[100]

The empirical evidence from these cases gives support to my argument. Boko Haram, a group that has rarely controlled territory and fights a higher-functioning democratic government, issues warnings for a greater percentage of its attacks. My theoretical framework produces no clear prediction as to which group, the Taliban or ISIL, should issue more warnings. Empirically, the Taliban issues warnings with greater frequency, but the practice is still relatively rare, and the warnings we do see tend to double as self-exculpatory propaganda and deterrents to sin.

Pledges for Social Control

My argument predicts that terrorists seeking social control over civilians will be more likely to issue pledges. All three jihadist groups seek social control as a core political goal. ISIL is first and foremost a state-building project, seeking to establish an Islamic caliphate where religious law governs behavior.[101] The Taliban have similar ambitions, seeking to reassert Deobandi theocracy over Afghanistan.[102] Boko Haram's self-described "aim is to Islamise Nigeria and ensure the rule of the majority Muslims in the country."[103] Given these three groups' aspirations for religious governance, we should expect them to threaten violence against civilians who violate religious rules and those who collaborate with the police, armed forces, civilian government, and Western NGOs. This logic plays out clearly in all three cases.

Boko Haram's social control-oriented threats range from the very general to the very specific. In proclaiming its resurrection in 2009, Boko Haram called "on all Northerners in the Islamic States to quit the followership [sic] of the wicked political parties leading the country, the corrupt, irresponsible, criminal, murderous political leadership, and join the struggle for Islamic Society that will be corruption free, Sodom free [sic], where security will be guaranteed and there will be peace under Islam." The same statement rattled off a list of social practices the group would abolish by violence: "the rights and privileges of Women, the idea of homosexualism, lesbianism, sanctions in cases of terrible crimes like drug trafficking, rape of infants, multi-party democracy in an overwhelmingly Islamic country like Nigeria, blue films, prostitution, drinking beer and alcohol."[104] Boko Haram shows a particular interest in abolishing Western education and the education of girls. The group abducted 276 schoolgirls from the town of Chibok and another 110 from the town of Dapchi.[105] (The latter attack was carried out by the group's ISWA faction.) These attacks demonstrate what can happen if Nigerians send their children to Western-style schools. They also enable the militants to issue credible threats against Nigerians who violate the same social prohibitions in the future. For example, when ISWA returned some of the kidnapped schoolgirls to their parents in Dapchi, they reminded villagers, "Don't ever put your daughters in school again."[106]

Boko Haram also uses threats to silence its critics. The group menaces Muslim clerics who speak out against its reactionary interpretation of Islam.[107] It threatens journalists—for reporting the group's atrocities, or conversely, for underreporting the group's military successes.[108] Boko Haram's leadership issues follow-on threats after successful attacks on the media, using the credibility generated by the initial attack to intimidate other news outlets. After an April 26, 2012, suicide attack on the offices of the newspaper *This Day*, Boko Haram threatened more attacks on the entire Nigerian media establishment. An eighteen-minute online video (beginning with footage of *This Day*'s burning offices) identified the *Punch*, *Daily Sun*, *Vanguard*, *Guardian*, *Nation*, *Tribune*, and *National Accord* papers as targets, as well as the Voice of America Hausa radio station. "All these media houses, we will attack them including their staff and offices," top leader Abubakar Shekau claimed.[109] Boko Haram did not carry out any of the threatened attacks.[110]

This incident raises an important question regarding Boko Haram's credibility. How do we interpret the group's sometimes-hyperbolic public statements? A report by the Institute for Strategic Studies notes a "proliferation of warnings" in Abubakar Shekau's propaganda videos. The Boko Haram leader goes on "extended rants in which he accuses essentially all opposed to him." Shekau's prolixity makes it "difficult to discern between a legitimate threat and bluster." Nonetheless, "a careful reading of the situation may determine what Boko Haram's next target could be, which is more likely to result in action when linked to a specific and articulated grievance." For example, Boko Haram previewed a 2012 arson campaign against Nigerian schools with a series of messages condemning the alleged mistreatment of Muslim students and teachers. Subsequent messages threatened escalation in response to more alleged abuses of Muslims. One message previewed the escalation from arson to nighttime bombing, and a second threatened further escalation from nighttime bombing to daylight attacks when schools were full. Boko Haram's spokesman let Nigerian Christians know precisely what was coming and why: "We attacked the schools at night because we don't want to kill pupils . . . we would attack the public school in daylight if any Tsangaya [Muslim] school is attacked again."[111] In the areas hardest hit by Boko Haram violence, the group's threats cause mass panic and the dislocation of religious outgroups. In January 2015 Boko Haram induced the spontaneous evacuation of hundreds of civilians from four towns rocked by a previous wave of suicide bombings. Witnesses recalled how Boko Haram cadres "asked people to leave—or else." Civilians fled toward Borno's provincial capital, Maiduguri, leaving the four smaller towns "almost empty."[112]

The Taliban issue their own pledges for social control. Like Boko Haram, they threaten schools that do not adhere to their religious line. In summer 2018 Taliban threats forced the closure of 103 schools serving sixty thousand students in Logar province. The Taliban shuttered schools in other provinces as well, depriving 3.7 million Afghan children of education.[113] The Taliban also use threats to intimidate journalists who report unflattering stories. In October 2015 the Taliban declared that they would treat Afghanistan's two largest television networks as "military objectives because of their disrespectful and hostile actions"—most notably, their stories reporting the rape of schoolgirls by Taliban agents.[114] A Taliban suicide bomber fulfilled the death threat in January 2016, driving an explosives-laden car into a bus full of Tolo TV employees, six of whom perished.[115] In addition, the Taliban threaten prominent women who defy the group's conservative dictates. The victims include Afghanistan's first female air force pilot and a rising women's football star, both of whom were forced to flee the country.[116] Khalida Popal, the footballer, recalls: "I had a choice—I could either stay in my own country and face the consequences, or leave and continue working towards my goal. And I didn't want to die."[117] The Taliban use threats to intimidate foreign aid workers as well, accusing them of espionage and pledging to kill them or trade them for militants held in government custody.[118]

The Taliban's night letters, already discussed for their warning content, also facilitate social control. They menace Afghans who might provide intelligence to security forces—or who might join security forces in their counterterrorism campaign.[119] Recently, the Taliban have begun to use electronic media to communicate threats. SMS text message chains distribute graphic execution videos, intimidating civilians who might consider collaborating with the government or otherwise violating the Taliban's social rules. Afghans interpret these SMS videos as serving the same social control function as the night letters, albeit with wider, less discriminate distribution.[120]

The Taliban often threaten civilians who associate with the Afghan government. The group pledges violence against civil servants at the start of each spring fighting season, hoping to intimidate those who support the Western-backed regime.[121] The Taliban also threaten the lives of civilians who vote. Because these threats are specific to an election taking place on a particular day, they may be thought of as warnings to reduce civilian casualties. However, there is an additional element of social control embedded in the threat: civilians are told not to go near any polling place on election day. This likely deters many Afghans from participating in the liberal system the Taliban seek to overthrow.[122] At the same time, the Taliban force Afghans to pay taxes to their quasi-governmental regime. A news report in 2018 describes how the Taliban's "Department of Tax and Revenue" collects tolls ranging from $250–310 for each large fuel truck and $70 for each light truck.[123] A similar system collects property taxes and other revenue from businesses and civilians in Taliban-controlled areas. News reports describe how "the Taliban regularly sends reminders and threats" to extract money from media agencies, and from entire towns. The district governor of Qara Bagh recalls: "After Qara Bagh district residents did not pay the taxes the Taliban demanded, the insurgents removed three [civilians] from a car and killed them."[124]

ISIL's social control is, if anything, more extensive than that of Boko Haram and the Taliban. On territory it does not control, ISIL issues threats to deter participation in liberal social practices such as elections.[125] On land it has conquered, ISIL imposes a grim form of law and order. After overrunning the city of Mosul, ISIL issued death threats against public employees who failed to report to their former jobs. One civil servant recalled: "We had no choice but to go back to work. . . . Except we were now serving a terrorist group."[126] Citizens of ISIL's caliphate faced a profusion of new rules governing personal matters such as sexual behavior, beard length, music, card playing, and smoking. These morality codes are backed by threats of punishment. A first-time offender may be let off with a written citation and a signed contract acknowledging that further violations will result in punishment. One contract recovered from former ISIL facilities in Mosul reads: "I, the undersigned, pledge not to cut or trim my beard again. . . . If I do that again, I will be subject to all kinds of punishments that the Hisba [morality] Center may take against me." When individual contracts of this kind are not adequate to change behavior, ISIL resorts to stark death threats. One Mosul resident recalls ISIL's reaction after he and his family attempted to flee to government-held areas: "Try this again and we'll kill every last one of you."[127]

In sum, the behavior of all three jihadist groups is consistent with my argument about pledges as tools of social control. In their religious state-building projects, Boko Haram, the Taliban, and ISIL seek to govern civilian populations according to conservative dictates. Each group threatens "justice" against those who violate its laws. When these groups punish violators, the fulfillment of their threats reinforces the terror that keeps other civilians in line.

Pledges for Negotiation

My argument predicts that terrorists seeking negotiations with the state will be more likely to pledge attacks on the government. We should expect more pledges from Boko Haram and the Taliban than from ISIL. This is because ISIL deliberately eschews negotiated political solutions. An ISIL propaganda video from 2015 addressed to the West explains: "We have decided to negotiate with you in the trenches and not in the hotels."[128] In contrast, Boko Haram and the Taliban have expressed a desire to negotiate with their state adversaries. News reports in 2012 revealed that Boko Haram had twice attempted to negotiate an end to the conflict with the Nigerian government. The group sent its "Head of Enlightenment," Abu Dardaa, as an emissary, but state forces arrested him.[129] Boko Haram launched fresh attacks and threatened more unless the government released Dardaa and other prisoners. The jihadists' spokesman, Abu Qaqa, told the press: "We are responsible for today's attacks on the military base and other places. We did it to teach the government a lesson because they deceived us to believe in their dialogue proposal, yet they kept arresting our members and refused to release them. We will continue to attack government and security agencies as long as they refuse to release our members in various cells and prisons." In the same statement pledging attacks and demanding the prisoners' release, Qaqa also expressed a desire for a "Sovereign National Conference" to negotiate a division of power between Christians and Muslims. Qaqa reiterated Boko Haram's position that until a political agreement is reached, all Christians remained "targets."[130] Weeks later, journalists reported that Boko Haram had authorized a second envoy, nationally renowned cleric Ibrahim Datti Ahmad, to put its diplomatic offers before the government.[131] Ahmad withdrew when his secret overture was revealed. Boko Haram then issued a blistering statement pledging revenge for the government's alleged role in exposing Ahmad's mission: "Almighty God has told us repeatedly that the unbelievers will never respect the promises they made. As such, henceforth, we will never respect any proposal for dialogue. . . . We are certain we will dismantle this government and establish Islamic government in Nigeria. . . . We are calling on all Muslims in this part of the world to accept the clarion call and fight for the restoration of the Caliphate."[132] As with Boko Haram's warnings and social control threats, there is some question about the truthfulness of the leadership's longer-winded rants against the state. In a February 2014 video some twenty-eight minutes in length, Abubakar Shekau threatened violence against Nigerian politicians, the state-run oil industry, and schools.[133] The threat against oil refineries seemed far-fetched, given the group's geographic position in the north of Nigeria, far from the country's southern oil infrastructure.[134] Boko Haram reiterated its threat in subsequent months, however, and in June 2014 a lone suicide bomber detonated herself at a fuel depot in Lagos.[135] This is one more example of Boko Haram making threats that seem implausible at the time. Yet the group usually follows through, rendering Boko Haram's messages "fairly accurate" overall.[136]

The Taliban make their own diplomatic overtures in public. The group has expressed willingness to speak directly with the United States about the terms of an American exit from Afghanistan.[137] The Taliban insist, however, that these negotiations be kept separate from peace talks with the Afghan government.[138] As the Trump administration took office, the Taliban ratcheted up the pressure. In a series of open letters, the Taliban demanded that the United States cut its involvement in Afghanistan, promising to inflict heavy casualties on any American forces who remained.[139] This harsh tone toward the United States was accompanied by a softening toward the Afghan government. In announcing their spring 2018 offensive, the Taliban pledged that "the American invaders and their intelligence agents" would be the "primary" target of attacks.[140] The group followed this tacit gesture of restraint toward the government with an explicit Eid-al-fitr ceasefire applying only to Afghan troops and police.[141] The Taliban stressed, however, that they would still attack foreign troops whenever opportunities arose.[142] By combining threats against foreigners and forbearance toward fellow Afghans, the Taliban have engaged in a sophisticated game of armed diplomacy. The strategy may yet pay off: a month after the Eid-al-Fitr ceasefire, the United States announced a policy shift to favor direct peace talks, rather than the multilateral talks that previous American governments had demanded.[143] The Trump administration and Taliban representatives apparently came close to reaching a deal, but the administration's concerns over bad press caused it to abandon negotiations—for now.[144] As of December 2019, the Taliban remained eager to talk.[145] President Trump or his successors could choose to reopen the channel.

The threat-laden diplomacy of Boko Haram and the Taliban is precisely what my argument would predict. A militant group seeking to bring the state to the bargaining table, to move the state back to the bargaining table after a breakdown of talks, or to motivate the state to give concessions at the bargaining table, should articulate threats about what will happen if the state holds out. ISIL's stated opposition to peace negotiations means that we do not observe similar threats from this group. However, there is one important context in which ISIL does use threats for negotiation: the kidnapping and ransoming of hostages. Like many violent nonstate actors, the Islamic State derives a portion of its income from ransoms. The group has extorted money from countries such as France and Spain, in exchange for the release of journalists captured in Syria.[146] ISIL's negotiation for hostages does not set it apart from the Taliban and Boko Haram. (The former kidnap and ransom aid workers, and the latter ransom captured schoolgirls.[147]) Nor do these hostage negotiations contradict ISIL's overall uncompromising stance against peace negotiations with the West. Some of the group's ransom demands are so high ($133 million for one kidnapped American journalist) that the offer of negotiation is best interpreted as an effort to build drama leading up to a videotaped beheading that all parties fully expect.[148] Nonetheless, the cases where ISIL has negotiated hostage releases for lesser sums show that even a group that eschews peace settlements will occasionally use pledges to negotiate lesser issues, when it is profitable to do so.

Self-Aggrandizing Threats

My argument predicts that groups with reputation deficits—smaller groups competing with more capable rivals, and organizations facing strategic reverses—will issue pledges and bluffs to aggrandize themselves. Groups with declining capabilities will also issue bluff threats to return themselves to prominence. None of the jihadist groups has had to compete against a more capable peer rival. Each has built a reputation through violence, with little need to talk itself up. Although the Taliban lost their territory and their state in 2001, they reemerged as Afghanistan's predominant insurgent group, overshadowing peers such as al-Qa'ida and Hizb-i-Islami.[149] These smaller groups have faded with time (leading Hizb-i-Islami to sign a separate peace with the Afghan government), but the Taliban have clawed back control of 15 percent of Afghanistan's political districts.[150] Boko Haram is similarly dominant in the field of Nigerian jihadism. The group has gained and lost territory, but it has always shown a persistent capacity for bombings, village raids, and attacks on Nigerian military outposts.[151] ISIL built its own fearsome reputation by conquering a large land area, hundreds of thousands of square kilometers, with a functioning bureaucracy and military rivaling those of many states.[152] Other jihadists in Iraq and Syria cannot claim such historic successes.

At their deepest military nadirs, however, Boko Haram and ISIL have felt the need to bolster their reputations by threatening revenge on their enemies. After Boko Haram was nearly destroyed by government forces in 2009, the group's surviving cadres issued a defiant public statement pledging revenge against "the wicked political parties leading the country, the corrupt, irresponsible, criminal, murderous political leadership" that extrajudicially executed the group's founder, Muhammad Yusuf.[153] Boko Haram regrouped and even managed to conquer territory in 2014, but a coalition of troops from Nigeria, Niger, Chad, and Cameroon retook the area. Again, Boko Haram's leaders issued self-aggrandizing threats to project their potency. A spokesman released a video depicting the mass execution of captives and vigorously disputing reports that Boko Haram had been run out of its stronghold in the Sambisa Forest: "Most of our territory is still under control. . . . I swear by Allah that I am talking right now from Sambisa. . . . Here in Sambisa you can travel more than four to five hours under the black flag of Islam by car or by motorbike. . . . We are uncountable in Sambisa. We are thousands of Mujahideen here."[154]

Boko Haram pledged, truthfully, to retaliate against its government antagonists by launching new attacks in southern Nigeria and across Nigeria's borders in Chad, Cameroon, and Niger.[155] The group also issued a bluff threat to extend its bombing campaign to South Africa if the government there did not intervene to stop xenophobic attacks against migrants.[156] This implausible threat was obviously not intended to open negotiations with South Africa, and it most likely had no impact on civilian behavior there. Yet it did grab headlines and project confidence at a time when observers could doubt the potency of Boko Haram.

More telling still, in terms of testing my argument, is the divergence in bluffing behavior between Abubakar Shekau's loyalists and the Barnawi-led ISWA, after the two factions split in 2016. ISWA's new leader, Barnawi, took with him the bulk of Boko Haram's troops, outnumbering Shekau's fifteen hundred or so men by a 2:1 or 3:1 ratio, depending on the estimate.

With its strength reduced, Shekau's faction has focused primarily on striking civilian soft targets, while ISWA has shown greater ability to confront state forces.[157] Now perceived as the "dominant" Boko Haram faction, ISWA has managed to control small portions of the Lake Chad basin.[158] Abubakar Shekau, no doubt sensing his new reputational deficit, has issued more frequent and more spectacular threats since the organizational split. In an August 2016 video, the first after ISWA's defection, Shekau threatened a massive expansion of Boko Haram's campaign. "Our coming out today is to fight the world, not just Nigeria, Niger, Cameroon, Chad or Africa alone. We have come out to fight the world."[159] Shekau's faction issued two videos the next month, promising to murder Nigerian President Muhammadu Buhari and "destroy what we never destroyed before."[160] More videos followed in November and December 2016, and in January, March, April, and June 2017.[161] In his January 2017 video, Shekau threatened that Boko Haram would "kill, chop, kidnap, and detonate bombs everywhere."[162] In the March video, Shekau promised that Boko Haram would "not back down until it establishes Sharia in Benin, Cameroon, Chad, Niger, Nigeria, and Mali."[163] Shekau's escalating threats during this period were a notable departure from Boko Haram's previous tendency to make threats it could conceivably fulfill. The threats also contrasted with ISWA's much more measured approach to propaganda. As one report noted, "ISWA's leaders are low-profile, not appearing in videos or claiming responsibility for attacks, possibly to avoid the international media, and the ire of regional governments."[164] This is what we should expect from the dominant group, which knows it can outcompete its smaller peer rival by carrying out more violence. Shekau's Boko Haram faction, weaker militarily and suffering an acute status deficit as a result, seeks to recapture the public imagination through bluster.

ISIL also turned to bluffing after 2015, as its caliphate was slowly reconquered by a coalition of major military powers.[165] In October 2017 ISIL's online propagandists distributed several doctored images threatening violence against the 2018 World Cup football tournament in Russia. The images depicted masked men looking out over a football stadium, with captions such as "We are the one who chooses the battlefield" and "I swear that the mujahideen's fire will burn you." The Russian World Cup games went on normally, with no sign that ISIL actually attempted to fulfill its threats. This was not the first time that ISIL had issued empty threats against football tournaments: the group also threatened the 2016 European

Championship and the 2017 Women's European Championship, both of which went forward without incident.[166] Other fanciful ISIL threats met widespread mockery on social media. Italians responded to ISIL's promise in 2015 to "conquer Rome" by tweeting tips on how to avoid rush hour traffic and which wines to pair with prosciutto (an offensive suggestion to an organization that forswears both alcohol and pork).[167] Spaniards likewise mocked ISIL's pledge to reconquer former Moorish territories from their country. Social media users dubbed satirical pop music over the ISIL video and offered advice on cooking the signature Andalusian rice dish, paella.[168]

The behavior of Boko Haram and ISIL in moments of desperation contrasts with the more measured pledges issued by the Taliban, whose fortunes have trended steadily upward since 2002. Every spring the Taliban announce the start of their fighting season with a detailed list of targets the group plans to attack. Foreign observers, including the NATO militaries fighting the Taliban, view these announcements as accurate predictors of the group's future actions.[169] For example, the communiqué announcing the 2014 fighting season promised attacks on "large and well fortified enemy bases with heavy weapons and missiles," as well as attacks on "the National Directorate that pursue and torture Mujahideen." The promised attacks would begin at 5:00 a.m. on Monday, May 12.[170] True to their word, the Taliban launched fourteen attacks that day, including a sophisticated three-bomber suicide attack on the Directorate of Justice, rocket attacks on Bagram air base and Kabul international airport, and coordinated assaults on three police checkpoints in Ghazni province by at least nine hundred armed assailants.[171]

By fulfilling their threats, the Taliban lend weight to their coercive demands on civilians and the state. (Recalling my speech/kinetic action model of terrorism, the fulfillment of a pledge generates credibility as a post-attack outcome.) The Taliban's spring press release announcing the 2014 fighting season also demanded that Afghans cease "backing the foreign infidel invaders" and that Western forces begin an "unconditional withdrawal."[172] Those demands seemed more forceful after the Taliban fulfilled pledges to attack the Directorate of Justice and security force installations. The broad pattern of behavior observed in these cases—consistently truthful pledges by the Taliban contrasting the hyperbolic bluffs of Boko Haram and ISIL in their times of decline—lends support to my theoretical argument.

Pledges and Bluffs for Advantage

My argument predicts that terrorists facing highly capable counterterrorism opponents will issue prophylactic threats to negate the state's security advantages. Prophylactic threats may be prospective or immediate, true or false, depending on the circumstances facing the terrorist group. For instance, a group confronting a powerful state security apparatus might use pledges and bluffs to force police to cover a wider variety of strategic targets. By spreading police resources out across many locations, the terrorist group makes it easier to launch operations at one or two locations of its choosing. Alternatively, a terrorist group attacking heavily fortified targets might use hoaxes to misdirect or distract police just as operations are commencing.

The three jihadist groups I analyze have all faced capable security forces. However, ISIL's security concerns have been primarily of a battlefield nature. The group routed Iraqi troops from much of the country in 2014, expanded into neighboring Syria, and proclaimed the sovereignty of its caliphate on both sides of the border.[173] ISIL's struggle has been to retain that territory despite pressure from ground troops and the air forces of major world powers, such as the United States and Russia. Those conventional military engagements are outside the scope of my argument, which concerns the symbolic use of violence and threats off the battlefield. However, Boko Haram and the Taliban have fought irregular wars, where the logic of my argument does apply. These groups seek to undermine the state's control of territory through terrorism and guerrilla violence. Both groups find themselves struggling against the same counterterrorism techniques used against groups like the IRA, ETA, and the MRTA. In areas of state control and contested control, the Taliban and Boko Haram worry about informants, infiltrators, and how to conduct surprise attacks before disappearing into the civilian population.[174] This is precisely the sort of environment in which prophylactic threats are useful. My argument thus leads us to expect more prophylactic threats from Boko Haram and the Taliban, and fewer from ISIL.

These predictions bear out well. Boko Haram and the Taliban use threats to "blind" their state opponents, threatening civilians and institutions that provide intelligence on the militants and their operations. For example, Boko Haram has issued threats against Nigerian mobile phone companies and the Nigeria Communication Commission (NCC), which it accuses of assisting government surveillance and capture efforts.[175] Boko Haram has also threatened to attack civilians who participate in the government's terror-reporting telephone hotline program. Counterterrorism officials encouraged Borno residents who received the threatening letter "to disregard or destroy it."[176] Yet Boko Haram's fearsome reputation in northern Nigeria is enough to make anyone think twice before denouncing the group to authorities. A publicly issued threat from 2012 underscores the risk informers run, even if they occupy social positions that theoretically render them immune under Islamic law. When Boko Haram believed it had uncovered a government plot to use women as spies, the group's spokesman, Abu Qaqa, issued this chilling injunction: "We are also aware of the activities of some women who have been recruited to spy on us. This is a final warning to all of them. By God, whenever we catch any woman spying on us, we would slaughter her like ram [sic]."[177]

Other prophylactic threats blur the line between casualty reduction and conditioning the combat environment. Prior to commencing operations against security forces, Boko Haram has distributed leaflets warning civilians to leave the area.[178] Although sparing civilians is surely part of Boko Haram's aim in distributing these leaflets, scaring off bystanders also has the prophylactic effect of isolating security forces from the civilian population, thereby making them easier to target.

One may also view Boko Haram's threats against Nigeria's neighbors, Chad, Niger, and Cameroon, as examples of strategic advantage seeking. Hemmed in by the security forces of four countries, Boko Haram sought to relieve some of the pressure by frightening one or more of its antagonists into leaving the counterinsurgent coalition. Boko Haram spokespeople pledged, truthfully, to extend the group's bombing campaign to Chad, Cameroon, and Niger if those countries joined Nigeria's fight against the jihadist group.[179] The terrorists followed up with statements directed to the citizens of Chad, Cameroon, and Niger, urging them to restrain their governments. A threat addressed to Chadians explained: "We are telling Chadian citizens that their government is leading them through a dark tunnel with its intervention in our land . . . no one should apportion blame on us if your country enters the vortex of civil war, as long as you do nothing to stop the tyranny of Chad and let your country slide into war against us."[180]

Like Boko Haram, the Taliban have threatened mobile phone companies in an effort to deny their state opponents useful intelligence. In certain provinces, the insurgents have convinced phone companies to shut down their services from 6:00 p.m. until 6:00 a.m.[181] The nocturnal phone blackout allows the Taliban to operate without fear of being given up by tipsters who might inform police about their movements.[182] After major military setbacks, the Taliban have extended the phone blackout to a full twenty-four hours.[183] Telecom companies who violate these blackouts are punished violently.[184] The Taliban have also used threats to interfere with the Afghan government's recruitment and retention of security personnel. (These threats blur the line between pledges for social control and pledges for strategic prophylaxis.) Night letters warn Afghans not to enlist in the police or army, or the Taliban "will take no further responsibility for what happens [to you] in the future."[185] When these deterrent threats fail, the Taliban direct menacing letters and phone calls to the homes of Afghans who have enlisted. One policeman recalls his interaction with a Taliban caller who rang him at home: "He said: 'If you don't leave your job in the next two or three days, we will find you and behead you.'"[186]

News reports also reveal how the Taliban use hoaxes for intelligence gathering, tactical prophylaxis, and come-ons to mitigate the technological advantages of their counterterrorism foes. Taliban bomb makers and field operatives find themselves in a cat-and-mouse game with Afghan government and NATO units tasked to detect and defuse improvised explosive devices (IEDs). When their opponents introduce a new bomb disposal device or vehicle, Taliban agents "lay hoax IEDs and watch to see how the coalition tackles them."[187] A U.S. Marine Corps training document explains that Taliban agents will "use/force local nationals to initiate a false report of a found IED" to draw in the bomb disposal team "and evaluate response times and TTPs [Tactics, Techniques and Procedures]" for dealing with suspected devices. This intelligence helps the Taliban to plan future attacks. The group issues additional hoaxes "to draw coalition forces into an ambush ... delay or harass convoys, or to place the convoy in a kill zone and can be incorporated into a coordinated or complex attack."[188]

ISIL, fighting a more conventional war with defined battle lines, has had less contact with domestic counterterrorism forces. However, it has issued advantage-seeking threats at a strategic level, seeking, unsuccessfully, to deter countries from joining the Western-led air campaign against Islamic State ground positions. Shortly after France commenced bombing operations against ISIL targets in Syria and Iraq, Islamic State propagandists released a twelve-minute video threatening attacks against any other country that joined the air campaign. The narrator of the video specifically threatened the United States, which was then considering whether to join the air campaign against ISIL in Syria and Iraq. "We swear that we will strike America at its heart—in Washington," the narrator pledged.[189] When such propaganda fails to deter countries from joining the air campaign, ISIL uses threats to blunt their operations. For example, ISIL's horrifying video depicting the immolation of a captured Jordanian Air Force pilot also made threats against the pilot's surviving colleagues. A news report explains: "Before his death, [1st Lieutenant] Kasasbeh was forced to reveal the names and workplaces of many fellow pilots in the Royal Jordanian Air Force. Their photographs appeared at the end of a 23-minute video depicting his death, along with an offer of a bounty of 100 gold dinars (roughly $20,000) for each pilot killed."[190]

This portion of the video may be interpreted as an effort to sabotage further Jordanian air operations—by inducing desertions, sapping morale, and deterring the air force from flying low altitude missions during which they, too, might be shot down and captured. Additionally, ISIL uses threats to deter foreign intelligence agencies from operating on its territory. In another disturbing execution video, a child soldier shoots an alleged Russian spy and speaks toward the camera: "My message to those who would come here to spy, I say to them repent to Allah before it's too late."[191]

The logic of my argument is borne out in these cases. Boko Haram and the Taliban often issue threats for strategic and tactical advantage. ISIL issues threats for strategic advantage, but it has fewer occasions to use tactical threats. This is likely to change in the future, however. As of December 2019, ISIL controls no territory. The group appears to be reverting to insurgent tactics in areas recaptured by state forces. If this trend persists, we should expect ISIL to adopt behaviors similar to those of Boko Haram and the Taliban: threatening civilian informants to deny the state intelligence, identifying chokepoints where police recruitment can be reduced by threats, and using threats to deny authorities the other essential ingredients for successful counterterrorism. With regard to advantage-seeking threats, ISIL's future is likely to look much like Boko Haram's and the Taliban's present.

This analysis of jihadist groups supports my theoretical predictions about when to expect different varieties of terrorist threats. Boko Haram gives warnings more often than the Taliban and ISIL do. This is what we anticipate from a group that depends on civilians for shelter and fights a more democratic state opponent. All three groups pledge violence against civilians who defy their pronouncements of religious law. Boko Haram and the Taliban pair their diplomatic overtures to state opponents with threats of what will happen if governments reject their demands. ISIL does not show the same tendency toward pledges and armed diplomacy. But ISIL has issued bluff threats as its fighting capabilities have declined. Boko Haram issued similar reputation-bolstering threats at its own military low points in 2009 and 2015. The Taliban, whose fortunes have trended upward since 2002, do not show the same tendency toward attention-grabbing bluffs. Finally, we see elaborate advantage-seeking threats by Boko Haram and the Taliban, groups that face off against capable police forces in areas of government control and contested control. ISIL, fighting a more conventional campaign with defined battle lines, has made less use of advantage-seeking threats—except for the occasional video attempting to deter airstrikes or induce desertions by air crews.

My analysis of Islamists shows some distinctive aspects of threats by religious groups. Religion seems to incentivize threats that blur the line between pledges and warnings. Threatening a category of sinful targets, without much specificity about the timing of the attack, deters the faithful from irreligious behavior, prevents some civilian casualties, and justifies any casualties on the grounds that the victims were not truly innocent. Although it pushes the boundaries of my typology, this elision of warnings and pledges shows the versatility of threats. It also shows the portability of my theoretical framework to religious contexts. Jihadists' language may be distinctive, and their threats may blur the line between the immediate and the prospective. But the functions of threats remain consistent. Terrorists use threats for casualty reduction and for social control more or less when my argument predicts that they should. The same theory of terrorist threats has explanatory power for religious and secular groups alike.

CHAPTER VI

Quantitative Analysis

When to Expect Truthful Warnings

In this chapter I use quantitative methods to test two key propositions from my argument: truthful warnings are more likely when terrorist groups seek legitimacy and when they pursue strategies of economic disruption.[1] I have three reasons for focusing particular attention on warnings: First, these threats have significant practical implications. Schools, government offices, religious organizations, and other institutions receive purported warnings on a regular basis. My analysis provides useful insights for those assessing these threats to determine their credibility. My insights in this chapter feed into the concluding chapter's discussion of how to evaluate terrorist threats and calibrate emergency responses to the degree of practical danger. My second reason for focusing on warnings is methodological. This type of threat presents a unique opportunity for statistical tests of my argument. There is a readily identifiable case universe since, by definition, warnings precede attacks. Existing data sources like the Global Terrorism Database give us a list of attacks, and a rigorous search protocol allows me to determine whether specific warnings were given for each of them.[2] In contrast, a statistical analysis of hoaxes might be plagued by uncertainty over whether certain threats were deliberately false or were instead truthful warnings of failed or aborted attacks. An analysis of warnings does not present these methodological hurdles. Building on this logic, a third reason for focusing on warnings is that doing so allows me to test my argument's application across ideological lines. The preceding chapters offer ideologically controlled comparisons—ethnic separatists versus other ethnic separatists, leftists versus leftists, and jihadists versus jihadists. That approach is useful for isolating the effects of political variables and showing how they incentivize different uses of threats, but it leaves open the question of what role, if any, ideology plays in shaping militants' threatening behavior. A large-N statistical analysis, including dozens of militant groups with varying belief systems, allows me to measure any effect ideology might have on terrorists' decisions to warn.

Using an existing resource, the Global Terrorism Database, I identify a sample of the most prolific terrorist organizations—131 groups that carried out twenty-five or more bombings during the period 1970–2016.[3] Together, these groups were responsible for nearly twenty thousand bombings of civilian targets.[4] My sample of terrorist groups includes secular and religious groups, ethnic nationalists, separatists, leftists, and reactionaries. If my argument is well specified, the variables that predicted warnings in my ideologically controlled case studies should also show significant effects in my analysis of groups with different fundamental beliefs. If terrorists' ideologies exert significant effects on their uses of threats, my argument will require revision to account for these variables.

Predictions from My Argument and Some Alternatives

Throughout this book I argue that terrorist groups issue warnings to mitigate their legitimacy concerns among the civilians whose towns and cities they attack. Militants also issue warnings to impose disruption on the state's economy. A third function of warnings is to seek tactical advantage over the state's security forces—for example, giving warnings to draw police into ambushes. I choose to focus this chapter on warnings' roles in legitimacy seeking and disruption. The terrorist-civilian relationship is theoretically complex and incompletely understood by the existing literature. A large body of scholarship makes claims quite different from mine, regarding the conditions that incentivize militant groups to spare or target civilians. To contribute to that debate, I concentrate my analysis on bombings of civilian targets, leaving aside the attacks on security forces where the advantage-seeking logic of warnings would otherwise play out. I test three hypotheses:

- Hypothesis 1a: Warnings are more likely when terrorist groups lack territory.
- Hypothesis 1b: Warnings are more likely when the state is a democracy.
- Hypothesis 2: Warnings are more likely when the attack targets the economy.

Hypotheses 1a and 1b follow from my first theoretical proposition: that terrorists will warn when they seek legitimacy among the civilian population. (A lack of territory and a democratic state opponent intensify the militant group's multiple audiences conundrum, forcing it to align its tactics with civilians' notions of legitimacy.) Hypothesis 2 follows from my second proposition: that terrorist groups will warn when they seek to disrupt the state's economy.

Aside from my own argument, there are several alternative theories that might explain terrorists' decision to warn before an attack. These alternatives suggest other variables to control for in my research design. They also make different predictions from my theory, regarding the likely effects of territory and democracy. Few authors argue, as I do, that the lack of territorial strongholds forces militants to restrain their violence.[5] More frequently, scholars argue the reverse: that territory *increases* legitimacy concerns and forces militants to behave with restraint.[6] By this logic, we would expect more warnings from terrorist groups with strongholds. However, context is important. The notion that territory encourages restraint emerges from the rebel governance literature—that is, the literature on how militants treat civilians on territory they control. Strategically, it makes sense to treat one's own civilian constituents well, offering them policy goods and protection in exchange for their loyalty and the support they provide in the fight against the state.[7] But much of the symbolic violence in terrorism is committed outside of one's strongholds, against civilians governed by the adversary. If anything, the possession of territory renders militants less accountable for abuses they commit against the state's civilians. (The terrorist group's own constituents will be unaffected, may not learn of the abuses, and may lack the ability to sanction the terrorist group for its behavior.) My argument about warnings applies most clearly to attacks on state territory, where the terrorist group carries out hit-and-run attacks and may issue warnings to mitigate casualties. The logic of responsible rebel governance does not apply in such settings. Still, it is worth noting the alternative argument. If hypothesis 1a is correct, it will represent a significant challenge to the more widely repeated claim that the possession of territory encourages restraint toward civilians.

The terrorism literature offers another alternative prediction regarding the role of democracy in militants' decisions to warn. There is broad debate about the role of democracy in shaping terrorist tactics.[8] A few authors argue, as I do, that democracy reduces civilian targeting because terrorists ratchet down casualties to appear more legitimate in citizens' eyes.[9] More commonly, authors argue that democracy makes militants *more likely* to target civilians. If terrorists see the electorate as complicit in the state's policies, they may view civilians as legitimate targets.[10] Terrorists may also target civilians strategically, assuming that the electorate will pressure the government to grant concessions.[11] If either of these alternative arguments holds, democracy should be associated with fewer warnings.

The civil war literature suggests other factors to include as control variables in my analysis. For instance, natural resource revenues might influence the decision to warn. If terrorists can fund themselves by selling drugs, gold, gems, or oil, they are less dependent on civilians' charity and less beholden to civilians' views on the legitimate conduct of violence. Resource-rich militant groups may also attract profit-driven recruits who are more likely to kill civilians, compared to ideologically driven recruits who are schooled to respect the population.[12] A related argument highlights the potential importance of state sponsorship. By offering funding and material support, foreign states render militants less dependent on civilians and less constrained by their taboos against indiscriminate violence.[13] If these arguments hold, we should expect fewer warnings from groups with resource endowments and state sponsors.

Another school of thought leaves issues of accountability aside and focuses on ideological factors that may influence terrorists' tactics. Conventional wisdom holds that religion exacerbates civilian targeting—by narrowing militants' political constituencies, creating dichotomies between the virtuous and the sinful, and generating social networks that encourage the transmission of deadly tactics such as suicide bombing.[14] Ethnic grievances may also incentivize civilian targeting to provoke an indiscriminate state response or to eliminate a hated ethnic outgroup.[15] Other research focuses on separatism, although the literature is equivocal as to whether this variable increases or decreases violence against civilians. (Separatism may encourage civilian targeting by narrowing militants' constituencies, or it may discourage civilian targeting by encouraging militants to seek international approval for their statehood.[16]) If any of these ideological factors exerts a significant effect on a terrorist group's propensity to warn, it may confound the effects of the variables I emphasize in my own argument.

Research Design

To test my hypotheses, I employ a dataset of 12,235 bombings drawn from the Global Terrorism Database (GTD), an open-source dataset published by the National Consortium for the Study of Terrorism and Responses to Terrorism (START).[17] I focus my analysis on bombings of nonmilitary targets because my argument concerns warnings as tools for civilian casualty reduction and economic disruption. With the bombing as the unit of analysis, I seek to determine which factors incentivize the perpetrator to give warnings in advance. To assess whether the perpetrators gave warnings before each attack, I consult journalistic and historical sources, particularly the LexisNexis searchable news database. I employed more than a dozen research assistants to create a dichotomous warning variable to merge with the GTD. My research assistants followed a detailed search and coding protocol, which provided them with Boolean search terms to pull relevant news stories from LexisNexis's archive of newspaper, wire service, magazine, radio, and television reportage. I instructed my research assistants to set a date range around each bombing: one day before the event through two days after. (Including dates before and after the event increases the likelihood of finding coverage of the bombing and any warnings given beforehand.) The terms for each search included the names, acronyms, and aliases of the perpetrator group and the terms "bomb!" and "warn!" If these initial searches did not return meaningful hits, my research assistants removed the term "warn!" from their search strings. They used any resulting hits from the broadened search to confirm that the attack had occurred and no warning was given.[18] When LexisNexis searches came up completely empty, I instructed my research assistants to consult other resources, including the annual *Significant Incidents of Political Violence Against Americans* report published by the U.S. State Department and the GTD's own "summary" field, which contains brief summaries of certain incidents.

I define my case universe to include terrorist incidents where the attack type (*attacktype1*) was "Bombing/Explosion" and target type (*targettype1*) was any category except "police," "military," "terrorists/non-state militia," or "violent political party." This filtering has the effect of excluding prophylactic warnings such as come-ons from my analysis. This is because the GTD codes the target of an attack based on the persons or property physically harmed in the incident.[19] Come-ons harm security forces, so the GTD codes them as attacks on military or police targets.

As a final restriction on the case universe, I include only attacks by militant groups that carried out at least twenty-five bombings in the years covered by my data: 1970 through 2016. I impose this restriction to avoid a type of underreporting bias that might occur with attacks by less prolific terrorist groups that do not draw as much media attention. Less interest by the press might imply fewer stories on a given bombing, and fewer words per story, so that the perpetrator's warnings might go unreported in news stories about the attack. This could lead to a systematic undercounting of warnings by less prolific terrorist groups. With the inclusion threshold set at twenty-five bombings, my sample of GTD incidents includes 19,310 bombings by 131 militant groups. My research assistants were able to find and code 12,235 of these incidents. Appendix table A.1 gives a list of the groups included in my analysis.

Measures

Dependent Variable: Warning

My dependent variable is a dichotomous (0/1) indicator of whether the perpetrator of an attack gave warning in advance. Warnings may include telephone calls to police, emergency services, or the owners of targeted businesses; alerts shouted to bystanders at the scene; and notes, signs, or graffiti alerting pedestrians to the presence of a bomb. I also code as a warning the tactic of forcibly removing people from the scene of an attack—for example, leading a building's security guard away at gunpoint before returning to detonate a bomb. I code nonspecific threats as pledges rather than warnings. Examples include threats of new violence if the government does not grant policy concessions and promises of consequences if business owners do not pay protection money. Thus extortion threats are not counted as warnings in my dataset. These restrictions notwithstanding, I do code certain categorical threats as warnings, if they are sufficiently detailed to allow civilians to escape harm. For example, a threat against polling sites during an upcoming election allows civilians to escape harm by avoiding the polls on election day. Appendix table A.1 shows the respective frequencies of warnings by each of the 131 terrorist groups in my sample.

Independent Variables

To operationalize the independent variables from my theoretical argument and the alternatives discussed previously, I draw on several additional resources: the Big, Allied, and Dangerous Dataset (BAAD, versions 1 and 2),[20] the Uppsala Conflict Data Program (UCDP) External Support in Armed Conflict Dataset,[21] and the Contraband Dataset.[22] I also employ reports from Stanford University's Mapping Militant Organizations project, the U.S. State Department, and journalistic sources.[23] I have used the BAAD datasets as the starting points for several of my independent variables. The BAAD data, however, cover a limited date range (1998–2012) and do not cover some groups in my analysis at all. For years and groups not covered in BAAD1 or BAAD2, I use the UCDP, Contraband, Stanford, State Department, and other secondary sources to code the relevant independent variables. The replication data files, available on my website, show the sources used to produce each coding.[24]

Given the importance of legitimacy seeking in my theoretical account of warnings, my independent variables include several factors that mediate militants' legitimacy concerns:

- *Territory*—a dichotomous indicator of whether the terrorist group possessed at least one territorial stronghold during the year of the attack. This variable is based on the *TerrStrong* and *Terrcntrl* variables in BAAD1 and BAAD2, respectively.
- *Polity2*—a scale ranging from -10 to 10, indicating a government's authority characteristics in a given year. This variable is drawn from the Polity IV Project.[25] Negative values indicate that a government was mostly autocratic in that year; positive values indicate that the government was mostly democratic. The *Polity2* coding for each bombing is that of the perpetrator group's primary target state in the year the attack took place. The target state is whichever country the militant group is attempting

to coerce. For example, the target state of ETA is Spain. The target state is usually but not always the state in which the physical attack took place. For example, ETA carried out some attacks on French soil, but it did so as part of a campaign to coerce Spain. All ETA attacks, regardless of their geographic location, are coded with Spain's *Polity2* score in the year the attack took place. Appendix table A.1 shows each militant group's target state.

- *Resources*—a dichotomous variable indicating whether the perpetrator group engaged in the sale or trafficking of drugs, gemstones, oil, or precious metals in that year. This variable is based on BAAD2's drug trafficking variable, *Fddrugtk*. Additional data on resource sales and trafficking are drawn from the Contraband Dataset and secondary sources.[26]
- *State Sponsored*—a dichotomous variable indicating whether a terrorist group received funding or material support from one or more governments in a given year. This variable is based on the BAAD1 and BAAD2 databases' *Statespond* and *Fdstate* variables.[27]

Several of my other independent variables relate to the political goals and ideologies of terrorist groups. These variables are dichotomous and not mutually exclusive. Hamas, for instance, is motivated by religion and the ethnic separatist grievances of Palestinians. The ideological and political variables include:

- *Separatist*—a variable indicating whether a group sought territorial secession. Groups coded "1" include ethnic separatists such as the IRA, ETA, and the Tamil Tigers; religious separatists like the Moro National Liberation Front; and secular multiethnic separatists such as the Niger Delta Avengers. Groups are coded "0" if their goal is full control or dissolution of the state. Examples include ISIL, the African National Congress (seeking the dissolution of South Africa's apartheid system), and Marxists attempting the overthrow of a government. Reactionary groups like the anti-IRA Ulster Volunteer Force (UVF) are also coded "0."
- *Religious*—derived from the *ContainRelig* and *Reli* variables in BAAD1 and BAAD2.[28]
- *Ethnic*—derived from the *ContainEthnic* and *Ethn* variables in BAAD1 and BAAD2.
- *Leftist*—derived from the *ContainLeft* and *Left* variables in BAAD1 and BAAD2.

- *Reactionary*—derived from BAAD1 and BAAD2 (as a residual category) and from secondary sources.

To test hypothesis 2, I include a set of dichotomous variables indicating the type of target bombed in each attack. If hypothesis 2 is correct and terrorist groups engaged in economic coercion are more likely to warn, we should see a higher probability of warnings for attacks on targets related to economic productivity, including businesses, tourist sites, and infrastructure. The target-type variables are derived from the GTD's *targtype1* variable:

- *Tourists*—where *targtype1* indicates an attack on "Tourists."
- *Business*—where *targtype1* indicates an attack on a "Business" target.
- *Government*—where *targtype1* gives the target as "Government (Diplomatic)" or "Government (General)."
- *Private Citizens*—where *targtype1* indicates an attack on "Private Citizens & Property."
- *Civil Society*—where *targtype1* indicates an attack on an "Educational Institution," "Journalists & Media," "Religious Figures/Institutions," or an "NGO."
- *Infrastructure*—where *targtype1* indicates an attack on "Airports and Aircraft," "Maritime," "Transportation," "Telecommunication," or "Food or Water Supply."
- *Utilities*—where *targtype1* indicates an attack on "Utilities."

The GTD's *targtype1* also indicates that some attacks were directed at "Other" and "Unknown" targets. These are not substantive categories, so in specifications using target-type variables, I omit attacks on "Other" and "Unknown" targets. This removes 852 observations from the analysis. I use *Utilities* as the base category in all models controlling for target types.

Some models include the dichotomous variable *Suicide*, drawn directly from the GTD. As the name implies, *Suicide* indicates whether a particular bombing used suicide tactics. I include this variable as a control, reasoning that the decision to use suicide tactics may have some bearing on the decision to warn. Assuming that a certain percentage of suicide attacks are motivated by a desire to get as close as possible to civilians and maximize casualties, we should expect fewer warnings before suicide attacks.[29]

TABLE 6.1
Descriptive Statistics

Variable Name	Observations	Mean	Std. Dev.	Min.	Max.
Warning	12,235	0.0531	0.2243	0	1
Territory	12,235	0.6310	0.4826	0	1
State Sponsored	12,235	0.3631	0.4809	0	1
Resources	12,235	0.4888	0.4999	0	1
Polity2	11,247	5.374	4.146	−9	10
Separatist	12,235	0.2877	0.4527	0	1
Religious	12,235	0.5389	0.4985	0	1
Ethnic	12,235	0.2585	0.4378	0	1
Leftist	12,235	0.2571	0.4371	0	1
Reactionary	12,235	0.0141	0.1181	0	1
Suicide	12,235	0.1147	0.3186	0	1
Utilities	12,235	0.0910	0.2876	0	1
Private Citizens	12,235	0.3251	0.4684	0	1
Government	12,235	0.1516	0.3587	0	1
Business	12,235	0.1726	0.3779	0	1
Civil Society	12,235	0.0826	0.2753	0	1
Infrastructure	12,235	0.1038	0.3050	0	1
Tourists	12,235	0.0034	0.0585	0	1

Analysis

I estimate logit regressions, given the dichotomous nature of my dependent variable. I employ a multilevel specification because my dataset comprises 12,235 bombings carried out by 131 terrorist groups.[30] The multilevel specification treats each group's bombings as related events. It assumes that each terrorist group has idiosyncrasies affecting its overall propensity to give warnings—and the extent to which certain variables influence its decision to warn in a given attack. The multilevel model addresses the first issue by estimating a different regression constant (i.e., random intercept) for each terrorist group. It addresses the second issue by allowing different slope coefficients (random slopes) on certain variables, assuming that their effects differ from group to group.[31] In general, the researcher's decision to allow a random slope on a particular variable is based on the variable's theoretical significance and whether the random slope specification explains more variance than a specification with random intercepts alone.[32] I allow random slopes on *Polity2* and *Suicide*, based on an exhaustive set of likelihood ratio tests demonstrating the superiority of models with random slopes on these variables.[33]

Table 6.2 presents the results of several different model specifications.[34] Model 1 contains *Territory* and *Polity2*, two variables relevant to my argument about legitimacy and the incentive to warn. It also includes *Resources* and *State Sponsored*, two variables that might decrease militants' legitimacy concerns and disincentivize warnings. Model 2 includes only the ideological variables: *Religious*, *Ethnic*, *Leftist*, *Reactionary*, and *Separatist*. Model 3 combines the variables of the previous two models. Model 4 adds the control variable *Suicide*. Model 5 introduces the target type variables relevant to hypothesis 2 and my argument that economic disruption strategies incentivize warnings. Because model 5 includes all the relevant variables and controls, this is the specification I interpret substantively.

The results in table 6.2 support my theoretical argument. Consistent with hypothesis 1a, the coefficients on *Territory* are always negative and are statistically significant at a 99 percent confidence level. Groups that possess territory are less likely to give warnings. Consistent with hypothesis 1b, the coefficients on *Polity2* are always positive and statistically significant at a 99 percent confidence level. Militant groups fighting democratic governments are more likely to give casualty-reducing warnings. Taken together, these findings support my theoretical proposition that militant groups facing elevated legitimacy concerns are more likely to give warnings. If a militant group lacks territory and is forced to hide among the state's civilians, or if a militant group fights a democratic regime, the group's legitimacy concerns are more pronounced and it is more likely to give warnings to reduce the number of civilians killed in its attacks.

The coefficients on the target type variables give support to hypothesis 2, regarding the strategy of economic coercion as an incentive to warn. The coefficients for all target types are positive, indicating a higher probability of warnings for attacks on these targets, compared to attacks on utilities. This makes intuitive sense because utility targets (power lines, water treatment facilities, etc.) are often empty of people, so there is no one at the scene to warn. With the exception of *Private Citizens*, the coefficients on all target types are statistically significant at 95 percent level or higher.

TABLE 6.2
Multilevel Logit Results

Probability of Warning	Model 1	Model 2	Model 3	Model 4	Model 5
Territory	−0.8227***		−0.8203***	−0.8057***	−0.8197***
	(0.23)		(0.23)	(0.23)	(0.23)
State Sponsored	0.2623		0.2473	0.3010	0.2862
	(0.27)		(0.27)	(0.27)	(0.27)
Resources	−0.5401**		−0.5413**	−0.5786**	−0.4464*
	(0.23)		(0.23)	(0.23)	(0.24)
Polity2	0.2062***		0.2017***	0.2138***	0.1995***
	(0.05)		(0.05)	(0.05)	(0.05)
Separatist		0.3706	−0.5056	−0.4820	−0.3976
		(0.74)	(0.84)	(0.82)	(0.77)
Religious		−1.285**	−0.6723	−0.6997	−0.6633
		(0.63)	(0.71)	(0.69)	(0.65)
Ethnic		0.1187	−0.4442	−0.4092	−0.4239
		(0.77)	(0.88)	(0.86)	(0.80)
Leftist		0.9802	0.4680	0.4591	0.4037
		(0.68)	(0.75)	(0.74)	(0.69)
Reactionary		−0.0063	−0.6653	−0.6700	−0.6626
		(1.1)	(1.5)	(1.5)	(1.4)
Suicide				−0.8412	−0.8614
				(0.64)	(0.65)
Private Citizens					0.7200*
					(0.40)
Government					0.9348**
					(0.40)

Probability of Warning	Model 1	Model 2	Model 3	Model 4	Model 5
Business					0.9638**
					(0.39)
Civil Society					1.013**
					(0.43)
Infrastructure					1.405***
					(0.40)
Tourists					3.638***
					(0.59)
Constant	−5.166***	−4.257***	−4.644***	−4.705***	−5.470***
	(0.45)	(0.67)	(0.78)	(0.76)	(0.78)
Var(Polity2)	0.0458		0.0448	0.0381	0.0319
	(0.02)		(0.02)	(0.01)	(0.01)
Var(Suicide)				1.988	1.981
				(1.4)	(1.4)
Var(constant)	2.361	3.871	1.997	1.997	1.589
	(0.92)	(0.91)	(0.81)	(0.83)	(0.70)
Log likelihood	−1517.38	−1695.71	−1513.23	−1504.86	−1411.29
Wald x2	38.25	18.31	45.48	50.26	103.3
N	11,247	12,235	11,247	11,247	10,441
Groups	129	131	129	129	129

Obs./group (min., avg., max.)—Models 1, 3 & 4: 1, 87.2, 1,852
Model 2: 1, 93.4, 1,962; Model 5: 1, 80.9, 1,709
*p < 0.1; **p < 0.05; ***p < 0.01

A closer look at the results shows the logic of hypothesis 2 at work. F-tests show that the coefficients on *Infrastructure* and *Tourists*, targets associated with economic activity, are statistically distinguishable from the smaller coefficient on *Private Citizens*.[35] The coefficients on the noneconomic target types *Civil Society* and *Government* are larger than that on *Private*

Citizens, but they are not statistically distinguishable from it. The coefficient on *Business* targets, though larger than that on *Private Citizens*, is not statistically distinguishable from it. This piece of evidence does not support hypothesis 2, but there may be explanations that do not necessarily cut against my argument. For example, my definition of warnings is conservative and does not include the extortion threats that militants commonly issue against business owners. It is likely that in excluding threats that involved extortion, I excluded threats that also served a casualty-limiting function when the businesses were eventually attacked. My data may thus understate the prevalence of warnings in attacks on business targets. Regardless, the greater coefficients on *Infrastructure* and *Tourists*, statistically distinguishable from the coefficient on *Private Citizens*, give strong support to hypothesis 2.

The results of my analysis do not support the various alternative theories that seek to explain civilian targeting based on militants' ideologies. The coefficients on *Religious* are negative in all specifications and statistically significant in model 2, but their significance disappears when controlling for *Territory* and *Polity2* in models 3–5. The ideological variables *Separatist*, *Ethnic*, *Leftist*, and *Reactionary* show no significant effects either. The null effect of *Religious* is worth examining because it defies the terrorism literature's conventional wisdom about religion and its alleged brutalizing effect on militants' behavior.[36] It is true that religious groups give warnings less frequently than secular groups do—1.7 percent of the time compared to 9.5 percent. But the relationship between religion and civilian victimization cannot be understood in isolation from other independent variables. Table 6.3's Pearson correlation matrix offers some clues as to why incorporating *Territory* and *Polity2* into the regression model renders *Religious*'s effect insignificant. *Religious* is positively correlated with *Territory*, indicating that religious militant groups are more likely to control territory than are secular groups. *Religious* is negatively correlated with *Polity2*, indicating that religious groups are, on average, less likely to fight democracies. The negative correlation between *Territory* and *Polity2* suggests that nondemocracies are also less effective at keeping their territory out of militants' hands. Taken together, this evidence suggests a nuanced explanation for religion's apparent association with bloody surprise attacks: religious militant groups are more likely to fight nondemocratic states with loose control of their territory. Emerging from illiberal and unstable places like Syria and Afghanistan, religious militant groups may face fewer political

TABLE 6.3
Pearson Correlation Matrix

	Religious	Territory	Polity2
Religious	1.0	0.3373	−0.3467
Territory		1.0	−0.2304
Polity2			1.0

consequences for engaging in indiscriminate violence. The issue has less to do with religion than with the low standard of legitimacy set by nondemocracies and the fact that militants can shelter in strongholds, escaping accountability that civilians might otherwise impose on them.

My results also stand somewhat at odds with previous findings linking state sponsorship and resource endowments to civilian abuse. The coefficients on *State Sponsored* are positive and statistically insignificant in all models, defying the conventional wisdom that state-sponsored militants are more brutal toward civilians.[37] The coefficients on *Resources* are always negative, a finding that appears to support the linkage between resource endowments and civilian victimization.[38] However, the effect of *Resources* is not statistically significant when controlling for *Territory*, *Polity2*, and the target types. Thus my results cannot be taken as support for these earlier studies' findings.

It is interesting to speculate about why territory should decrease militants' propensity to warn, while state sponsorship and resources do not. In theory, all three of these endowments reduce terrorists' accountability to the state's civilians; the militants no longer depend on the state's population for shelter, funding, and material. But perhaps terrorist groups, like humans, have a "hierarchy of needs."[39] Some needs may be more important and harder to offset. A group without territory must depend on civilians for shelter regardless of whether the group has smuggling revenues or a foreign state sponsor providing money and weapons.[40] The need for shelter may thus be a more powerful lever of accountability. It allows civilians to turn the tables on terrorists, threatening to evict them if they kill indiscriminately.

The control variable *Suicide* has a negative coefficient in all models where it appears. The coefficient is never statistically significant, however. It is not common to pair the two tactics, but roughly 1 percent of the 1,403 suicide attacks in my data were preceded by warnings. ISIL, for instance, has given warnings prior to suicide attacks on Iraqi polling places.[41] These warnings were given days in advance, foreshadowing attacks on polling sites but not specifying precisely which sites would be attacked. Devout Muslims knew to avoid voting. Those who do not heed the warning were, by the Islamic State's reckoning, legitimate targets worthy of death in suicide attacks that, because of the warnings' general character, maintained some of their tactical advantage.

Robustness

The book's appendix presents several alternative models to confirm the robustness of my findings. Table A.5 replaces the multilevel model specification with a conventional logit with fixed effects for each terrorist group. Table A.6 shows multilevel models with additional control variables. One of these variables accounts for the fact that certain attacks target sites that are likely to be vacant at the time (e.g., businesses "after hours"). One would expect warnings to be unnecessary in some of these cases. Another model controls for the extent of press freedom in the country where each attack occurred (because a restricted press may not reliably report warnings). A third alternative specification in the table employs a *Polity2* measure based on the *Polity2* score of the country where the attack took place, not the *Polity2* score of the perpetrator group's target state. Table A.7 raises the dataset's inclusion threshold, omitting groups that carried out fewer than fifty, seventy-five, or one hundred attacks. Table A.8 incorporates alternative measures of democracy in place of *Polity2*: the Political Terror Scale (PTS), Freedom House civil liberties (CL) and political rights (PR) scores, the democracy (*democ*) component score of *Polity2*, and the autocracy (*autoc*) component of *Polity2*.[42] These respecifications and adjustments to the dataset do not change the significance levels or substantially alter the magnitudes of the effects shown in my main results in table 6.2, model 5.

Marginal Effects

The signs and significance levels of regression coefficients can help us to assess my theoretical argument in general. But we gain more substantive insight by examining the average marginal effects (AMEs) of key variables and determining how the predicted probability of warnings changes when these variables change. Setting all of model 5's independent variables to zero, the predicted probability of warning is just 0.9 percent. If we hold all the variables at their means (see table 6.1), the probability of warning is slightly higher, at 2.6 percent. This scenario closely resembles several groups in my dataset. For example, Turkey's Kurdistan Workers' Party (PKK) has average *Territory* and *Polity2* values (0.838 and 4.47) close to the sample averages of 0.63 and 5.37. The PKK gave warnings for 2.9 percent of its 241 attacks.

Figure 6.1 plots the average marginal effects of the independent variables in model 5. *Territory*, the independent variable relevant to hypothesis 1a, decreases the probability of warning by 2.9 percent. With all other variables held at their means, the predicted probabilities of warning are 6.7 percent for groups without territory and 3.8 percent for groups with territory. Boko Haram, one the groups analyzed in chapter 5, illustrates the within-case variation that can occur when a group gains or loses its territorial strongholds. The group's average *Territory* value is 53 percent (slightly below the sample average), and it gave warnings for 4.6 percent of its 459

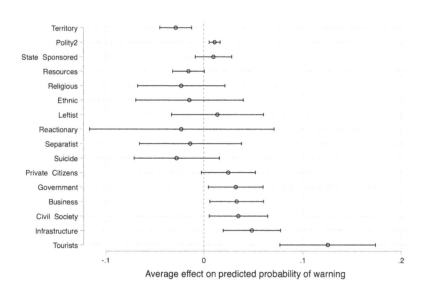

Figure 6.1 Average Marginal Effects

attacks. Looking closer, however, one sees the logic of hypothesis 1a at work: Boko Haram's frequency of warning was 7.4 percent in years when it possessed no territory and just 2.1 percent when it possessed territory.

Considering the marginal effects of *Polity2*, the independent variable of hypothesis 1b, ascending one point on the scale increases the predicted probability of warning by 1.1 percent. With all other variables fixed at their means, the probability of warning is 0.5 percent at *Polity2* = -10 and 10 percent at *Polity2* = 10. It is also interesting to consider the changes that occur with varying levels of democracy and a given realization of *Territory*. Figure 6.2 displays the predicted probabilities for all values of *Polity2* and *Territory*, holding other variables at their means. At *Polity2* = -10 and *Territory* = 1, the probability of warning is just 0.4 percent. Substantively, this situation resembles that of the Free Syrian Army, which always held territory and had an average *Polity2* score of -8.9 across its thirty-eight bombings. The FSA gave warnings for none of these attacks. Even in a hypothetical scenario where the FSA fought a liberal democracy with a *Polity2* score of 10, the possession of territory would still mitigate the group's accountability to civilian audiences. The predicted probability of warning would rise modestly to about 8 percent. But for groups with no strongholds, there is

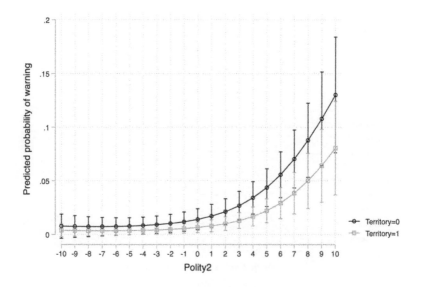

Figure 6.2 Predicted Probability of Warning, by *Territory* and *Polity2* Score

more upside in the probability of warnings as democracy increases. When *Territory* = 0, the probability of warnings is less than 1 percent at *Polity2* = -10, but it rises to 13 percent at *Polity2* = 10. This approximates the situation of several groups that never held territory and fought governments with *Polity2* averages of 9 or greater: Turkey's Dev Sol, which gave warnings for 13 percent of its thirty-two attacks; Greece's November 17 Revolutionary Organization, which gave warnings for 11 percent of its thirty-seven attacks; and the Puerto Rican separatist group FALN, which gave warnings for 9 percent of its ninety-two attacks.

Not all the variation in warning behavior can be explained by *Territory* and *Polity2*. ETA and the IRA, for instance, never held territory and fought states with average *Polity2* scores of 9.85 and 10, respectively. ETA gave warnings for 45 percent of its 309 attacks; the IRA gave warnings for 44 percent of its 360. These groups' high frequencies of warning may be partly attributable to target selection (the logic of hypothesis 2). For example, roughly 5 percent of ETA's attacks targeted tourist sites. As figure 6.1 shows, the average marginal effect of selecting tourism targets is substantial, increasing the probability of warning by roughly 12.5 percent. Overall, 48 percent of all tourism-related attacks in my data were preceded by warnings.

There is still something distinctive about ETA, however. Looking at the group's tourism-related attacks, the frequency of warning is an astonishingly high 86 percent. Even in its nontourism bombings, ETA gave warnings 42 percent of the time. The group's high rate of warning is, to some degree, driven by idiosyncratic factors that cannot be modeled—most notably, the Basque public's distinctive willingness to sanction a group that engages in indiscriminate violence.[43] We can find bloody counterexamples to contrast with ETA—groups that give far fewer warnings than we might expect, given their realizations of key variables. Consider ISIL and Colombia's FARC. These groups possessed territory for nearly all their attacks, but their respective *Polity2* averages (5.14 and 7.18) give us reason to expect a moderate frequency of warnings—2 percent for a group with ISIL's realizations of *Territory* and *Polity2* and 4 percent for FARC's realizations. Empirically, however, ISIL and FARC gave warnings 0.5 percent and 0.7 percent of the time. In sum, there is considerable variation in groups' baseline propensities to warn, and in their responsiveness to key independent variables such as *Polity2*. This is why we need a multilevel model to provide accurate estimates of key variables' effects.

Discussion

This analysis generally supports my argument concerning the use of warnings to reduce casualties and disrupt the state's economy. It shows that terrorist organizations are likely to give truthful warnings under three political conditions: when the group lacks territory, when the state is a democracy, and when the group is engaged in a campaign of economic coercion. The result regarding territory is remarkable because it cuts against conventional wisdom in the civil war literature. That literature argues that territory moderates militants' behavior toward civilians. But this moderating logic plays out in the militants' own strongholds, not on the state's territory, where terrorist bombings typically occur. My results suggest that attacks on the state's civilians become more brutal and indiscriminate when terrorists possess strongholds of their own. My findings show the need to qualify existing claims about territory. What holds true in the civil war literature more generally does not always hold true in the strategic setting of terrorism.

This chapter's large-N quantitative research design complements the qualitative approaches of chapters 3–5. The comparative case studies in those chapters treated the ideologies and political goals of militants as constants. This chapter treats ideology and political goals as variables in their own right. Even when ideologies and political goals vary, the same factors emphasized in my theory—territory, the democratic legitimacy of the state, and economic coercion strategies—are significant predictors of preattack warnings.

My results contradict the conventional wisdom that religion increases militants' propensity to target civilians. A closer analysis of the results suggests that we may need to revisit that conventional wisdom in light of the role of territory and regime type. Without controlling for these variables, religion does show a raw association with no-warning attacks. But introducing territory and regime type washes out the apparent significance of religion's effect. A correlational analysis shows why this is the case. Religious and secular terrorist groups tend to come from different political environments. Religious groups' adversaries are generally less democratic and less effective at denying militants control of territory. Because of these situational factors, religious terrorist groups may feel less pressure to uphold humanitarian standards in their conflict behavior. It is no surprise, then, that when we control for territory and democracy, religion exerts no significant effect on terrorists' propensities to warn. These findings give us reason to scrutinize claims elsewhere in the terrorism literature concerning religion's supposed brutalizing effect. Any study making this assertion about religion, without controlling for territorial strongholds and the regime type of the state, should be taken with a grain of salt.

    The analysis in this chapter also offers some practical guidance for interpreting immediate threats. What makes a purported warning believable? My quantitative analysis identifies the political factors (a lack of territory, democracy) that encourage terrorist groups to warn truthfully. A purported warning from a terrorist group without territory or a group fighting a democracy has greater plausibility, ex ante. The analysis also suggests that warnings are more credible when issued against economic targets such as infrastructure and tourism. Warnings are less credible when issued against utility targets and private citizens, a finding that offers some reassurance to individuals receiving anonymous death threats. The concluding chapter develops these insights further. It offers specific recommendations for assessing any given threat, based on the capabilities of the militant group, the group's incentives for threatening truthfully or falsely, and the likelihood that anyone could impersonate the terrorist group and issue hoax threats in its name.

Conclusion

Findings, Recommendations, and Predictions

Threats and violence are the two halves of terrorists' coercive tool kit. By reframing our understanding of terrorism and giving threats equal analytical priority, I seek to enrich our account of this subject. This book shows how terrorists achieve their strategic goals. As nonstate actors, terrorists cannot easily overpower governments, but they can issue threats to manipulate perceptions, induce fear, and obtain concessions. Terrorists also use threats to impose social control. By menacing civilians who undertake proscribed activities—collaborating with the state, violating religious edicts, and so on—terrorists shape personal and political behavior. Whether issued against state or society, threats are a crucial link between terrorist violence and its political outcomes.

This book also calls attention to threats' integral role in the attack. By helping to determine the consequences of violence, or by substituting for violence, threats ensure that each action advances terrorists' messaging strategy. I develop these insights by highlighting the multiple audiences conundrum that terrorists face. Violent actions taken to coerce the enemy risk alienating terrorists' supporters. Threats help to alleviate this problem. Warnings and hoaxes enable terrorists to destroy property and destabilize the state while sparing civilians from harm. They split terrorism's signal, projecting images of strength to enemies and images of restraint to friendly civilian audiences. Immediate threats can also draw security forces into traps or interfere with their actions so that physical attacks are more likely to succeed. When violence alone would achieve suboptimal messaging outcomes, terrorists use threats to adjust the pattern of damage, ensuring that the optimal message is sent.

Summary of Findings

I developed the theoretical basis for my argument in chapter 1. My theoretical framework conceptualizes terrorism as consisting of threats and violence. It disaggregates terrorism into several temporal moments: preattack, attack, and postattack, with the postattack outcomes creating conditions for future episodes of terrorism. My theory also distinguishes four categories of threats. Warnings and hoaxes threaten immediate violence. These are tactical threats issued at the moment of the attack. They disrupt the economy, increase or decrease bloodshed, and interfere with security forces' operations. Pledges and bluffs threaten violence prospectively. These are coercive threats issued in the preattack moment. They intimidate civilians, aggrandize the terrorist group, and build credibility for political bargaining with the state. A single threat may serve more than one function. For example, religious terrorist groups may warn their coreligionists not to frequent sinful establishments such as bars and secular schools. These threats serve as tools of social control, means of casualty reduction, and means of justifying civilian casualties that result from attacks on the threatened targets. The fulfillment of a threat builds credibility as a postattack outcome. By increasing the credibility of its future threats, the terrorist group enhances its leverage to extract concessions from the state and civilians in the future. My analysis leads to six propositions about when terrorists will issue particular types of threats:

1. Terrorists will issue warnings when they seek political legitimacy.
2. Terrorists will issue warnings and/or hoaxes when they seek to disrupt the state's economy.
3. Terrorists will issue pledges and/or bluffs (against civilians) when they seek social control.
4. Terrorists will issue pledges and/or bluffs (against the state) when they seek negotiations.

5. Terrorists will issue pledges and/or bluffs when they seek to aggrandize their reputations.
6. Terrorists will issue warnings, hoaxes, pledges, and/or bluffs to seek advantage against strong counterterrorist opponents.

Chapter 2 presented a case study of the IRA, showing all the functions that threats perform. IRA tacticians integrated warnings and hoaxes with their violence. They bombed buildings, causing physical and financial damage, but their warnings allowed civilians to escape. Follow-on hoaxes imposed additional economic disruption and could be used to lure police into deadly ambushes. The IRA employed these tactics because it had multiple political audiences to consider: the British state adversary and supportive civilians in Ireland and the United States. Economic attrition and attacks on security forces coerced the British state into negotiations over Northern Ireland's political future. Civilian casualty reduction, via warnings, signaled humanitarian restraint to the IRA's supporters. This signal splitting could work only if British authorities responded to IRA threats. To ensure a police response to warnings and a political response to the IRA's diplomatic overtures, the IRA created an elaborate set of trust-building institutions. These included third-party intermediaries and code words that demonstrated the IRA Army Council's ability to control its cells. The system showed that the IRA could ratchet the level of violence up or down, depending on whether the British state accepted or rejected IRA peace terms.

The next three chapters presented contrasting case studies of different terrorist groups, matched to control for ideological factors. Chapter 3 compared ETA and the Tamil Tigers (LTTE), two ethnic separatist groups. This case pair highlighted the divergent uses of threats that arise from groups with different legitimacy concerns, different emphases on economic disruption, and different levels of counterterrorism pressure to overcome. The incentive structure of ETA (depending on civilians for shelter, fighting a democracy, and attempting a strategy of economic coercion) pushed this group to give more warnings than the LTTE did. ETA also issued more hoaxes, although it ceased this practice after an incident in which police disbelieved a truthful bomb warning and twenty-one civilians perished. ETA also had greater incentives to issue prophylactic threats. Spanish police were far more competent counterterrorists, compared to Sri Lanka's historically ineffective police. Consistent with expectations, ETA made more extensive use of prophylactic threats to distract, misdirect, and otherwise interfere with Spanish counterterrorism. However, the LTTE's use of prophylactic bluffs increased toward the end of the Sri Lankan civil war as the group's military fortunes waned. By threatening soft civilian targets, the LTTE sought to draw security resources away from the military front and away from political targets the group was planning to attack. ETA and the LTTE had similar incentives with regard to social control and negotiation with the state. Both groups issued pledges against civilian and state targets, coupled with their coercive demands.

Chapter 4 compared the MRTA and the Shining Path, two Marxist rebel groups in Peru. The discussion showed how different incentives for legitimacy seeking, disruption, social control, negotiation, and aggrandizement shape militants' uses of threats. Compared to the Shining Path, the MRTA faced a more intense multiple audiences conundrum. It lacked territory and operated in Peru's cities. The Shining Path held rural territory where it could arrange its own shelter. The MRTA also showed a greater tendency to target Peru's economy, particularly the local branches of U.S. companies. Consistent with my theoretical argument, the MRTA gave more frequent warnings. The incentives of the MRTA and the Shining Path also diverged with regard to prospective threats. The Shining Path had far more extensive social control aims, seeking to regulate the minute details of Peruvians' lives. The MRTA did not seek the same degree of social control, but it did seek to open negotiations with the Peruvian state. Consistent with the logic of my argument, we see a more extensive pattern of Shining Path pledges against civilians, and a pattern of MRTA pledges against the state. In fact, we also see bluff threats by the MRTA against the state. This is what my argument leads us to expect from a group that was always in the shadow of the Shining Path, seeking to attract attention away from its militarily more prolific rival. The MRTA's boastful, sometimes false threats were not matched by a similar pattern from the Shining Path until late in the conflict. As the Maoists' rural formations found themselves under counterterrorism pressure and their capabilities began to decline, Abimael Guzmán promised a dramatic escalation of violence against Peruvian cities. Guzmán hoped that, through bluster, the Shining Path could provoke the government into a counterproductive crackdown that would restore support for the terrorist group. His gamble failed.

Chapter 5 compared three jihadist groups: the Afghan Taliban, ISIL, and Boko Haram. These cases showed the remarkable consistency of social control threats by groups with similar state-building projects. All three groups couple their proclamations of religious law with explicit threats against civilians who defy their behavioral demands. Despite these similarities, the jihadist cases also showed the different patterns of threats that arise from groups with divergent incentives for legitimacy seeking, negotiation, aggrandizement, and advantage seeking. Boko Haram faces a more intense multiple audiences conundrum owing to its difficulty controlling territory and the relatively democratic example set by the Nigerian state. The Taliban and ISIL have controlled large swathes of territory (although ISIL has lost its strongholds recently). The Taliban and ISIL have both fought governments that were largely autocratic or dysfunctional. In keeping with my theoretical argument, we see more warnings from Boko Haram. Regarding negotiation, Boko Haram and the Taliban have both sought to bargain political issues with their state opponents. Both have coupled their demands with threats against their adversary states. ISIL, which disavows negotiation, has issued fewer threats of this sort. Regarding aggrandizement, the Taliban have followed a consistent upward trajectory in military strength since 2002. They do not engage in boastful bluffing, but their truthful pledges are useful in building credibility for negotiation-oriented threats against their state enemies. ISIL had good military fortunes until 2015, when an international coalition began to degrade the group's ground forces and territorial strongholds. Since then, ISIL has issued implausible bluff threats, even promising to conquer entire European countries. Boko Haram's incentives for self-aggrandizement have varied with its changing military status, from near-oblivion in 2009 to an apogee of territorial control in 2014–2015, and a return to underground insurgency since. The pattern of threats is consistent with my argument: Boko Haram, particularly the Shekau faction, issued flurries of boastful bluff threats at its nadirs in 2009 and 2016–2017. Finally, my argument leads us to expect more advantage-seeking threats by Boko Haram and the Taliban than from ISIL. This is because Boko Haram and the Taliban fight in areas of state control and contested control, where police are able to interdict terrorist operations. ISIL has fought a more conventional war, with clearly delineated battle lines. As my argument would predict, Boko Haram and the Taliban issue more prophylactic, advantage-seeking threats. This may change, however, as a postcaliphate ISIL reverts to a strategy of insurgency and finds prophylactic threats to be more useful.

Chapter 6 used large-N quantitative methods to test my theoretical propositions about warnings. This was useful for several reasons. First, large-N methods allowed me to test hypotheses on a much wider cross section of militant groups across a greater span of history. Second, the comparative case studies presented in previous chapters were grouped by ideology, obscuring any possible role ideological variables might play in mediating warning behavior. By comparing 131 terrorist groups of varying ideologies, chapter 6's analysis served as an important check on the qualitative chapters' findings. Third, warnings are a type of threat that merits emergency action to save lives. Determining which factors compel a group to warn brings us closer to understanding what makes immediate threats credible. The empirical analysis in chapter 6 provided strong support for my argument. Terrorists issue warnings when they face legitimacy concerns, specifically when they lack territory and when they fight democracies. Terrorists are also more likely to warn when they attack economic targets. The chapter does not support alternative hypotheses derived from other terrorism literature—for instance, that religious groups are more likely to employ brutal tactics such as no-warning bombings. In my analysis of warnings, ideology makes no difference. Additionally, my finding about territory suggests a need to qualify the common assertion that territorial holdings moderate militants' behavior toward civilians.[1] With regard to terrorist bombings of civilian targets (a mode of violence generally carried out on state-controlled territory), the possession of strongholds encourages more brutal, no-warning attacks.

Academic Impact: The Importance of Threats and the Effectiveness of Terrorism

These findings are significant to the field of terrorism studies. They demonstrate the centrality of threats to our understanding of terrorism. Although academic studies of terrorism regard threats and violence as "equally important" in the abstract,[2] the vast majority of the terrorism literature has focused on the violent half of terrorists' coercive tool kit.[3] This is a significant oversight. As the international crisis diplomacy literature shows, coercion operates not through violence but through the threat of more violence to come.[4] By explaining the role of pledges and bluffs in coercion, this book shows how terrorism works politically. It brings the terrorism literature in line with terrorist practice, which has always involved the use of coercive threats.

This book also shows how threats mitigate the multiple audiences conundrum, a pervasive problem faced by terrorist groups. The same attack that signals strength to terrorists' enemies may inadvertently signal brutality to friendly audiences, jeopardizing terrorists' access to shelter, funding, and other vital resources. To alleviate the multiple audiences conundrum, terrorists incorporate threats into their tactical plans. They use warnings and hoaxes to reduce the number of civilian casualties, focus harm on security forces, and achieve bloodless economic disruption by shutting down commercial centers and infrastructure. Threats alter the pattern of damage so that a single attack signals strength to enemies and restraint to friends. Signal splitting of this kind may render terrorism politically sustainable in the long term. These findings are important additions to the literature on terrorists' communication with their audiences. Terrorist communication is enabled by violence, but it is rendered more precise and more potent with the use of threats.

Another major contribution of this book concerns the issue of effectiveness. My analysis suggests that terrorism is more effective than existing studies appreciate. A substantial body of empirical scholarship finds that terrorism generally fails to deliver political results.[5] One reason is that terrorists often target civilians, provoking backlash.[6] Terrorism against civilians is also "useless for taking or holding territory" ruled by the government.[7] My analysis of threats raises useful critiques of these arguments. First, they suppose a narrow definition of terrorism as indiscriminate violence against civilians. I argue that terrorism should be understood more broadly as *violence and threats*. I show how terrorist groups like the IRA, ETA, the MRTA, and Boko Haram use threats to render violence more discriminate and less harmful to civilians. If we consider only indiscriminate attacks on civilians ("pure hurting," in Thomas Schelling's words[8]) we restrict our focus to the least sophisticated and most alienating variety of terrorism. It is no wonder that empirical studies using this definition show terrorism to be ineffective.

When terrorists mix violence and threats, they appear more legitimate and are able to sustain their campaigns for longer stretches of time. This persistence, enabled by threats, is actually a measure of success. Another measure is the ability to force the state into negotiations. The IRA, ETA, the LTTE, and the Taliban dragged governments to the bargaining table through a combination of physical violence and threats. This is an impressive feat for relatively weak nonstate actors. The IRA actually extracted some concessions from the British government. ETA and the LTTE might have extracted concessions, but they were stubborn negotiators, refusing to accept anything short of sovereign statehood.[9] Terrorism could have been successful in these cases, even by the lofty standard set by the literature, if ETA and the LTTE had accepted limited gains rather than holding out for territorial concessions virtually no state is willing to give.

We should also acknowledge terrorists' success at coercing civilians. This subject is easily overlooked by terrorism studies that focus on violence while ignoring threats. Social control is arguably the area in which terrorism is most effective. Civilians are vulnerable targets, nearly defenseless and in most cases easy to follow home to where they lay their heads. Terrorists obtain a remarkable degree of social control through threats. Consider just a few examples from my case studies: the IRA coercing drug dealers to show up for kneecapping by appointment, ETA forcing the abandonment of a nearly completed nuclear power plant, the Shining Path reorganizing entire villages, Boko Haram and the Taliban closing down school systems and telephone grids, ISIL and the LTTE imposing highly bureaucratized state-like regimes. Whether we regard these outcomes as terrorist successes depends on how much attention we pay to threats. If we understand threats as part of terrorists' tool kit, we can appreciate the effectiveness of terrorism in controlling civilian populations.

Scholars have offered some rules and recommendations for militants seeking to increase their political effectiveness.[10] My analysis suggests an important addition: militants who use terrorism should take full advantage of threats. Threats bring results. They are supremely effective at intimidating civilians. They are effective at shaping the physical consequences of violence—sparing bystanders, victimizing security forces, and disrupting the economy. Threats help militant groups to persist. Eventually, they may bring the government to the bargaining table. Threats may not secure major policy concessions such as full statehood, but they can earn limited concessions if militants are pragmatic enough to accept them.

Practical Impact: When Are Threats Dangerous?

My analysis also produces practical guidance for people who receive threats. I believe that these recommendations will become increasingly important with time, owing to the likely proliferation of threats as we live more of our lives through laptops and smart devices. Here, a personal anecdote may be useful to illustrate the point. In 2017, as I was writing the early portions of this book, I received several online death threats from alt-right trolls and individuals claiming to represent white supremacist "patriot" groups. I considered what to do—adjust my daily routine, report the threats, or ignore them. I ultimately decided to ignore the threats, but not before reflecting on how best to determine the actual danger they presented. Was there a way of estimating the credibility of a threat, based on the content of the message and some prior knowledge of the militant landscape? I believe there is a way, emerging from the analysis in this book.

We can identify three dimensions of credibility in terrorist threats. Each represents an issue that the receiver should consider when assessing whether a given threat is likely to be true. The first issue is the capability of the purported terrorist group making the threat. The second issue is truthfulness—whether the terrorist group has reasons to issue truthful threats when attacking, and to abstain from false threats when not attacking. The third issue is whether the sender of the message is who they claim to be. As Republican #2 points out in chapter 2, "some person, with a few beers in them or not, might decide for any one of one hundred thousand reasons, to issue a few bomb warnings."[11] The receiver of a threat must determine, to the best of their ability, whether the sender is just "some person" or an actual militant with the capability to do harm.

Regarding the first issue, capability, the question is whether the militant group referenced in the threat possesses the physical ability to carry out the threatened action at the time and place foreshadowed in the message. To demonstrate the importance of capability, consider an episode that unfolded in Los Angeles city schools in 2015. On December 15 "a crudely written email threat," referencing ISIL, caused the Los Angeles Board of Education to shutter all nine hundred schools in its system.[12] Some 640,000 students were kept out of class and droves of police were sent to search the schools, but nothing suspicious was found.[13] Los Angeles parents later questioned the city's response, as did representatives of the New York City Police Department. Days earlier, the NYPD had "dismissed a nearly identical threat from the same sender as an obvious hoax."[14] Why? One reason was the content of the threat, promising a nerve gas attack by no fewer than thirty-two jihadists.[15] ISIL had never demonstrated a capability to use nerve gas, let alone in the United States. Granting that there is a first time for everything, it is usually possible to assess a threat's plausibility based on abilities the militant group has already shown.[16] If the details of a threat suggest novelty or a nonlinear jump in capabilities, one should view the threat with skepticism.

Considering the second issue, truthfulness, the receiver of a threat should assess whether the issuer has incentives to speak accurately or to mislead. If the issuers were actually planning to carry out the threatened attack, would they tip their hand in advance? Conversely, if the terrorist group were not planning to carry out the attack, would it have reason to threaten falsely? Earlier in this book I discussed the "helpful" threats that terrorists sometimes give, warning civilians away from attacks that are only intended to harm the state or its economy. Chapter 6 showed that two key incentives for warning are the lack of territorial bases and the high legitimacy threshold that comes from fighting a democracy. If the audience receiving a threat knows that the issuer's incentives are for casualty reduction or economic disruption, they should expect truthful warnings with some probability. The probability of hoaxes decreases as incentives for casualty reduction increase, since the group will seek to preserve the credibility of its warnings. (An American school district receiving a threat from ISIL can take reassurance from the fact that this group has low incentives for warning truthfully.) With regard to prospective threats, we expect terrorists to issue pledges and bluffs to achieve social control and to squeeze policy concessions from the state. But this assumes that the militant group has social control aims or concrete political demands to negotiate. A purported pledge from a millennialist group like ISIL, outside of the group's claimed caliphate, should also be viewed with skepticism. Even groups with negotiable aims may bluff from time to time, but the incentive to bluff decreases if the militant group believes negotiation could prove fruitful in the future. The IRA spent considerable effort at the height of its campaign developing a reputation for truthfulness so that its warnings and pledges would be believed. But during the disarmament process, the IRA's time horizons shortened and it issued bluffs such as the one following the Northern Bank robbery. Anyone receiving a threat from a declining group should stop to ask whether the group still cares about its credibility or whether it is merely hoping to project potency or spend down reputational capital for last minute concessions while it can still get them.

The third issue, the identity of the threatener, is particularly thorny. It is often impossible for terrorists to communicate face-to-face or through other direct channels because they face the risk of arrest or imprisonment.

This introduces credibility problems not foreseen in the literature on coercive diplomacy, in which each country generally knows it is dealing with the other country's authorized representative.[17] Sometimes a group that wants to be believed will find its own ways around the anonymity problem. The IRA used an elaborate system of intermediaries and code words that could authenticate pledges and demonstrate the probable truthfulness of warnings. ETA employed intermediaries, dead drops, special maps, and electronic instruments that altered the voices of those making bomb threats. Boko Haram's approach is simultaneously high tech and low tech. The group communicates prospective pledges in online videos, with the image and voice of a spokesman like Abubakar Shekau demonstrating the authenticity of the message. Boko Haram transmits warnings verbally and in leaflets. These low-tech threats induce civilian evacuations and general terror among the population. They have also spawned an epidemic of copycat hoaxes.

Nigeria provides an example of a society coming to grips with credibility questions and hoaxes in the presence of a real militant group that often issues truthful threats. It falls to civil society to determine what to do with purported Boko Haram messages. Over time, Nigerian institutions have arrived at something resembling my protocol for assessing threats based on the three criteria of capability, truthfulness, and the ability to discern the identity of the sender. The learning process has been difficult and costly. For example, in September 2011 southern Nigeria was roiled by an email threat promising bomb attacks at twenty different universities between the 12th and 17th of the month. The threat induced police mobilizations, roadblocks, auto searches, and a wave of absences, but no attack was ultimately detected at any of the campuses.[18] We can sympathize with the difficult position of school administrators and police, facing the coincidence of a bomb threat and an insurgency by a militant group that warns truthfully and attacks schools.[19] Nonetheless, there were red flags that should have raised greater skepticism about whether this particular threat actually originated with Boko Haram. First, the threat was sent to the registrar at the University of Benin, located in Edo State, an area that Boko Haram had not previously attacked.[20] Boko Haram had managed a handful of attacks as far south as Abuja, but UniBen was nearly 500 kilometers south of that. There was reason to doubt whether Boko Haram could attack a university in southern Nigeria—let alone twenty universities, as the threat promised. Moreover, the threat originated from a dubious Ewe-language email account, bokoharamewe@yahoo.com.[21] Boko Haram typically communicates in Hausa, Kanuri, or Fulfulde, but not Ewe, a language rarely spoken in northern Nigeria.[22] In retrospect, it is not surprising that the threat turned out to be false. Even at the time, there was ample reason to suspect that the sender was a hoax artist, possibly a UniBen student trying to trick the registrar into canceling classes. The universities overreacted.

Subsequent hoaxes targeted Nigerian secondary schools, institutions already on edge following Boko Haram's abduction of more than two hundred schoolgirls from Chibok. In these cases, school officials took a more measured approach. When the principal at a boys' school in Makurdi, Benue State, received a letter threatening "to abduct some boys to marry the school girls in [Boko Haram's] custody," administrators opted to keep the school open. Meanwhile, police established a heavily armed security cordon outside.[23] The schoolmaster's skepticism was well founded: Makurdi is over 800 kilometers from Chibok by road—a prohibitively long drive to unite hundreds of kidnapped boys with their would-be brides. Moreover, Boko Haram has never attacked schools in Benue State.[24] There was reason to doubt whether the group could even have delivered the threatening letter (written, uncharacteristically, in pidgin English) to the principal's office without being detected.[25] The Makurdi school's muted reaction was appropriate, as was the skeptical reaction of schools in nearby Lafia when they received similar threats just weeks later.[26]

Nigeria's schools and universities, particularly those outside of Boko Haram's northern heartland, have adopted a sensible attitude of heavily secured skepticism with regard to threats. In late September 2016 administrators at the University of Ibadan (Oyo State) dismissed a bomb threat as "the handiwork of mischievous individuals who wanted to cause commotion." The threat, sent to administrators and staff via email and WhatsApp, warned: "Most of you are going to die before Independence Day [October 1]. . . . Detonation will start going from tomorrow till Independence Day and there is nothing you can do as we are among you."[27] The wording of the threat raised questions about its truthfulness and supposed origin. If Boko Haram were truly intent on killing so many people, why would it tell them—while simultaneously asserting that there is nothing they can do to save themselves? Administrators reacted with increased security measures and public reassurances about the threat's implausibility. The university's director of public relations told the press his assessment of the threat: "I also got it. Anyone could instigate such [a] thing. Some people could be mischievous. Our international students are having their carnival on the campus and everywhere is peaceful. I attribute it to the handiwork of mischievous individuals and vehemently deny any commotion." Police, likewise, encouraged "members of the public to go about their lawful businesses" and disregard the threat, which ultimately amounted to nothing.[28]

We can see in these Nigerian examples an evolution of best practices to assess threats and respond in the least disruptive fashion appropriate to the level of risk. A standard approach to assessing threats can be helpful as well. Three steps—considering the militant group's demonstrated capability, its incentives for truthfulness, and the likelihood that the issuer actually represents the organization—can help the receiver of threats determine which are worth heeding and which can be dismissed. Often the most frightening threats are those that come out of the blue, like the supposed Boko Haram threat to UniBen and the supposed ISIL threat to Los Angeles. The messages are frightening because they defy established patterns and expectations. Fortunately, these threats are also the least likely to be true.

The Future: Threats and Terrorism Research

Threats are inherent to terrorism, and they will persist as long as terrorism remains a useful political strategy for nonstate armed groups. The most instructive predictions about the future will concern the character of threats we are likely to see. My case studies of Boko Haram, the Taliban, and ISIL show how communication technology multiplies the pathways for issuing threats. Boko Haram and its copycats use every possible medium: WhatsApp, email, long-form videos, spoken word, and the group's handwritten notes. The Taliban, which used to rely on night letters, can now transmit videos that are shared virally among Afghan civilians. ISIL takes advantage of social media's viral potential as well, circulating visual memes that reference future attacks on distant targets in Europe. These latter examples show an important trend: the line between threats and incitement is blurring.

Terrorism scholars note a trend toward "crowdsourced" terrorism: the central hub of an organization, via its online publications and social media accounts, calls for attacks, hoping that like-minded individuals will act on the message.[29] Individual terrorists and the autonomous cells of militant groups use this model as well. ISIL's threat against the 2018 World Cup football tournament in Russia, an image of masked jihadists at a football stadium, was both a threat and an incitement for ISIL's international supporters to attack sporting events.[30] The online milieu of the alt-right, neo-nazis, and white supremacists shows a similar convergence of viral threats and incitement. The "echoes" Twitter meme, bracketing a person's name with triple parentheses, can be interpreted as hate speech (identifying and disparaging the person as a Jew), as a veiled threat against the target, and as an invitation for others to attack them.[31] Likewise, tweeting a threatening image at someone—a white supremacist meme, or perhaps a photograph of the person and their physical address—represents a direct threat and an invitation for others to attack. This is the sort of online interaction I had with the alt-right trolls and "patriots" in 2017. One article describes how Twitter trolls labeling journalists with the (((echoes))) meme precipitated a deluge of "death threats, anti-Semitic cartoons, images of concentration camp ovens and executed Jews, threatening emails, even home phone calls."[32] As online communication becomes increasingly visual, symbolic, and viral, we can expect the convergence of threats and incitement to continue. This is a fruitful area of future research on terrorism and threats.

Another trend, likely to continue in the future, is the democratization of threats. The omnipresence of networked communication technology and the expansion of the individual's online presence make it easier for any person or political organization to communicate threats. At the same time, the growing connectivity of institutions via multiple online platforms increases each institution's exposure to threats. Compared to the heyday of the IRA and ETA, when the means of threatening (and of being threatened) consisted of phone, letter, and the spoken word, the potential vectors for threats are more numerous and diverse. Nigerian universities may be menaced by email, mobile messaging, and social media, by Boko Haram or any of the 1.9 million university students in the country.[33] For countries with active insurgencies, it is more important than ever to have a rigorous protocol for evaluating threats and discerning the dangerous messages from an increasingly high volume of pranks. In countries without large, active insurgencies, the ratio of nuisance threats to real danger will be even more lopsided.[34] Institutions and individuals can expect to receive a greater volume of threats, with a lower percentage of them being true. As we sort through the welter of threats in our collective future, it will help to have some guidance for interpreting what we see.

This book is one step in that direction. It offers an analysis of how real terrorists' threats work. It develops a basic system for evaluating the credibility of any given threat. The remaining piece is to inform the "priors" of that system. What is the local landscape of militancy in any given country? Which groups and individuals are capable of carrying out violence? Whom would they attack, and would they issue truthful threats beforehand? What sort of media, procedures, or other cues would real terrorists use to identify their own threats and make them stand out from the background noise of pranks? This kind of research, specific to a given context, will be essential to assessing risk in a threat-filled future. Outside of active conflict zones, the future, like the present, is likely to be relatively safe for most of us, with terrorism posing far less danger than preventable disease, road accidents, and extreme weather.[35] Still, it is important to understand the actual risks that exist in a given milieu—geographic, political, or cultural—in order to communicate both reassurance and recommendations for appropriate action on occasions when a threat merits a response. Scholars can do a great deal of useful work in this area.

Appendix

This appendix contains an overview of the interviews I conducted for the IRA portions of this study, a description of my recruitment and interview procedures, sample interview questions, and the human subjects protections I employed during my research.

Qualitative Methods and Human Subjects Protections

The IRA portions of this study are derived from personal interviews of former conflict participants in Northern Ireland. I conducted these interviews on location in 2012–2013. The subject population, including those interviewed for background only, comprised the following:

- Nine former members of the Irish Republican Army (IRA)
- Eight former members of the Royal Ulster Constabulary and British Army reserves
- Ten journalists who reported on Northern Ireland during the 1969–1998 conflict
- Three switchboard operators from charity groups or businesses
- Three current or former government officials

My research subjects all faced personal risks in giving interviews. The risks included physical violence, prosecution, and personal or professional repercussions resulting from the revelation of individuals' participation in conflict activities. Because of these risks, most subjects requested anonymity. Others requested to be kept exclusively "on background," with no quoting of their remarks. The Institutional Review Board–approved research protocol (Columbia University Morningside IRB protocol AAAJ3551) required that all subjects' interview transcripts remain in the exclusive possession of the author. The reasons are described here.

All the IRA members previously served prison sentences for violent crime or membership in proscribed organizations. Several had been released from prison under the condition that they not participate in further illegal activity. In Northern Ireland, release "on license" as part of the Good Friday Agreement (1998) does not guarantee freedom from prosecution for crimes committed during the conflict if individuals were not previously prosecuted and pardoned for those offenses. The revelation of new information is dangerous for former IRA members. Several of the journalists and switchboard operators served as intermediaries for communication between the IRA and British security forces in the past. Because those conversations concerned illegal activity, speaking with researchers carries legal and personal risks. Law enforcement and military interviewees face a threat of assassination by paramilitary groups still active in Northern Ireland. The most recent assassination in Northern Ireland occurred in March 2016 with the car bombing of corrections officer Adrian Ismay.

At the time when these interviews were conducted, the Police Service of Northern Ireland (PSNI) was actively investigating crimes committed during the Troubles. Such crimes included alleged murders by IRA agents. In one case, the PSNI Historical Enquiries Team obtained data collected by Boston College researchers, via an international subpoena executed by the U.S. Department of Justice. A U.S. Supreme Court ruling held that Boston College researchers' data, including interviews of IRA members, could not be withheld on grounds of academic freedom or journalistic privilege. The interview data provided to PSNI led to several high-profile arrests in relation to open murder investigations.

Because of the legal and personal risks to interview subjects, particularly when speaking to academic researchers, most interviewees chose to speak on condition of anonymity. In keeping with their wishes, I collected no identified data and I describe them generically—for instance,

"Republican #1." I provide as much contextual information as subjects allow, for instance, the rank at which a police officer retired. Other interviewees have allowed me to use their names. In these cases, I maintain the confidentiality of interview data. The Institutional Review Board–approved research protocol specifies that "interview data, recordings, and draft manuscripts" shall be encrypted and retained exclusively by the author, who will "never release this information, unless specifically compelled to do so by law." The data cannot be released in full, but I provide as much information as possible to clarify the intended meaning of each subject's remarks.

Sample Interview Questions

FOR IRA INTERVIEWEES

1. What sort of threats did the IRA issue?
2. Who was the target of these threats?
3. What was the political purpose of issuing threats? Did they communicate a message to anyone other than the immediate target?
4. Did threats influence the physical outcomes of attacks—for instance, making them more or less likely to succeed or determining who was harmed?
5. Would the IRA ever issue false threats? (If so, what was the purpose?)
6. Was credibility of threats important to the IRA? (If so, how?)
7. How did the IRA issue threats—directly to the target, or through some other means?
8. Why did the IRA choose this means of conveying threats?
9. Did the IRA's use of threats change as the conflict progressed?

FOR RUC INTERVIEWEES

1. What was the content of IRA threats—i.e., who was threatened and what was threatened against them?
2. How specific were the threats as to the time, location, or target of the attack?
3. In what form did these threats arrive? Did they come directly from the IRA?
4. Why did the IRA choose this means of conveying threats?

5. How often did the IRA issue false threats?
6. Was there any way of telling truthful threats from false?
7 Did police respond to all threats?
8. How did police respond to threats?
9. What were the safety concerns associated with responding to threats?

FOR JOURNALISTS AND SWITCHBOARD OPERATORS

1. What was the content of IRA threats?
2. How were these threats received?
3. Were there standard procedures for what to do if a threat was received?
4. Was there any way to know if a threat would be true?
5. Was there any way to know if the person communicating the threat actually represented the IRA?
6. Were some threats treated more seriously than others? Were any ignored?
7. Did the IRA approach media organizations in advance to let them know they would be receiving threats later?
8. Did police ever approach intermediaries to coordinate a system of communication?

My interview procedures and questionnaires were similar in Spain, Sri Lanka, and Peru. The subject populations, including interviewees on background, comprised the following:

- Three anonymous Tamil activists
- Two Sri Lankan political figures
- A former top leader of ETA
- Two Spanish/Basque political figures (a politician and a peace negotiator)
- Two members of the Guardia Civil
- Two former associates of Peruvian paramilitary groups
- A civilian witness to Shining Path atrocities
- Two members of the Peruvian Truth and Reconciliation Commission (CVR)

As in my Northern Ireland fieldwork, many of the interviewees requested to be kept anonymous or on background. I am limited in what I can say about these interviewees. When interviewees allowed me to quote them, however, I provide as much information as possible to contextualize their remarks.

SUMMARY OF INTERVIEWS

1. Republican #1, Belfast, June 2012
2. Republican #2, Newry, July 2012
3. Republican #3, Belfast, June 2012
4. Republican #4, Belfast, July 2012
5. Republican (background only), Belfast, July 2012
6. Séanna Walsh, Belfast, June 2012
7. John O'Hagan, Belfast, July 2012
8. Robert McClanahan, Belfast, July 2012
9. Danny Morrison, Andersonstown, July 2012
10. "Very high-ranking RUC Special Branch" member, Belfast, January 2013
11. RUC Special Branch intelligence expert, Belfast, January 2013
12. RUC chief superintendent, Belfast, July 2012
13. RUC superintendent, Belfast, January 2013
14. RUC (background only), Belfast, August 2012
15. RUC (background only), Belfast, January 2013
16. RUC (background only), Belfast, January 2013
17. Retired army, Belfast, January 2013
18. "Civil servant," Belfast, July 2012
19. Retired cabinet official (background only), London, June 2012
20. Peace negotiator for Tony Blair government, London, July 2012
21. Journalist #1, Belfast, July 2012
22. Journalist #2, Belfast, July 2012
23. Journalist #3 (retired BBC reporter), London, June 2012
24. Journalist #4, Holywood, June 2012
25. Journalist #5 (background only), Dublin, June 2012
26. Journalist #6, Belfast, June 2012
27. Journalist #7, Belfast, July 2012
28. Journalist #8 (background only), Belfast, January 2013
29. Journalist #9 (background only), Belfast, January 2013
30. Eamonn Mallie, Belfast, November 2012

31. Samaritans volunteer #1 (background only), Dublin, February 2013
32. Samaritans volunteer #2 (background only), Belfast, February 2013
33. Taxi dispatcher (background only), Belfast, January 2013
34. M. A. Sumanthiran, Colombo, August 2013
35. Retired Sri Lankan diplomat, Colombo, August 2013
36. Tamil activist (background only), Colombo, August 2013
37. Tamil activist (background only), New York, September 2013
38. Tamil activist (background only), New York, February 2014
39. Antxon Etxebeste, Donostia, October 2013
40. Basque politician (background only), Donostia, October 2013
41. Former peace negotiator (background only), Bilbao, October 2013
42. Retired Guardia Civil (background only), Madrid, October 2013
43. Retired Guardia Civil (background only), Madrid, October 2013
44. Former PCP-SL member (background only), Lima, November 2013
45. Former MRTA paramilitary (background only), Lima, December 2013
46. Civilian conflict witness (background only), Lima, December 2013
47. CVR member, Lima, December 2013
48. CVR member (background only), Lima, December 2013

Summary Statistics and Robustness Checks for Chapter 6

Tables A.1–A.3 contain summary statistics of the logit models' independent and dependent variables, as realized for each of the 131 militant groups in the analysis. Table A.1 also lists the target state of each militant group. (The target state's *Polity2* score is applied to each attack committed by the terrorist group in that year.) Several of the variables used in the robustness checks also bear explaining.

Vacant Site is a 0/1 indicator of whether an attack targeted a location likely to be empty of people at the time of the attack. Examples include bombing under-construction buildings, abandoned buildings, summer vacation resorts closed for the winter, and businesses on bank holidays or "after hours" (for my purposes, 11:00 p.m.–5:00 a.m.). *Vacant Site* is coded based on the same LexisNexis data, State Department reports, and Global Terrorism Database (GTD) summaries used to code the dependent variable *Warning*. Targets are coded 1 based on their ex ante likelihood of being vacant—not based on whether people actually occupied the target at the moment of the attack. For instance, an attack on a seaside resort in June during business hours would not qualify as an attack on a vacant site, even if the building happened to be vacant at the time of the explosion. The intuition of this variable is that militants may not give warnings when attacking structures *they believe will be vacant* at the time of the attack.

Free Press is a 0/1 indicator of press freedom in the country on whose soil an attack took place. (The location of the attack is obtained from the GTD's *country_txt* variable.) *Free Press* is derived from Whitten-Woodring and Van Belle's Global Media Freedom Dataset. The authors assign a yearly media score to each country, with values of 1 ("Free"), 2 ("Imperfectly Free"), and 3 ("Not Free"). In studies using media freedom as an independent variable, the authors "recommend using a dichotomous version of the variable where the categories of free media and imperfectly free media are collapsed into functionally free media vs. not free media." *Free Press* follows this convention, collapsing the 1 and 2 categories of the original media score into a 1 category ("functionally free") and scores of 3 into a 0 category ("not free").

Political Terror Scale (*PTS*)—a 1–5 scale indicating the extent of physical integrity violations perpetrated by a government within its borders. A score of 1 indicates that political murder, torture, forced disappearance, and arbitrary imprisonment are "rare or exceptional"; a score of 5 indicates that such abuse "has expanded to the whole population," and that leaders "place no limits" on the coercive tools they use to shape citizens' behavior. For each incident in my dataset, *PTS* indicates the score of the militant group's target state in the year the attack took place.

Democ and *Autoc* are the two components of *Polity2*. The variables are coded on a 0–10 scale, with higher scores representing greater degrees of democracy or autocracy, respectively.

Freedom House PR and *Freedom House CL* are the political rights and civil liberties component scores for Freedom House's yearly country and territory freedom ratings. The PR and CL scores are coded on a 1–7 scale, with low values representing greater protections for political rights and civil liberties and high values representing poorer protections for rights. To merge these variables with my data, I used Amanda B. Edgell's long-format Stata Friendly Freedom House Data, 1973–2018, dataset.

Polity2 (local) is a variant of *Polity2*, based not on the perpetrator group's target state but on the yearly *Polity2* score of the country on whose soil the attack took place.

TABLE A.1
Codings of Militant Groups (numbers are averages)

Group	Obs.	Warning	Target State	Polity2	PTS
Abu Sayyaf	151	0.053	Philippines	8	3.72
Action Directe	24	0.042	France	8.17	2
African National Congress	73	0	S. Africa	4.03	3.90
Ajnad Misr	6	0	Egypt	−4	4
Al-Aqsa Martyrs Brigade	73	0	Israel	6	4.77
Al-Naqshabandiya Army	17	0	Iraq	6	5
Al-Nusrah Front	89	0.011	Syria	−9	5
Al-Qa'ida	34	0.029	USA	10	2.18
Al-Qa'ida in the Arabian Peninsula	126	0	Yemen	0.905	4.26
Al-Qa'ida in the Islamic Maghreb	47	0	Algeria	2	3.26
Al-Shabaab	394	0.018	Somalia	4.51	4.73
Ansar Allah (Houthis)	356	0	Yemen	0.053	4.98
Ansar al-Sharia	27	0	Libya	0	5
Ansar Bayt al-Maqdis	20	0	Egypt	−3.95	3.95
April 6th Liberation Movement	24	0	Philippines	−9	4
Armed Forces of National Liberation (FALN)	92	0.087	United States	10	1
Armed Islamic Group	34	0	Algeria	−3.09	4.85
Armenian Secret Army for the Liberation of Armenia	24	0.042	Turkey	1	4

Baloch Liberation Army	57	0	Pakistan	2.25	4.21
Baloch Liberation Front	8	0	Pakistan	6.88	4.25
Baloch Republican Army	172	0	Pakistan	6.76	4.24
Bangladesh Nationalist Party	27	0	Bangladesh	3.19	3.89
Bangsamoro Islamic Freedom Movement	72	0	Philippines	8	3.58
Barqa Province of the Islamic State	50	0	Libya	0	5
Black September	10	0	Israel	9	4
Boko Haram	459	0.046	Nigeria	5.52	4.51
Breton Liberation Front	6	0	France	8.83	2
Communist Party of India–Maoist	346	0.066	India	9	3.99
Conspiracy of Cells of Fire	23	0.217	Greece	10	2.30
Corsican National Liberation Front	312	0.035	France	8.60	1.88
Corsican National Liberation Front—Historic Channel	115	0	France	9	1.08
Democratic Front for the Liberation of Palestine	11	0	Israel	6.27	4.36
Dev Sol	32	0.125	Turkey	9	4.09
Dishmish Regiment	37	0	India	8	3
Donetsk People's Republic	9	0	Ukraine	4	4
Euskadi Ta Askatasuna	309	0.450	Spain	9.85	2.22
Farabundo Marti National Liberation Movement	60	0.033	El Salvador	5.72	4.33
First of October Antifascist Resistance Group	33	0.303	Spain	9.76	1.82

(*continued*)

TABLE A.1
Codings of Militant Groups (numbers are averages) *(continued)*

Group	Obs.	Warning	Target State	Polity2	PTS
Free Aceh Movement (GAM)	34	0.118	Indonesia	6.12	4.03
Free Galician People's Guerrilla Army	6	0	Spain	10	2
Free Syrian Army	38	0	Syria	−8.95	5
Garo National Liberation Army	13	0	India	9	4
Great Eastern Islamic Raiders Front	13	0.077	Turkey	7.15	4
Guerrilla Army of the Poor	3	0	Guatemala	−5.67	5
Hamas	133	0.023	Israel	6	4.56
Haqqani Network	38	0	Afghanistan	−1	4.68
Hizb-I-Islami	11	0	Afghanistan	†	4.64
Hizballah	60	0.017	Israel	6	4.02
Hizbul Mujahideen	16	0	India	9	3.88
Indian Mujahideen	43	0	India	9	4
Informal Anarchist Federation	21	0	Italy	10	1.95
Iparretarrak	6	0.333	France	8.83	1.83
Irish National Liberation Army	10	0.2	U.K.	10	1.7
Irish Republican Army	360	0.444	U.K.	10	1.54
Islamic Front	18	0	Syria	−9	5
Islamic State/Al-Qa'ida in Iraq	1,962	0.005	Iraq	5.14	4.91
Jamaat-E-Islami	16	0	Bangladesh	2.19	3.94

Jaysh al-Islam	21	0	Syria	−9	5
Jemaah Islamiya	68	0	Indonesia	6.53	3.82
Jewish Defense League	23	0	United States	9.30	1
Kangleipak Communist Party	27	0	India	9	4
Karen National Union	28	0	Myanmar	−5.54	4.25
Khmer Rouge	8	0.25	Cambodia	1	3.38
Khorasan Chapter of the Islamic State	32	0	Afghanistan	−1	5
Kurdistan Workers' Party	241	0.029	Turkey	4.47	3.76
Lashkar-e-Islam	22	0	Pakistan	6.09	4.82
Lashkar-e-Jhangvi	30	0	Pakistan	5.37	4.57
Lashkar-e-Taiba	31	0.065	India	9	3.74
Liberation Tigers of Tamil Eelam	215	0.014	Sri Lanka	5.49	4.48
Lorenzo Zelaya Revolutionary Front	3	0	Honduras	6	4
Luhansk People's Republic	7	0	Ukraine	4	4
Manuel Rodriguez Patriotic Front	136	0.029	Chile	−0.051	3.53
Montoneros	12	0	Argentina	6	5
Moro Islamic Liberation Front	139	0.007	Philippines	7.95	3.96
Moro National Liberation Front	16	0	Philippines	1.625	4
Movement for Oneness and Jihad in West Africa	14	0	Mali	5	3.79
Movement for the Emancipation of the Niger Delta	40	0.10	Nigeria	4.08	4.03
Movement of April 19th (M-19)	33	0.061	Colombia	8	4.76
Movement of the Revolutionary Left	59	0.068	Chile	−4.69	3.97

(continued)

TABLE A.1
Codings of Militant Groups (numbers are averages) *(continued)*

Group	Obs.	Warning	Target State	Polity2	PTS
Mozambique National Resistance	4	0	Mozambique	−7	3
Mujahedin-e Khalq	16	0	Iran	1.44	3.38
National Democratic Front of Bodoland	40	0.05	India	8.95	4.05
National Liberation Army of Colombia	165	0.018	Colombia	7.2	4.46
National Union for the Total Independence of Angola	58	0	Angola	−5.40	4.14
New People's Army	113	0.088	Philippines	7.55	3.78
New World Liberation Front	18	0.056	United States	10	1
Nicaraguan Democratic Force	15	0	Nicaragua	−2.07	2.87
Niger Delta Avengers	48	0.042	Nigeria	7	5
November 17 Revolutionary Organization	37	0.108	Greece	9.95	2.22
Óglaigh na hÉireann	12	0.167	UK	10	1.25
Omega-7	21	0.048	United States	10	1
Palestine Liberation Organization	7	0	Israel	6.86	2.86
Palestinian Islamic Jihad	104	0	Israel	6	4.62
Pattani United Liberation Organization	21	0	Thailand	−0.667	3.71
People's Liberation Army	22	0	India	9	4
People's Liberation Front (JVP)	24	0.042	Sri Lanka	5	4.29
People's War Group	14	0	India	9	3.79
Popular Front for the Liberation of Palestine	54	0.037	Israel	6.72	4.39

Popular Liberation Army	1	0	Colombia	8	4
Popular Resistance Committees	35	0	Israel	6	4.54
Real Irish Republican Army	20	0.45	UK	10	1.85
Red Army Faction	15	0.2	W. Germany	10	1.73
Red Brigades	9	0	Italy	10	1.56
Resistenza	60	1	France	9	1.78
Revolutionary Armed Forces of Colombia (FARC)	597	0.007	Colombia	7.18	4.69
Revolutionary Cells	10	0	W. Germany	10	1.7
Revolutionary Organization of People in Arms	1	0	Guatemala	−7	5
Revolutionary People's Army (ERP)	6	0	Argentina	6	6
Revolutionary People's Struggle (ELA)	1	1	Greece	10	2
Runda Kumpulan Kecil	82	0.024	Thailand	−0.646	3.57
Salafist Group for Preaching and Fighting	23	0	Algeria	−0.174	4.30
Sanaa Province of the Islamic State	23	0	Yemen	0	5
Sandinista National Liberation Front	12	0.75	Nicaragua	3.75	3.33
Shining Path	616	0.005	Peru	6.44	4.46
Simon Bolivar Guerrilla Coordinating Board	3	0.333	Colombia	9	5
Sinai Province of the Islamic State	33	0	Egypt	−4	4
Sindhu Desh Liberation Army	53	0	India	6.25	4.87
South–West Africa People's Organization	10	0	Namibia	4	3.9

(continued)

TABLE A.1
Codings of Militant Groups (numbers are averages) *(continued)*

Group	Obs.	Warning	Target State	Polity2	PTS
Sudan People's Liberation Movement North	21	0	Sudan	−4	5
Taliban	1,159	0.027	Afghanistan	−1	4.71
Tawhid and Jihad	16	0	Iraq	†	5
Tehrik-i-Taliban Pakistan	375	0.056	Pakistan	5.89	4.77
Terra Lliure	14	0	Spain	10	2
Tripoli Province of the Islamic State	41	0	Libya	0	5
Túpac Amaru Revolutionary Movement	84	0.06	Peru	6.86	4.49
Ulster Freedom Fighters	29	0.034	UK	10	1.45
Ulster Volunteer Force	46	0.043	UK	10	1.83
United Baloch Army	52	0	Pakistan	6.85	4.38
United Liberation Front of Assam	180	0.028	India	8.99	3.68
United Popular Action Movement	23	0.217	Chile	8	3
Weather Underground	22	0.318	United States	8.55	1

† No observations for *Polity2* due to missing data in relevant country-years.

TABLE A.2
Codings of Militant Groups (numbers are averages)

Group	Territory	State-Sponsored	Resources	Separatist	Suicide
Abu Sayyaf	0.656	0.026	0.570	1	0.02
Action Directe	0	0	0	0	0
African National Congress	1	1	0	0	0
Ajnad Misr	0	0	0	0	0
Al-Aqsa Martyrs Brigade	0	0.932	0	1	0.425
Al-Naqshabandiya Army	0	0	0	0	0.176
Al-Nusrah Front	0	0	0	0	0.281
Al-Qa'ida	0.029	0	0.882	0	0.294
Al-Qa'ida in the Arabian Peninsula	0.984	0	0.587	0	0.198
Al-Qa'ida in the Islamic Maghreb	0.383	0	1	0	0.255
Al-Shabaab	1	1	0.033	0	0.173
Ansar Allah (Houthis)	1	1	0	0	0.003
Ansar al-Sharia	1	0	0	0	0
Ansar Bayt al-Maqdis	0	0	0	0	0.1
April 6th Liberation Movement	0	0	0	0	0
Armed Forces of National Liberation (FALN)	0	0	0	1	0

(*continued*)

TABLE A.2
Codings of Militant Groups (numbers are averages) *(continued)*

Group	Territory	State-Sponsored	Resources	Separatist	Suicide
Armed Islamic Group	0	0	0.853	0	0
Armenian Secret Army for the Liberation of Armenia	0	1	1	0	0
Baloch Liberation Army	0	0	0	1	0.018
Baloch Liberation Front	0	0	0	1	0
Baloch Republican Army	0	0	0	1	0
Bangladesh Nationalist Party	0	0	0	1	0
Bangsamoro Islamic Freedom Movement	0	0	0.042	1	0
Barqa Province of the Islamic State	1	0	0	0	0.28
Black September	0	1	0	1	0
Boko Haram	0.529	0	0	1	0.501
Breton Liberation Front	0	0	0	1	0
Communist Party of India–Maoist	0.607	0	0	0	0
Conspiracy of Cells of Fire	0	0	0	0	0
Corsican National Liberation Front	0	0	0	1	0
Corsican National Liberation Front—Historic Channel	0	0	0	1	0
Democratic Front for the Liberation of Palestine	1	0.273	0	1	0
Dev Sol	0	0	0.781	0	0
Dishmish Regiment	0	0	0	1	0

Donetsk People's Republic	1	1	0	1	0
Euskadi Ta Askatasuna	0	0	0.071	1	0
Farabundo Marti National Liberation Movement	1	1	0	0	0
First of October Antifascist Resistance Group	0	0	0	0	0
Free Aceh Movement (GAM)	1	0	1	1	0
Free Galician People's Guerrilla Army	0	0	0	1	0
Free Syrian Army	1	0.974	0	0	0.026
Garo National Liberation Army	0	0	0	1	0
Great Eastern Islamic Raiders Front	0	0	0	0	0.154
Guerrilla Army of the Poor	1	0	0	0	0
Hamas	0.263	1	0.053	1	0.346
Haqqani Network	1	1	0.895	0	0.711
Hizb-I-Islami	0.455	0	1	0	0.091
Hizballah	0.8	1	1	0	0.117
Hizbul Mujahideen	1	1	0	1	0
Indian Mujahideen	0	1	0	0	0
Informal Anarchist Federation	0	0	0	0	0
Iparretarrak	0	0	0	1	0
Irish National Liberation Army	0	0	0	1	0
Irish Republican Army	0	0.036	0.017	1	0
Islamic Front	1	1	0	0	0

(continued)

TABLE A.2
Codings of Militant Groups (numbers are averages) *(continued)*

Group	Territory	State-Sponsored	Resources	Separatist	Suicide
Islamic State/Al-Qa'ida in Iraq	0.988	0.55	1	0	0.217
Jamaat-E-Islami	0	1	0	0	0
Jaysh al-Islam	1	1	0	0	0
Jemaah Islamiya	0	0	0	0	0.118
Jewish Defense League	0	0	0	0	0
Kangleipak Communist Party	0	0	0	1	0
Karen National Union	0.607	0.107	0	1	0
Khmer Rouge	1	0	1	0	0
Khorasan Chapter of the Islamic State	0	0	0	0	0.313
Kurdistan Workers' Party	0.838	0.228	0.614	1	0.037
Lashkar-e-Islam	0.773	0	0.636	0	0
Lashkar-e-Jhangvi	0	0	0.3	0	0.633
Lashkar-e-Taiba	0.484	1	0	1	0.065
Liberation Tigers of Tamil Eelam	1	0.051	0.944	1	0.144
Lorenzo Zelaya Revolutionary Front	0	0	0	0	0
Luhansk People's Republic	1	1	0	1	0
Manuel Rodriguez Patriotic Front	0	0	0	0	0
Montoneros	0	0	0	0	0

Moro Islamic Liberation Front	0	0	0.022	1	0.022
Moro National Liberation Front	1	1	0	1	0
Movement for Oneness and Jihad in West Africa	0	0	0	0	0.143
Movement for the Emancipation of the Niger Delta	0	0	1	0	0
Movement of April 19th (M-19)	0	1	0	0	0
Movement of the Revolutionary Left	0	1	0	0	0
Mozambique National Resistance	1	1	0	0	0
Mujahedin-e Khalq	0.938	0.813	0	0	0
National Democratic Front of Bodoland	0	0	0	1	0
National Liberation Army of Colombia	0.964	0.133	0.903	0	0
National Union for the Total Independence of Angola	1	1	1	0	0
New People's Army	0.717	0.150	0	0	0
New World Liberation Front	0	0	0	0	0
Nicaraguan Democratic Force	1	1	1	0	0
Niger Delta Avengers	0	0	0	1	0
November 17 Revolutionary Organization	0	0	0	0	0
Óglaigh na hÉireann	0	0	0.25	1	0
Omega-7	0	0	0	0	0
Palestine Liberation Organization	1	1	0	1	0.143
Palestinian Islamic Jihad	1	1	0	1	0.25
Pattani United Liberation Organization	0.190	0	0	1	0

(*continued*)

TABLE A.2
Codings of Militant Groups (numbers are averages) *(continued)*

Group	Territory	State-Sponsored	Resources	Separatist	Suicide
People's Liberation Army	0	0	0	1	0
People's Liberation Front (JVP)	0	0	0	0	0
People's War Group	0	0	1	0	0
Popular Front for the Liberation of Palestine	1	0.481	0	1	0.074
Popular Liberation Army	0	0	1	0	0
Popular Resistance Committees	0	0	0	1	0
Real Irish Republican Army	0	0	0	1	0
Red Army Faction	0	1	0	0	0
Red Brigades	0	1	0	0	0
Resistenza	0	0	0	1	0
Revolutionary Armed Forces of Colombia (FARC)	1	0.101	1	0	0
Revolutionary Cells	0	0	0	0	0
Revolutionary Organization of People in Arms	1	0	0	0	0
Revolutionary People's Army (ERP)	1	0	0	0	0
Revolutionary People's Struggle (ELA)	0	0	0	0	0
Runda Kumpulan Kecil	0	0	0	1	0
Salafist Group for Preaching and Fighting	0.087	0	0.174	0	0

Sanaa Province of the Islamic State	1		1	0.478
Sandinista National Liberation Front	0.25	0	0	0
Shining Path	0.953	0.25	0	0
Simon Bolivar Guerrilla Coordinating Board	1	0	0.99	0
Sinai Province of the Islamic State	0	0	0	0.121
Sindhu Desh Liberation Army	0	0	0	0
South-West Africa People's Organization	1	1	0	0
Sudan People's Liberation Movement North	1	0	0	0
Taliban	1	1	1	0.209
Tawhid and Jihad	0	0	0	0.625
Tehrik-i-Taliban Pakistan	1	0	0.749	0.2
Terra Lliure	0	0	0	0
Tripoli Province of the Islamic State	0.927	0	0	0.195
Túpac Amaru Revolutionary Movement	0	1	0.583	0
Ulster Freedom Fighters	0	0	0.138	0
Ulster Volunteer Force	0	0	0.087	0
United Baloch Army	0	0	0	0
United Liberation Front of Assam	0	0.661	0.656	0.022
United Popular Action Movement	0	0	0	0
Weather Underground	0	0	0	0

TABLE A.3
Codings of Militant Groups

Group	Religious	Ethnic	Leftist	Reactionary
Abu Sayyaf	1	0	0	0
Action Directe	0	0	1	0
African National Congress	0	1	0	0
Ajnad Misr	1	0	0	0
Al-Aqsa Martyrs Brigade	0	1	0	0
Al-Naqshabandiya Army	1	0	0	0
Al-Nusrah Front	1	0	0	0
Al-Qa'ida	1	0	0	0
Al-Qa'ida in the Arabian Peninsula	1	0	0	0
Al-Qa'ida in the Islamic Maghreb	1	0	0	0
Al-Shabaab	1	0	0	0
Ansar Allah (Houthis)	1	0	0	0
Ansar al-Sharia	1	0	0	0
Ansar Bayt al-Maqdis	1	0	0	0
April 6th Liberation Movement	0	0	0	0
Armed Forces of National Liberation (FALN)	0	1	0	0
Armed Islamic Group	1	0	0	0
Armenian Secret Army for the Liberation of Armenia	0	1	0	0
Baloch Liberation Army	0	1	0	0
Baloch Liberation Front	0	1	0	0
Baloch Republican Army	0	1	0	0
Bangladesh Nationalist Party	1	0	0	0
Bangsamoro Islamic Freedom Movement	1	1	0	0
Barqa Province of the Islamic State	1	0	0	0

Group	Religious	Ethnic	Leftist	Reactionary
Black September	0	1	0	0
Boko Haram	1	0	0	0
Breton Liberation Front	0	1	0	0
Communist Party of India-Maoist	0	0	1	0
Conspiracy of Cells of Fire	0	0	1	0
Corsican National Liberation Front	0	1	0	0
Corsican National Liberation Front—Historic Channel	0	1	0	0
Democratic Front for the Liberation of Palestine	0	1	1	0
Dev Sol	0	0	1	0
Dishmish Regiment	0	1	0	0
Donetsk People's Republic	0	1	0	0
Euskadi Ta Askatasuna	0	1	0	0
Farabundo Marti National Liberation Movement	0	0	1	0
First of October Antifascist Resistance Group	0	0	1	0
Free Aceh Movement (GAM)	1	1	0	0
Free Galician People's Guerrilla Army	0	1	0	0
Free Syrian Army	0	0	0	0
Garo National Liberation Army	0	1	0	0
Great Eastern Islamic Raiders Front	1	0	0	0
Guerrilla Army of the Poor	0	0	1	0
Hamas	1	1	0	0
Haqqani Network	1	0	0	0
Hizb-I-Islami	1	0	0	0

(continued)

TABLE A.3
Codings of Militant Groups *(continued)*

Group	Religious	Ethnic	Leftist	Reactionary
Hizballah	1	0	0	0
Hizbul Mujahideen	1	0	0	0
Indian Mujahideen	1	0	0	0
Informal Anarchist Federation	0	0	1	0
Iparretarrak	0	1	0	0
Irish National Liberation Army	0	1	0	0
Irish Republican Army	0	1	0	0
Islamic Front	1	0	0	0
Islamic State/Al-Qa'ida in Iraq	1	0	0	0
Jamaat-E-Islami	1	0	0	0
Jaysh al-Islam	1	0	0	0
Jemaah Islamiya	1	0	0	0
Jewish Defense League	1	1	0	0
Kangleipak Communist Party	0	1	1	0
Karen National Union	0	1	0	0
Khmer Rouge	0	0	1	0
Khorasan Chapter of the Islamic State	1	0	0	0
Kurdistan Workers' Party	0	1	1	0
Lashkar-e-Islam	1	0	0	0
Lashkar-e-Jhangvi	1	0	0	0
Lashkar-e-Taiba	1	0	0	0
Liberation Tigers of Tamil Eelam	0	1	0	0
Lorenzo Zelaya Revolutionary Front	0	0	1	0
Luhansk People's Republic	0	1	0	0
Manuel Rodriguez Patriotic Front	0	0	1	0

Group	Religious	Ethnic	Leftist	Reactionary
Montoneros	0	0	1	0
Moro Islamic Liberation Front	1	1	0	0
Moro National Liberation Front	1	1	0	0
Movement for Oneness and Jihad in West Africa	1	0	0	0
Movement for the Emancipation of the Niger Delta	0	0	0	0
Movement of April 19th (M-19)	0	0	1	0
Movement of the Revolutionary Left	0	0	1	0
Mozambique National Resistance	0	0	0	1
Mujahedin-e Khalq	1	0	1	0
National Democratic Front of Bodoland	0	1	0	0
National Liberation Army of Colombia	0	0	1	0
National Union for the Total Independence of Angola	0	0	0	1
New People's Army	0	0	1	0
New World Liberation Front	0	0	1	0
Nicaraguan Democratic Force	0	0	0	1
Niger Delta Avengers	0	0	0	0
November 17 Revolutionary Organization	0	0	1	0
Óglaigh na hÉireann	0	1	0	0

(continued)

TABLE A.3
Codings of Militant Groups (*continued*)

Group	Religious	Ethnic	Leftist	Reactionary
Omega-7	0	0	0	1
Palestine Liberation Organization	0	1	0	0
Palestinian Islamic Jihad	1	0	0	0
Pattani United Liberation Organization	1	1	0	0
People's Liberation Army	0	0	1	0
People's Liberation Front (JVP)	0	0	1	0
People's War Group	0	0	1	0
Popular Front for the Liberation of Palestine	0	1	1	0
Popular Liberation Army	0	0	1	0
Popular Resistance Committees	0	1	0	0
Real Irish Republican Army	0	1	0	0
Red Army Faction	0	0	1	0
Red Brigades	0	0	1	0
Resistenza	0	1	0	0
Revolutionary Armed Forces of Colombia (FARC)	0	0	1	0
Revolutionary Cells	0	0	1	0
Revolutionary Organization of People in Arms	0	0	1	0
Revolutionary People's Army (ERP)	0	0	1	0
Revolutionary People's Struggle (ELA)	0	0	1	0
Runda Kumpulan Kecil	1	1	0	0
Salafist Group for Preaching and Fighting	1	0	0	0

Group	Religious	Ethnic	Leftist	Reactionary
Sanaa Province of the Islamic State	1	0	0	0
Sandinista National Liberation Front	0	0	1	0
Shining Path	0	0	1	0
Simon Bolivar Guerrilla Coordinating Board	0	0	1	0
Sinai Province of the Islamic State	1	0	0	0
Sindhu Desh Liberation Army	0	1	0	0
South-West Africa People's Organization	0	0	1	0
Sudan People's Liberation Movement North	0	0	1	0
Taliban	1	0	0	0
Tawhid and Jihad	1	0	0	0
Tehrik-i-Taliban Pakistan	1	0	0	0
Terra Lliure	0	1	0	0
Tripoli Province of the Islamic State	1	0	0	0
Túpac Amaru Revolutionary Movement	0	0	1	0
Ulster Freedom Fighters	0	1	0	1
Ulster Volunteer Force	1	1	0	1
United Baloch Army	0	1	0	0
United Liberation Front of Assam	0	0	1	0
United Popular Action Movement	0	0	1	0
Weather Underground	0	0	1	0

TABLE A.4
Descriptive Statistics for Robustness Checks

Variable Name	Obs.	Mean	Std. Dev.	Min.	Max.
Vacant Site	12,235	0.0434	0.2038	0	1
Free Press	12,235	0.4772	0.4995	0	1
Democ	10,644	6.395	2.711	0	10
Autoc	10,644	0.7192	1.663	0	9
Freedom House PR	12,235	4.081	1.929	1	7
Freedom House CL	12,235	4.511	1.668	1	7
Polity2 "local"	11,237	5.127	4.561	−10	10
PTS	12,235	4.111	1.139	1	5

Table A.5
Logit Results with Group Fixed Effects

Probability of Warning	Model 1	Model 2	Model 3
Territory	−1.022***	−1.002***	−1.006***
	(0.24)	(0.24)	(0.25)
Polity2	0.1452***	0.1591***	0.1544***
	(0.04)	(0.04)	(0.04)
State Sponsored	0.4598	0.4412	0.4880
	(0.29)	(0.29)	(0.30)
Resources	−0.7408***	−0.7682***	−0.6392**
	(0.24)	(0.24)	(0.25)
Suicide		−0.8314**	−0.7208**
		(0.33)	(0.33)
Private Citizens			0.6066
			(0.41)
Government			0.8427**
			(0.41)

Probability of Warning	Model 1	Model 2	Model 3
Business			0.8813**
			(0.40)
Civil Society			0.8887**
			(0.44)
Infrastructure			1.331***
			(0.41)
Tourists			3.390***
			(0.60)
Constant	−4.152***	−4.249***	−4.216***
	(0.78)	(0.78)	(0.79)
Log likelihood	−1394.47	−1390.78	−1302.30
Pseudo R^2	0.3286	0.3303	0.3432
N	8,727	8,727	8,121

*$p < 0.1$; **$p < 0.05$; ***$p < 0.01$. Coefficients for group dummy variables not shown.

TABLE A.6
Multilevel Logit Results: Vacant Sites, Press Freedom, *Polity2* "Local"

Probability of Warning	Model 1	Model 2	Model 3
Territory	−0.8207***	−0.8235***	−0.8273***
	(0.23)	(0.23)	(0.23)
State Sponsored	0.2612	0.2854	2.778
	(0.27)	(0.27)	(0.27)
Resources	−0.4255*	−0.4469*	−0.4357*
	(0.24)	(0.24)	(0.24)
Polity2	0.1997***	0.2021***	
	(0.05)	(0.05)	
Polity2 "local"			0.1728***
			(0.04)
Separatist	−0.3710	−0.3824	−0.2666
	(0.75)	(0.77)	(0.75)
Religious	−0.7388	−0.6666	−0.5697
	(0.64)	(0.65)	(0.62)
Ethnic	−0.4083	−0.4305	−0.4108
	(0.79)	(0.81)	(0.78)
Leftist	0.3485	0.4090	0.5263
	(0.68)	(0.69)	(0.66)
Reactionary	−0.7328	−0.6467	−0.5754
	(1.4)	(1.4)	(1.3)
Suicide	−0.8731	−0.8631	−0.8828
	(0.65)	(0.65)	(0.66)
Vacant Site	−2.073***		
	(0.44)		
Free Press		−0.0548	
		(0.30)	

Probability of Warning	Model 1	Model 2	Model 3
Constant	−5.421***	−5.459***	−5.429***
	(0.77)	(0.79)	(0.75)
Var(*Polity2*)	0.0301	0.0319	
	(0.01)	(0.01)	
Var(*Polity2* "local")			0.0316
			(0.01)
Var(*Suicide*)	1.969	1.985	2.118
	(1.4)	(1.4)	(1.4)
Var(constant)	1.548	1.613	1.413
	(0.68)	(0.71)	(0.65)
Log likelihood	−1392.90	−1411.28	−1411.92
Wald x^2	125.16	103.16	104.62
N	10,441	10,441	10,433
Groups	129	129	129

Note: Target-type coefficients not shown owing to space constraints.
Models 1 and 2: Observations/group: minimum: 1, average: 80.9, maximum: 1,709.
Model 3: Observations/group: minimum: 1, average: 80.9, maximum: 1,712.
*p < 0.1; **p < 0.05; ***p < 0.01.

TABLE A.7
Multilevel Logit Results with Higher Inclusion Thresholds

Probability of Warning	50+ attacks	75+ attacks	100+ attacks
Territory	−0.8624***	−0.8682***	−0.9743***
	(0.23)	(0.23)	(0.24)
State Sponsored	0.3209	0.2534	0.2547
	(0.28)	(0.27)	(0.28)
Resources	−0.5602**	−0.5872**	−0.6517***
	(0.24)	(0.24)	(0.24)
Polity2	0.1936***	0.1820***	0.1768***
	(0.05)	(0.05)	(0.05)
Separatist	−0.6856	−0.5617	−0.5128
	(0.77)	(0.75)	(0.73)
Religious	−0.3899	−0.2317	−0.3441
	(0.75)	(0.75)	(0.77)
Ethnic	−0.2600	−0.5141	−0.5016
	(0.85)	(0.83)	(0.82)
Leftist	0.6352	0.4859	0.0148
	(0.79)	(0.76)	(0.81)
Reactionary	−0.6484	†	†
	(1.9)		
Suicide	−0.7340	−0.7133	−0.6267
	(0.64)	(0.63)	(0.63)
Constant	−5.399***	−5.059***	−4.703***
	(0.88)	(0.85)	(0.88)
Var(Polity2)	0.0307	0.0204	0.0205
	(0.01)	(0.01)	(0.01)
Var(Suicide)	2.003	1.896	1.889
	(1.4)	(1.3)	(1.3)

Probability of Warning	50+ attacks	75+ attacks	100+ attacks
Var(constant)	1.109	0.6672	0.5436
	(0.62)	(0.43)	(0.38)
Log likelihood	−1263.36	−1208.37	−1164.29
Wald x^2	101.72	104.38	94.44
N	9,593	8,973	8,630
Groups	78	57	45

Note: Target-type coefficients not shown owing to space constraints.
Model 1: Observations/group: minimum: 1, average: 123.0, maximum: 1,709.
Model 2: Observations/group: minimum: 1, average: 157.4, maximum: 1,709.
Model 3: Observations/group: minimum: 6, average: 191.8, maximum: 1,709.
*$p < 0.1$; **$p < 0.05$; ***$p < 0.01$; † Variable omitted because it predicts failure perfectly.

TABLE A.8
Multilevel Logit Results with Different Democracy/Autocracy Measures

Probability of Warning	Model 1	Model 2	Model 3	Model 4	Model 5
Territory	−0.8653***	−0.8160***	−0.7916***	−0.8755***	−0.7756***
	(0.23)	(0.23)	(0.24)	(0.24)	(0.24)
State Sponsored	0.2735	0.2452	0.4607*	0.3318	0.3875
	(0.27)	(0.27)	(0.27)	(0.27)	(0.28)
Resources	−0.5738**	−0.5035**	−0.5587**	−0.4858**	−0.5748**
	(0.24)	(0.24)	(0.24)	(0.24)	(0.24)
PTS	−0.4072**				
	(0.14)				
Polity Democ		0.2026***			
		(0.06)			
Polity Autoc			−1.064***		
			(0.33)		
Freedom House PR				−0.4168***	
				(0.12)	
Freedom House CL					−0.5399***
					(0.13)
Separatist	0.3744	−0.5046	−0.1573	0.2242	0.2115
	(0.74)	(0.27)	(0.74)	(0.77)	(0.81)
Religious	−0.7707	−0.5442	−0.9703	−0.8775	−0.8357
	(0.62)	(0.64)	(0.65)	(0.69)	(0.69)
Ethnic	−0.1486	−0.5198	−0.1051	−0.0933	−0.1960
	(0.76)	(0.84)	(0.77)	(0.79)	(0.83)
Leftist	0.9951	0.2993	0.3542	0.4939	0.6575
	(0.67)	(0.69)	(0.70)	(0.73)	(0.75)
Reactionary	−0.4269	−0.7885	−0.2673	−0.4427	−0.6010
	(1.1)	(1.4)	(1.2)	(1.2)	(1.2)

Probability of Warning	Model 1	Model 2	Model 3	Model 4	Model 5
Suicide	−1.131*	−0.8583	−0.6456	−1.113*	−1.103*
	(0.61)	(0.64)	(0.62)	(0.61)	(0.62)
Constant	−3.454***	−5.482***	−3.898***	−3.402***	−2.834***
	(0.84)	(0.82)	(0.77)	(0.87)	(0.91)
Var(PTS)	0.1035				
	(0.05)				
Var(Polity Democ)		0.0397			
		(0.02)			
Var(Polity Autoc)			0.4195		
			(0.38)		
Var(Freedom House PR)				0.1087	
				(0.07)	
Var(Freedom House CL)					0.1494
					(0.06)
Var(Suicide)	1.795	1.884	1.643	1.815	1.877
	(1.2)	(1.3)	(1.3)	(1.2)	(1.3)
Var(constant)	1.920	1.373	3.078	2.594	2.229
	(0.66)	(0.65)	(0.79)	(0.78)	(0.77)
Log likelihood	−1559.09	−1408.13	−1406.75	−1554.96	−1546.49
Wald x^2	115.54	93.63	99.18	111.06	121.55
N	11,383	9,876	9,876	11,383	11,383
Groups	131	125	125	131	131

Models 1, 4, and 5: Observations/group: minimum: 1, average: 86.9, maximum: 1,817.
Models 2 and 3: Observations/group: minimum: 1, average: 79.0, maximum: 1,709.
*$p < 0.1$; **$p < 0.05$; ***$p < 0.01$; target-type coefficients not shown due to space constraints.

Notes

Introduction

1. William E. Schmidt, "1 Dead, 40 Hurt as a Blast Rips Central London," *New York Times*, April 25, 1993.
2. Nick Cohen et al., "The Bishopsgate Bomb: One Bomb: £1bn Devastation: Man Dead After City Blast—Two More Explosions Late Last Night," *Independent* (London), April 25, 1993.
3. Martin Dillon, *25 Years of Terror: The IRA's War Against the British* (New York: Bantam Books, 1996), 292.
4. Tony Geraghty, *The Irish War: The Hidden Conflict Between the IRA and British Intelligence* (Baltimore: Johns Hopkins University Press, 2000), 218; Toby Harnden, *Bandit Country* (London: Hodder and Stoughton, 1999), 337.
5. Harnden, *Bandit Country*, 337.
6. Geraghty, *The Irish War*, 218.
7. Harnden, *Bandit Country*, 503.
8. Chas Early, "April 24, 1993: IRA's Bishopsgate Bomb Devastates the Heart of the City of London," http://home.bt.com/news/on-this-day/april-24-1993-iras-bishopsgate-bomb-devastates-the-heart-of-the-city-of-london-11363977172852; Schmidt, "1 Dead, 40 Hurt."
9. David Norris and Bill Mouland, "'Fire and Plague Did Not Beat Us. Neither Will the IRA'; London Blitzed, as a New Pall of Evil Shrouds the City, Church Sounds Its Ancient Bell of Hope and Inspiration, Defiance Rings Out in the Ruins," *Daily Mail* (London), April 26, 1993.

10. Cohen et al., "The Bishopsgate Bomb." There is some disagreement as to the extent of the financial damage. Estimates range from £350 million (Early, "April 24, 1993") to £1 billion or more (Geraghty, *The Irish War*, 218).
11. Jon Coaffee, *Terrorism, Risk and the City: The Making of a Contemporary Urban Landsape* (London: Routledge, 2017).
12. Richard English, *Armed Struggle: The History of the IRA* (New York: Oxford University Press, 2003), 279.
13. Stewart Tendler and Nicholas Watt, "Low Risk, Maximum Effect," *Times* (London), April 19, 1997.
14. Kim Sengupta, "Phone Codes That Prove Bomb Threats Are Real," *Independent* (London), March 30, 1997.
15. See, for example, Bruce Hoffman, *Inside Terrorism* (New York: Columbia University Press, 2006); and Walter Laqueur, *The New Terrorism: Fanaticism and the Arms of Mass Destruction* (New York: Oxford University Press, 2000).
16. Brian M. Jenkins, *International Terrorism: A New Kind of Warfare* (Santa Monica, Calif.: RAND Corporation, 1974), 4.
17. Hoffman, *Inside Terrorism*; Laqueur, *New Terrorism*; U.S. Joint Chiefs of Staff, *Antiterrorism*, Joint Publication 3-07.2 (Arlington, Va.: U.S. Department of Defense, 2010). Quote from William Shakespeare, *Macbeth* (London: Arden Shakespeare, 1997), 154.
18. See Mia M. Bloom and John Horgan, "Missing Their Mark: The IRA Proxy Bomb Campaign," *Social Research* 75, no. 2 (2008): 80–94; and Walter Enders and Todd Sandler, "Causality Between Transnational Terrorism and Tourism: The Case of Spain," *Terrorism* 14, no. 1 (1991): 49–58.
19. See Charles W. Mahoney, "Empty Threats: How Extremist Organizations Bluff in Terrorist Campaigns," *Studies in Conflict & Terrorism* (October 2018), https://doi.org/10.1080/1057610X.2018.1514093; and Nicole A. Tishler, "Fake Terrorism: Examining Terrorist Groups' Resort to Hoaxing as a Mode of Attack," *Perspectives on Terrorism* 12, no. 4 (2018): 3–13.
20. Joseph M. Brown, "Force of Words: The Role of Threats in Terrorism," *Terrorism and Political Violence* (August 2018), https://doi.org/10.1080/09546553.2018.1486301.
21. Andrew H. Kydd and Barbara F. Walter, "The Strategies of Terrorism," *International Security* 31, no. 1 (2006): 49–80; David A. Lake, "Rational Extremism: Understanding Terrorism in the Twenty-First Century," *Dialogue IO* 1, no. 1 (2002): 15–29.
22. Kydd and Walter, "Strategies of Terrorism"; Harvey E. Lapan and Todd Sandler, "Terrorism and Signalling," *European Journal of Political Economy* 9, no. 3 (1993): 383–97; Per Baltzer Overgaard, "The Scale of Terrorist Attacks as a Signal of Resources," *Journal of Conflict Resolution* 38, no. 3 (1994):

452–78; John Ginkel and Alastair Smith, "So You Say You Want a Revolution: A Game Theoretic Explanation of Revolution in Repressive Regimes," *Journal of Conflict Resolution* 43, no. 3 (1999): 291–316; Bruce Hoffman and Gordon H. McCormick. "Terrorism, Signaling, and Suicide Attack." *Studies in Conflict and Terrorism* 27, no. 4 (2004): 243–81.

23. On suicide bombings, see Mia M. Bloom, *Dying to Kill: The Allure of Suicide Terror* (Philadelphia: University of Pennsylvania Press, 2005); and Robert Pape, *Dying to Win: The Strategic Logic of Suicide Terrorism* (New York: Random House, 2005). On pursuit of weapons of mass destruction, see Laqueur, *New Terrorism*; and Jessica Stern, *The Ultimate Terrorists* (Cambridge, Mass.: Harvard University Press, 2001). On claiming credit, see Max Abrahms, "What Terrorists Really Want: Terrorist Motives and Counterterrorism Strategy," *International Security* 32, no. 4 (2008): 78–105; and Aaron Hoffman, "Voice and Silence: Why Groups Take Credit for Acts of Terror," *Journal of Peace Research* 47, no. 5 (2010): 1–22.
24. Aron Nimzowitsch, *My System Chess Praxis: His Landmark Classics* (Alkmaar, Netherlands: New in Chess, 2016).
25. See Brown, "Force of Words," for an early version of the speech/kinetic action model of terrorism.
26. In fact, some authors restrict their definitions of terrorism to the use of kinetic violence, leaving out threats entirely. For example, see Virginia Page Fortna, "Do Terrorists Win? Rebels' Use of Terrorism and Civil War Outcomes," *International Organization* 69, no. 3 (2015): 519–56.
27. The possibility of hoax attacks is increasingly accepted in major terrorism data collection projects, including the Global Terrorism Database (GTD) and the International Terrorism: Attributes of Terrorist Events (ITERATE) dataset. See Edward F. Mickolus et al., *International Terrorism: Attributes of Terrorist Events (ITERATE), 1968–2016*, V1 (2017), distributed by Harvard Dataverse, https://doi.org/10.7910/DVN/ZOGPHC; and National Consortium for the Study of Terrorism and Responses to Terrorism (START), *GTD: Global Terrorism Database—Codebook: Inclusion Criteria and Variables* (College Park: University of Maryland, 2019), https://www.start.umd.edu/gtd/downloads/Codebook.pdf.
28. For example, to test proposition 1, about legitimacy concerns incentivizing warnings, we need to know which factors give rise to legitimacy concerns. What makes a multiple audiences conundrum particularly intense, incentivizing a terrorist group to warn and spare civilians? By helping to operationalize concepts like the multiple audiences conundrum, the IRA case study permits more precise measurements of the ex ante conditions in my subsequent theory-testing case studies and quantitative analysis.
29. "Maze Emptied as Terrorist Prisoners Walk Free," *Guardian*, July 28, 2000.

30. The database is introduced in Joseph M. Brown, "Correlates of Warning: Territory, Democracy, and Casualty Aversion in Terrorist Tactics," *International Organization* (March 2020), https://doi.org/10.1017/S002081832000003X.
31. Hoffman, *Inside Terrorism*, 9; Bloom, *Dying to Kill*; Laqueur, *New Terrorism*; Pape, *Dying to Win*; Stern, *Ultimate Terrorists*.
32. For analogous arguments in the international conflict literature, see James D. Fearon, "Domestic Political Audience Costs and the Escalation of International Disputes," *American Political Science Review* 88, no. 3 (1994): 577–92; James D. Fearon, "Signaling Foreign Policy Interests: Tying Hands Versus Sinking Costs," *Journal of Conflict Resolution* 41, no. 1 (1997): 68–90; Robert L. Jervis, *Perception and Misperception in International Politics* (Princeton, N.J.: Princeton University Press, 1976); and Thomas C. Schelling, *Arms and Influence* (New Haven, Conn.: Yale University Press, 1966).
33. Kydd and Walter, "Strategies of Terrorism."
34. Kydd and Walter, "Strategies of Terrorism"; Lapan and Sandler, "Terrorism and Signalling"; Overgaard, "Scale of Terrorist Attacks"; Ginkel and Smith, "So You Say You Want a Revolution"; Hoffman and McCormick, "Terrorism, Signaling, and Suicide Attack."
35. Fearon, "Domestic Political Audience Costs"; Fearon, "Signaling Foreign Policy Interests"; Alexandra Guisinger and Alastair Smith, "Honest Threats: The Interaction of Reputation and Political Institutions in International Crises," *Journal of Conflict Resolution* 46, no. 2 (2002): 175–200; Jervis, "Perception and Misperception"; Jonathan Mercer, *Reputation and International Politics* (Ithaca, N.Y.: Cornell University Press, 1996).
36. Max Abrahms, *Rules for Rebels: The Science of Victory in Militant History* (New York: Oxford University Press, 2018).
37. Abrahms, *Rules for Rebels*; Daniel G. Arce and Todd Sandler, "Strategic Analysis of Terrorism," in *Mathematical Methods In Counterterrorism*, ed. Nasrulla Memon et al. (New York: Springer-Verlag/Wien, 2009), 333–48.
38. On communiqués, see Neville Bolt, *The Violent Image: Insurgent Propaganda and the New Revolutionaries* (New York: Columbia University Press, 2012); Emma Louise Briant, *Propaganda and Counter-Terrorism: Strategies for Global Change* (Manchester, UK: Manchester University Press, 2015); Christopher C. Harmon and Randall G. Bowdish, *The Terrorist Argument: Modern Advocacy and Propaganda* (Washington, D.C.: Brookings Institution, 2018); Walter Laqueur, *Voices of Terror: Manifestos, Writings, and Manuals of Al Qaeda, Hamas, and Other Terrorists from Around the World and Throughout the Ages* (Naperville, Ill.: Sourcebooks, 2004); Michael Loadenthal, *The Politics of Attack: Communiqués and Insurrectionary Violence* (Manchester, UK: Manchester University Press, 2017); and Matteo Re, "The Red Brigades' Communiqués: An Analysis of the Terrorist Group's Propaganda,"

Terrorism and Political Violence (September 2017), https://doi.org/10.1080 /09546553.2017.1364639.

On websites, see Anne Aly et al., eds., *Violent Extremism Online: New Perspectives on Terrorism and the Internet* (Abingdon: Routledge, 2016).

On propaganda videos, see Max Abrahms, Nicholas Beauchamp, and Joseph Mroszczyk, "What Terrorist Leaders Want: A Content Analysis of Terrorist Propaganda Videos," *Studies in Conflict and Terrorism* 40, no. 11 (2016): 899–916; and Mia M. Bloom, John Horgan, and Charlie Winter, "Depictions of Children and Youth in the Islamic State's Martyrdom Propaganda, 2015–2016," *CTC Sentinel* 9, no. 2 (2016): 29–32.

On claims of credit, see Max Abrahms and Justin Conrad, "The Strategic Logic of Credit Claiming: A New Theory for Anonymous Terrorist Attacks," *Security Studies* 26, no. 2 (2017): 279–304; Joseph M. Brown, "Notes to the Underground: Credit Claiming and Organizing in the Earth Liberation Front," *Terrorism and Political Violence* (September 2017), https://doi.org/10 .1080/09546553.2017.1364637; and Hoffman, "Voice and Silence."

39. The notion of "propaganda by the deed" is traceable to the writings of early anarchists. See Paul Brousse, "Propaganda by the Deed," in *Anarchism: A Documentary History of Libertarian Ideas*, vol. 1: *From Anarchy to Anarchism (200 CE to 1939)*, ed. Robert Graham (New York: Black Rose Books, 2005), 150–51. See also Carlo Pisacane, "Political Testament," in *Anarchism: A Documentary History of Libertarian Ideas*, vol. 1: *From Anarchy to Anarchism (200 CE to 1939)*, ed. Robert Graham (New York: Black Rose Books, 2005), 67–68.

40. John Bew, Martyn Frampton, and Íñigo Gurruchaga. *Talking to Terrorists: Making Peace in Northern Ireland and the Basque Country* (London: Hurst, 2009); Jonathan Powell, *Talking to Terrorists: How to End Armed Conflicts* (New York: Vintage, 2015).

41. Jervis, *Perception and Misperception*; Mercer, *Reputation and International Politics*; Schelling, *Arms and Influence*.

42. Brown, "Force of Words"; Erin M. Kearns, Brendan Conlon, and Joseph K. Young, "Lying About Terrorism," *Studies in Conflict and Terrorism* 37, no. 5 (2014): 422–39; Mahoney, "Empty Threats"; Tishler, "Fake Terrorism."

43. On suicide bombing, see Mia M. Bloom, "Palestinian Suicide Bombing: Public Support, Market Share, and Outbidding," *Political Science Quarterly* 119, no. 1 (2004): 61–88; Simon Collard-Wexler, Costantino Pischedda, and Michael G. Smith, "Do Foreign Occupations Cause Suicide Attacks?," *Journal of Conflict Resolution* 58, no. 4 (2014): 625–57; Hoffman and McCormick, "Terrorism, Signaling, and Suicide Attack"; Michael C. Horowitz, "Nonstate Actors and the Diffusion of Innovations: The Case of Suicide Terrorism," *International Organization* 64, no. 1 (2010): 33–64; and Pape, *Dying to Win*. On pursuit of weapons, see Laqueur, *New Terrorism*; Stern, *Ultimate Terrorists*.

44. An exception in the terrorism literature is Abrahms, *Rules for Rebels*. On civilian targeting in civil war, see Tanisha M. Fazal, *Wars of Law: Unintended Consequences in the Regulation of Armed Conflict* (Ithaca, N.Y.: Cornell University Press, 2018); Michael L. Gross, *The Ethics of Insurgency: A Critical Guide to Just Guerrilla Warfare* (New York: Cambridge University Press, 2015); Stathis Kalyvas, *The Logic of Violence in Civil War* (New York: Cambridge University Press, 2006); Jessica A. Stanton, *Violence and Restraint in Civil War: Civilian Targeting in the Shadow of International Law* (New York: Cambridge University Press, 2016).
45. On religion, see Assaf Moghadam, *The Globalization of Martyrdom: Al Qaeda, Salafi Jihad, and the Diffusion of Suicide Attacks* (Baltimore: Johns Hopkins University Press, 2011). On ethnic grievances, see Roger D. Petersen, *Understanding Ethnic Violence: Fear, Hatred, and Resentment in Twentieth-Century Eastern Europe* (New York: Cambridge University Press, 2002). On separatism, see Fazal, *Wars of Law*; Stanton, *Violence and Restraint*. On state sponsorship, see Idean Salehyan, David Siroky, and Reed M. Wood, "External Rebel Sponsorship and Civilian Abuse: A Principal-Agent Analysis of Wartime Atrocities," *International Organization* 68, no. 3 (2014): 633–61.
46. On the limited danger of terrorism, see John Mueller, "Six Rather Unusual Propositions About Terrorism," *Terrorism and Political Violence*, 17, no. 4 (2005): 487–505; and John Mueller and Mark G. Stewart, "Terrorism and Bathtubs: Comparing and Assessing the Risks," *Terrorism and Political Violence* (October 2018), https://doi.org/10.1080/09546553.2018.1530662.

1. Threats

1. An early version of this framework appears in Joseph M. Brown, "Force of Words: The Role of Threats in Terrorism," *Terrorism and Political Violence* (August 2018), https://doi.org/10.1080/09546553.2018.1486301.
2. Alex P. Schmid and Albert J. Jongman, *Political Terrorism: A New Guide to Actors, Authors, Concepts, Data Bases, Theories and Literature* (New York: Transaction Books, 1988).
3. Brian M. Jenkins, *International Terrorism: A New Kind of Warfare* (Santa Monica, Calif.: RAND Corporation, 1974), 4.
4. Paul Brousse, "Propaganda by the Deed," in *Anarchism: A Documentary History of Libertarian Ideas*, vol. 1: *From Anarchy to Anarchism (200 CE to 1939)*, ed. Robert Graham (New York: Black Rose Books, 2005), 150–51. See also Carlo Pisacane, "Political Testament," in *Anarchism: A Documentary History of Libertarian Ideas*, vol. 1: *From Anarchy to Anarchism (200 CE to 1939)*, ed. Robert Graham (New York: Black Rose Books, 2005), 67–68.

5. Bruce Hoffman, *Inside Terrorism* (New York: Columbia University Press, 2006); Ignacio Sánchez-Cuenca and Luis de la Calle, "Domestic Terrorism: The Hidden Side of Political Violence," *Annual Review of Political Science* 12 (2009): 31–49.
6. Virginia Page Fortna, "Do Terrorists Win? Rebels' Use of Terrorism and Civil War Outcomes," *International Organization* 69, no. 3 (2015): 519–56.
7. Michel Foucault, *Discipline and Punish: The Birth of the Prison* (New York: Vintage Books, 1995); Maximilien Robespierre, "Discours par Maximilien Robespierre—17 Avril 1792–27 Juillet 1794" (Project Gutenberg, September 2009), http://www.gutenberg.org/ebooks/29887; Thomas C. Schelling, *Arms and Influence* (New Haven, Conn.: Yale University Press, 1966). For an example of empirical data collection on "political terror," see Mark Gibney et al., *The Political Terror Scale 1976–2018* (October 26, 2019), Political Terror Scale website, http://www.politicalterrorscale.org.
8. Fortna, "Do Terrorists Win?"; U.S. Department of State, *Patterns of Global Terrorism—2000*, report by the Office of the Coordinator for Counterterrorism (Washington, D.C.: U.S. Department of State, 2001), https://web.archive.org/web/20061115204446/http://www.state.gov/s/ct/rls/crt/2000/2419.htm.
9. "Woolwich Attack: The Terrorist's Rant," *Daily Telegraph* (London), May 23, 2013.
10. See Fortna, "Do Terrorists Win?"; and Hoffman, *Inside Terrorism*, 9. See also Walter Laqueur, *The New Terrorism: Fanaticism and the Arms of Mass Destruction* (New York: Oxford University Press, 2000); and U.S. Joint Chiefs of Staff, *Antiterrorism*, Joint Publication 3-07.2 (Arlington, Va.: U.S. Department of Defense, 2010).
11. Andrew H. Kydd and Barbara F. Walter, "The Strategies of Terrorism," *International Security* 31, no. 1 (2006): 49–80; David A. Lake, "Rational Extremism: Understanding Terrorism in the Twenty-First Century," *Dialogue IO* 1, no. 1 (2002): 15–29.
12. John Ginkel and Alastair Smith, "So You Say You Want a Revolution: A Game Theoretic Explanation of Revolution in Repressive Regimes," *Journal of Conflict Resolution* 43, no. 3 (1999): 291–316; Bruce Hoffman and Gordon H. McCormick, "Terrorism, Signaling, and Suicide Attack," *Studies in Conflict and Terrorism* 27, no. 4 (2004): 243–81; Kydd and Walter, "Strategies of Terrorism"; Harvey E. Lapan and Todd Sandler, "Terrorism and Signalling," *European Journal of Political Economy* 9, no. 3 (1993): 383–97; Per Baltzer Overgaard, "The Scale of Terrorist Attacks as a Signal of Resources," *Journal of Conflict Resolution* 38, no. 3 (1994): 452–78.
13. On varieties of violence, see Mia M. Bloom, *Dying to Kill: The Allure of Suicide Terror* (Philadelphia: University of Pennsylvania Press, 2005); Laqueur,

New Terrorism; Robert Pape, *Dying to Win: The Strategic Logic of Suicide Terrorism* (New York: Random House, 2005); and Jessica Stern, *The Ultimate Terrorists* (Cambridge, Mass.: Harvard University Press, 2001).

On claiming credit, see Max Abrahms, "What Terrorists Really Want: Terrorist Motives and Counterterrorism Strategy," *International Security* 32, no. 4 (2008): 78–105; Max Abrahms and Justin Conrad, "The Strategic Logic of Credit Claiming: A New Theory for Anonymous Terrorist Attacks," *Security Studies* 26, no. 2 (2017): 279–304; Aaron Hoffman, "Voice and Silence: Why Groups Take Credit for Acts of Terror," *Journal of Peace Research* 47, no. 5 (2010): 1–22; and Erin M. Kearns, "When to Take Credit for Terrorism? A Cross-National Examination of Claims and Attributions," *Terrorism and Political Violence* (January 2019), https://doi.org/10.1080/09546553.2018.1540982.

14. James D. Fearon, "Domestic Political Audience Costs and the Escalation of International Disputes," *American Political Science Review* 88, no. 3 (1994): 577–92; James D. Fearon, "Signaling Foreign Policy Interests: Tying Hands Versus Sinking Costs," *Journal of Conflict Resolution* 41, no. 1 (1997): 68–90; Robert L. Jervis, *Perception and Misperception in International Politics* (Princeton, N.J.: Princeton University Press, 1976); Schelling, *Arms and Influence*.
15. Schelling, *Arms and Influence*, 2–3.
16. Abrahms, "What Terrorists Really Want."
17. John Bew, Martyn Frampton, and Íñigo Gurruchaga, *Talking to Terrorists: Making Peace in Northern Ireland and the Basque Country* (London: Hurst, 2009); Jonathan Powell, *Talking to Terrorists: How to End Armed Conflicts* (New York: Vintage, 2015).
18. Ethan Bueno de Mesquita, "The Quality of Terror," *American Journal of Political Science* 49, no. 3 (2005): 515–30; Daniel Masters, "The Origin of Terrorist Threats: Religious, Separatist, or Something Else?," *Terrorism and Political Violence* 20, no. 3 (2008): 396–414; Edieal J. Pinker, "A Mathematical Analysis of Short-Term Responses to Threats of Terrorism," in *Mathematical Methods in Counterterrorism*, ed. Nasrulla Memon et al. (New York: Springer-Verlag/Wien, 2009), 141–60; Jeffrey D. Simon, *Lone Wolf Terrorism: Understanding the Growing Threat*, (Amherst, N.Y.: Prometheus Books, 2016).
19. Schelling, *Arms and Influence*, 74.
20. Max Abrahms, "Why Terrorism Does Not Work," *International Security* 31, no. 2 (2006): 42–78; Max Abrahms, *Rules for Rebels: The Science of Victory in Militant History* (New York: Oxford University Press, 2018); Daniel G. Arce and Todd Sandler, "Strategic Analysis of Terrorism," in *Mathematical Methods in Counterterrorism*, ed. Nasrulla Memon et al. (New York: Springer-Verlag/Wien, 2009), 333–48; Tanisha M. Fazal, "Rebellion, War Aims and the Laws of War," *Daedalus* 146, no. 1 (2017): 71–82; Tanisha M. Fazal, *Wars of Law: Unintended Consequences in the Regulation of Armed Conflict* (Ithaca, N.Y.:

Cornell University Press, 2018); Jessica A. Stanton, "Terrorism in the Context of Civil War," *Journal of Politics* 75, no. 4 (2013): 1009–22; Jessica A. Stanton, *Violence and Restraint in Civil War: Civilian Targeting in the Shadow of International Law* (New York: Cambridge University Press, 2016).
21. Stanton, "Terrorism in the Context of Civil War"; Stanton, *Violence and Restraint*.
22. See, for example, the attacks on Madrid's train system in 2004, killing 191, reported in Fernando Reinares, "Evidence of Al-Qaʻida's Role in the 2004 Madrid Attack," *CTC Sentinel* 5, no. 3 (2012): 1–6. See also the Colombian ELN's 1998 bombing of a Segovia pipeline, killing 48, incident 199810180002 in National Consortium for the Study of Terrorism and Responses to Terrorism (START), The Global Terrorism Database (October 26, 2019), distributed by the University of Maryland, https://www.start.umd.edu/gtd/. Terrorists may also have difficulty distinguishing civilians from state agents. See Stathis N. Kalyvas, *The Logic of Violence in Civil War* (New York: Cambridge University Press, 2006); and Stathis N. Kalyvas and Ignacio Sánchez-Cuenca, "Killing Without Dying: The Absence of Suicide Missions," in *Making Sense of Suicide Missions*, ed. Diego Gambetta (New York: Oxford University Press, 2005), 209–31.
23. Mia M. Bloom and John Horgan, "Missing Their Mark: The IRA Proxy Bomb Campaign," *Social Research* 75, no. 2 (2008): 80–94; Walter Enders and Todd Sandler, "Causality Between Transnational Terrorism and Tourism: The Case of Spain," *Terrorism* 14, no. 1 (1991): 49–58.
24. Bloom and Horgan, "Missing Their Mark"; Enders and Sandler, "Causality."
25. I introduced an early version of this speech/kinetic action model in Brown, "Force of Words."
26. Major terrorism data collection projects like ITERATE and the Global Terrorism Database allow the possibility that hoaxes could constitute terrorist incidents. In practice, however, coders have included very few hoaxes in the dataset. See Edward F. Mickolus et al., *International Terrorism: Attributes of Terrorist Events (ITERATE), 1968–2016*, V1 (2017), distributed by Harvard Dataverse, https://doi.org/10.7910/DVN/ZOGPHC; and START, Global Terrorism Database.
27. Kydd and Walter, "Strategies of Terrorism."
28. Less desirable, from the militant's perspective, is the possibility that the government can step in to thwart the attack if warnings are given.
29. A terrorist group could also use warnings or hoaxes to draw civilians into ambushes. One might see such tactics in a protracted ethnic conflict, in which militants' supporters tolerate bloodshed—provided that it is the other ethnic group's blood.
30. I borrow the term *prophylaxis* from chess texts advising the player to precondition the board in a way that restricts one's opponent to moves benefiting

oneself. See Aron Nimzowitsch, *My System Chess Praxis: His Landmark Classics* (Alkmaar, Netherlands: New in Chess, 2016).
31. Fearon, "Domestic Political Audience Costs"; Jervis, *Perception and Misperception*; Schelling, *Arms and Influence*. This sort of threat is addressed in somewhat less detail by the costly signaling terrorism literature. See Bruce Hoffman and Gordon H. McCormick, "Terrorism, Signaling, and Suicide Attack," *Studies in Conflict and Terrorism* 27, no. 4 (2004): 243–81; Kydd and Walter, "Strategies of Terrorism"; Pape, *Dying to Win*.
32. By discouraging forbidden behavior, pledges may reduce civilian casualties—if only by saving the militant group the trouble of fulfilling the threat.
33. Kydd and Walter, "Strategies of Terrorism."
34. Thomas E. Ricks, *The Gamble: General David Petraeus and the American Military Adventure in Iraq, 2006–2008* (New York: Penguin, 2009).

2. The Provisional IRA

1. "Maze Emptied as Terrorist Prisoners Walk Free," *Guardian*, July 28, 2000; "The Agreement," text of the Belfast Agreement, April 10, 1998, published by U.K. Northern Ireland Office, https://assets.publishing.service.gov.uk/government/uploads/system/uploads/attachment_data/file/136652/agreement.pdf.
2. An early version of this analysis appears in Joseph M. Brown, "Force of Words: The Role of Threats in Terrorism," *Terrorism and Political Violence* (August 2018), https://doi.org/10.1080/09546553.2018.1486301.
3. Landon Hancock, *Northern Ireland: Troubles Brewing* (Derry, Northern Ireland: Conflict Archive on the Internet [CAIN], 1998), https://cain.ulster.ac.uk/othelem/landon.htm.
4. John Lynch, *A Tale of Three Cities: Comparative Studies in Working-Class Life* (London: Macmillan, 1998); Denis O'Hearn, "Catholic Grievances, Catholic Nationalism: A Comment," *British Journal of Sociology* 34, no. 3 (1983): 438–45.
5. Richard English, *Armed Struggle: The History of the IRA* (New York: Oxford University Press, 2003).
6. Although several republican groups carried out the "armed struggle," the Provisional Irish Republican Army carried out most of the violence on the republican side.
7. I leave post-1998 violence by Irish republican dissidents for future studies.
8. Martin Dillon, *The Enemy Within* (London: Transworld, 1994); Toby Harnden, *Bandit Country* (London: Hodder and Stoughton, 1999).

9. The first casualty, Bobby Sands, stood for and won a Westminster Parliament seat during his strike, prior to his death.
10. "Armalite" AR-15 and AR-180 assault rifles were favorite weapons of IRA shooters. The "ballot paper" quote is generally attributed to Sinn Féin activist Danny Morrison, speaking at Sinn Féin's 1981 Ard Fheis party conference.
11. Harnden, *Bandit Country*, 108.
12. Harnden, *Bandit Country*, 5–10, 343–47.
13. These negotiations are described at length in John Bew, Martyn Frampton, and Íñigo Gurruchaga, *Talking to Terrorists: Making Peace in Northern Ireland and the Basque Country* (London: Hurst, 2009); and Jonathan Powell, *Talking to Terrorists: How to End Armed Conflicts* (New York: Vintage, 2015).
14. See "The Agreement" text at https://assets.publishing.service.gov.uk/government/uploads/system/uploads/attachment_data/file/136652/agreement.pdf. As this book goes to press, it is not clear what impact the United Kingdom's exit from the European Union will have on the peace settlement's key provisions, including the "soft" border between Northern Ireland and the Republic of Ireland.
15. The Coiste na nIarchimí Republican ex-prisoners support group made several former IRA prisoners available for interviews.
16. Sam Trotter, *Constabulary Heroes: 1826–2011* (Coleraine and Ballycastle, Northern Ireland: Impact, 2012).
17. The Northern Ireland Retired Police Officers Association (NIRPOA) provided background information on policing during the Troubles.
18. The Samaritans organization, which maintains a twenty-four-hour anonymous suicide prevention hotline, also received IRA threats. Members of the organization discussed their role on background.
19. Svend Brinkmann, *Qualitative Interviewing* (New York: Oxford University Press, 2013), 21–25.
20. Anton J. Kuzel, "Sampling In Qualitative Inquiry," in *Doing Qualitative Research*, ed. Benjamin F. Crabtree and William L. Miller, 2nd ed. (Thousand Oaks, Calif.: Sage, 1999), 33–46.
21. English, *Armed Struggle*, 125.
22. Republican #1 interview, Belfast, June 2012.
23. Ed Moloney, *A Secret History of the IRA*, 2nd ed. (New York: Penguin, 2007), 100; William E. Schmidt, "1 Dead, 40 Hurt as a Blast Rips Central London," *New York Times*, April 25, 1993.
24. Republican #2 interview, Newry, July 2012.
25. Ed Moloney, *Voices from the Grave: Two Men's War in Northern Ireland* (New York: Public Affairs, 2010), 66.
26. Mao Zedong, *On Guerrilla Warfare*, published as U.S.Marine Corps FMFRP 12–18 (1989), 93.

27. Walsh interview, Belfast, June 2012. Walsh delivered the Provisional IRA's final public statement, distributed July 27, 2005, confirming the group's disarmament and the disbanding of its organizational structures for waging war. He delivered the statement without a mask, the only time after 1972 that an IRA spokesman did so. Angelique Chrisafis, "After 35 Years of Bombs and Blood, a Quiet Voice Ends the IRA's War," *Guardian* (London), July 28, 2005.
28. McClanahan interview, Belfast, July 2012.
29. Bowyer Bell, *The Secret Army: The IRA* (New Brunswick, N.J.: Transaction, 1997), 438–39.
30. McClanahan interview, Belfast, July 2012.
31. Brendan Anderson, *Joe Cahill: A Life in the IRA* (Dublin: O'Brien Press, 2002); Ed Moloney, *A Secret History of the IRA*, 1st ed. (New York: Norton, 2002); Moloney, *Voices from the Grave*; Andrew J. Wilson, *Irish America and the Ulster Conflict, 1968–1995* (Washington, D.C.: Catholic University of America Press, 1995).
32. Wilson, *Irish America*, 42–46.
33. Wilson, *Irish America*, 77.
34. In another public relations victory for the IRA, U.S. politicians, clergy, and activists advocated against the extradition of IRA gunman Joe Doherty from a New York City jail to Northern Ireland for killing a British Army captain. The pro-Doherty campaign rested on an assertion of "political prisoner" status—a proposition anathema to British policy but endorsed by 132 congressional representatives, Senator Orrin Hatch (R-UT), and the New York City Council, which named a street corner after Doherty. Efforts by Prime Minister Margaret Thatcher and President Ronald Reagan to extradite Doherty dragged on for eight embarrassing years. See Wilson, *Irish America*, 261.
35. Moloney, *A Secret History* (2002), 420.
36. Walsh interview, Belfast, June 2012.
37. Republican #3 interview, Belfast, June 2012.
38. Morrison interview, Andersonstown, July 2012.
39. Republican #1 interview, Belfast, June 2012.
40. Walsh interview, Belfast, June 2012.
41. Morrison interview, Andersonstown, July 2012.
42. Moloney, *A Secret History* (2007), 111.
43. "Bloody Friday: What Happened," *BBC News*, July 16, 2002; David McKittrick et al., *Lost Lives: The Stories of the Men, Women, and Children Who Died as a Result of the Northern Ireland Troubles* (London: Mainstream, 2001).
44. Moloney, *A Secret History* (2002), 117; Moloney, *Voices from the Grave*, 104.
45. Anderson, *Joe Cahill*, 257–58; Moloney, *A Secret History* (2002), 117.
46. Wilson, *Irish America*, 42–46.

47. "Very high-ranking RUC Special Branch veteran" interview, Belfast, January 2013.
48. Wilson, *Irish America*, 42–46.
49. Anderson, *Joe Cahill*, 267–68.
50. McClanahan interview, Belfast, July 2012.
51. Walsh interview, Belfast, June 2012.
52. RUC Special Branch intelligence expert interview, Belfast, January 2013.
53. These incendiary devices drew inspiration from a different kind of risk management. So-called "French letters" consisted of a flammable charge packed into the shell of a VHS cassette along with a sugar-coated, sulfuric acid-filled condom. Taking advantage of the fine manufacturing tolerances of condoms, IRA bomb makers determined the length of time it took for the acid to eat through the latex and react with the incendiary material. French letters could be hidden in shops immediately before the close of business, igniting hours later and setting fire to the store when the building was empty. (Danny Morrison, who provided these insights, stresses that his remarks are not based on direct participation in or observation of IRA activities.)
54. "Countdown to Terror," *BBC News*, June 21, 2006; Jennifer Williams, "Manchester Bomb: June 15, 1996. A Day That Changed Our City Forever," *Manchester Evening News* (U.K.), June 15, 2016.
55. Williams, "Manchester Bomb."
56. "Context: A Quest for Real Peace," *Manchester Evening News*, March 28, 2007; "Countdown to Terror."
57. Harnden, *Bandit Country*, 503.
58. The April 10, 1992, bomb at London's Baltic Exchange used a similarly large 2,000-pound truck bomb, causing £350 million in damage and killing three people. The February 9, 1996, bombing of London's Canary Wharf used a 3,000-pound device, causing £150 million in damage and killing two. See Harnden, *Bandit Country*.
59. The Remembrance Day bombing at Enniskillen in 1987 is one example of a deliberate no-warning attack. The incident killed twelve people. See Moloney, *A Secret History* (2007), 340–41.
60. Moloney, *A Secret History* (2002), 172.
61. Statistics derived from National Consortium for the Study of Terrorism and Responses to Terrorism (START), Global Terrorism Database, October 26, 2019, distributed by the University of Maryland, https://www.start.umd.edu/gtd/. These numbers likely underestimate the IRA's degree of discrimination when attempting to spare civilians. Many of the fatalities in IRA commercial bombings were actually police and army personnel involved in evacuating civilians and attempting to defuse the bombs.

62. START, Global Terrorism Database. The actual number of bombings is almost certainly higher because incidents that did not cause casualties may be underreported in the journalistic sources consulted by Global Terrorism Database coders.
63. William E. Schmidt, "I.R.A. Bombs and Motives," *New York Times*, February 20, 1991.
64. Stewart Tendler and Ray Clancy, "BR Struggles to End Confusion After IRA Blast," *Times* (London), December 17, 1991.
65. Republican #2 interview, Newry, July 2012.
66. Morrison interview, Andersonstown, July 2012. Morrison stresses that his remarks are not based on direct observation of IRA activity.
67. Stewart Tendler and Nicholas Watt, "Low Risk, Maximum Effect," *Times* (London), April 19, 1997.
68. Tendler and Watt, "Low Risk, Maximum Effect."
69. O'Hagan interview, Belfast, July 2012. For the allegations of O'Hagan's involvement in IRA intelligence, see David McKittrick, "John Major's Details Found in Files of 'IRA Officer,'" *Independent* (London), December 3, 2002.
70. Tendler and Watt, "Low Risk, Maximum Effect."
71. See examples throughout Trotter, *Constabulary Heroes*.
72. "Very high-ranking RUC Special Branch veteran" interview, Belfast, January 2013.
73. Chris Ryder, *A Special Kind of Courage* (London: Methuen, 2005).
74. The IRA employed similar tactics against military medics arriving at the scenes of earlier ambushes. The most famous example is its ambush of a military patrol and the follow-up medical triage team at Warrenpoint on August 27, 1979. The initial improvised explosive device killed six soldiers and the follow-up device, aimed at medics, killed twelve. See English, *Armed Struggle*, 220–21.
75. O'Hagan interview, Belfast, July 2012.
76. RUC Special Branch intelligence expert interview, Belfast, January 2013.
77. Royal Ulster Constabulary, *Chief Constable's Report* (Belfast: Police Authority for Northern Ireland, 1996, 1998); Ryder, *A Special Kind of Courage*.
78. Ryder, *A Special Kind of Courage*.
79. Republican #4 interview, Belfast, July 2012.
80. "Omagh Bomb Warnings Released," *BBC News*, August 18, 1998.
81. Ryder, *A Special Kind of Courage*.
82. John McGuffin, *Internment* (Tralee, Ireland: Anvil Books, 1973).
83. I borrow the term *prophylaxis* from Aron Nimzowitsch's discussion of chess strategy. See Aron Nimzowitsch, *My System Chess Praxis: His Landmark Classics* (Alkmaar, Netherlands: New in Chess, 2016).
84. Morrison interview, Andersonstown, July 2012.

85. Tony Geraghty, *The Irish War: The Hidden Conflict Between the IRA and British Intelligence* (Baltimore: Johns Hopkins University Press, 2000), 84.
86. "Very high-ranking RUC Special Branch veteran" interview, Belfast, January 2013.
87. RUC chief superintendent interview, Belfast, July 2012.
88. RUC chief superintendent interview, Belfast, July 2012.
89. Stathis N. Kalyvas, *The Logic of Violence in Civil War* (New York: Cambridge University Press, 2006); Stathis N. Kalyvas and Matthew Adam Kocher, "The Dynamics of Violence in Vietnam: An Analysis of the Hamlet Evaluation System (HES)," *Journal of Peace Research* 46, no. 3 (2009): 335–55; Thomas E. Ricks, *The Gamble: General David Petraeus and the American Military Adventure in Iraq, 2006–2008* (New York: Penguin, 2009).
90. Republican #2 interview, Newry, July 2012.
91. See the IRA's "Green Book" for new recruits, reprinted in Tim Pat Coogan, *The IRA* (London: HarperCollins, 1993).
92. English, *Armed Struggle*, 131.
93. Republican #3 interview, Belfast, June 2012.
94. "I.R.A. Mortars Kill 9 at Ulster Base," Associated Press, March 1, 1985.
95. Andrew H. Kydd and Barbara F. Walter, "The Strategies of Terrorism," *International Security* 31, no. 1 (2006): 49–80.
96. Kalyvas and Kocher, "Dynamics of Violence in Vietnam."
97. English, *Armed Struggle*, 135.
98. Bell, *The Secret Army*, 382; Thomas R. Mockaitis, *British Counterinsurgency in the Post-Imperial Era* (Manchester, U.K.: Manchester University Press, 1995).
99. English, *Armed Struggle*, 160–61.
100. Bell, *The Secret Army*, 378.
101. English, *Armed Struggle*, 166, 175–79.
102. Thomas C. Schelling, *Arms and Influence* (New Haven, Conn.: Yale University Press, 1966), 78, 80.
103. Jacey Fortin, "Margaret Thatcher and the 1984 Brighton Bomb: When the IRA Almost Killed the Iron Lady," *International Business Times*, April 9, 2013. Journalist #1 interview, Belfast, July 2012.
104. Journalist #1 interview, Belfast, July 2012; Fortin, "Margaret Thatcher."
105. Moloney, *A Secret History* (2007); Fraser Nelson, "Crisis as IRA Vows to Keep Weapons," *Scotsman* (Edinburgh), February 3, 2005.
106. P. O'Neill, "Text of Irish Republican Army (IRA) Statement in Response to Political Developments Following the 'Northern Bank Robbery' 2 February 2005," originally published in *An Phoblacht* (Republican news), February 3, 2005, compiled by Martin Melaugh for the Conflict Archive on the Internet (CAIN), http://cain.ulst.ac.uk/othelem/organ/ira/ira020205.htm.
107. Nelson, "Crisis as IRA Vows to Keep Weapons."

108. English, *Armed Struggle*, 157–58.
109. For example, see Moloney, *A Secret History* (2007), 260. The tendency toward delegation by the IRA and other groups is discussed at length in Jacob N. Shapiro, *The Terrorist's Dilemma: Managing Violent Covert Organizations* (Princeton, N.J.: Princeton University Press, 2013).
110. Republican #4 interview, Belfast, July 2012.
111. Morrison interview, Andersonstown, July 2012.
112. O'Hagan interview, Belfast, July 2012.
113. Republican #2 interview, Newry, July 2012.
114. McKittrick et al., *Lost Lives*, 229–30.
115. The RUC chief constable described these hoaxes as "a dreadful menace. . . . Each hoax necessitated evacuation of buildings and diversion of traffic and considering that several areas of the city might be affected at any one time it can readily be appreciated the large number of police required daily for this work." See Royal Ulster Constabulary, *Chief Constable's Report* (1972).
116. Peter Gurney, *Braver Men Walk Away: Memoirs of the World's Top Bomb-Disposal Expert* (London: Harper Collins, 1993).
117. Republican #2 interview, Newry, July 2012.
118. Short-fused bombs raised their own safety concerns. If the bomb went off prematurely or the bombers failed to set it down before the timer reached zero, the operation effectively became a no-warning attack—and a disaster for the bombers. The October 23, 1993, Shankill Road fish shop attack is one infamous example. Two IRA volunteers disguised as deliverymen brought a bomb into Frizzell's Fish Shop, hidden under a tray of fish. The IRA's intended target was a meeting of the Ulster Defence Association (a loyalist paramilitary group), purportedly taking place in a room above the shop. The bomb's eleven-second fuse went off before the IRA men could shout a warning. The attack killed nine civilians, including two girls, ages seven and thirteen, and one of the bombers. See Moloney, *A Secret History* (2007), 414–15.
119. McClanahan interview, Belfast, July 2012.
120. RUC Special Branch intelligence expert interview, Belfast, January 2013. The twelve deaths in the La Mon House hotel bombing in 1978 appear to have resulted from IRA operatives' carelessness in failing to identify a functioning pay phone in advance of their attack. See Moloney, *A Secret History* (2002), 172.
121. RUC Special Branch intelligence expert interview, Belfast, January 2013.
122. However, if a bomber left a device on the wrong street, parked a car bomb on the wrong side of the building, got stuck in traffic, or was stopped at a police checkpoint, the battalion commander would not know this. The warning would include the details of the operation as originally planned, not the detail of the operation as executed. The twenty-nine fatalities in the Omagh

bombing of 1998 (carried out by dissident Republicans who rejected the peace agreement) appear to have resulted from this type of failure: the warning caused police to clear civilians onto the street corner with the bomb, not away from it. (See "Omagh Bomb Warnings Released," *BBC News*.)
123. The examples of taxi and insurance companies were offered by a former taxi dispatcher and journalist #2.
124. McClanahan interview, Belfast, July 2012.
125. Journalist #2 interview, Belfast, July 2012.
126. Republican #3 interview, Belfast, June 2012. According to Republican #2, the redundancy of warning calls also hedged against any "misunderstanding or difficulty in forwarding the communication" to police (Republican #2 interview, Newry, July 2012).
127. McClanahan interview, Belfast, July 2012.
128. Journalist #3, a former BBC reporter who worked in Belfast, recalled another, more complicated system involving two codes within the same message. A call would follow the form: "Hello. This is Paddy. There's a bomb at [the location of the attack]. The code word is [e.g., 'Excalibur']." The caller would conclude by promising to bomb one of three specific locations known by BBC reporters as de facto code words. The BBC reporter would not identify the locations and could recall only one of the locations being used in a warning during the reporter's tenure at the BBC's Belfast office. Yet the reporter was confident that the two other locations would have been recognized by BBC operators as IRA code words at that time.
129. "Excalibur" provided by an anonymous journalist. For other words, see Harnden, *Bandit Country*, 5; Stewart Tendler, "Harrods Bombers Will Be Brought to Trial, Hucklesby Tells Inquest," *Times*, November 15, 1984; and "TV Station Received Warning Calls," *Telegraph* (London), September 7, 2000.
130. Journalist #2 interview, Belfast, July 2012.
131. On at least one occasion, a newspaper reporting on a bombing at London's Heathrow airport printed the IRA code word used to make the warning phone call. See David Leigh, "Bomb Wrecks 50 Cars in Parking Building at Heathrow Terminal After Telephone Warning," *Times*, May 20, 1974.
132. O'Hagan interview, Belfast, July 2012.
133. Journalist #2 interview, Belfast, July 2012.
134. RUC chief superintendent interview, Belfast, July 2012.
135. Gurney, *Braver Men Walk Away*.
136. RUC superintendent interview, Belfast, January 2013.
137. "Very high-ranking RUC Special Branch veteran" interview, Belfast, January 2013.

138. RUC superintendent interview, Belfast, January 2013.
139. Tendler and Watt, "Low Risk, Maximum Effect."
140. "Bloody Friday: What Happened."
141. RUC Special Branch intelligence expert interview, Belfast, January 2013.
142. Republican #3 interview, Belfast, June 2012.
143. Using intermediaries to make the warning public imposes a sort of audience cost on police if they fail to respond. This is not unlike the public crisis bargaining scenarios discussed in the international relations literature. That literature argues that leaders will leverage their own accountability to structure their future payoffs, making it impossible for them to back down from deterrent threats. See James D. Fearon, "Domestic Political Audience Costs and the Escalation of International Disputes," *American Political Science Review* 88, no. 3 (1994): 577–92. The IRA's phone procedures used a variation on the conventional audience cost logic: giving warnings through intermediaries to leverage their *opponents*' accountability, structuring police's future payoffs so that failing to respond to a warning carried prohibitively high political costs.
144. Journalist #2 interview, Belfast, July 2012.
145. Tendler and Clancy, "BR Struggles to End Confusion After IRA Blast."
146. "Very high-ranking RUC Special Branch veteran" interview, Belfast, January 2013.
147. Mallie interview, Belfast, November 2012.
148. On competitive credit claiming, see Aaron Hoffman, "Voice and Silence: Why Groups Take Credit for Acts of Terror," *Journal of Peace Research* 47, no. 5 (2010): 1–22.
149. Journalist #2 recalls receiving such statements by telephone "from somebody who was using a code word to authenticate that the person who was making that call was genuine."
150. On the issue of spoiling, see Kydd and Walter, "Strategies of Terrorism."
151. RUC Special Branch intelligence expert interview, Belfast, January 2013.

3. ETA and the Tamil Tigers

1. John Bew, Martyn Frampton, and Íñigo Gurruchaga, *Talking to Terrorists: Making Peace in Northern Ireland and the Basque Country* (London: Hurst, 2009), 169; Mark Kurlansky, *The Basque History of the World* (New York: Walker, 1999).
2. Kurlansky, *The Basque History of the World*.

3. These atrocities included the infamous aerial bombing of Gernika in 1937, estimated to have killed 1,654 people. See Xabier Irujo, *Gernika, 1937: The Market Day Massacre* (Reno: University of Nevada Press, 2015), 117.
4. Jacqueline Urla, *Reclaiming Basque: Language, Nation, and Cultural Activism* (Reno: University of Nevada Press, 2012), 55–57.
5. Marianne Heiberg, *The Making of the Basque Nation* (New York: Cambridge University Press, 1987), 112; Urla, *Reclaiming Basque*, 59.
6. Heiberg, *The Making of the Basque Nation*, 108. Basque identity, ETA reasoned, was not inherited but inculcated by teaching the next generation to speak the language (Heiberg, *The Making of the Basque Nation*, 115–17; Urla, *Reclaiming Basque*, 59). The survival of the Basque people required a renewed emphasis on Basque-language education.
7. Urla, *Reclaiming Basque*, 63. A linguistic definition of ethnicity meant that immigrants could, in principle, become Basque by learning the language of their new home. But the sheer number of immigrants and the government's official anti-Basque position complicated this task. Hard-line Basque nationalists lamented the "genocidal efficiency" of Franco introducing this wave of immigrants (Heiberg, *The Making of the Basque Nation*, 113).
8. Urla, *Reclaiming Basque*, 65.
9. Heiberg, *The Making of the Basque Nation*, 109–10.
10. Bew, Frampton, and Gurruchaga, *Talking to Terrorists*, 180.
11. Michel Wievorka, "ETA and Basque Political Violence," in *The Legitimization of Violence*, ed. David E. Apter (New York: New York University Press, 1997), 292–349.
12. Heiberg, *The Making of the Basque Nation*, 120–28.
13. Bew, Frampton, and Gurruchaga, *Talking to Terrorists*, 190–91.
14. Bew, Frampton, and Gurruchaga, *Talking to Terrorists*, 196.
15. Attack totals derived from searches of National Consortium for the Study of Terrorism and Responses to Terrorism (START), Global Terrorism Database (October 26, 2019), distributed by the University of Maryland, https://www.start.umd.edu/gtd/. Fatality totals derived from Ministerio del Interior, *Victimas de ETA* (2010), statistical resource published online by the Spanish government (Gobierno de España), archived at https://web.archive.org/web/20100915224606/http://www.mir.ed/DGRIS/Terrorismo_de_ETA/ultimas_victimas/p12b-esp.htm. These aggregate statistics include a handful of attacks committed in the years 1970–1974.
16. Erin Miller and Kathleen Smarick, *Background Report: ETA Ceasefires by the Numbers* (College Park, Md.: National Consortium for the Study of Terrorism and Responses to Terrorism, 2011), https://www.start.umd.edu/sites/default/files/files/publications/br/ETACeasefires.pdf.
17. Bew, Frampton, and Gurruchaga, *Talking to Terrorists*, 236.

18. Raphael Minder, "Basque Group ETA Disbands, After Terrorist Campaign Spanning Generations," *New York Times*, May 2, 2018; Ministerio del Interior, *Víctimas de ETA*.
19. Gordon Weiss, *The Cage: The Fight For Sri Lanka and the Last Days of the Tamil Tigers* (New York: Bellevue Literary Press, 2012), 41–43.
20. H. P. Chattopadhyahya, *Ethnic Unrest in Modern Sri Lanka: An Account of Tamil-Sinhalese Race Relations* (New Delhi: M.D. Publications, 1994); "Sri Lanka Profile—A Chronology of Key Events," *BBC News*, April 25, 2019, https://www.bbc.com/news/world-south-asia-12004081.
21. Chattopadhyahya, *Ethnic Unrest in Modern Sri Lanka*; *Report to Congress on Incidents During the Recent Conflict in Sri Lanka* (Washington, D.C.: U.S. Department of State, 2009), 6; "Up to 100,000 Killed in Sri Lanka's Civil War: UN," Australian Broadcasting Corporation, May 20, 2009; Weiss, *The Cage*.
22. M. R. Narayan Swamy, *Tigers of Lanka: From Boys to Guerrillas* (Colombo: Vijitha Yapa, 2008), 89–91, 93.
23. Weiss, *The Cage*.
24. Swamy, *Tigers of Lanka*, 133, 138, 149–50.
25. Swamy, *Tigers of Lanka*, 106–11, 115–18, 132, 238–40; Weiss, *The Cage*.
26. Indo-Lanka Accord, agreement signed by the governments of India and Sri Lanka, Colombo, Sri Lanka, July 29, 1987.
27. Swamy, *Tigers of Lanka*, 250–316.
28. Swamy, *Tigers of Lanka*, 319.
29. Weiss, *The Cage*.
30. Swamy, *Tigers of Lanka*, 360.
31. Zachariah Cherian Mampilly, *Rebel Rulers: Insurgent Governance and Civilian Life During War* (Ithaca, N.Y.: Cornell University Press, 2011).
32. Weiss, *The Cage*, 72–85.
33. John Sullivan, *ETA and Basque Nationalism: The Fight for Euskadi, 1980–1986* (New York: Routledge, 1988), 153.
34. Wievorka, "ETA and Basque Political Violence," 306.
35. Heiberg, *The Making of the Basque Nation*.
36. Wievorka, "ETA and Basque Political Violence," 305.
37. Wievorka, "ETA and Basque Political Violence," 305.
38. Teresa Whitfield, *Endgame for ETA: Elusive Peace in the Basque Country* (New York: Oxford University Press, 2014), 84.
39. See, for example, the July 1997 kidnapping and killing of Miguel Ángel Blanco, an Ermua councilor from the anti-ETA Partido Popular. The incident was condemned by many Basques, including thousands who turned out in the street to protest ETA's violence (Bew, Frampton, and Gurruchaga, *Talking to Terrorists*, 220–21).

40. "Zaragoza: cinco ataúdes blancos," *El País*, August 2, 2009. A similar incident on May 29, 1991, in the city of Vic killed nine people, including five children. See "Vic (Barcelona) recordará hoy a las víctimas del atentado de ETA en su casa cuartel," *El Economista*, June 13, 2009.
41. Bew, Frampton, and Gurruchaga, *Talking to Terrorists*, 211.
42. When the so-called *Mesa de Argel* talks broke down, the Spanish government had Etxebeste exiled to Latin America and imprisoned. He lost his leadership role sometime in the 1990s, when it became clear that the Spanish government would not allow his release and would no longer use him as an intermediary to convey messages to the rest of ETA.
43. Etxebeste interview, Donostia, October 2013.
44. Statistics from START, Global Terrorism Database.
45. "ETA hace estallar dos bombas en la playa de Laredo y otras dos en Noja en menos de tres horas," *El Correo*, July 20, 2008.
46. Bew, Frampton, and Gurruchaga, *Talking to Terrorists*, 205.
47. "Igor Portu fue el que avisó del atentado de la T-4 del aeropuerto de Barajas," *La Vanguardia*, May 5, 2010.
48. Statistics based on an analysis of attacks listed in START, Global Terrorism Database. See chapter 6 for a discussion of the data and coding methodology.
49. Etxebeste interview, Donostia, October 2013.
50. "ETA hace estallar dos bombas," *El Correo*.
51. Walter Enders and Todd Sandler, "Causality Between Transnational Terrorism and Tourism: The Case of Spain," *Terrorism* 14, no. 1 (1991): 49–58.
52. "Igor Portu fue el que avisó," *La Vanguardia*.
53. Anna Argemi, "El Estado, condenado por negligencia policial en el atentado de Hipercor," *El País*, May 21, 1994.
54. START, Global Terrorism Database.
55. START, Global Terrorism Database.
56. Etxebeste interview, Donostia, October 2013.
57. Jan Mansvelt-Beck, *Territory and Terror: Conflicting Nationalisms in the Basque Country* (New York: Routledge, 2005), 64–66. The continuity of Spanish counterterrorism is symbolized by the Guardia Civil's retention of *fasces* heraldry to the present day.
58. Bew, Frampton, and Gurruchaga, *Talking to Terrorists*, 200, 205.
59. Etxebeste interview, Donostia, October 2013.
60. Statistics generated from START, Global Terrorism Database.
61. See Paul A. Povlock, "The Guerrilla War at Sea: The Sri Lankan Civil War," *Small Wars Journal*, September 9, 2011. What stronghold populations and smuggling could not provide, the LTTE was able to collect from an international diaspora in places such as the United Kingdom, Canada, and the United

States. Although persuasion becomes more important when fundraising in a diaspora, extortion is still possible, and the LTTE definitely showed a willingness to raise funds coercively when necessary. See Jo Becker, *Funding the "Final War": LTTE Intimidation and Extortion in the Tamil Diaspora* (Washington, D.C.: Human Rights Watch, 2006).

62. Monty G. Marshall, Keith Jaggers, and Ted Robert Gurr, *POLITY IV Project Dataset Users' Manual* (Vienna, Va.: Center for Systemic Peace, 2018).

63. Polity IV Project, *Political Regime Characteristics and Transitions, 1800–2018* (October 27, 2019), distributed by the Center for Systemic Peace, http://www.systemicpeace.org/inscr/p4v2018.xls.

64. Mark Gibney et al., *The Political Terror Scale 1976–2018* (October 26, 2019), from the Political Terror Scale website, http://www.politicalterrorscale.org. These scores are from the Amnesty International–derived variant of PTS. Scores from the U.S. State Department–derived variant are virtually identical. See the PTS codebook for further explanation.

65. Gibney et al., *Political Terror Scale*; Polity IV Project, *Political Regime Characteristics*.

66. Weiss, *The Cage*.

67. Sumanthiran interview, Colombo, August 2013.

68. Sumanthiran interview, Colombo, August 2013. With regard to diaspora fundraising, the Tigers' mistreatment of Sinhalese civilians did not pose much of a political problem either. During the Sri Lankan Civil War, the Tamil Tigers drew funds and weapons from large Tamil communities in the United Kingdom, Canada, the United States, and elsewhere. Many Tamils in the diaspora communities were refugees, having fled Sri Lanka following the "Black July" pogroms of 1983. Many members of the Tamil diaspora bore an understandable grudge against the Sri Lankan government and Sinhalese people generally. Those who did not might still be willing to overlook LTTE atrocities because the Tigers were the only rebel group capable of wresting an independent Eelam out of the Sri Lankan state. At any rate, diaspora Tamils learned much of what they knew about the Sri Lankan war through nationalist news outlets such as Tamilnet, which maintained a close relationship with LTTE spokespeople. As the only viable militant group, with the ability to craft a propaganda narrative and shape the flow of information to an emotionally engaged base, the Tigers were able to commit atrocities and still raise millions of dollars abroad.

69. START, Global Terrorism Database.

70. Bibhu Prasad Routray and Ajit Kumar Singh, "The Pawns of War," *South Asia Intelligence Review: Weekly Assessments and Briefings*, October 2, 2006; M. R. Narayan Swamy, *Prabhakaran: Inside An Elusive Mind* (Delhi: Konark, 2003), 123; "Tamils Kill 110 Muslims at 2 Sri Lankan Mosques,"

Associated Press, August 5, 1990; Chris Kamalendra, "Pre-dawn Horror in Ampara," *Sunday Times* (Colombo), September 19, 1999.
71. Swamy, *Tigers of Lanka*, 329.
72. "Tamil Tigers Blamed for Bus Garage Blast," *BBC News*, April 21, 1987.
73. Chris Morris, "Velupillai Pirabaharan (Interview with Chris Morris)," *BBC News*, September 1, 1991.
74. "Fifty Dead in Sri Lanka Suicide Bombing," *BBC News*, January 31, 1996; "Tamil Arrested in Sri Lanka Train Bombing," *New York Times*, September 4, 1996.
75. Emily Wax, "Sri Lanka's War on Several Fronts," *Washington Post*, February 22, 2009.
76. Statistics based on chapter 6's analysis of attacks listed in START, Global Terrorism Database.
77. Weiss, *The Cage*, 35–36.
78. Weiss, *The Cage*, 82–83.
79. I conducted open-ended LexisNexis searches for evidence of prophylactic warnings and hoaxes. The format of the searches was *(LTTE or Tamil Tigers or Liberation Tigers) and (threat! or warn! or hoax!)*.
80. Following a botched suicide attack on Sri Lankan cabinet ministers, the would-be assassins fled on foot. A civilian witness recalled: "I saw five armed men running. . . . They were all armed. They threatened everyone and kept on running." See Dilshika Jayamaha, "Tamil Suicide Bomb Kills 19," *Sunday Telegraph* (Sydney), March 12, 2000.
81. Edward F. Mickolus et al., *International Terrorism: Attributes of Terrorist Events (ITERATE), 1968–2016*, V1 (2017), distributed by Harvard Dataverse, https://doi.org/10.7910/DVN/ZOGPHC.
82. Even if the LTTE had targeted shops or infrastructure with hoaxes, the absence of truthful warnings for attacks on such targets might have rendered hoaxes unconvincing and ineffective as a tactic.
83. See descriptions of ETA hoaxes on October 15, 1984; April 26, 1985; June 1, 1986; and June 2, 1986, in Mickolus et al., *International Terrorism*.
84. See the codebook accompanying Mickolus et al., *International Terrorism*.
85. Etxebeste interview, Donostia, October 2013.
86. Paul Delaney, "Spain Fears Bombing May Herald an Increase in Terrorist Attacks," *New York Times*, June 23, 1987.
87. Mickolus et al., *International Terrorism*.
88. Etxebeste interview, Donostia, October 2013.
89. I conducted the Guardia Civil interviews in Madrid in October 2013, prior to the final disbandment of ETA. For safety and professional reasons, the interviewees wished to remain anonymous and would not allow the use of quotations.

90. Etxebeste interview, Donostia, October 2013.
91. Etxebeste interview, Donostia, October 2013.
92. Etxebeste interview, Donostia, October 2013.
93. Etxebeste interview, Donostia, October 2013.
94. "ETA hace estallar dos bombas," *El Correo*.
95. Etxebeste interview, Donostia, October 2013.
96. Iñaki Barcena et al., "Institutionalisation and Radicalisation in the Organisational Evolution of the Basque Ecologist Movement (1975–1999): Between Virtue and Necessity," paper presented at the European Consortium for Political Research conference, Colchester, U.K., April 2000.
97. "El fantasma de la autovía de Leizarán se cierne sobre la 'Y vasca,'" *Vasco Press*, December 3, 2008.
98. Barcena et al., "Institutionalisation and Radicalisation."
99. Bew, Frampton, and Gurruchaga, *Talking to Terrorists*, 215.
100. Aitor Guenaga, "Recibir la carta de extorsión de ETA era como si te diagnosticaran cáncer," *El Diario* (Spain), March 11, 2017.
101. Bew, Frampton, and Gurruchaga, *Talking to Terrorists*, 197, 235.
102. Guenaga, "Recibir la carta de extorsión de ETA."
103. Mampilly, *Rebel Rulers*, 136–37, 141–48.
104. Weiss, *The Cage*, 76–80.
105. Edward A. Gargan, "Batticaloa Journal; Atrocity by Atrocity, a Priest Chronicles War," *New York Times*, September 3, 1991.
106. Weiss, *The Cage*, 61, 62, 83.
107. Weiss, *The Cage*, 74–75.
108. Weiss, *The Cage*, 71.
109. Bew, Frampton, and Gurruchaga, *Talking to Terrorists*, 213.
110. Bew, Frampton, and Gurruchaga, *Talking to Terrorists*, 211–14.
111. Bew, Frampton, and Gurruchaga, *Talking to Terrorists*, 236–37.
112. "Igor Portu fue el que avisó," *La Vanguardia*.
113. Bew, Frampton, and Gurruchaga, *Talking to Terrorists*, 220–21.
114. Bew, Frampton, and Gurruchaga, *Talking to Terrorists*, 200.
115. Kasun Ubayasiri, "An Illusive Leader's Annual Speech," *EJournalist: A Refereed Media Journal* 6, no. 1 (2006): 1–27.
116. Weiss, *The Cage*, 80.
117. Ubayasiri, "An Illusive Leader's Annual Speech," 2, 23.
118. Velipullai Prabhakaran, "Leader V Prabakaran's Heroes Day Speech 2002," public remarks, November 27, 2002; Velipullai Prabhakaran, "Leader V Prabakaran's Heroes Day Speech 2003," public remarks, November 27, 2003; Velipullai Prabhakaran, "Leader V Prabakaran's Heroes Day Speech 2004," public remarks, November 27, 2004; Velipullai Prabhakaran, "Leader V Prabakaran's Heroes day speech 2005," public remarks, November 27, 2005.

119. "A Warning by High Security Zone Residents' Liberation Force," *Asian Tribune*, December 8, 2005.
120. Joe Ariyaratnam, "Suspected Rebel Fronts Threaten Sri Lankan Army," Reuters, December 15, 2005.
121. Justin Huggler, "Thousands Flee as Air Force Attacks Sri Lankan Rebels," *Independent* (London), April 27, 2006.
122. Simon Gardner, "Sri Lanka Battle Traps Civilians, South Threatened," Reuters, August 14, 2006.
123. Simon Gardner, "Suspected Rebel Front May Target Sri Lanka Hospitals," Reuters, November 6, 2006.
124. I conducted open-ended LexisNexis searches for such threats, finding no clear examples.
125. Urla, *Reclaiming Basque*, 57.
126. Heiberg, *The Making of the Basque Nation*, 109–10.
127. Bew, Frampton, and Gurruchaga, *Talking to Terrorists*, 181, 191.
128. Bew, Frampton, and Gurruchaga, *Talking to Terrorists*, 181–82.
129. Bew, Frampton, and Gurruchaga, *Talking to Terrorists*, 181.
130. START, Global Terrorism Database.
131. See incidents 197807070001 and 197901130003 in START, Global Terrorism Database. See also María José Grech, "ETA asesina a un guardia civil, un exmiembro de ETA, un coronel retirado y un expolicía," *Libertad Digital* blog post, June 3, 2011, http://blogs.libertaddigital.com/in-memoriam/eta-asesina-a-un-guardia-civil-un-exmiembro-de-eta-un-coronel-retirado-y-un-expolicia-9744/; and María José Grech, "Txomin Merino, supuesto confidente, un guardia civil y un teniente del Ejército," *Libertad Digital* blog post, July 5, 2011, http://blogs.libertaddigital.com/in-memoriam/txomin-merino-supuesto-confidente-un-guardia-civil-y-un-teniente-del-ejercito-9939/.
132. Bew, Frampton, and Gurruchaga, *Talking to Terrorists*, 194.
133. The search strings included the following terms: *(ETA or ETA-m or ETA-pm or Euskadi) and (threat! or warn!)*.
134. John Hooper, "ETA Offers to Lift Olympics Terror Threat," *Guardian* (London), July 11, 1992.
135. Hooper, "ETA Offers to Lift Olympics Terror Threat."
136. "Eta Rebuffed," Reuters, July 13, 1992; Miller and Smarick, *Background Report*.
137. Sumanthiran interview, Colombo, August 2013.
138. Weiss, *The Cage*, 63.
139. START, Global Terrorism Database.
140. I conducted LexisNexis searches with the following terms: *(LTTE or Tamil Tigers or Liberation Tigers) and (threat! or warn!)*.

141. "LTTE Rebels in Sri Lanka Abduct Tamil Party Leader," *BBC News*, October 13, 1990.
142. D. B. S. Jeyaraj, "'Sinna Bala' and the Tamil National Struggle," *Sunday Leader* (Colombo), October 17, 2004.
143. "South Indian Police Ordered to Track Down Tamil Rebels," Xinhua General Overseas News Service, February 8, 1993.
144. Tom Farrell, "Tamil Tigers Vow to Take Revenge on Army," *Daily Telegraph* (London), July 18, 2007.
145. Bew, Frampton, and Gurruchaga, *Talking to Terrorists*, 189.
146. Etxebeste interview, Donostia, October 2013.
147. "Zaragoza: cinco ataúdes blancos," *El País*.
148. "Vic (Barcelona) recordará hoy a las víctimas del atentado de ETA en su casa cuartel," *El Economista*, June 13, 2009.
149. Bew, Frampton, and Gurruchaga, *Talking to Terrorists*, 211.
150. Weiss, *The Cage*, 80.
151. Weiss, *The Cage*, 80, 83–84.
152. Gardner, "Suspected Rebel Front May Target Sri Lanka Hospitals."
153. Huggler, "Thousands Flee."
154. Matthew Weaver and Gethin Chamberlain, "Sri Lanka Declares End to War with Tamil Tigers," *Guardian* (London), May 19, 2009.
155. Delaney, "Spain Fears Bombing May Herald an Increase in Terrorist Attacks."
156. Moloney, *A Secret History* (2002), 172; Moloney, *A Secret History* (2007), 414–15; McKittrick et al., *Lost Lives*, 229–30; "Omagh Bomb Warnings Released," *BBC News*, August 18,1998.
157. Delaney, "Spain Fears Bombing May Herald an Increase in Terrorist Attacks."

4. The MRTA and the Shining Path

1. Comisión de la Verdad y Reconciliación (CVR), *Hatun Willakuy: Abbreviated Version of the Final Report of the Truth and Reconciliation Commission* (Lima: Transfer Commission of the Truth and Reconciliation Commission of Peru, 2014), 5.
2. CVR, *Hatun Willakuy*, 122–23.
3. Gordon H. McCormick, *Sharp Dressed Men: Peru's Túpac Amaru Revolutionary Movement* (Santa Monica, Calif.: RAND Corporation, 1993), 7.
4. Tom Marks, "Making Revolution with Shining Path," in *The Shining Path of Peru*, ed. David Scott Palmer (London: Hurst, 1992), 209–23; David Scott Palmer, "Introduction," in *The Shining Path of Peru*, ed. David Scott Palmer (London: Hurst, 1992), 1–32.

5. CVR, *Hatun Willakuy*, 12–13, 70, 122.
6. CVR, *Hatun Willakuy*, 17, 42–52, 167–68.
7. CVR, *Hatun Willakuy*, 50, 95; Michael L. Smith, "Shining Path's Urban Strategy: Ate Vitarte," in *The Shining Path of Peru*, ed. David Scott Palmer (London: Hurst, 1992), 145–65.
8. CVR, *Hatun Willakuy*, 43, 51–53.
9. CVR, *Hatun Willakuy*; U.S. Department of State, Bureau of International Narcotics and Law Enforcement Affairs, "Narcotics Rewards Program: Victor Quispe Palomino," 2014, archived at https://web.archive.org/web/20170220171559/https://www.state.gov/j/inl/narc/rewards/144801.htm; Hector Tobar, "Peru to Tighten Security for Bush," *Los Angeles Times*, March 22, 2002.
10. CVR, *Hatun Willakuy*, 122–30.
11. See a full discussion of this issue in Stathis N. Kalyvas, *The Logic of Violence in Civil War* (New York: Cambridge University Press, 2006).
12. Miguel Rincón, *Testimonio a la Comisión de la Verdad y Reconciliación* (Lima: Comisión de la Verdad y Reconciliación, 2002).
13. "Accionar Tupacamarista," *Cambio* (Lima). February 7, 1991.
14. "Atentados Remueven Toda la Capital," *Cambio*, February 7, 1991.
15. Statistical data from National Consortium for the Study of Terrorism and Responses to Terrorism (START), Global Terrorism Database, October 26, 2019, distributed by the University of Maryland, https://www.start.umd.edu/gtd/.
16. Event counts taken from START, Global Terrorism Database, as well as Bureau of Diplomatic Security, *Significant Incidents of Political Violence Against Americans—1990*, publication 9869 (Washington, D.C.: U.S. Department of State, 1991), and Bureau of Diplomatic Security, *Significant Incidents of Political Violence Against Americans—1991*, publication 9953 (Washington, D.C.: U.S. Department of State, 1992). The MRTA also attacked *yanqi* businesses directly supporting the "corporate and fascist" Peruvian government. See Víctor Polay, *Testimonio a la Comisión de la Verdad y Reconciliación* (Lima: Comisión de la Verdad y Reconciliación, 2002), 41. On February 5, 1991, the MRTA attacked a facility belonging to the Pesevisa Company, a subsidiary of the U.S.-based Wackenhut security contractor. MRTA commandos approached the parking area in front of the building, spraying automatic weapons fire at the building and planting a bomb that killed two security guards and wounded as many as one hundred people. See Bureau of Diplomatic Security, *Significant Incidents—1991*, 9.
17. McCormick, *Sharp Dressed Men*, 52, 55.
18. CVR, *Hatun Willakuy*, 246.
19. CVR, *Hatun Willakuy*, 84.

20. The MRTA, in its few ill-fated forays into the country, wore military garb, specifically to prevent government retaliation against civilians.
21. CVR, *Hatun Willakuy*, 255–56.
22. Statistical data from START, Global Terrorism Database.
23. CVR, *Hatun Willakuy*, 102–4, 333.
24. Guzmán, *Síntesis de entrevista*, 17; CVR, *Hatun Willakuy*, 80.
25. Rincón, *Testimonio*, 49.
26. Polay, *Testimonio*, 41.
27. "Atentados Remueven Toda La Capital," *Cambio*.
28. Bureau of Diplomatic Security, *Significant Incidents—1991*.
29. Citibank was a favorite target of the MRTA, as were American chain restaurants. The MRTA carried out at least six attacks on Kentucky Fried Chicken restaurants, on March 20, 1985 (when three restaurants were attacked simultaneously); June 5, 1990; February 2, 1991; and February 16, 1991. See START, Global Terrorism Database; Bureau of Diplomatic Security, *Significant Incidents—1990*; and Bureau of Diplomatic Security, *Significant Incidents—1991*. The MRTA also frequently attacked BNC facilities. Between June 25, 1987, and August 22, 1991, it attacked BNCs as many as sixteen times (START, Global Terrorism Database). The attacks tended to occur at night or in the early morning hours when the buildings were less likely to be occupied. In certain daytime attacks, however, the BNC facilities did receive bomb warnings, by telephone or from MRTA members verbally as they overpowered security guards and began placing bombs inside the buildings. See Bureau of Diplomatic Security, *Significant Incidents of Political Violence Against Americans—1987*, publication 9644 (Washington, D.C.: U.S. Department of State, 1988); Bureau of Diplomatic Security, *Significant Incidents of Political Violence Against Americans—1989*, publication 9767 (Washington, D.C.: U.S. Department of State, 1990); Bureau of Diplomatic Security, *Significant Incidents—1990*; and Bureau of Diplomatic Security, *Significant Incidents—1991*.
30. These statistics are based on analyses of attacks listed in START, Global Terrorism Database. See chapter 6 for a discussion of the coding methods.
31. "Bomb at Gas Station Kills Seven in Peru," *Toledo Blade*, September 7, 1992; CVR, *Hatun Willakuy*, 52; START, Global Terrorism Database (incident 199209060008); "Truck Bomb Outside Lima TV Station Kills 5," United Press International, June 5, 1992.
32. CVR, *Hatun Willakuy*, 59; Abimael Guzmán, *Síntesis de Entrevista, Abimael Guzmán Reynoso y Elena Iparraguirre, 27 de enero del 2003* (Lima: Comisión de la Verdad y Reconciliación, 2003), 17.
33. Cynthia McClintock, "Theories of Revolution and the Case of Peru," in *The Shining Path of Peru*, ed. David Scott Palmer (London: Hurst, 1992), 230.

34. A survey of the ITERATE international terrorism database shows one hoax threat claimed by the MRTA and no hoaxes attributed to the Shining Path. See Edward F. Mickolus et al., *International Terrorism: Attributes of Terrorist Events (ITERATE), 1968–2016*, V1 (2017), distributed by Harvard Dataverse, https://doi.org/10.7910/DVN/ZOGPHC.
35. Bureau of Diplomatic Security, *Significant Incidents—1991*; "Peru Attacks on US and British Interests Reported," *BBC Summary of World Broadcasts*, February 4, 1991.
36. "Atentados Remueven Toda La Capital," *Cambio*; Bureau of Diplomatic Security, *Significant Incidents—1991*.
37. "Peru Attacks on US and British Interests Reported," *BBC Summary of World Broadcasts*.
38. "Bomb Threat Delays," *Journal of Commerce*, Aviation Briefs (from Wire and Staff Reports), December 30, 1988; Michael Reid, "Lima Explosion as Presidents Arrive / Car Blown Up Outside Military Headquarters in Peruvian Capital," *Guardian* (London), July 29, 1985; Vidal Silva, "Peruvian Police Attacked During Armed Strike," United Press International, May 29, 1991.
39. McCormick, *Sharp Dressed Men*.
40. "Accionar Tupacamarista," *Cambio*.
41. "Atentados Remueven Toda La Capital," *Cambio*.
42. Bureau of Diplomatic Security, *Significant Incidents—1989*, 16.
43. Bureau of Diplomatic Security, *Significant Incidents—1991*, 9, 11, 14.
44. Bureau of Diplomatic Security, *Significant Incidents—1989*; Bureau of Diplomatic Security, *Significant Incidents—1990*; Bureau of Diplomatic Security, *Significant Incidents—1991*.
45. José E. Gonzales, "Guerrillas and Coca in the Upper Huallaga Valley," in *The Shining Path of Peru*, ed. David Scott Palmer (London: Hurst, 1992), 129.
46. Gonzales, "Guerrillas and Coca," 129.
47. CVR, *Hatun Willakuy*, 84.
48. CVR, *Hatun Willakuy*, 271.
49. Palmer, "Introduction," 27.
50. CVR, *Hatun Willakuy*, 85.
51. CVR, *Hatun Willakuy*, 215.
52. Smith, "Shining Path's Urban Strategy," 149.
53. Carlos Ivan Degregori, "The Origins and Logic of the Shining Path: Two Views," in *The Shining Path of Peru*, ed. David Scott Palmer (London: Hurst, 1992), 51–52.
54. CVR, *Hatun Willakuy*, 111.
55. Smith, "Shining Path's Urban Strategy," 160. For a sample communiqué announcing an armed strike, see Partido Comunista del Perú (PCP)—Mantaro Valley Base, *Paro Armado en Junín y Pasco*, communiqué dated

May 1, 1992, archived by el Centro de Documentación de los Movimientos Armados (CEDEMA), http://www.cedema.org/ver.php?id=8033.
56. CVR, *Hatun Willakuy*, 111.
57. This insight drawn from an interview of a witness to one burning (Civilian conflict witness interview, Lima, October 2013). See also Marks, "Making Revolution with Shining Path," 196.
58. In some cases, the political messaging may be more subtle: pledges of violence associated with assertions that the terrorist group is prepared to engage in talks.
59. McCormick, *Sharp Dressed Men*, 7, 52, 55.
60. CVR, *Hatun Willakuy*, 125. The Shining Path, meanwhile, increased its level of provocation, seeking to "unmask" the García regime by inducing repression. See CVR, *Hatun Willakuy*, 97.
61. CVR, *Hatun Willakuy*, 125.
62. MRTA, *Primera Conferencia Clandestina: Suspensión de Acciones Militares*, transcript of press conference, released August 1, 1985, archived by CEDEMA, http://www.cedema.org/ver.php?id=3432.
63. MRTA, "La Violencia: El Derecho del Agredido," *Venceremos* 6 (September 1, 1985), archived by CEDEMA, http://www.cedema.org/ver.php?id= 3481.
64. MRTA, *¡Sin Justicia ni Libertad, la Rebelión Avanzará!* communiqué dated February 20, 1986, archived by CEDEMA, http://www.cedema.org/ver.php?id=6629.
65. CVR, *Hatun Willakuy*, 125.
66. For example, in the early 1990s MRTA agents sought the mediation of the ICRC to negotiate the release of several policemen captured by the MRTA in a raid. The MRTA affirmed the Red Cross's view that the conflict in Peru "must be conducted with the strictest respect for the norms of international humanitarian law." In the end, however, the MRTA failed to secure the release of its members and was forced to release the police unilaterally. See "San Martín: Entre el Fuego y las Negociaciones," *Cambio* (Lima), May 30, 1991.
67. CVR, *Hatun Willakuy*, 115.
68. CVR, *Hatun Willakuy*, 115, 74.
69. Some speculate that Guzmán's peace overtures were a calculated move to reestablish communication with his organization and direct its revolution from behind the prison walls. If so, his gambit failed spectacularly. See Palmer, "Introduction," 31.
70. PCP, *¡Reafirmarse en la Base de Unidad Partidaria!*, statement of the Central Committee, February 1, 1994, archived by CEDEMA, http://www.cedema.org/ver.php?id=709; PCP, *¡Viva el Presidente Gonzalo y su Todopoderoso*

Pensamiento!, statement of the Central Committee, February 1, 1994, archived by CEDEMA, http://www.cedema.org/ver.php?id=710; PCP, *Directiva Internacional del PCP al Movimiento Popular Perú*, statement of the Central Committee, December 1, 1993, archived by CEDEMA, http://www.cedema.org/ver.php?id=707.

71. PCP, *Lineamiento para Documento de Bases*, statement of the Central Directorate, November 1, 1993, archived by CEDEMA, http://www.cedema.org/ver.php?id=5290.
72. Statistics from START, Global Terrorism Database.
73. McCormick, *Sharp Dressed Men*, 57.
74. PCP, *Comenzamos a Derrumbar los Muros y a Desplegar la Aurora*, statement of the Second Plenary Session of the Central Committee, March 28, 1980, archived by CEDEMA, http://www.cedema.org/ver.php?id=631.
75. CVR, *Hatun Willakuy*, 335.
76. PCP, *¡A Nuestro Heroico Pueblo Combatiente!*, statement of the Central Committee, January 1, 1981, archived by CEDEMA, http://www.cedema.org/ver.php?id=635; PCP, *¡Viva la Lucha Armada de Nuestro Pueblo! ¡Abajo la Patraña Reaccionaria!*, communiqué dated September 8, 1981, archived by CEDEMA, http://www.cedema.org/ver.php?id=636.
77. PCP, *Desarrollar la Guerra Popular Sirviendo a la Revolución Mundial*, statement of the Central Committee, August 1, 1986, archived by CEDEMA, http://www.cedema.org/ver.php?id=640; PCP, *¡Elecciones, No! ¡Guerra Popular, Sí!*, statement of the Central Committee, May 1, 1990, archived by CEDEMA, http://www.cedema.org/ver.php?id=647.
78. PCP, *Día de la Heroicidad*, resolution of the Central Committee, June 19, 1986, archived by CEDEMA, http://www.cedema.org/ver.php?id=639; PCP, *¡Viva el Maoísmo!*, statement of the Central Committee, August 1, 1993, archived by CEDEMA, http://www.cedema.org/ver.php?id=704.
79. Abimael Guzmán, *Dar la Vida por el Partido y la Revolución*, communiqué signed as "Presidente Gonzalo," June 1, 1987, archived by CEDEMA, http://www.cedema.org/ver.php?id=642.
80. PCP, *Documentos Fundamentales*, statement of the Central Committee, January 1, 1988, archived by CEDEMA, http://www.cedema.org/ver.php?id=5460; PCP, *Linea de Construcción de los Tres Instrumentos de la Revolución*, communiqué dated January 1, 1988, archived by CEDEMA, http://www.cedema.org/ver.php?id=646.
81. McCormick, *Sharp Dressed Men*; CVR, *Hatun Willakuy*, 30, 125, 127.
82. MRTA, *La Situación Actual y las Tareas en el Proceso de la Guerra Revolucionaria del Pueblo*, communiqué dated May 1, 1984, archived by CEDEMA, http://www.cedema.org/ver.php?id=3922.

83. MRTA, *El MRTA y la Revolución Peruana*, communiqué dated May 1, 1985, archived by CEDEMA, http://www.cedema.org/ver.php?id=5618.
84. MRTA, "Balance y Perspectivas: Campaña Militar del Frente Guerrillero Nor Oriental," *Voz Rebelde* 9 (January 1, 1988), archived by CEDEMA, http://www.cedema.org/ver.php?id=6012. In fact, by the time the communiqué was issued, the government had already discovered and smashed the MRTA cadres in San Martín (CVR, *Hatun Willakuy*, 126). The MRTA's next attempt to concentrate forces, in 1989, also ended in disaster: a column of fifty-eight guerrillas encountered an army patrol in the town of Molinos and was completely annihilated (CVR, *Hatun Willakuy*, 128).
85. "Atentados Remueven Toda La Capital," *Cambio*; "Dos Veces en su Misma Casa—En Forma Reiterada, los Subversivos Atacaron la Embajada Norteamericana, Pese a la Redoblada Seguridad Policial," *Cambio* (Lima), February 7, 1991.
86. CVR, *Hatun Willakuy*, 65, 104–8.
87. CVR, *Hatun Willakuy*, 106, 107.
88. CVR, *Hatun Willakuy*, 30.
89. CVR, *Hatun Willakuy*, 175.
90. Palmer, "Introduction," 24.
91. CVR, *Hatun Willakuy*, 30.
92. CVR, *Hatun Willakuy*, 106–8, 175.

5. The Taliban, ISIL, and Boko Haram

1. Jessica A. Stanton, "Terrorism in the Context of Civil War," *Journal of Politics* 75, no. 4 (2013): 1009–22.
2. Bruce Hoffman, *Inside Terrorism* (New York: Columbia University Press, 2006).
3. Hoffman, *Inside Terrorism*.
4. Zachary Laub, "The Taliban in Afghanistan," Council on Foreign Relations online report, July 4, 2014, https://www.cfr.org/backgrounder/taliban-afghanistan; "The Taliban," Council on Foreign Relations infoguide, https://www.cfr.org/interactives/taliban?cid=marketing_use-taliban_infoguide-012115#!/taliban?cid=marketing_use-taliban_infoguide-012115.
5. Ahmed Rashid, *Taliban: Militant Islam, Oil and Fundamentalism in Central Asia* (New Haven, Conn.: Yale University Press, 2000), 1–2, 35, 88–90.
6. Laub, "The Taliban in Afghanistan."
7. Council on Foreign Relations, "The Taliban"; Laub, "The Taliban in Afghanistan."
8. Rashid, *Taliban*, 35, 43–51.

9. Council on Foreign Relations, "The Taliban"; Rashid, *Taliban*, 41–79.
10. Council on Foreign Relations, "The Taliban"; Laub, "The Taliban in Afghanistan"; Rashid, *Taliban*, 50–51.
11. Laub, "The Taliban in Afghanistan."
12. Council on Foreign Relations, "The Taliban"; Laub, "The Taliban in Afghanistan."
13. Council on Foreign Relations, "The Taliban"; Laub, "The Taliban in Afghanistan."
14. Council on Foreign Relations, "The Taliban."
15. Thomas H. Johnson, "The Taliban Insurgency and an Analysis of Shabnamah (Night Letters)," *Small Wars and Insurgencies* 18, no. 3 (2007): 317–44.
16. Council on Foreign Relations, "The Taliban."
17. Alia Chughtai, "Afghanistan: Who Controls What," Al-Jazeera, June 5, 2018.
18. Matin Sahak, "Families Flee as Taliban Battle Islamic State in Northern Afghanistan," Reuters, July 17, 2018.
19. Mujib Mashal and Eric Schmitt, "White House Orders Direct Taliban Talks to Jump-Start Afghan Negotiations," *New York Times*, July 15, 2018; Shereena Qazi, "Afghanistan: Taliban Resume Fighting as Eid Ceasefire Ends," Al-Jazeera, June 18, 2018; Sahak, "Families Flee as Taliban Battle Islamic State"; "Taliban Leader: No Peace Without Foreigners Leaving," Al-Jazeera, June 2, 2016.
20. Robert Burns, Deb Reichmann, and Matthew Lee, "Trump Says Peace Talks with Taliban Are Now 'Dead,'" Associated Press, September 10, 2019.
21. Asif Shahzad, Jibran Ahmad, and Charlotte Greenfield, "Pakistan and Taliban Call for U.S. to Resume Afghan Peace Talks," Reuters, October 3, 2019.
22. Fawaz A. Gerges, *ISIS: A History* (Princeton, N.J.: Princeton University Press, 2016), 63–68.
23. Zachary Laub, "The Islamic State," Council on Foreign Relations online report, August 10, 2016, https://www.cfr.org/backgrounder/islamic-state.
24. Gerges, *ISIS*, 73.
25. Laub, "The Islamic State."
26. Ayman Al-Zawahiri, "Letter from al-Zawahiri to al-Zarqawi," July 9, 2005, trans. and released by U.S. Office of the Director of National Intelligence, https://fas.org/irp/news/2005/10/dni101105.html.
27. Laub, "The Islamic State."
28. Mapping Militant Organizations, "The Islamic State," Stanford University (last modified September 2019), https://cisac.fsi.stanford.edu/mappingmilitants/profiles/islamic-state.
29. Thomas E. Ricks, *The Gamble: General David Petraeus and the American Military Adventure in Iraq, 2006–2008* (New York: Penguin, 2009).

30. Mapping Militant Organizations, "The Islamic State."
31. Laub, "The Islamic State"; Mapping Militant Organizations, "The Islamic State."
32. Mapping Militant Organizations, "The Islamic State."
33. Selene Assir, "Iraqis, Saudis Call the Shots in ISIS 'Capital' Raqqa," Agence France-Presse, June 20, 2014; Suadad Al-Salhy and Tim Arango, "Sunni Militants Drive Iraqi Army Out of Mosul," *New York Times*, June 10, 2014; "Iraq Government Loses Control of Fallujah," Al-Jazeera, January 4, 2014.
34. Rukmini Callimachi, "The ISIS Files," *New York Times*, April 4, 2018.
35. Michael Pizzi, "In Declaring Itself a Caliphate, Islamic State Draws a Line in the Sand," Al-Jazeera America, June 30, 2014.
36. Laub, "The Islamic State."
37. Rukmini Callimachi, "Not 'Lone Wolves' After All: How ISIS Guides World's Terror Plots From Afar," *New York Times*, February 4, 2017; Mapping Militant Organizations, "The Islamic State."
38. Joseph M. Brown, "Notes to the Underground: Credit Claiming and Organizing in the Earth Liberation Front," *Terrorism and Political Violence* (September 2017), https://doi.org/10.1080/09546553.2017.1364637.
39. Laub, "The Islamic State."
40. Bethan McKernan, "Isis Defeated, US-Backed Syrian Democratic Forces Announce," *Guardian* (London), March 23, 2019.
41. Rukmini Callimachi and Karam Shoumali, "ISIS Names New Leader and Confirms al-Baghdadi's Death," *New York Times*, October 31, 2019.
42. "Hundreds of ISIL Prisoners Escape Syrian Camp, Kurds Say," Al-Jazeera, October 13, 2019.
43. Alissa J. Rubin, "ISIS, Weakened, Finds New Bombers: Cows Wearing Explosive Vests," *New York Times*, September 4, 2019.
44. Rukmini Callimachi, "Fight to Retake Last ISIS Territory Begins," *New York Times*, September 11, 2018; Callimachi, "Not 'Lone Wolves' After All."
45. Scott MacEachern, *Searching for Boko Haram: A History of Violence in Central Africa* (New York: Oxford University Press, 2018), 11.
46. Alexander Thurston, *Boko Haram: The History of an African Jihadist Movement* (Princeton, N.J.: Princeton University Press, 2018), 83, 87.
47. *International Religious Freedom Report 2008: Nigeria* (Washington, D.C.: U.S. Department of State, 2008); MacEachern, *Searching for Boko Haram*, 9–10.
48. Thurston, *Boko Haram*, 98, 106, 111, 115.
49. Thurston, *Boko Haram*, 134–40.
50. Quoted in Thurston, *Boko Haram*, 143–44.
51. MacEachern, *Searching for Boko Haram*, 13; Thurston, *Boko Haram*, 152–53.
52. Thurston, *Boko Haram*, 156–57.
53. MacEachern, *Searching for Boko Haram*, 13; Thurston, *Boko Haram*, 159.

54. Thurston, *Boko Haram*, 168–69, 173–76.
55. Thurston, *Boko Haram*, 157.
56. MacEachern, *Searching for Boko Haram*, 11; Thurston, *Boko Haram*, 182.
57. Thurston, *Boko Haram*, 157, 182.
58. MacEachern, *Searching for Boko Haram*, 13; Thurston, *Boko Haram*, 240.
59. Thurston, *Boko Haram*, 224–28.
60. Thurston, *Boko Haram*, 230–40.
61. MacEachern, *Searching for Boko Haram*, 14; Thurston, *Boko Haram*, 272–74.
62. Thurston, *Boko Haram*, 276.
63. MacEachern, *Searching for Boko Haram*, 11–12; Thurston, *Boko Haram*, 277.
64. Thurston, *Boko Haram*, 277–79.
65. Lauren Ploch Blanchard and Katia T. Cavigelli, *Boko Haram and the Islamic State's West Africa Province* (Washington, D.C.: Congressional Research Service, 2018); Paul Carsten and Ahmed Kingimi, "Islamic State Ally Stakes Out Territory Around Lake Chad," Reuters, April 29, 2018.
66. "Death Toll in Boko Haram attack on Nigerian Base Rises to 48," Al-Jazeera, September 3, 2018; "Nigeria: Boko Haram Kills 19 Villagers in Borno State," Al-Jazeera, August 20, 2018; "Nigeria Mosque Attack Death Toll Rises to 86," Al-Jazeera, May 2, 2018.
67. Blanchard and Cavigelli, *Boko Haram*.
68. Carsten and Kingimi, "Islamic State Ally Stakes Out Territory."
69. David Blair, "Boko Haram Is Now a Mini-Islamic State, with Its Own Territory," *Telegraph* (London), January 10, 2015; "Boko Haram HQ Gwoza in Nigeria 'Retaken,'" *BBC News*, March 27, 2015; "Nigeria Boko Haram: Militants 'Technically Defeated'—Buhari." *BBC News*, December 24, 2015.
70. Mapping Militant Organizations, "The Islamic State"; Mapping Militant Organizations, "Afghan Taliban," Stanford University (last modified June 2018), https://cisac.fsi.stanford.edu/mappingmilitants/profiles/afghan-taliban.
71. Monty G. Marshall, Keith Jaggers, and Ted Robert Gurr, *POLITY IV Project Dataset Users' Manual* (Vienna, Va.: Center for Systemic Peace, 2018).
72. See the Polity IV Project, *Political Regime Characteristics and Transitions, 1800–2018* (October 27, 2019), distributed by the Center for Systemic Peace, http://www.systemicpeace.org/inscr/p4v2018.xls.
73. Statistics in this paragraph are from National Consortium for the Study of Terrorism and Responses to Terrorism (START), The Global Terrorism Database (October 26, 2019), distributed by the University of Maryland, https://www.start.umd.edu/gtd/.
74. Attacks on commercial-related targets were also rare. One attack targeted tourists, two targeted the food/water supply, and forty-seven targeted transportation.

75. Two attacks targeted tourists, ten targeted the food/water supply, sixty-four targeted transportation, and 111 targeted utilities.
76. Incorporating attacks by ISIL's precursors, the Islamic State of Iraq (ISI) and Al-Qa'ida in Iraq (AQI), does not substantially alter the distribution of attacks. Of 7,235 attacks by ISIL and its precursor groups, 374 (5.2 percent) targeted businesses. Quasi-economic attacks include 4 on tourists, 11 on the food/water supply, 79 on transportation, 11 on airports and aircraft, and 114 on utilities. The modal category was attacks on private citizens (3,305), followed by the military (1,906 attacks) and police (1,003 attacks).
77. Quasi-commercial attacks included five on tourists, 122 on transportation, 34 on airports or aircraft, 11 on the food/water supply, and 32 on utilities.
78. Omar S. Mahmood, *More than Propaganda: A Review of Boko Haram's Public Messages* (Pretoria, South Africa: Institute for Security Studies, 2017), 10.
79. Mahmood, *More than Propaganda*, 7.
80. Yahaya Ibrahim, "Four Killed in Borno Beer Parlour Attack," *Daily Trust* (Abuja), September 14, 2011.
81. Sani Tukur, "Boko Haram Warned Before Attacking Ganye Prison—Residents," *Premium Times* (Abuja), March 21, 2013.
82. Jaiyeola Andrews, Michael Olugbode, and Emmanuel Ugwu, "Boko Haram Challenges Army, Threatens Second Chibok Attack," *This Day* (Lagos), June 17, 2014.
83. See chapter 6 for further information on coding procedures.
84. Mahmood, *More than Propaganda*.
85. Mahmood, *More than Propaganda*, 19; "Nigerian Bombers Blame U.N. for 'Oppression' of Muslims," CNN, August 31, 2011.
86. Mahmood, *More than Propaganda*, 19; Sunny Nwankwo, "Why We Attacked Maiduguri Market—Boko Haram," *Leadership* (Abuja), February 22, 2012.
87. "Boko Haram Threatens to Bomb Government Buildings in 19 Northern States," *Premium Times* (Abuja, Nigeria), May 17, 2012.
88. Based on searches of START, Global Terrorism Database, and additional searches of secondary news coverage of each incident. See chapter 6 for further information.
89. "Afghanistan: Kandahar Braced for Taliban Attack as Thousands Flee," *Guardian* (London), June 17, 2008.
90. "Taliban Attacks Target Afghan Polls," Al-Jazeera, September 18, 2010.
91. Johnson, "The Taliban Insurgency."
92. See examples described in Johnson, "The Taliban Insurgency."
93. Aryn Baker and Muhib Habibi, "Deadly Notes in the Night: How the Taliban Is Using a New Kind of Terrorist Threat to Intimidate Afghans," *Time*, July 5, 2006.
94. Johnson, "The Taliban Insurgency."

95. Statistics are derived from the warnings dataset, discussed in chapter 6.
96. "Iraq Jihadists Blow Up Muslim Shrine in Mosul: Official," *Legal Monitor Worldwide*, July 26, 2014.
97. "Indian Nurses Caught in Iraq Crisis Return to Kochi, Reunited with Families," *India Blooms*, July 5, 2014.
98. "Suicide Bombers Target Polling Sites," *Herald* (Glasgow), April 29, 2014.
99. See START, Global Terrorism Database, incident 201407030059.
100. See summaries for incidents 201510100002, 201507180045, and 201607020002 in START, Global Terrorism Database.
101. Joby Warrick, *Black Flags: The Rise of ISIS* (New York: Doubleday, 2015).
102. Laub, "The Taliban in Afghanistan."
103. "Boko Haram Resurrects, Declares Total Jihad," *Vanguard Nigeria* (Lagos), August 14, 2009.
104. "Boko Haram Resurrects," *Vanguard Nigeria*.
105. "110 Nigerian Schoolgirls Still Missing After Attack: Minister," Al-Jazeera, February 25, 2018; Andrews, Olugbode, and Ugwu, "Boko Haram Challenges Army."
106. "Boko Haram Issues Threat as It Returns Abducted Schoolgirls," *Irish Times*, March 21, 2018.
107. Heather Murdock, "Nigeria's Boko Haram Threatens Oil Refineries, Muslim Clerics," *Voice of America News*, February 20, 2014.
108. "Boko Haram Targets Media in Nigeria," United Press International, May 2, 2012; "Nigerian Reporter Threatened Over Boko Haram Coverage," Committee to Protect Journalists online alert, March 19, 2012, http://cpj.org/2012/03/nigerian-journalist-threatened-over-boko-haram-cov.php.
109. "Boko Haram Targets Media in Nigeria," United Press International.
110. No such attacks appear in START, Global Terrorism Database.
111. Mahmood, *More than Propaganda*, 10–11.
112. Aminu Abubakar, "Hundreds Flee Nigeria Villages 'After Boko Haram Warning,'" Agence France-Presse, January 20, 2015.
113. "103 Schools Shut in Central Afghanistan Due to Taliban Threats," *Gulf Times*, July 14, 2018.
114. David Jolly and Jawad Sukhanyar, "Following Up on Threat, Taliban Strike at Bus Carrying TV Employees," *New York Times*, January 21, 2016.
115. Jolly and Sukhanyar, "Following Up on Threat."
116. Luke Brown, "Taliban, death threats and not giving up: Afghanistan's football pioneer Khalida Popal tells her harrowing yet heroic tale," *Independent* (London), December 28, 2017; Jane Dalton, "Afghanistan's First Female Military Pilot Granted Asylum in US After Fleeing Taliban Death Threats," *Independent* (London), May 4, 2018.
117. Brown, "Taliban, death threats and not giving up."

118. Paula Newton, "Taliban Threaten to Kill Aid Workers as Spies," CNN, March 15, 2009.
119. Spencer Ackerman, "Taliban Texts Terror to Afghan Phones," *Wired*, March 17, 2011; Baker and Habibi, "Deadly Notes in the Night"; Johnson, "The Taliban Insurgency."
120. Ackerman, "Taliban Texts Terror to Afghan Phones."
121. Amir Shah, "Taliban suicide bomber kills 17," Associated Press, June 11, 2013.
122. Shashank Bengali, "Afghans Vote Despite Rain, Taliban Threats," *Los Angeles Times*, April 5, 2014; Nathan Hodge and Margherita Stancati, "Taliban Threaten to Attack Voters in Afghan Election," *Wall Street Journal*, March 10, 2014; "Six Killed, 22 Injured in Attacks on Afghan Presidential Contender's Convoy," Afghan Islamic Press, June 6, 2014; "Taliban Attacks Target Afghan Polls," Al-Jazeera.
123. Ruchi Kumar, "From Road Tax to Courts: The Taliban's Attempts at State-Building," Al-Jazeera, August 26, 2018.
124. Mohammad Habibzada, "Taliban Rebels Impose Taxes on Media Outlets in Restive Ghazni," *Voice of America News*, February 21, 2018.
125. "Suicide Bombers Target Polling Sites," *Herald* (Glasgow).
126. Callimachi, "The ISIS Files."
127. Callimachi, "The ISIS Files."
128. John Bacon and Oren Dorell, "ISIL's Haunting Threat: 'We Will Strike America at Its Heart,'" *USA Today*, November 17, 2015.
129. Mahmood, *More than Propaganda*, 12.
130. "We Did It, Sokoto Is Next—Sect," *Nigerian Voice*, February 8, 2012.
131. "Boko Haram: Intermediary Pulls Out of Talks with Govt," Agence France-Press, March 17, 2012.
132. Ibrahim Mshelizza, "UPDATE 2—Boko Haram Rules Out Talks with Nigeria Government," Reuters, March 20, 2012.
133. Ola' Audu, "Boko Haram Leader, Shekau, Speaks; Vows to Attack Nigerian Reineries, Buhari, Babangida, Others," *Premium Times* (Abuja), February 20, 2014.
134. Mahmood, *More than Propaganda*, 11.
135. Mahmood, *More than Propaganda*; START, Global Terrorism Database, incident 201406250083.
136. Mahmood, *More than Propaganda*, 27.
137. Mashal and Schmitt, "White House Orders Direct Taliban Talks."
138. "Taliban Leader: No Peace Without Foreigners Leaving," Al-Jazeera.
139. "Taliban Letter to Trump Urges US to Leave Afghanistan," Al-Jazeera, August 15, 2017; "Taliban Responds to Trump's Afghan Strategy," Al-Jazeera, August 22, 2017; "Time to Leave Afghanistan, Taliban Tell Donald Trump," Al-Jazeera, January 25, 2017.

140. Ayaz Gul, "Afghan Taliban Launches New Spring Offensive," *Voice of America*, April 25, 2018.
141. Qazi, "Afghanistan: Taliban Resume Fighting."
142. Qazi, "Afghanistan: Taliban Resume Fighting."
143. Mashal and Schmitt, "White House Orders Direct Taliban Talks."
144. Burns, Reichmann, and Lee, "Trump Says Peace Talks with Taliban Are Now 'Dead.'"
145. Shahzad, Ahmad, and Greenfield, "Pakistan and Taliban Call for U.S. to Resume Afghan Peace Talks."
146. Karen DeYoung and Adam Goldman, "After Foley Killing, U.S. Defends Refusal to Pay Ransom To Terrorist Groups That Kidnap," *Washington Post*, August 21, 2014.
147. "110 Nigerian Schoolgirls Still Missing After Attack: Minister," *Al-Jazeera*, February 25, 2018; Newton, "Taliban Threaten to Kill Aid Workers as Spies."
148. DeYoung and Goldman, "After Foley Killing, U.S. Defends Refusal to Pay Ransom."
149. Seth G. Jones, "The Rise of Afghanistan's Insurgency: State Failure and Jihad," *International Security* 32, no. 4 (2008): 7–40.
150. "Afghanistan: Ghani, Hekmatyar Sign Peace Deal," *Al-Jazeera*, September 29, 2016; Chughtai, "Afghanistan: Who Controls What"; Joshua Partlow, "In Afghanistan, Taliban Leaving al-Qaeda Behind," *Washington Post*, November 11, 2009.
151. "Death Toll in Boko Haram Attack on Nigerian Base Rises to 48," *Al-Jazeera*; "Nigeria: Boko Haram Kills 19 Villagers in Borno State," *Al-Jazeera*; "Nigeria Mosque Attack Death Toll Rises to 86," *Al-Jazeera*.
152. Callimachi, "The ISIS Files."
153. "Boko Haram Resurrects," *Vanguard Nigeria*.
154. Jerome Starkey, "Suicide Bomber Kills 50 in Nigeria," *Times* (London), June 3, 2015.
155. "Boko Haram Kills 40 in Diffa, Southeast Niger," Anadolu News Agency, June 18, 2015; "Nigerian Troops Rescue Over 330 Women, Children Held by Boko Haram," Agence France-Presse, October 28, 2015.
156. "Terror Threat to Durban; Al-Shabaab: 'We Will Enter Durban'; Boko Haram: 'End Attacks or Face Bombing'; SA Vehicles Stoned in Mozambique; Malawi Boycotts Goods," *Independent on Saturday* (South Africa), April 18, 2015.
157. Blanchard and Cavigelli, *Boko Haram*; Carsten and Kingimi, "Islamic State Ally Stakes Out Territory."
158. Carsten and Kingimi, "Islamic State Ally Stakes Out Territory."
159. Abdulwasiu Hassan, "Shekau's Boko Haram Threatens Buhari, Abuja," *Daily Trust* (Abuja), August 8, 2016.

160. "Embattled Boko Haram Leader Resurfaces in Video After Claims of Being 'Fatally Wounded,'" *Telegraph* (London), September 25, 2016; "New Boko Haram Video Threatens to Kill Nigeria's President," Canadian Press, September 14, 2016.
161. "Boko Haram leader Shekau threatens more bombings in new video," *Nation* (Nigeria), March 17, 2017; "Boko Haram Leader Warns Trump 'War Has Just Begun,'" Agence France-Presse, November 14, 2016; "Boko Haram Threatens to Behead President Paul Biya of Cameroon," *PM News*, April 3, 2017; Katie Mansfield, "Boko Haram—'The battle Is Just Beginning' Threatens Leader in Chilling New Video," *Daily Express* (London), January 2, 2017; Philip Nwosu, "Breaking: Boko Haram Leader Resurfaces in New Video Says Group Not Crushed," *Sun* (Nigeria), December 29, 2016.
162. Mansfield, "Boko Haram."
163. "Boko Haram leader Shekau threatens more bombings," *Nation*.
164. Carsten and Kingimi, "Islamic State Ally Stakes Out Territory."
165. Liz Sly and Mustafa Salim, "ISIS Is Making a Comeback in Iraq Just Months After Baghdad Declared Victory," *New York Times*, July 17, 2018.
166. Marissa Payne, "Pro-ISIS Poster Threatening World Cup Terrorist Attack Depicts Lionel Messi Crying Blood," *Washington Post*, October 24, 2017.
167. Rob Crilly, "Italians Laugh Off Isil Terror Threat with Travel Tips," *Independent* (London), February 21, 2015.
168. Lucy Pasha-Robinson, "Isis Fighter Relentlessly Mocked on Spanish Twitter After Threatening Further Violence," *Independent* (London), August 26, 2017.
169. Glenn A. Fine, Steve A. Linick, and Ann Calvaresi Barr, *Operation Freedom's Sentinel: Report to the United States Congress, April 1, 2018-June 30, 2018*, Office of the Inspector General of the Department of Defense, June 30, 2018, https://www.stateoig.gov/system/files/lig_oco_ofs3_jun2018_508_r2.pdf; Animesh Roul, "Taliban Demonstrates Resilience with Afghan Spring Offensive," *Terrorism Monitor* 16, no. 11 (June 2, 2018): 3–5.
170. Taliban (Islamic Emirate of Afghanistan), "Statement of Leadership Council of Islamic Emirate Regarding the Commencement of the Annual Spring Operation Named 'Khaibar,'" press release, May 12, 2014, http://manusiaonline.blogspot.com/2014/05/statement-of-leadership-council-of.html.
171. START, Global Terrorism Database (incidents 201405120030, 201405120028, 201405120029, 201405120043, 201405120042, and 201405120038).
172. Taliban, "Statement of Leadership Council."
173. Gerges, *ISIS*, 170–201.
174. For a discussion of these problems, see Stathis N. Kalyvas, *The Logic of Violence in Civil War* (New York: Cambridge University Press, 2006); and Stathis N. Kalyvas and Ignacio Sánchez-Cuenca, "Killing Without Dying:

The Absence of Suicide Missions," in *Making Sense of Suicide Missions*, ed. Diego Gambetta (New York: Oxford University Press, 2005), 209–31.
175. Yahaya Ibrahim, "Nigeria: Boko Haram Threaten to Attack GSM Providers," *Daily Trust* (Abuja), February 13, 2012.
176. "Disregard Threat Messages from Boko Haram, JTF Tells Residents in Maiduguri," Channels Television, August 29, 2012.
177. "Spy on Us We Slaughter You like Rams Says Boko Haram," *Bulawayo 24 News*, August 2, 2012.
178. "Nigeria: Gunmen in Another Attack on Police Station," *Telegraph* (London), January 29, 2012.
179. "Boko Haram Kills 40 in Diffa," Anadolu News Agency.
180. "Boko Haram Asks Chad to Stop Military Intervention, Threatens Civil War," BBC Monitoring Africa, February 17, 2015.
181. Noor Zahid, "Taliban Warns Phone Companies to Shut Down Their Coverage in Ghazni," Voice of America, October 10, 2017.
182. Yaroslav Trofimov, "Cell Carriers Bow to Taliban Threat," *Wall Street Journal*, March 22, 2010.
183. Sifatullah Zahidi, "Civilians Suffer as Taliban Threats Shut Down Telecom Services in Helmand," *Salaam Times*, April 24, 2018.
184. Noor Khan, "Taliban Destroy Afghan Phone Towers," *Washington Post*, March 2, 2008.
185. "Afghans Buy Fake Taliban Threat Letters," Associated Press, November 23, 2015.
186. Scott Peterson, "How Taliban Are Evolving to Compete in Afghanistan," *Christian Science Monitor*, October 26, 2017.
187. Saeed Shah, "U.S. Vehicles Destroy Afghan Bombs by Rolling Over Them," McClatchy Newspapers, September 2, 2010.
188. "Improvised Explosive Device (IED) B3L0487XQ-DM Student Handout" (Camp Barrett, Va.: United States Marine Corps, Basic School—Marine Corps Training Command, 2016), 13.
189. Bacon and Oren Dorell, "ISIL's Haunting Threat."
190. Martin Chulov and Shiv Malik, "Jordan Executes Would-Be Suicide Bomber Wanted for Release by Islamic State," *Guardian* (London), February 4, 2015.
191. Sam Webb, "Shocking New ISIS Video Claims to Show Young Boy Execute Two 'Russian Spies,'" *Irish Mirror* (Dublin), January 13, 2015.

6. Quantitative Analysis

1. An article-length version of this research appears in Joseph M. Brown, "Correlates of Warning: Territory, Democracy, and Casualty Aversion in

Terrorist Tactics," *International Organization* (March 2020), https://doi.org/10.1017/S002081832000003X.
2. National Consortium for the Study of Terrorism and Responses to Terrorism (START), The Global Terrorism Database, October 26, 2019, distributed by the University of Maryland, https://www.start.umd.edu/gtd/.
3. START, Global Terrorism Database. See the section on my research design for a description of coding procedures.
4. The Global Terrorism Database records 19,310 bombings of civilian targets by these groups. Using secondary sources and the search protocol described in this chapter, my research assistants were able to code 12,235 of these bombings for inclusion in my dataset.
5. Ignacio Sánchez-Cuenca and Luis de la Calle, "Domestic Terrorism: The Hidden Side of Political Violence," *Annual Review of Political Science* 12 (2009): 31–49.
6. Kyle Beardsley, Kristian Skrede Gleditsch, and Nigel Lo, "Roving Bandits? The Geographic Evolution of Armed Conflicts," *International Studies Quarterly* 59, no. 3 (2015): 503–16; Zachariah Cherian Mampilly, *Rebel Rulers: Insurgent Governance and Civilian Life During War* (Ithaca, N.Y.: Cornell University Press, 2011); Mancur Olson, "Dictatorship, Democracy, and Development," *American Political Science Review* 87, no. 3 (1993): 567–76; Megan A. Stewart, "Civil War as State-Making: Strategic Governance in Civil War," *International Organization* 72, no. 1 (2018): 205–26.
7. Beardsley, Gleditsch, and Lo, "Roving Bandits?"; Mampilly, *Rebel Rulers*; Olson, "Dictatorship, Democracy, and Development"; Stewart, "Civil War as State-Making."
8. Erica Chenoweth, "Democratic Competition and Terrorist Activity," *Journal of Politics* 72, no. 1 (2010): 16–30; Seung-Whan Choi, "Fighting Terrorism Through the Rule of Law?," *Journal of Conflict Resolution* 54, no.6 (2010): 940–66.
9. Stathis N. Kalyvas and Ignacio Sánchez-Cuenca, "Killing Without Dying: The Absence of Suicide Missions," in *Making Sense of Suicide Missions*, ed. Diego Gambetta (New York: Oxford University Press, 2005), 209–31.
10. Jeff Goodwin, "A Theory of Categorical Terrorism," *Social Forces* 84, no. 4 (2006): 2027–46.
11. Kristine Eck and Lisa Hultman, "One-Sided Violence Against Civilians in War: Insights from New Fatality Data," *Journal of Peace Research* 44, no. 2 (2007): 233–46; Goodwin, "A Theory of Categorical Terrorism"; Robert Pape, *Dying to Win: The Strategic Logic of Suicide Terrorism* (New York: Random House, 2005); Jessica A. Stanton, "Terrorism in the Context of Civil War," *Journal of Politics* 75, no. 4 (2013): 1009–22.

12. Jeremy Weinstein, *Inside Rebellion: The Politics of Insurgent Violence* (New York: Cambridge University Press, 2006).
13. Idean Salehyan, David Siroky, and Reed M. Wood, "External Rebel Sponsorship and Civilian Abuse: A Principal-Agent Analysis of Wartime Atrocities," *International Organization* 68, no. 3 (2014): 633–61.
14. Stanton, "Terrorism in the Context of Civil War"; Bruce Hoffman, *Inside Terrorism* (New York: Columbia University Press, 2006); Mark Juergensmeyer, *Terror in the Mind of God: The Global Rise of Religious Violence* (Berkeley: University of California Press, 2017); Michael C. Horowitz, "Nonstate Actors and the Diffusion of Innovations: The Case of Suicide Terrorism," *International Organization* 64, no. 1 (2010): 33–64; Assaf Moghadam, *The Globalization of Martyrdom: Al Qaeda, Salafi Jihad, and the Diffusion of Suicide Attacks* (Baltimore: Johns Hopkins University Press, 2011).
15. Reed M. Wood, "Rebel Capability and Strategic Violence Against Civilians," *Journal of Peace Research* 47, no. 5 (2010): 601–14; Chaim D. Kaufmann, "Possible and Impossible Solutions to Ethnic Wars," *International Security* 20, no. 4 (1996): 136–75; Roger D. Petersen, *Understanding Ethnic Violence: Fear, Hatred, and Resentment in Twentieth-Century Eastern Europe.* (New York: Cambridge University Press, 2002); Barry R. Posen, "The Security Dilemma and Ethnic Conflict," *Survival* 35, no. 1 (1993): 27–47.
16. Stanton, "Terrorism in the Context of Civil War"; Tanisha M. Fazal, "Rebellion, War Aims and the Laws of War," *Daedalus* 146, no. 1 (2017): 71–82; Tanisha M. Fazal, *Wars of Law: Unintended Consequences in the Regulation of Armed Conflict* (Ithaca, N.Y.: Cornell University Press, 2018).
17. My dataset is introduced in Brown, "Correlates of Warning."
18. Research assistants broadened the search further if necessary, searching for the name of the perpetrator within a month of the attack.
19. National Consortium for the Study of Terrorism and Responses to Terrorism, *GTD: Global Terrorism Database—Codebook: Inclusion Criteria and Variables* (College Park: University of Maryland, 2019).
20. Victor H. Asal and R. Karl Rethemeyer, "The Nature of the Beast: Terrorist Organizational Characteristics and Organizational Lethality," *Journal of Politics* 70, no. 2 (2008): 437–49; Victor H. Asal and R. Karl Rethemeyer, Big Allied and Dangerous Dataset, V2, October 28, 2019, distributed by the National Consortium for the Study of Terrorism and Responses to Terrorism, University of Maryland, http://www.start.umd.edu/baad/database.
21. Stina Högbladh, Therése Pettersson, and Lotta Themnér, "External Support in Armed Conflict 1975–2009—Presenting New Data," paper presented at the International Studies Association annual convention, Montreal, Canada, March 2011.

22. James Igoe Walsh et al., "Funding Rebellion: The Rebel Contraband Dataset," *Journal of Peace Research* 55, no. 5 (2018): 699–707.
23. Mapping Militant Organizations, "Mapping Militants," Stanford University, https://cisac.fsi.stanford.edu/mappingmilitants, accessed October 28, 2019.
24. My website is https://www.josephmbrown.com.
25. Polity IV Project, *Political Regime Characteristics and Transitions, 1800–2018*, October 27, 2019, distributed by the Center for Systemic Peace, http://www.systemicpeace.org/inscr/p4v2018.xls.
26. Walsh et al., "Funding Rebellion."
27. I have also used UCDP to supplement BAAD—for instance, coding as 1 cases where BAAD recorded no state support but UCDP showed support.
28. All but two of the religious groups in my sample are motivated by Islam. The exceptions are the Jewish Defense League (JDL) and Ulster Volunteer Force (UVF).
29. Bruce Hoffman and Gordon H. McCormick, "Terrorism, Signaling, and Suicide Attack," *Studies in Conflict and Terrorism* 27, no. 4 (2004): 243–81.
30. Andrew Gelman and Jennifer Hill, eds., *Data Analysis Using Regression and Multilevel/Hierarchical Models* (New York: Cambridge University Press, 2007).
31. Andrew Gelman, "Multilevel (Hierarchical) Modeling: What It Can and Cannot Do," *Technometrics* 48, no.3 (2006): 432–35.
32. Gelman and Hill, *Data Analysis*, 283, 549.
33. The likelihood ratio tests can be recreated via the replication files, linked from my website, https://www.josephmbrown.com.
34. The analysis was conducted using Stata/SE 16.0 for Mac. Replication results may vary slightly with different software.
35. The null hypothesis is that the coefficients are equal. The F-tests can be recreated via the replication files at https://www.josephmbrown.com.
36. Hoffman, *Inside Terrorism*; Horowitz, "Nonstate Actors and the Diffusion of Innovations"; Moghadam, *The Globalization of Martyrdom*; Stanton, "Terrorism in the Context of Civil War."
37. For this argument, see Salehyan, Siroky, and Wood, "External Rebel Sponsorship and Civilian Abuse."
38. See, for example, Weinstein, *Inside Rebellion*.
39. Abraham H. Maslow, "A Theory of Human Motivation," *Psychological Review* 50, no. 4 (1943): 370–96.
40. In cases where a foreign government hosts the militant group on its territory, I have coded the militant group as possessing territory.
41. "Suicide Bombers Target Polling Sites," *Herald* (Glasgow), April 29, 2014.
42. For the Political Terror Scale, see Mark Gibney et al., The Political Terror Scale 1976–2018, October 26, 2019, http://www.politicalterrorscale.org.

43. John Bew, Martyn Frampton, and Íñigo Gurruchaga, *Talking to Terrorists: Making Peace in Northern Ireland and the Basque Country* (London: Hurst, 2009), 211, 220–21; "Vic (Barcelona) recordará hoy a las víctimas del atentado de ETA en su casa cuartel," *El Economista*, June 13, 2009; Teresa Whitfield, *Endgame for ETA: Elusive Peace in the Basque Country* (New York: Oxford University Press, 2014), 84; "Zaragoza: cinco ataúdes blancos," *El País*, August 2, 2009.

Conclusion

1. Kyle Beardsley et al., "Roving Bandits? The Geographic Evolution of Armed Conflicts," *International Studies Quarterly* 59, no. 3 (2015): 503–16; Zachariah Cherian Mampilly, *Rebel Rulers: Insurgent Governance and Civilian Life During War* (Ithaca, N.Y.: Cornell University Press, 2011); Mancur Olson, "Dictatorship, Democracy, and Development," *American Political Science Review* 87, no. 3 (1993): 567–76; Megan A. Stewart, "Civil War as State-Making: Strategic Governance in Civil War," *International Organization* 72, no. 1 (2018): 205–26.
2. Bruce Hoffman, *Inside Terrorism* (New York: Columbia University Press, 2006), 9.
3. Mia M. Bloom, *Dying to Kill: The Allure of Suicide Terror* (Philadelphia: University of Pennsylvania Press, 2005); Walter Laqueur, *The New Terrorism: Fanaticism and the Arms of Mass Destruction* (New York: Oxford University Press, 2000); Robert Pape, *Dying to Win: The Strategic Logic of Suicide Terrorism* (New York: Random House, 2005); Jessica Stern, *The Ultimate Terrorists* (Cambridge, Mass.: Harvard University Press, 2001).
4. James D. Fearon, "Domestic Political Audience Costs and the Escalation of International Disputes," *American Political Science Review* 88, no. 3 (1994): 577–92; James D. Fearon, "Signaling Foreign Policy Interests: Tying Hands Versus Sinking Costs," *Journal of Conflict Resolution* 41, no. 1 (1997): 68–90; Robert L. Jervis, *Perception and Misperception in International Politics* (Princeton, N.J.: Princeton University Press, 1976); Thomas C. Schelling, *Arms and Influence* (New Haven, Conn.: Yale University Press, 1966).
5. Max Abrahms, "Why Terrorism Does Not Work," *International Security* 31, no. 2 (2006): 42–78; Max Abrahms, "What Terrorists Really Want: Terrorist Motives and Counterterrorism Strategy," *International Security* 32, no. 4 (2008): 78–105; Erica Chenoweth and Maria J. Stephan, "Why Civil Resistance Works: The Strategic Logic of Nonviolent Conflict," *International Security* 33, no. 1 (2008): 7–44; Virginia Page Fortna, "Do Terrorists Win? Rebels' Use of Terrorism and Civil War Outcomes," *International Organization* 69, no. 3 (2015): 519–56.

6. Max Abrahms, *Rules for Rebels: The Science of Victory in Militant History* (New York: Oxford University Press, 2018); Chenoweth and Stephan, "Why Civil Resistance Works."
7. Fortna, "Do Terrorists Win?," 549.
8. Schelling, *Arms and Influence*, 14.
9. John Bew, Martyn Frampton, and Íñigo Gurruchaga. *Talking to Terrorists: Making Peace in Northern Ireland and the Basque Country* (London: Hurst, 2009); Gordon Weiss, *The Cage: The Fight For Sri Lanka and the Last Days of the Tamil Tigers* (New York: Bellevue Literary Press, 2012).
10. Abrahms, *Rules for Rebels*; Chenoweth and Stephan, "Why Civil Resistance Works."
11. Republican #2 interview, Newry, July 2012.
12. Quoted text from Haily Branson-Potts, Stephen Ceaser, and Howard Blume, "L.A. schools to Reopen Wednesday; Threat Against Schools Was 'Not Credible,' Officials Say," *Los Angeles Times*, December 15, 2015. See also Kate Mather, Richard Winton, and Joel Rubin, "L.A. Defends Response to Threat That New York Dismissed as a Hoax," *Los Angeles Times*, December 16, 2015.
13. Mather, Winton, and Rubin, "L.A. Defends Response to Threat."
14. Branson-Potts, Ceaser, and Blume, "L.A. Schools to Reopen."
15. Branson-Potts, Ceaser, and Blume, "L.A. Schools to Reopen." The email's spelling out of the word "Allah," without capitalization in one instance, also suggested that the message was a prank.
16. Recall that the costly signaling paradigm views terrorism as a process of information revelation, with terrorists striving to make their capabilities as clear as possible to observers. See Andrew H. Kydd and Barbara F. Walter, "The Strategies of Terrorism," *International Security* 31, no. 1 (2006): 49–80.
17. There may be some question about whether an emissary has spoken out of turn or promised more than the head of state intended. For examples, see Robert Jervis, *The Logic of Images in International Relations* (New York: Columbia University Press, 1970). In general, however, if a government has concerns about the emissary sent by another state, the government can send the emissary home and request that a new one be sent.
18. Ola Ajayi and Gabriel Enogholase, "Boko Haram Threatens to Bomb UI, Uni-Ben, 18 Others," *Vanguard* (Lagos), September 13, 2011.
19. One can also sympathize with the press, which reported the threat as if it had come from the militant group and not hoax artists.
20. Ajayi and Enogholase, "Boko Haram Threatens to Bomb UI." For the locations of Boko Haram attacks predating the September 2011 threat, see National Consortium for the Study of Terrorism and Responses to Terrorism (START), The Global Terrorism Database, October 26, 2019, distributed by the University of Maryland, https://www.start.umd.edu/gtd/.

21. Tunde Fatunde, "Nigeria: Campus Security Reviewed After Threats," *University World News*, September 25, 2011.
22. Omar S. Mahmood, *More than Propaganda: A Review of Boko Haram's Public Messages* (Pretoria, South Africa: Institute for Security Studies, 2017).
23. Hope Abah, "Benue Schools Alarmed Over Boko Haram Threat," *Daily Trust* (Abuja), May 18, 2014.
24. Conclusion based on searches of START, Global Terrorism Database.
25. Abah, "Benue Schools Alarmed." Just 5 percent of Boko Haram's external communications are written in English, and this includes online content clearly intended for international audiences. (See Mahmood, *More than Propaganda*.)
26. "What Police Is Doing Over Boko Haram Threat Letter to Secondary School," *New Telegraph* (Lagos), July 4, 2014.
27. "Terrorists Threaten to Bomb UI before October 1," *Punch* (Lagos), September 24, 2016.
28. "Terrorists Threaten to Bomb UI," *Punch*.
29. Joseph M. Brown, "Notes to the Underground: Credit Claiming and Organizing in the Earth Liberation Front," *Terrorism and Political Violence* (September 2017), https://doi.org/10.1080/09546553.2017.1364637. Politically minded hacker communities also use this model, inciting distributed denial-of-service (DDoS) attacks by posting image files with instructions for when and how to take down a particular target. See Parmy Olson, *We Are Anonymous: Inside the Hacker World of LulzSec, Anonymous, and the Global Cyber Insurgency* (New York: Back Bay Books, 2013).
30. Marissa Payne, "Pro-ISIS Poster Threatening World Cup Terrorist Attack Depicts Lionel Messi Crying Blood," *Washington Post*, October 24, 2017.
31. Cooper Fleishman and Anthony Smith, "(((Echoes))), Exposed: The Secret Symbol Neo-Nazis Use to Target Jews Online," *Mic*, June 1, 2016.
32. Fleishman and Smith, "(((Echoes))), Exposed."
33. Bayo Wahab, "NUC Says There Are 1.9m Students in Nigerian Universities," *Pulse Nigeria*, May 8, 2018.
34. Notwithstanding the considerable discussion of lone wolf and autonomous cell terrorism among terrorism scholars of the past decade, the population ratio of actual militants to unscrupulous hoaxers remains quite favorable to the hoaxers, and the barriers to hoaxing are lower than ever. On autonomous cell and lone wolf terrorism, see Jeffrey Kaplan, Heléne Lööw, and Leena Malkki, "Introduction to the Special Issue on Lone Wolf and Autonomous Cell Terrorism," *Terrorism and Political Violence* 26, no. 1 (2014): 1–12; George Michael, *Lone Wolf Terror and the Rise of Leaderless Resistance* (Nashville, Tenn.: Vanderbilt University Press, 2012); Marc Sageman, *Leaderless Jihad: Terror Networks In the Twenty-First Century* (Philadelphia: University of

Pennsylvania Press, 2008); and Ramón Spaaij, *Understanding Lone Wolf Terrorism: Global Patterns, Motivations and Prevention* (Dortrecht, Netherlands: Springer, 2012).

35. John Mueller, "Six Rather Unusual Propositions About Terrorism," *Terrorism and Political Violence*, 17, no. 4 (2005): 487–505; John Mueller and Mark G. Stewart, "Terrorism and Bathtubs: Comparing and Assessing the Risks," *Terrorism and Political Violence* (October 2018) https://doi.org/10.1080/09546553.2018.1530662.

Bibliography

Abrahms, Max. *Rules for Rebels: The Science of Victory in Militant History.* New York: Oxford University Press, 2018.
——. "What Terrorists Really Want: Terrorist Motives and Counterterrorism Strategy." *International Security* 32, no. 4 (2008): 78–105.
——. "Why Terrorism Does Not Work." *International Security* 31, no. 2 (2006): 42–78.
Abrahms, Max, Nicholas Beauchamp, and Joseph Mroszczyk. "What Terrorist Leaders Want: A Content Analysis of Terrorist Propaganda Videos." *Studies in Conflict and Terrorism* 40, no. 11 (2016): 899–916.
Abrahms, Max, and Justin Conrad. "The Strategic Logic of Credit Claiming: A New Theory for Anonymous Terrorist Attacks." *Security Studies* 26, no. 2 (2017): 279–304.
Ackerman, Spencer. "Taliban Texts Terror to Afghan Phones." *Wired*, March 17, 2011.
Ajayi, Ola, and Gabriel Enogholase. "Boko Haram Threatens to Bomb UI, Uni-Ben, 18 Others." *Vanguard* (Lagos), September 13, 2011.
Al-Salhy, Suadad, and Tim Arango. "Sunni Militants Drive Iraqi Army Out of Mosul." *New York Times*, June 10, 2014.
Al-Zawahiri, Ayman. "Letter from al-Zawahiri to al-Zarqawi," July 9, 2005. Translated and released by U.S. Office of the Director of National Intelligence. https://fas.org/irp/news/2005/10/dni101105.html.
Aly, Anne, Stuart Macdonald, Lee Jarvis, and Thomas Chen, eds. *Violent Extremism Online: New Perspectives on Terrorism and the Internet.* Abingdon, U.K.: Routledge, 2016.

Anderson, Brendan. *Joe Cahill: A Life in the IRA*. Dublin: O'Brien Press, 2002.
Arce, Daniel G., and Todd Sandler. "Strategic Analysis of Terrorism." In *Mathematical Methods in Counterterrorism*, ed. Nasrulla Memon, Jonathan David Farley, David L. Hicks, and Torben Rosenorn, 333–48. New York: Springer-Verlag/Wien, 2009.
Asal, Victor H., and R. Karl Rethemeyer. Big Allied and Dangerous Dataset. V2. October 28, 2019. Distributed by National Consortium for the Study of Terrorism and Responses to Terrorism (START) at the University of Maryland. http://www.start.umd.edu/baad/database.
———. "The Nature of the Beast: Terrorist Organizational Characteristics and Organizational Lethality." *Journal of Politics* 70, no. 2 (2008): 437–49.
Baker, Aryn, and Muhib Habibi. "Deadly Notes in the Night: How the Taliban Is Using a New Kind of Terrorist Threat to Intimidate Afghans." *Time*, July 5, 2006.
Barcena, Iñaki, Eunate Guarrotxena, Jon Torre, and Pedro Ibarra. 2000. "Institutionalisation and Radicalisation in the Organisational Evolution of the Basque Ecologist Movement (1975–1999): Between Virtue and Necessity." Paper presented at the European Consortium for Political Research conference, Colchester, U.K., April 2000.
Beardsley, Kyle, Kristian Skrede Gleditsch, and Nigel Lo. "Roving Bandits? The Geographic Evolution of Armed Conflicts." *International Studies Quarterly* 59, no. 3 (2015): 503–16.
Becker, Jo. *Funding the "Final War": LTTE Intimidation and Extortion in the Tamil Diaspora*. Washington, D.C.: Human Rights Watch, 2006. https://www.hrw.org/report/2006/03/14/funding-final-war/ltte-intimidation-and-extortion-tamil-diaspora.
Bell, J. Bowyer. *The Secret Army: The IRA*. New Brunswick, N.J.: Transaction, 1997.
Bew, John, Martyn Frampton, and Íñigo Gurruchaga. *Talking to Terrorists: Making Peace in Northern Ireland and the Basque Country*. London: Hurst, 2009.
Blanchard, Lauren Ploch, and Katia T. Cavigelli. *Boko Haram and the Islamic State's West Africa Province*. Washington, D.C.: Congressional Research Service, 2018.
Bloom, Mia M. *Dying to Kill: The Allure of Suicide Terror*. Philadelphia: University of Pennsylvania Press, 2005.
———. "Palestinian Suicide Bombing: Public Support, Market Share, and Outbidding." *Political Science Quarterly* 119, no. 1 (2004): 61–88.
Bloom, Mia M., and John Horgan. "Missing Their Mark: The IRA Proxy Bomb Campaign." *Social Research* 75, no. 2 (2008): 80–94.
Bloom, Mia M., John Horgan, and Charlie Winter. "Depictions of Children and Youth in the Islamic State's Martyrdom Propaganda, 2015–2016." *CTC Sentinel* 9, no. 2 (2016): 29–32.

Bolt, Neville. *The Violent Image: Insurgent Propaganda and the New Revolutionaries.* New York: Columbia University Press, 2012.

Briant, Emma Louise. *Propaganda and Counter-Terrorism: Strategies for Global Change.* Manchester, U.K.: Manchester University Press, 2015.

Brinkmann, Svend. *Qualitative Interviewing.* New York: Oxford University Press, 2013.

Brousse, Paul. "Propaganda by the Deed." In *Anarchism: A Documentary History of Libertarian Ideas*, vol. 1: *From Anarchy to Anarchism (200 CE to 1939)*, ed. Robert Graham, 150–51. New York: Black Rose Books, 2005.

Brown, Joseph M. "Correlates of Warning: Territory, Democracy, and Casualty Aversion in Terrorist Tactics." *International Organization.* July 2020. https://doi.org/10.1017/S002081832000003X.

——. "Force of Words: The Role of Threats in Terrorism." *Terrorism and Political Violence.* August 2018. https://doi.org/10.1080/09546553.2018.1486301.

——. "Notes to the Underground: Credit Claiming and Organizing in the Earth Liberation Front." *Terrorism and Political Violence.* September 2017. https://doi.org/10.1080/09546553.2017.1364637.

Bueno de Mesquita, Ethan. "The Quality of Terror." *American Journal of Political Science* 49, no. 3 (2005): 515–30.

Chattopadhyahya, H. P. *Ethnic Unrest in Modern Sri Lanka: An Account of Tamil-Sinhalese Race Relations.* New Delhi: M.D. Publications, 1994.

Chenoweth, Erica. "Democratic Competition and Terrorist Activity." *Journal of Politics* 72, no. 1 (2010): 16–30.

Chenoweth, Erica, and Maria J. Stephan. "Why Civil Resistance Works: The Strategic Logic of Nonviolent Conflict." *International Security* 33, no. 1 (2008): 7–44.

Choi, Seung-Whan. "Fighting Terrorism through the Rule of Law?" *Journal of Conflict Resolution* 54, no. 6 (2010): 940–66.

Coaffee, Jon. *Terrorism, Risk and the City: The Making of a Contemporary Urban Landsape.* London: Routledge, 2017.

Collard-Wexler, Simon, Costantino Pischedda, and Michael G. Smith. "Do Foreign Occupations Cause Suicide Attacks?" *Journal of Conflict Resolution* 58, no. 4 (2014): 625–57.

Comisión de la Verdad y Reconciliación (CVR). *Hatun Willakuy: Abbreviated Version of the Final Report of the Truth and Reconciliation Commission.* Lima: Transfer Commission of the Truth and Reconciliation Commission of Peru, 2014.

Committee to Protect Journalists "Nigerian Reporter Threatened Over Boko Haram Coverage." Online alert, March 19, 2012. http://cpj.org/2012/03/nigerian-journalist-threatened-over-boko-haram-cov.php.

Coogan, Tim Pat. *The IRA.* London: HarperCollins, 1993.

Council on Foreign Relations. "The Taliban." Infoguide. https://www.cfr.org/interactives/taliban?cid=marketing_use-taliban_infoguide-012115#!/

taliban?cid=marketing_use-taliban_infoguide-012115. Accessed October 27, 2019.

Degregori, Carlos Ivan. "The Origins and Logic of the Shining Path: Two Views." In *The Shining Path of Peru*, ed. David Scott Palmer, 51–75. London: Hurst, 1992.

Dillon, Martin. *The Enemy Within*. London: Transworld, 1994.

———. *25 Years of Terror: The IRA's War Against the British*. New York: Bantam Books, 1996.

Early, Chas. "April 24, 1993: IRA's Bishopsgate Bomb Devastates the Heart of the City of London." BT.com. http://home.bt.com/news/on-this-day/april-24-1993-iras-bishopsgate-bomb-devastates-the-heart-of-the-city-of-london-11363977172852.

Eck, Kristine, and Lisa Hultman. "One-Sided Violence Against Civilians in War: Insights from New Fatality Data." *Journal of Peace Research* 44, no. 2 (2007): 233–46.

Edgell, Amanda B. "Data." https://acrowinghen.com/data/. Accessed October 29, 2019.

Enders, Walter, and Todd Sandler. "Causality Between Transnational Terrorism and Tourism: The Case of Spain." *Terrorism* 14, no. 1 (1991): 49–58.

English, Richard. *Armed Struggle: The History of the IRA*. New York: Oxford University Press, 2003.

Fazal, Tanisha M. "Rebellion, War Aims and the Laws of War." *Daedalus* 146, no. 1 (2017): 71–82.

———. *Wars of Law: Unintended Consequences in the Regulation of Armed Conflict*. Ithaca, N.Y.: Cornell University Press, 2018.

Fearon, James D. "Domestic Political Audience Costs and the Escalation of International Disputes." *American Political Science Review* 88, no. 3 (1994): 577–92.

———. "Signaling Foreign Policy Interests: Tying Hands Versus Sinking Costs." *Journal of Conflict Resolution* 41, no. 1 (1997): 68–90.

Fine, Glenn A., Steve A. Linick, and Ann Calvaresi Barr. *Operation Freedom's Sentinel: Report to the United States Congress, April 1, 2018–June 30, 2018*. Report by the Office of the Inspector General of the Department of Defense. June 30, 2018. https://www.stateoig.gov/system/files/lig_oco_ofs3_jun2018_508_r2.pdf.

Fleishman, Cooper, and Anthony Smith. "(((Echoes))), Exposed: The Secret Symbol Neo-Nazis Use to Target Jews Online." *Mic*, June 1, 2016.

Fortna, Virginia Page. "Do Terrorists Win? Rebels' Use of Terrorism and Civil War Outcomes." *International Organization* 69, no. 3 (2015): 519–56.

Foucault, Michel. *Discipline and Punish: The Birth of the Prison*. New York: Vintage, 1995.

Freedom House. "Freedom in the World Data and Resources." Freedom House, October 29, 2019. https://freedomhouse.org/content/freedom-world-data-and-resources.

Gelman, Andrew. "Multilevel (Hierarchical) Modeling: What It Can and Cannot Do." *Technometrics* 48, no. 3 (2006): 432–35.

Gelman, Andrew, and Jennifer Hill, eds. *Data Analysis Using Regression and Multilevel/Hierarchical Models*. New York: Cambridge University Press, 2007.

Geraghty, Tony. *The Irish War: The Hidden Conflict Between the IRA and British Intelligence*. Baltimore: Johns Hopkins University Press, 2000.

Gerges, Fawaz A. *ISIS: A History*. Princeton, N.J.: Princeton University Press, 2016.

Gibney, Mark, Linda Cornett, Reed Wood, Peter Haschke, Daniel Arnon, Attilio Pisanò, and Gray Barrett. The Political Terror Scale 1976–2018. October 26, 2019. http://www.politicalterrorscale.org.

Ginkel, John, and Alastair Smith. "So You Say You Want a Revolution: A Game Theoretic Explanation of Revolution in Repressive Regimes." *Journal of Conflict Resolution* 43, no. 3 (1999): 291–316.

Gonzales, José E. "Guerrillas and Coca in the Upper Huallaga Valley." In *The Shining Path of Peru*, ed. David Scott Palmer, 123–43. London: Hurst, 1992.

Goodwin, Jeff. "A Theory of Categorical Terrorism." *Social Forces* 84, no. 4 (2006): 2027–46.

Grech, María José. "ETA asesina a un guardia civil, un exmiembro de ETA, un coronel retirado y un expolicía." *Libertad Digital* (blog post). June 3, 2011. http://blogs.libertaddigital.com/in-memoriam/eta-asesina-a-un-guardia-civil-un-exmiembro-de-eta-un-coronel-retirado-y-un-expolicia-9744/.

——. "Txomin Merino, supuesto confidente, un guardia civil y un teniente del Ejército." *Libertad Digital* (blog post). July 5, 2011. http://blogs.libertaddigital.com/in-memoriam/txomin-merino-supuesto-confidente-un-guardia-civil-y-un-teniente-del-ejercito-9939/.

Gross, Michael L. *The Ethics of Insurgency: A Critical Guide to Just Guerrilla Warfare*. New York: Cambridge University Press, 2015.

Guisinger, Alexandra, and Alastair Smith. "Honest Threats: The Interaction of Reputation and Political Institutions in International Crises." *Journal of Conflict Resolution* 46, no. 2 (2002): 175–200.

Gurney, Peter. *Braver Men Walk Away: Memoirs of the World's Top Bomb-Disposal Expert*. London: Harper Collins, 1993.

Guzmán, Abimael. *Dar la Vida por el Partido y la Revolución*. Communiqué signed as "Presidente Gonzalo." June 1, 1987. Archived by el Centro de Documentación de los Movimientos Armados (CEDEMA). http://www.cedema.org/ver.php?id=642.

——. *Síntesis de Entrevista, Abimael Guzmán Reynoso y Elena Iparraguirre, 27 de Enero del 2003*. Lima: Comisión de la Verdad y Reconciliación, 2003.

Habibzada, Mohammad. "Taliban Rebels Impose Taxes on Media Outlets in Restive Ghazni." *Voice of America News*. February 21, 2018.

Hancock, Landon. *Northern Ireland: Troubles Brewing*. Derry, Northern Ireland: Conflict Archive on the Internet (CAIN), 1998. https://cain.ulster.ac.uk/othelem/landon.htm.

Harmon, Christopher C., and Randall G. Bowdish. *The Terrorist Argument: Modern Advocacy and Propaganda*. Washington, D.C.: Brookings Institution, 2018.

Harnden, Toby. *Bandit Country*. London: Hodder and Stoughton, 1999.

Heiberg, Marianne. *The Making of the Basque Nation*. New York: Cambridge University Press, 1987.

Hoffman, Aaron. "Voice and Silence: Why Groups Take Credit for Acts of Terror." *Journal of Peace Research* 47, no. 5 (2010): 1–22.

Hoffman, Bruce. *Inside Terrorism*. New York: Columbia University Press, 2006.

Hoffman, Bruce, and Gordon H. McCormick. "Terrorism, Signaling, and Suicide Attack." *Studies in Conflict and Terrorism* 27, no. 4 (2004): 243–81.

Högbladh, Stina, Therése Pettersson, and Lotta Themnér. "External Support in Armed Conflict 1975–2009—Presenting New Data." Paper presented at the International Studies Association annual convention, Montreal, Canada, March 2011.

Horowitz, Michael C. "Nonstate Actors and the Diffusion of Innovations: The Case of Suicide Terrorism." *International Organization* 64, no. 1 (2010): 33–64.

Indo-Lanka Accord. Text of agreement between the government of India and the government of Sri Lanka. Signed in Colombo, Sri Lanka, July 29, 1987. https://peacemaker.un.org/sites/peacemaker.un.org/files/IN%20LK_870729_Indo-Lanka%20Accord.pdf.

Irujo, Xabier. *Gernika, 1937: The Market Day Massacre*. Reno: University of Nevada Press, 2015.

Jenkins, Brian M. *International Terrorism: A New Kind of Warfare*. Santa Monica, Calif.: RAND Corporation, 1974.

Jervis, Robert L. *The Logic of Images in International Relations*. New York: Columbia University Press, 1970.

———. *Perception and Misperception in International Politics*. Princeton, N.J.: Princeton University Press, 1976.

Johnson, Thomas H. "The Taliban Insurgency and an Analysis of Shabnamah (Night Letters)." *Small Wars and Insurgencies* 18, no. 3 (2007): 317–44.

Jones, Seth G. "The Rise of Afghanistan's Insurgency: State Failure and Jihad." *International Security* 32, no. 4 (2008): 7–40.

Journal of Commerce. "Bomb Threat Delays." Aviation Briefs (from wire and staff reports). December 30, 1988.

Juergensmeyer, Mark. *Terror in the Mind of God: The Global Rise of Religious Violence*. Berkeley: University of California Press, 2017.

Kalyvas, Stathis. *The Logic of Violence in Civil War*. New York: Cambridge University Press, 2006.

Kalyvas, Stathis N., and Matthew Adam Kocher. "The Dynamics of Violence in Vietnam: An Analysis of the Hamlet Evaluation System (HES)." *Journal of Peace Research* 46, no. 3 (2009): 335–55.

Kalyvas, Stathis N., and Ignacio Sánchez-Cuenca. "Killing Without Dying: The Absence of Suicide Missions." In *Making Sense of Suicide Missions*, ed. Diego Gambetta, 209–31. New York: Oxford University Press, 2005.

Kaplan, Jeffrey, Heléne Lööw, and Leena Malkki. "Introduction to the Special Issue on Lone Wolf and Autonomous Cell Terrorism." *Terrorism and Political Violence* 26, no. 1 (2014): 1–12.

Kaufmann, Chaim D. "Possible and Impossible Solutions to Ethnic Wars." *International Security* 20, no. 4 (1996): 136–75.

Kearns, Erin M. "When to Take Credit for Terrorism? A Cross-National Examination of Claims and Attributions." *Terrorism and Political Violence*. January 2019. https://doi.org/10.1080/09546553.2018.1540982.

Kearns, Erin M., Brendan Conlon, and Joseph K. Young. "Lying About Terrorism." *Studies in Conflict and Terrorism* 37, no. 5 (2014): 422–39.

Kurlansky, Mark. *The Basque History of the World*. New York: Walker, 1999.

Kuzel, Anton J. "Sampling In Qualitative Inquiry." In *Doing Qualitative Research*, ed. Benjamin F. Crabtree and William L. Miller, 33–46. 2nd ed. Thousand Oaks, Calif.: Sage, 1999.

Kydd, Andrew H., and Barbara F. Walter. "The Strategies of Terrorism." *International Security* 31, no. 1 (2006): 49–80.

Lake, David A. "Rational Extremism: Understanding Terrorism in the Twenty-First Century." *Dialogue IO* 1, no. 1 (2002): 15–29.

Lapan, Harvey E., and Todd Sandler. "Terrorism and Signalling." *European Journal of Political Economy* 9, no. 3 (1993): 383–97.

Laqueur, Walter. *The New Terrorism: Fanaticism and the Arms of Mass Destruction*. New York: Oxford University Press, 2000.

——. *Voices of Terror: Manifestos, Writings, and Manuals of Al Qaeda, Hamas, and Other Terrorists from Around the World and Throughout the Ages*. Naperville, Ill.: Sourcebooks, 2004.

Laub, Zachary. "The Islamic State." Council on Foreign Relations. Online report, August 10, 2016. https://www.cfr.org/backgrounder/islamic-state.

——. "The Taliban in Afghanistan." Council on Foreign Relations. Online report, July 4, 2014. https://www.cfr.org/backgrounder/taliban-afghanistan.

Loadenthal, Michael. *The Politics of Attack: Communiqués and Insurrectionary Violence*. Manchester, U.K.: Manchester University Press, 2017.

Lynch, John. *A Tale of Three Cities: Comparative Studies in Working-Class Life*. London: Macmillan, 1998.

MacEachern, Scott. *Searching for Boko Haram: A History of Violence in Central Africa*. New York: Oxford University Press, 2018.

Mahmood, Omar S. *More than Propaganda: A Review of Boko Haram's Public Messages*. Pretoria, South Africa: Institute for Security Studies, 2017. https://issafrica.org/research/west-africa-report/more-than-propaganda-a-review-of-boko-harams-public-messages.

Mahoney, Charles W. "Empty Threats: How Extremist Organizations Bluff in Terrorist Campaigns." *Studies in Conflict & Terrorism*. October 2018. https://doi.org/10.1080/1057610X.2018.1514093.

Mampilly, Zachariah Cherian. *Rebel Rulers: Insurgent Governance and Civilian Life During War*. Ithaca, N.Y.: Cornell University Press, 2011.

Mansvelt-Beck, Jan. *Territory and Terror: Conflicting Nationalisms in the Basque Country*. New York: Routledge, 2005.

Mao, Zedong. *On Guerrilla Warfare*. Published as U.S. Marine Corps FMFRP 12–18. 1989. https://www.marines.mil/Portals/1/Publications/FMFRP%2012-18%20%20Mao%20Tse-tung%20on%20Guerrilla%20Warfare.pdf.

Mapping Militant Organizations. "Afghan Taliban." Stanford University. Last modified June 2018. https://cisac.fsi.stanford.edu/mappingmilitants/profiles/afghan-taliban.

——. "Boko Haram." Stanford University. Last modified March 2018. https://cisac.fsi.stanford.edu/mappingmilitants/profiles/boko-haram.

——. "The Islamic State." Stanford University. Last modified September 2019. https://cisac.fsi.stanford.edu/mappingmilitants/profiles/islamic-state.

——. "Mapping Militants." Stanford University. https://cisac.fsi.stanford.edu/mappingmilitants. Accessed October 28, 2019.

Marks, Tom. "Making Revolution with Shining Path." In *The Shining Path of Peru*, ed. David Scott Palmer, 209–23. London: Hurst, 1992.

Marshall, Monty G., Keith Jaggers, and Ted Robert Gurr. *POLITY IV Project Dataset Users' Manual*. Vienna, Va.: Center for Systemic Peace, 2018. http://www.systemicpeace.org/inscr/p4manualv2018.pdf.

Maslow, Abraham H. "A Theory of Human Motivation." *Psychological Review* 50, no. 4 (1943): 370–96.

Masters, Daniel. "The Origin of Terrorist Threats: Religious, Separatist, or Something Else?" *Terrorism and Political Violence* 20, no. 3 (2008): 396–414.

McClintock, Cynthia. "Theories of Revolution and the Case of Peru." In *The Shining Path of Peru*, ed. David Scott Palmer, 243–58. London: Hurst, 1992.

McCormick, Gordon H. *Sharp Dressed Men: Peru's Túpac Amaru Revolutionary Movement*. Santa Monica, Calif.: RAND Corporation, 1993.

McGuffin, John. *Internment*. Tralee, Ireland: Anvil Books, 1973.

McKittrick, David, Seamus Kelters, Brian Feeney, and Chris Thornton. *Lost Lives: The Stories of the Men, Women, and Children Who Died as a Result of the Northern Ireland Troubles*. London: Mainstream, 2001.

McMurtrie, Beth. "Secrets from Belfast." *Chronicle of Higher Education*, January 26, 2014.

Mercer, Jonathan. *Reputation and International Politics*. Ithaca, N.Y.: Cornell University Press, 1996.

Michael, George. *Lone Wolf Terror and the Rise of Leaderless Resistance*. Nashville, Tenn.: Vanderbilt University Press, 2012.

Mickolus, Edward F., Todd Sandler, Jean M. Murdock, and Peter A. Flemming. *International Terrorism: Attributes of Terrorist Events (ITERATE), 1968–2016*. VI. 2017. Distributed by Harvard Dataverse. https://doi.org/10.7910/DVN/ZOGPHC.

Miller, Erin and Kathleen Smarick. *Background Report: ETA Ceasefires by the Numbers*. College Park, Md.: National Consortium for the Study of Terrorism and Responses to Terrorism (START), 2011. https://www.start.umd.edu/sites/default/files/files/publications/br/ETACeasefires.pdf.

Ministerio del Interior. *Victimas de ETA*. Statistical resource published online by the Spanish government (*Gobierno de España*). 2010. https://web.archive.org/web/20100915224606/http://www.mir.ed/DGRIS/Terrorismo_de_ETA/ultimas_victimas/p12b-esp.htm.

Mockaitis, Thomas R. *British Counterinsurgency in the Post-Imperial Era*. Manchester, U.K.: Manchester University Press, 1995.

Moghadam, Assaf. *The Globalization of Martyrdom: Al Qaeda, Salafi Jihad, and the Diffusion of Suicide Attacks*. Baltimore: Johns Hopkins University Press, 2011.

——. "Motives for Martyrdom: Al-Qaida, Salafi Jihad, and the Spread of Suicide Attacks." *International Security* 33, no. 3 (2008): 46–78.

Moloney, Ed. *A Secret History of the IRA*. 1st ed. New York: Norton, 2002.

——. *A Secret History of the IRA*. 2nd ed. New York: Penguin Books, 2007.

——. *Voices from the Grave: Two Men's War in Northern Ireland*. New York: Public Affairs, 2010.

Movimiento Revolucionario Túpac Amaru (MRTA). "Balance y Perspectivas: Campaña Militar del Frente Guerrillero Nor Oriental." *Voz Rebelde* 9 (January 1, 1988). Archived by el Centro de Documentación de los Movimientos Armados (CEDEMA). http://www.cedema.org/ver.php?id=6012.

——. *El MRTA y la Revolución Peruana*. Communiqué dated May 1, 1985. Archived by el Centro de Documentación de los Movimientos Armados (CEDEMA). http://www.cedema.org/ver.php?id=5618.

——. *La Situación Actual y las Tareas en el Proceso de la Guerra Revolucionaria del Pueblo*. Communiqué dated May 1, 1984. Archived by el Centro de Documentación de los Movimientos Armados (CEDEMA). http://www.cedema.org/ver.php?id=3922.

———. "La Violencia: El Derecho del Agredido." *Venceremos* 6 (September 1, 1985). Archived by el Centro de Documentación de los Movimientos Armados (CEDEMA). http://www.cedema.org/ver.php?id= 3481.

———. *Primera Conferencia Clandestina: Suspensión de Acciones Militares.* Transcript of press conference. Released August 1, 1985. Archived by el Centro de Documentación de los Movimientos Armados (CEDEMA). http://www.cedema.org/ver.php?id=3432.

———. *¡Sin Justicia ni Libertad, la Rebelión Avanzará!* Communiqué dated February 20, 1986. Archived by el Centro de Documentación de los Movimientos Armados (CEDEMA). http://www.cedema.org/ver. php?id=6629.

Mueller, John. "Six Rather Unusual Propositions about Terrorism." *Terrorism and Political Violence*, 17, no. 4 (2005): 487–505.

Mueller, John, and Mark G. Stewart. "Terrorism and Bathtubs: Comparing and Assessing the Risks." *Terrorism and Political Violence*. October 2018. https://doi.org/10.1080/09546553.2018.1530662.

National Consortium for the Study of Terrorism and Responses to Terrorism (START). *The Global Terrorism Database*. October 26, 2019. Distributed by the University of Maryland. https://www.start.umd.edu/gtd/.

———. *GTD: Global Terrorism Database—Codebook: Inclusion Criteria and Variables.* College Park: University of Maryland, 2019. https://www.start.umd.edu/gtd/downloads/Codebook.pdf.

Nimzowitsch, Aron. *My System Chess Praxis: His Landmark Classics.* Alkmaar, Netherlands: New in Chess, 2016.

O'Hearn, Denis. "Catholic Grievances, Catholic Nationalism: A Comment." *British Journal of Sociology* 34, no. 3 (1983): 438–45.

Olson, Mancur. "Dictatorship, Democracy, and Development." *American Political Science Review* 87, no. 3 (1993): 567–76.

Olson, Parmy. *We Are Anonymous: Inside the Hacker World of LulzSec, Anonymous, and the Global Cyber Insurgency.* New York: Back Bay Books, 2013.

O'Neill, P. "Text of Irish Republican Army (IRA) Statement in Response to Political Developments Following the 'Northern Bank Robbery' 2 February 2005." Originally published in *An Phoblacht* (Republican News), February 3, 2005. Compiled by Martin Melaugh for the Conflict Archive on the Internet (CAIN) Web Service at the University of Ulster. http://cain.ulst.ac.uk/othelem/organ/ira/ira020205.htm.

Overgaard, Per Baltzer. "The Scale of Terrorist Attacks as a Signal of Resources." *Journal of Conflict Resolution* 38, no. 3 (1994): 452–78.

Palmer, David Scott. "Introduction." In *The Shining Path of Peru*, ed. David Scott Palmer, 1–32. London: Hurst, 1992.

Pape, Robert. *Dying to Win: The Strategic Logic of Suicide Terrorism.* New York: Random House, 2005.

———. "The Strategic Logic of Suicide Terrorism." *American Political Science Review* 97, no. 3 (2003): 343–61.

Partido Comunista del Perú (PCP). *¡A Nuestro Heroico Pueblo Combatiente!* Statement of the Central Committee. January 1, 1981. Archived by el Centro de Documentación de los Movimientos Armados (CEDEMA). http://www.cedema.org/ver.php?id=635.

———. *Comenzamos a Derrumbar los Muros y a Desplegar la Aurora.* Statement of the Second Plenary Session of the Central Committee. March 28, 1980. Archived by el Centro de Documentación de los Movimientos Armados (CEDEMA). http://www.cedema.org/ver.php?id=631.

———. *Desarrollar la Guerra Popular Sirviendo a la Revolución Mundial.* Statement of the Central Committee. August 1, 1986. Archived by el Centro de Documentación de los Movimientos Armados (CEDEMA). http://www.cedema.org/ver.php?id=640.

———. *Día de la Heroicidad.* Resolution of the Central Committee. June 19, 1986. Archived by el Centro de Documentación de los Movimientos Armados (CEDEMA). http://www.cedema.org/ver.php?id=639.

———. *Directiva Internacional del PCP al Movimiento Popular Perú.* Statement of the Central Committee. December 1, 1993. Archived by el Centro de Documentación de los Movimientos Armados (CEDEMA). http://www.cedema.org/ver.php?id=707.

———. *Documentos Fundamentales.* Statement of the Central Committee. January 1, 1988. Archived by el Centro de Documentación de los Movimientos Armados (CEDEMA). http://www.cedema.org/ver.php?id=5460.

———. *¡Elecciones, No! ¡Guerra Popular, Sí!* Statement of the Central Committee. May 1, 1990. Archived by el Centro de Documentación de los Movimientos Armados (CEDEMA). http://www.cedema.org/ver.php?id=647.

———. *Linea de Construcción de los Tres Instrumentos de la Revolución.* Communiqué dated January 1, 1988. Archived by el Centro de Documentación de los Movimientos Armados (CEDEMA). http://www.cedema.org/ver.php?id=646.

———. *Lineamiento para Documento de Bases.* Statement of the Central Directorate. November 1, 1993. Archived by el Centro de Documentación de los Movimientos Armados (CEDEMA). http://www.cedema.org/ver.php?id=5290.

———. *¡Reafirmarse en la Base de Unidad Partidaria!* Statement of the Central Committee. February 1, 1994. Archived by el Centro de Documentación de los Movimientos Armados (CEDEMA). http://www.cedema.org/ver.php?id=709.

———. *¡Viva el Maoísmo!* Statement of the Central Committee. August 1, 1993. Archived by el Centro de Documentación de los Movimientos Armados (CEDEMA). http://www.cedema.org/ver.php?id=704.

———. *¡Viva el Presidente Gonzalo y su Todopoderoso Pensamiento!* Statement of the Central Committee. February 1, 1994. Archived by el Centro de Documentación de los Movimientos Armados (CEDEMA). http://www.cedema.org/ver.php?id=710.

———. *¡Viva la Lucha Armada de Nuestro Pueblo! ¡Abajo la Patraña Reaccionaria!* Commuiqué dated September 8, 1981. Archived by el Centro de Documentación de los Movimientos Armados (CEDEMA). http://www.cedema.org/ver.php?id=636.

Partido Comunista del Perú (PCP)—Mantaro Valley Base. *Paro Armado en Junín y Pasco.* Commuiqué dated May 1, 1992. Archived by el Centro de Documentación de los Movimientos Armados (CEDEMA). http://www.cedema.org/ver.php?id=8033

Petersen, Roger D. *Understanding Ethnic Violence: Fear, Hatred, and Resentment in Twentieth-Century Eastern Europe.* New York: Cambridge University Press, 2002.

Pinker, Edieal J. "A Mathematical Analysis of Short-Term Responses to Threats of Terrorism." In *Mathematical Methods in Counterterrorism*, ed. Nasrulla Memon, Jonathan David Farley, David L. Hicks, and Torben Rosenorn, 141–60. New York: Springer-Verlag/Wien, 2009.

Pisacane, Carlo. "Political Testament." In *Anarchism: A Documentary History of Libertarian Ideas*, vol. 1: *From Anarchy to Anarchism (200 CE to 1939)*, ed. Robert Graham, 67–68. New York: Black Rose Books, 2005.

Polay, Víctor. *Testimonio a la Comisión de la Verdad y Reconciliación.* Lima: Comisión de la Verdad y Reconciliación, 2002.

Polity IV Project. *Political Regime Characteristics and Transitions, 1800–2018.* October 27, 2019. Distributed by the Center for Systemic Peace. http://www.systemicpeace.org/inscr/p4v2018.xls.

Posen, Barry R. "The Security Dilemma and Ethnic Conflict." *Survival* 35, no. 1 (1993): 27–47.

Povlock, Paul A. "The Guerrilla War at Sea: The Sri Lankan Civil War." *Small Wars Journal*, September 9, 2011.

Powell, Jonathan. *Talking to Terrorists: How to End Armed Conflicts.* New York: Vintage, 2015.

Prabhakaran, Velipullai. "Leader V Prabakaran's Heros Day Speech 2002." November 27, 2002. http://www.eelamview.com/2012/11/07/leader-v-prabakarans-heros-day-speech-2002-2/.

———. "Leader V Prabakaran's Heros Day Speech 2003." November 27, 2003. http://www.eelamview.com/2012/11/07/leader-v-prabakarans-heros-day-speech-2003-2/.

———. "Leader V Prabakaran's Heros Day Speech 2004." November 27, 2004. http://www.eelamview.com/2012/11/07/leader-v-prabakarans-heros-day-speech-2004-2/.

———. "Leader V Prabakaran's Heros Day Speech 2005." November 27, 2005. http://www.eelamview.com/2012/11/08/leader-v-prabakarans-heros-day-speech-2005-2/.

Rashid, Ahmed. *Taliban: Militant Islam, Oil and Fundamentalism in Central Asia.* New Haven, Conn.: Yale University Press, 2000.

Re, Matteo. "The Red Brigades' Communiqués: An Analysis of the Terrorist Group's Propaganda." *Terrorism and Political Violence.* September 2017. https://doi.org/10.1080/09546553.2017.1364639.

Reinares, Fernando. "Evidence of Al-Qa'ida's Role in the 2004 Madrid Attack." *CTC Sentinel* 5, no. 3 (2012): 1–6.

Ricks, Thomas E. *The Gamble: General David Petraeus and the American Military Adventure in Iraq, 2006–2008.* New York: Penguin, 2009.

Rincón, Miguel. *Testimonio a la Comisión de la Verdad y Reconciliación.* Lima: Comisión de la Verdad y Reconciliación, 2002.

Robespierre, Maximilien. "Discours par Maximilien Robespierre—17 Avril 1792–27 Juillet 1794." Project Gutenberg, September 2009. http://www.gutenberg.org/ebooks/29887.

Roul, Animesh. "Taliban Demonstrates Resilience with Afghan Spring Offensive." *Terrorism Monitor* 16, no. 11 (June 2018): 3–5.

Routray, Bibhu Prasad, and Ajit Kumar Singh. "The Pawns of War." *South Asia Intelligence Review: Weekly Assessments and Briefings,* October 2, 2006.

Royal Ulster Constabulary. *Chief Constable's Report.* Belfast: Police Authority for Northern Ireland, 1972.

———. *Chief Constable's Report.* Belfast: Police Authority for Northern Ireland, 1996.

———. *Chief Constable's Report.* Belfast: Police Authority for Northern Ireland, 1998.

Ryder, Chris. *A Special Kind of Courage.* London: Methuen, 2005.

Sageman, Marc. *Leaderless Jihad: Terror Networks in the Twenty-First Century.* Philadelphia: University of Pennsylvania Press, 2008.

Salehyan, Idean, David Siroky, and Reed M. Wood. "External Rebel Sponsorship and Civilian Abuse: A Principal-Agent Analysis of Wartime Atrocities." *International Organization* 68, no. 3 (2014): 633–61.

Sánchez-Cuenca, Ignacio, and Luis de la Calle. "Domestic Terrorism: The Hidden Side of Political Violence." *Annual Review of Political Science* 12 (2009): 31–49.

Schelling, Thomas C. *Arms and Influence.* New Haven, Conn.: Yale University Press, 1966.

Schmid, Alex P., and Albert J. Jongman. *Political Terrorism: A New Guide to Actors, Authors, Concepts, Data Bases, Theories and Literature.* New York: Transaction Books, 1988.

Shakespeare, William. *Macbeth.* London: Arden Shakespeare, 1997.

Shapiro, Jacob N. *The Terrorist's Dilemma: Managing Violent Covert Organizations.* Princeton, N.J.: Princeton University Press, 2013.

Simon, Jeffrey D. *Lone Wolf Terrorism: Understanding the Growing Threat.* Amherst, N.Y.: Prometheus Books, 2016.

Smith, Michael L. "Shining Path's Urban Strategy: Ate Vitarte." In *The Shining Path of Peru*, ed. David Scott Palmer, 145–65. London: Hurst, 1992.

Spaaij, Ramón. *Understanding Lone Wolf Terrorism: Global Patterns, Motivations and Prevention.* Dortrecht, Netherlands: Springer, 2012.

Stanton, Jessica A. "Terrorism in the Context of Civil War." *Journal of Politics* 75, no. 4 (2013): 1009–22.

——. *Violence and Restraint in Civil War: Civilian Targeting in the Shadow of International Law.* New York: Cambridge University Press, 2016.

Stern, Jessica. *The Ultimate Terrorists.* Cambridge, Mass.: Harvard University Press, 2001.

Stewart, Megan A. "Civil War as State-Making: Strategic Governance in Civil War." *International Organization* 72, no. 1 (2018): 205–26.

Sullivan, John. *ETA and Basque Nationalism: The Fight for Euskadi, 1980–1986.* New York: Routledge, 1988.

Swamy, M. R. Narayan. *Prabhakaran: Inside An Elusive Mind.* Delhi: Konark, 2003.

——. *Tigers of Lanka: From Boys to Guerrillas.* Colombo: Vijitha Yapa, 2008.

Taliban (Islamic Emirate of Afghanistan). *Statement of Leadership Council of Islamic Emirate Regarding the Commencement of the Annual Spring Operation Named "Khaibar."* Press release, May 12, 2014. http://manusiaonline.blogspot.com/2014/05/statement-of-leadership-council-of.html.

Thurston, Alexander. *Boko Haram: The History of an African Jihadist Movement.* Princeton, N.J.: Princeton University Press, 2018.

Tishler, Nicole A. "Fake Terrorism: Examining Terrorist Groups' Resort to Hoaxing as a Mode of Attack." *Perspectives on Terrorism* 12, no. 4 (2018): 3–13.

Trotter, Sam. *Constabulary Heroes: 1826–2011.* Coleraine and Ballycastle, Northern Ireland: Impact, 2012.

Ubayasiri, Kasun. "An Illusive Leader's Annual Speech." *EJournalist: A Refereed Media Journal* 6, no. 1 (2006): 1–27.

United Kingdom Northern Ireland Office. "The Agreement." Text of the Belfast Agreement, signed April 10, 1998. https://assets.publishing.service.gov.uk/government/uploads/system/uploads/attachment_data/file/136652/agreement.pdf.

United States Department of State. *International Religious Freedom Report 2008: Nigeria.* Washington, D.C.: U.S. Department of State, 2008. https://2009-2017.state.gov/j/drl/rls/irf/2008/108385.htm.

——. *Patterns of Global Terrorism—2000.* Report by the Office of the Coordinator for Counterterrorism. Washington, D.C.: U.S. Department of State, 2001. https://web.archive.org/web/20061115204446/http://www.state.gov/s/ct/rls/crt/2000/2419.htm.

———. *Report to Congress on Incidents During the Recent Conflict in Sri Lanka.* Washington, D.C.: U.S. Department of State, 2009. https://web.archive.org/web/20161013022320/http://www.state.gov/documents/organization/131025.pdf.

United States Department of State, Bureau of Diplomatic Security. *Significant Incidents of Political Violence Against Americans—1987.* Publication 9644. Washington, D.C.: U.S. Department of State, 1988.

———. *Significant Incidents of Political Violence Against Americans—1989.* Publication 9767. Washington, D.C.: U.S. Department of State, 1990.

———. *Significant Incidents of Political Violence Against Americans—1990.* Publication 9869. Washington, D.C.: U.S. Department of State, 1991.

———. *Significant Incidents of Political Violence Against Americans—1991.* Publication 9953. Washington, D.C.: U.S. Department of State, 1992.

United States Department of State, Bureau of International Narcotics and Law Enforcement Affairs. "Narcotics Rewards Program: Victor Quispe Palomino." 2014. https://web.archive.org/web/20170220171559/https://www.state.gov/j/inl/narc/rewards/144801.htm.

United States Joint Chiefs of Staff. *Antiterrorism.* Joint Publication 3-07.2. Arlington, Va.: U.S. Department of Defense, 2010.

United States Marine Corps. "Improvised Explosive Device (IED) B3L0487XQ-DM Student Handout." Camp Barrett, Va.: United States Marine Corps, Basic School—Marine Corps Training Command, 2016. https://www.trngcmd.marines.mil/Portals/207/Docs/TBS/B3L0487XQ-DM%20Improvised%20Explosive%20Device.pdf?ver=2016-01-11-164337-777.

Urla, Jacqueline. *Reclaiming Basque: Language, Nation, and Cultural Activism.* Reno: University of Nevada Press, 2012.

Walsh, James Igoe, Justin M. Conrad, Beth Elise Whitaker, and Katelin M. Hudak. "Funding Rebellion: The Rebel Contraband Dataset." *Journal of Peace Research* 55, no. 5 (2018): 699–707.

Warrick, Joby. *Black Flags: The Rise of ISIS.* New York: Doubleday, 2015.

Weinstein, Jeremy. *Inside Rebellion: The Politics of Insurgent Violence.* New York: Cambridge University Press, 2006.

Weiss, Gordon. *The Cage: The Fight for Sri Lanka and the Last Days of the Tamil Tigers.* New York: Bellevue Literary Press, 2012.

Whitfield, Teresa. *Endgame for ETA: Elusive Peace in the Basque Country.* New York: Oxford University Press, 2014.

Whitten-Woodring, Jenifer. *Guidelines for Using the Global Media Freedom Dataset.* Codebook distributed by the University of Massachusetts Lowell. http://faculty.uml.edu/Jenifer_whittenwoodring/documents/GuidelinesforusingtheGlobalMediaFreedomDataset_001.pdf. Accessed October 29, 2019.

Whitten-Woodring, Jenifer, and Douglas A. Van Belle. "The Correlates of Media Freedom: An Introduction of the Global Media Freedom Dataset." *Political Science Research and Methods* 5, no. 1 (January 2017): 179–88.

Wievorka, Michel. "ETA and Basque Political Violence." In *The Legitimization of Violence*, ed. David E. Apter, 292–49. New York: New York University Press, 1997.

Wilson, Andrew J. *Irish America and the Ulster Conflict, 1968–1995.* Washington, D.C.: Catholic University of America Press, 1995.

Wood, Reed M. "Rebel Capability and Strategic Violence Against Civilians." *Journal of Peace Research* 47, no. 5 (2010): 601–14.

Index

Note: Page numbers in italics indicate figures; those with a *t* indicate tables.

Adams, Gerry, 32, 36–37. *See also* Sinn Féin
Afghanistan, 11–12, 125, 158; ISIL in, 118, 120; NATO in, 117, 128, 142; Soviet invasion of, 117. *See also* Taliban
African National Congress, 152
aggrandizement, 8, 26, 27t, 167; by ETA/LTTE, 86–90; by IRA, 9, 47–49; by jihadist groups, 136–39; by MRTA/Shining Path, 108–11
Ahmad, Ibrahim Datti, 134–35
airstrikes, 119, 120, 143
Alianza Popular Revolucionaria Americana (APRA), 95, 106–7, 111–12, 114
al-Qa'ida, 117, 119, 136
al-Qa'ida in Iraq (AQI). *See* ISIL
al-Qa'ida in the Islamic Maghreb (AQIM), 122
Amnesty International, 238n64
anti-Semitism, 179

armed forces, 19–21, 26; of Afghanistan, 132, 139, 142; of India, 66, 89; of Iraq, 120, 140; of Jordan, 143; of Nigeria, 122, 134, 137, 141; of Peru, 111, 112; of Russia, 120; of Spain, 72, 84; of Sri Lanka, 65, 75–76, 86, 89, 91; of Syria, 120; of United Kingdom, 19–20, 31–34, 44–45, 53, 56, 57; of United States, 118–19
audience costs, 234n143

BAAD (Big, Allied, and Dangerous Dataset), 151–53, 260n27
Baghdadi, Abu Bakr al-, 119, 120
Barcelona Olympics (1992), 88
Barnawi, Abu Mus'ab al-, 122, 123, 137–38
Basques, 62–64; environmentalism of, 80; language of, 64, 235n6; nationalism of, 62, 64, 69, 80, 87, 235n6; politics of, 69, 80, 83, 84, 87, 93; views on violence of, 69, 80, 93, 163

Belfast agreement (1998), 32
Benin, 138
Binational Centers (BNCs) (Peru-U.S.), 99, 102, 244n29
Bin Laden, Osama, 117, 119
Bishopsgate bombing (1993), 1–3, 41
"Black July" riots (1983), 65, 73, 238n68
Blair, Tony, 32
Blanco, Miguel Ángel, 84, 236n39
"Bloody Friday" bombings (1972), 38, 39, 53, 58, 93
"Bloody Sunday" incident (1972), 36, 39
bluffs, 25–27, 108–9, 124, 140–43, 167–68; aggrandizement and, 136; functions of, 8, 18; objectives of, 5t, 27t; pledges and, 47–51, 90–92, 171; prophylactic, 10, 168; speech/kinetic action model of, 6–8, 7; for strategic advantage, 90–92. *See also* hoaxes
Boko Haram, 8–9, 115–16, 123–44, 169–70, 176–77; history of, 121–23; hoaxes by, 125–29; incentives of, 123t; legitimacy concerns of, 125; negotiations by, 124, 134–36; official name of, 121; Shekau faction of, 122–23, 131, 135–39, 170, 176; social control by, 130–34, 173; suicide bombings by, 121–23; tactics of, 11–12, 176; warnings by, 126–28, 161–62. *See also* jihadist groups
Brexit, 227n14
Buddhism, 65, 74
Buhari, Muhammadu, 138

Cahill, Joe, 36
Cameroon, 122, 137, 138, 141
capital punishment, 19
Carrero Blanco, Luis, 64
Castro, Fidel, 95

caudillismo, 100
Centro de Documentación de los Movimientos Armados (CEDEMA), 246n55
Chad, 122, 137, 138, 141
Citibank, 99, 244n29
Clinton, Bill, 36–37
cocaine trade, 96, 97, 104
codes: of ETA, 79; of IRA, 54–60, 176, 233n128
Coiste na nIarchimí, 227n15
Colombia, 163
come-on attacks, 44–45, 51–52, 150, 230n74
Comisión de la Verdad y Reconciliación (CVR), 95–96, 99, 101, 104–5, 109–12
Conflict Archive on the Internet (CAIN), 231n106
Contraband Dataset, 151, 152
copycat hoaxes, 176, 178
costly signaling, 4, 13, 20–22, 24, 262n16
counterterrorism, 5–8, 10, 12, 25, 27, 90; in Afghanistan, 132, 140, 142; in Iraq, 142–43; in Nigeria, 140, 141; in Northern Ireland, 61; in Peru, 94, 113, 114; in Spain, 67, 68, 72, 77, 90–91, 168–69, 237n57; in Sri Lanka, 73, 75, 76, 90, 168; in Syria, 142–43
credibility, 14–15, 20; of Boko Haram, 127, 131; of ETA, 77; of IRA, 51–60; of Taliban, 139; of threats, 174–80; truth-telling and, 52, 76–79

Dawlah al-Islāmiyah fī 'l-'Irāq was-sh-Shām. *See* ISIL
Deng Xiaoping, 105
Deobandism, 130
diplomacy: coercive, 25, 171, 176; crisis bargaining and, 50, 234n143

[282] INDEX

disappearances, 19, 73, 96, 106, 187
disruption. *See* economic disruption
distributed denial-of-service (DDoS) attacks, 263n29
Doherty, Joe, 228nn34–35
drug traffickers: Afghan, 118; IRA and, 48, 61, 152; Shining Path and, 96, 97, 104

economic disruption, 8, 27t, 147, 153; by ETA, 70–71, 76; by IRA, 2–3, 34, 37–46, 229n58; by jihadist groups, 126, 251nn74–77
Eelam People's Revolutionary Liberation Front, 88
Egypt, 120
environmental movement (Basque), 80
EROS (Eelam Revolutionary Organization of Students), 89
ETA (Euskadi Ta Askatasuna), 10, 62–93, 168–69; aggrandizement by, 86–90; attacks in France by, 152; bluffs by, 90–92; codes of, 79; disbandment of, 239n89; economic disruption by, 70–71, 76; ethnic separatism of, 10, 62–64, 69, 80, 168; extortion by, 76, 79–81; factions of, 87; guerrilla warfare by, 64, 76–77; history of, 63–65; hoaxes by, 76–79; incentives of, 67t; IRA and, 64, 70, 76, 93, 163; legitimacy concerns of, 68–69; multiple audiences conundrum of, 68–69; negotiations by, 64–65, 70, 82–86, 88, 172–73; predictions for, 68t; social control by, 79–82, 173; tactics of, 10, 176; warnings by, 68–73, 163
ethnic separatism, 146, 148, 152; ETA and, 10, 62–64, 69, 79–80, 168; IRA and, 31; LTTE and, 10, 62, 65, 80, 168

Etxebeste, Eugenio "Antxon," 70–73, 77–79, 83, 90
European Championship football tournament (2016), 138–39
European Women's Championship football tournament (2017), 139
Euskal Herria (Basque homeland), 63
Explosive Ordnance Disposal (EOD), 44–46, 53
extortion, 76, 79–82, 136, 150, 158, 238n61

FALN (Fuerzas Armadas de Liberación Nacional), 163
FARC (Fuerzas Armadas Revolucionarias de Colombia), 163
Fonseka, Sarath, 86
Franco, Francisco, 63, 64, 235n7
Free Syrian Army (FSA), 162
"French letters," 229n53
Fujimori, Alberto, 96

Gálvez, Alberto, 111–12
Gandhi, Rajiv, 66
García, Alan, 106–7
Global Terrorism Database (GTD), 145–46, 149–50, 219n22, 219n27, 229n61; jihadists and, 126; MRTA and, 99; Shining Path and, 100; target types in, 153
Good Friday agreement. *See* Belfast agreement
Greece, 163
Guardia Civil (Spain), 72, 77–78, 87, 90, 237n57
guerrilla warfare, 19; by ETA, 64, 76–77; by IRA, 32, 34–38; by jihadist groups, 140; by LTTE, 66, 81; by MRTA, 95, 99, 104–5, 109–10, 248n84; by Shining Path, 96, 100, 104–5, 109, 113

INDEX [283]

Guevara, Ernesto "Che," 95
Gurney, Peter, 56
Guzmán, Abimael, 95, 96, 114, 169; "Gonzalo Thought" of, 107–8; tactics of, 110–11, 113, 246n69

Hamas, 152
Hatch, Orrin, 228n34
Henty, Ed, 2, 41
Herri Batasuna (ETA's political wing), 80, 83
High Security Zone Residents' Liberation Force (HSZRLF), 85–86, 91–92
Hinduism, 65
Hizb-i-Islami, 136
hoaxes, 7, 165, 167–68, 263n34; come-on, 44–45, 51–52, 150, 230n74; copycat, 176, 178; by ETA, 76–79; functions of, 8, 18; for intelligence gathering, 46–47; by IRA, 3–4, 42–47, 52; by jihadist groups, 125–34, 174–75; by MRTA, 102–3, 245n34; objectives of, 5t, 27t; with signal splitting, 6, 13, 14, 166–68; speech/kinetic action model of, 6–8, 7. *See also* bluffs
Hughes, Brendan, 35
hunger strikes, 31, 227n9
Hussein, Saddam, 118

improvised explosive device (IED): of IRA, 230n74; of Taliban, 142
India, 66, 89
Indian Peacekeeping Force (IPKF), 66
Indo-Lanka Accord (1987), 236n26
Institute for Strategic Studies, 131
International Red Cross, 71, 78, 107, 246n66
International Terrorism: Attributes of Terrorist Events (ITERATE) database, 76–77, 219n27

IRA (Irish Republican Army), 29–61; code words of, 55–60, 176, 233n128; credibility of, 51–60; drug traffickers and, 48, 53, 61; economic disruption by, 2–3, 34, 37–44, 229n58; ETA and, 64, 70, 76, 93, 163; guerrilla warfare by, 32, 34–38; history of, 29–33; hoaxes by, 3–4, 42–47, 52; hunger strikes by, 31, 227n9; legitimacy concerns of, 40–42; multiple audiences conundrum and, 37–40; negotiations by, 50–51, 172–73; "Official IRA" versus, 49, 59; pledges by, 47–51; research on, 32–37; risk management by, 41; signal splitting by, 40–42, 60; social control by, 9, 47–48, 173; strategies of, 3–4, 9–10, 34–37, 168; supporters of, 35–37; tactical prophylaxis and, 45–46; targets of, 34; threats by, 40; warnings by, 40–46, 163; weapons decommissioning by, 51
Iraq, 11–12, 99, 103, 118; al-Qa'ida in, 119; Polity2 score for, 125
Irish Americans, 35–36, 39, 42
Irish Northern Aid (Noraid), 36, 39
Irish Revolution (1919), 30
ISIL (Islamic State of Iraq and the Levant), 115–16, 123–44, 158–60, 169–70; Afghanistan and, 118, 120; Arabic name of, 119; extortion by, 136; history of, 118–20, 252n76; hoaxes by, 130–34, 174–75; incentives of, 123t; negotiations by, 134–36; Nigeria and, 120; Russia and, 178–79; social control by, 130–34, 173; tactics of, 11–12, 252n76. *See also* jihadist groups
Islamic State in West Africa (ISWA), 122, 130

Jama'at al-Tawhid w'al-Jihad (organization), 118–19. *See also* ISIL

Jama'atu Ahlis Sunna Lidda'awati w'al Jihad. *See* Boko Haram

Janatha Vimukthi Peramuna (JVP), 75

Jenkins, Brian, 3, 19

Jewish Defense League (JDL), 260n28

jihadist groups, 11–12, 115–44, 158–60, 169–70; aggrandizement by, 136–39; bluffs by, 125–34, 140–43, 174–75; economic disruption by, 126, 251nn74–77; multiple audiences conundrum of, 115, 170; negotiations by, 124, 134–36; social control by, 130–34, 173; suicide bombings by, 119, 121–23, 129, 132, 160; warnings by, 123–29, 163

Kennedy, Edward "Ted," 36

Kentucky Fried Chicken bombings, 99, 101–3, 244n29

Kenya, 117

"kneecappings," 48, 53, 61

Kurds, 120, 161

La Mon House bombing (1978), 42, 93, 232n120

legitimacy concerns, 5t, 8; of Boko Haram, 125; of ETA, 68–69; of IRA, 40–42; of MRTA, 98–99; warnings and, 15, 27t, 146–49, 219n28

LexisNexis database, 149, 239n79

Libya, 120

LTTE (Liberation Tigers of Tamil Eelam), 10, 62–68, 73–76, 80–92, 168–69; aggrandizement by, 86–90; bluffs by, 90–92; credibility concerns of, 77; extortion by, 80–82, 238n61; guerrilla warfare by, 66, 81; history of, 65–66; incentives of, 67t; negotiations by, 66, 82–86, 172, 173;

predictions for, 68t; recruitment efforts by, 81–82; rival organizations of, 88; social control by, 80–82, 173; suicide bombings, 75, 76, 89; tactics of, 10, 68, 73–76, 76

Lucanamarca massacre (1983), 100, 105

Mac Stíofáin, Seán, 58

Major, John, 32

Mali, 138

Mallie, Eamonn, 59

Mao Zedong, 35, 109

Maoists, 95, 100, 102, 104–7, 109, 113. *See also* Shining Path

McClanahan, Robert "Dinker," 35, 36, 39, 54, 55

McGuinness, Martin, 32

Mesa de Argel negotiations, 83, 237n42

methodology, 8–13, 145–46, 149–50

Mitchell, George, 37, 55

Mormons, 104

Moro National Liberation Front, 152

Morrison, Danny, 37, 38, 43, 46, 52, 227n10

MRTA (Movimiento Revolucionario Túpac Amaru): aggrandizement by, 108–11; economic disruption by, 99–104, 244n29; guerrilla warfare by, 95, 99, 104–5, 109–10, 248n84; history of, 95–97; hoaxes by, 102–3, 245n34; incentives of, 97–98, 97t; multiple audiences conundrum and, 98–99, 169; negotiations by, 11, 64, 105–8; predictions for, 98t; Shining Path and, 11, 94–114, 169; social control by, 103–5; tactics of, 11, 98–103

mujahideen, 117, 137–39

multiple audiences conundrum, 6, 22, 172, 219n28; of ETA, 68–69; of IRA, 37–40; of jihadist groups, 115, 170; of MRTA, 98–99, 169; of religious groups, 116

National Consortium for the Study of Terrorism and Responses to Terrorism (START). *See* Global Terrorism Database
nationalism: Basque, 62, 64, 69, 80, 87; of IRA, 30–32, 38, 49; of MRTA, 99; Tamil, 65, 88. *See also* ethnic separatism
NATO (North Atlantic Treaty Organization), 117, 128, 142
negotiations, 5t, 8, 27t, 167; by ETA, 64–65, 70, 82–86, 88, 172–73; by IRA, 50–51, 172–73; by jihadist groups, 124, 134–36, 170, 172; by LTTE, 66, 82–86, 172, 173; by MRTA, 11, 64, 105–8; by Shining Path, 107–8
Niger, 122, 137, 138, 141
Niger Delta Avengers, 152
Nigeria, 11–12, 176–79; democracy in, 125; ISIL and, 120. *See also* Boko Haram
"night letters," 128, 129
Nimzowitsch, Aron, 230n83
Northern Bank Robbery (U.K.), 51, 175
Northern Ireland Retired Police Officers Association (NIRPOA), 227n17
Northern Ireland's "Troubles" (1969–1998), 29–33, 38
nuclear power plants, 80, 173

"Official IRA," 49, 59. *See also* IRA
O'Hagan, John, 43, 44, 52, 55–56
Olympic Games (1992), 88
Omagh bombing (1998), 93
Omar, Mohammed, 117
"Operation Motorman" (1972), 38–39
opium trade, 118. *See also* drug traffickers

Partido Comunista del Perú–Sendero Luminoso (PSP-SL). *See* Shining Path
Persian Gulf War (1990–1991), 99, 103. *See also* Iraq
Peru, 11, 90, 94–114
pledges, 25–27, 150, 167–68; bluffs and, 47–51, 90–92; functions of, 8, 18; for negotiation, 50–51, 82–86, 124, 134–36; objectives of, 5t, 27t; for social control, 79–82, 130–34; speech/kinetic action model of, 6–8, 7; for strategic advantage, 90–92. *See also* warnings
Polay, Víctor, 96, 101, 106, 111–12
police, 6, 24–25, 140, 146, 150; in Afghanistan, 126, 135, 139, 142, 170; in Britain, 1–2, 41–43, 53, 55, 56; in Iraq, 143, 252n76; in Nigeria, 121, 123, 170, 176–78; in Northern Ireland, 9, 10, 29–34, 43–49, 52–59, 168; in Peru, 96, 99, 100, 111–13, 168, 246n66; in Spain, 69–73, 77–79, 87, 90, 91, 93; in Sri Lanka, 74–76; in Syria, 143, 252n76; in United States, 174
Political Terror Scale (PTS), 73, 238n64
Polity2 scale, 125–26, 151–52, 160–63, *161, 162*
Polity IV Project, 73, 151
Popal, Khalida, 132
Pope, Martha, 55
Prabhakaran, Velupillai, 75, 85, 91
"propaganda by the deed," 14, 19, 221n39
prophylaxis, 91, 150, 230n83; strategic, 6, 27, 63; tactical, 6, 24, 27t, 45–46, 75, 76
Provisional IRA. *See* IRA
Puerto Rico, 163

[286] INDEX

Qaqa, Abu, 126, 134, 141

Rajapaksa, Gotabaya, 76
Reagan, Ronald, 228n35
"Real IRA," 93. *See also* IRA
rebel groups, terrorist versus, 19
Red Cross, 71, 78, 107, 246n66
reputation. *See* aggrandizement
Rigby, Lee, 19–20
Rincón, Miguel, 99, 101, 111–12
rondas campesinas (peasant militias), 110
Royal Irish Regiment (RIR), 34
Royal Ulster Constabulary (RUC), 33, 34, 39, 41; bomb threats and, 46, 53, 58–59
Russia, 120, 179

Salafism, 121
Samaritans (organization), 54, 227n18
Sambisa Forest (Nigeria), 137
Sands, Bobby, 227n9
Schelling, Thomas, 20–21, 172
Sendero Luminoso. *See* Shining Path
separatism. *See* ethnic separatism
September 11th attacks, 117, 262n20
sharia: in Afghanistan, 117; in Nigeria, 121, 127
Shekau, Abubakar, 122–23, 131, 135–38, 170, 176. *See also* Boko Haram
Shining Path (Sendero Luminoso): aggrandizement by, 108–11; drug trafficking and, 96, 97, 104; guerrilla warfare by, 96, 100, 104–5, 109, 113; history of, 95–97; incentives of, 97–98, 97t; Maoism of, 95, 100–105, 107, 109, 113, 169; MRTA and, 11, 94–114, 169; negotiations by, 107–8, 246n69; predictions for, 98t; social control by, 11, 103–5, 173; tactics of, 11, 100–103, 246n69
signaling. *See* costly signaling

signal splitting, 13–14, 18, 24, 166–67, 172; definition of, 6, 18; by IRA, 40–42, 60, 168; by LTTE, 85
Significant Incidents of Political Violence Against Americans reports, 149
Sinhalese people, 65, 73–75, 82, 85, 92; language of, 65
Sinn Féin, 31–32, 36–37, 40, 43, 48, 51, 227n10
social control, 5t, 8, 27t, 169–70, 173; by ETA, 80–82, 173; by IRA, 9, 47–48, 173; by jihadist groups, 130–34, 173; by LTTE, 81–82, 173; by MRTA, 103–5; pledges for, 79–82, 130–34; by Shining Path, 11, 103–5, 173
Social Democratic Labour Party (Ireland), 50
South Africa, 152
Spain, 10; constitution of, 69; democratization of, 63, 69; Guardia Civil of, 72, 77–78, 87, 90, 237n57; Political Terror Scale for, 73
speech/kinetic action model of terrorism, 6–8, 7, 23–25, 139, 219n25, 225n25; definition of, 18
Sri Lanka: civil war in, 10, 65–66, 90, 91, 169; Tamil diaspora of, 238n68. *See also* LTTE
Stanford University's Mapping Militant Organizations project, 151
statistical analysis, 145–66; average marginal effects, 161, 161–64, 162; multilevel logit results, 155–58, 156–57t; Pearson correlation matrix, 158–59, 159t; regression coefficients, 160
Study of Terrorism and Responses to Terrorism (START). *See* Global Terrorism Database
suicide bombings, 15, 153; by HSZRLF, 85, 92; by jihadist groups, 119, 121–23, 129, 132, 160; by LTTE, 75, 76, 89

Sumanthiran, M. A., 74
Syria, 119, 120, 125–26, 158, 162

Taliban, 115–16, 123–44, 169–70; history of, 116–18; hoaxes by, 125–29; incentives of, 123t; negotiations by, 124, 134–36, 172; predictions for, 124t; social control by, 130–34, 173; suicide bombings by, 132; tactics of, 11–12; warnings by, 128–29. *See also* jihadist groups
Tamil Eelam (proposed state), 65, 82
Tamil Eelam Liberation Organization, 88
Tamil Nadu, 66
Tamil National Alliance (TNA), 74
Tamils, 65–66, 73–74, 84–85, 238n68
Tamil Tigers. *See* LTTE
Tanzania, 117
target selection, 22, 34, 153
terrorism, 18–28; autonomous cell, 263n34; "crowdsourced," 17, 178; definitions of, 3, 18–20, 219n26; effectiveness of, 171–73; future research on, 178–80; logic of, 21; lone wolf, 263n34; risks of, 21; as signaling, 13–14; speech/kinetic action model of, 6–8, 7, 23–24, 139, 219n25, 225n25; as theater, 3, 19
Thamilselvan, S. P., 89
Thatcher, Margaret, 50, 228n35
theoretical saturation, 33
Thimpu Declaration, 84
threats, 3–4, 20–28, 40; advantages of, 5t; assessment of, 60–61, 173–80; credibility of, 174–80; democratization of, 179; effectiveness of, 171–73; false, 14–15; future research on, 178–80; immediate, 18; multiple audiences conundrum and, 172; objectives of, 5t; political

outcomes of, 5; prophylactic, 25, 68, 94, 140, 168; propositions about, 8, 167–68; prospective, 18; by religious groups, 116; speech/kinetic action model of, 6–8, 7; types of, 5–6, 167
torture, 19, 73, 104, 106, 139, 238n64
Trump, Donald, 118, 135
Truth and Reconciliation Commission. *See* Comisión de la Verdad y Reconciliación
truth-telling, 52, 76–79. *See also* credibility
Túpac Amaru II (José Gabriel Condorcanqui), 99
Túpac Amaru Revolutionary Movement. *See* MRTA
Turkey, 161, 163

UCDP (Uppsala Conflict Data Program), 151, 260n27
Ulster Defence Association, 232n118
Ulster Defence Regiment (UDR), 34
Ulster Volunteer Force (UVF), 152
Urla, Jacqueline, 63
USSR-Afghan war, 117

violence, 106–7; as coercion, 20–22; discriminate/indiscriminate, 172; political outcomes of, 5; speech/kinetic action model of, 6–8, 7

Walsh, Séanna, 35, 37–40, 228n27
warnings, 145–46, 167–68, 175; functions of, 8, 18; hypotheses about, 146–48; legitimacy concerns and, 15, 40–42, 219n28; objectives of, 5t, 27t; predicted probability of, *161*, *162*, 162–63; research design for, 32–33, 149–50, 170–71; with signal splitting, 6, 13, 14, 24, 40,

166–68; speech/kinetic action model of, 6–8, 7; types of, 150. *See also* pledges

weapons of mass destruction, 15

white supremacist groups, 174, 179

World Cup football tournament (2018), 138, 178–79

Yemen, 120

Yusuf, Muhammad, 121, 137

Zapatero, José Luis Rodríguez, 83

Zaragoza bombing (1987), 69, 90–91

Zarqawi, Abu Musab al-, 118–19

Zawahiri, Ayman al-, 119

Printed in Australia
Ingram Content Group Australia Pty Ltd
AUHW020615061224
403865AU00004B/66